TAKING ANBAR

A Frontline Account of the Hunt for

Iraq's Lethal Insurgency

CAPTAIN MICHAEL J. GIFFORD

USAR, 1997-2005

*To my father, Mike, who tried to tame me,
and for my mother, Tina, who tried to warn me.*

Contents

All Gave Some, Some Gave All.................vii
CHAPTER 1 1
CHAPTER 2 43
CHAPTER 3 61
CHAPTER 4 95
CHAPTER 5 177
CHAPTER 6 195
CHAPTER 7 203
CHAPTER 8 241
CHAPTER 9: 295
CHAPTER 10 303
CHAPTER 11 331
CHAPTER 12 337
CHAPTER 13 349
CHAPTER 14 355
Afterthoughts 371
Epilogue 377
The Soapbox.............................. 391

ALL GAVE SOME. SOME GAVE ALL.

AUGUST 4, 2004. It's a day I'll never forget, but one I barely remember.

At about 4 a.m. on that remarkably humid morning, 166 soldiers from the 94th Military Police Company boarded four, luxurious chartered buses and started the long journey from Ft. Drum, New York, back to our base in New Hampshire. Some had gone to bed early in preparation for the pre-dawn departure, carefully packing their bags and getting some rest. But most had stayed up straight through the night, continuing the days-long celebration following our official release from an Active duty deployment spanning nearly two years. Noticeably sluggish as they stowed their gear, they shuffled onto the bus and fell into their seats, a crumpled but happy mess. In about three hours, most would be having their first hangover in nearly a year and a half.

Eight hours after stepping onto those buses at Ft. Drum, the 94th marched into Manchester's JFK Coliseum to the thunderous screams and applause of hundreds of families and friends, local and national news teams, senators and state representatives, and a handful of curious locals. We'd been deployed and served together since the fall of 2002, but within 45 minutes, all the soldiers in the 94th—men and women who had met as strangers nearly two years before—would go their separate ways, falling into the arms of loved ones in a dizzying homecoming ceremony on that hot summer afternoon.

About 15 months earlier in May of 2003, the 94th had crossed the border from Kuwait into Iraq, literally hours after the fall of the Hussein Regime and the war's unofficial end. I clearly remember seeing the President's humanitarian case for war in the beaming faces of the little Iraqi kids: children were cheering and waving at our convoy as it roared into southern Iraq, fearlessly running alongside our trucks for a chance to touch a soldier from this magnificent, benevolent foreign army. And although the war was technically over at that point, I could also see the uncertainty of what awaited us in the faces of my fellow soldiers. The Iraqi Army had collapsed within weeks, and few prisoners had been taken. Gently—and somewhat reluctantly—we placed our lives in each other's hands. The 94th had rolled between the coiled, barbed concertina wire and massive tank ditches separating Kuwait from Iraq, with absolutely no idea what was waiting for us on the other side.

Now, the war was over for our small New England Army Reserve unit. We were civilians again, and looking forward to getting back to our work as carpenters, students, firemen, police officers, and businessmen. We had several new fathers in our company eager to spend time with their little ones, and a handful of weddings had been postponed due to the deployment. There were thousands of joyous days ahead.

But would they be? What exactly do you do when you get home from war? How are you supposed to feel? How do you actually celebrate the fact you survived, when so many others were killed? What do you do with the rest of your precious time on Earth? At first, there was the temporary relief of simply being out of harm's way, and a few cold beers were enough. I knew more of the difficult thoughts and emotions would come later, but I had the rest of my life to figure those out.

The rest of my life.

I was a platoon leader with the Londonderry, New Hampshire-based 94th, who fought in the Al Anbar Province of Iraq for over a year. The 94th holds the unenviable record—as of the date of this writing—as the Army Reserve's longest serving unit since World War II, with a nearly two-year continuous Active duty deployment in support of Operations Noble Eagle and Iraqi Freedom 1 and 2. At one time we were the longest serving unit—Active or Reserve—in the United States Central Command, with 15 straight months in a combat zone.[1]

We entered Iraq in early May of 2003, and over the next 15 months would be spectators to the rise of an insurgency that would give our military the greatest challenge it has seen since the Vietnam conflict. The 94th found itself on the roads and in the cities of Al Anbar almost daily, dealing with its local governments, police and people on so many levels it made our collective head spin. From the first hours of post-war Iraq, we witnessed the "ground truth" results of the strategic, operational and tactical decisions made by military leadership, and how those choices began to shape the broader conflict. It was this rare exposure that gave us an excellent but often dangerous and unsettling view of all you've seen, heard and read about in the news and editorials. It also gave me the insight to write

---

1 The U.S. Army ended up introducing a mandatory 15-month deployment cycle for active duty soldiers in April 2007.

this book. Because of our work with just about every branch of the Army, we were presented with a unique perspective on this war, a depth of involvement few other soldiers would ever experience. It was an interesting position to be in as a junior officer in the United States military to say the least; especially as a Reservist who had never planned on seeing much in the way of close combat in his career.

As "MPs" attached to a combat arms unit of the United States Army, we found ourselves involved in nearly every major tactical aspect of Operation Iraqi Freedom. At the outset, we were working hand-in-hand with the 3rd Armored Cavalry Regiment, a.k.a. *the* 3rd *ACR*, and their attachments throughout Al Anbar. For the first six months of our time overseas, the 94th was heavily involved with escorting supplies along its major highways and patrolling its towns and cities. Like a teenager with a new license, we'd poke around Iraqi's landscape with a youthful curiosity, one that quickly gave way after reports of fatal ambushes and roadside bombs began to fill our daily meetings. We'd soon find ourselves working side-by-side with the fledgling Iraqi Police Force (IPF), most of whom weren't even in uniform yet, grappling with trust issues, thorny tribal politics, and an invisible enemy gaining strength in the shadows. This tenuous new partnership led to an all-out, exhaustive 24-hour gun battle in one of Anbar's most peculiar cities, a muddled firefight in which we just didn't know whom to trust.

As the danger grew, so did our reliance on the 3rd ACR's aviation and armor assets. Our bonds with these helicopter pilots and tank gunners would be some of the strongest we would make in our time overseas, their conventional machinery a welcomed complement to our often door-to-door pursuit of our unpredictable insurgent foe. Given the complexity of our rapidly-evolving and malicious environment, we'd become well acquainted with the tactical human intelligence teams working their sources in the cities near, and including, Ramadi. Their labors were critical in revealing the insurgency's infrastructure, and aiding us in our own efforts to develop informants; a network of courageous locals who helped eventually turn the tide of the war in Al Anbar.

With a better understanding of our enemies—and friends—in the province, we found our communication and image with the Iraqi people beginning to improve after working with the U.S. Army's Psychological Operations Command. A community outreach plan like no other, "PSYOPS" were often the first American voices most Iraqis had ever heard, actively challenging the empty dogma Saddam had shoved down their throats for decades. All the while, we were escorting the U.S. Army's Civil Affairs Teams to their meetings with tribal, political, law enforcement and military leaders throughout Anbar. The camouflaged diplomats of the U.S. military, civil affairs had the challenging and often thankless task of charting a course for the aimless, burgeoning provincial leadership, and along the way discovering what the Iraqis *really* thought of the American way of life. A high profile mission in August of 2003 with U.S. Army Special Forces to capture a team of insurgent killers would test our professionalism, as we came face to face with a surprisingly pathetic and feeble enemy. These experiences would give us a tremendous insight into the customs, traditions, beliefs and people of Iraq, as well as a terrifying snapshot of our increasingly lethal rebel adversary.

And that was just the first six months.

In October of 2003, we'd be tasked by our new bosses—the 82nd Airborne Division—to help run the *Al Anbar Security College*, a police academy for the Iraqi Police Forces of the Anbar Province. That mission would end up giving us a privileged insight as to what was going on in the police stations around the province—as well in the head of the average Iraqi police officer—and would end up yielding both surprising and tragic results. As we began to notice an influx of insurgent spies into our academy, we became wary of even our closest Iraqi police allies, which eventually led to the arrest and interrogation of Fallujah's own Chief of Police. With the introduction of a covert intelligence collection program, several brave cadets would come forward and give us invaluable information on the brutal practices within the IPF, intelligence no other unit was able to gather in the field. Unfortunately, as is often the case when "fearless" clashes with "ruthless," some would pay with their lives.

The experience would bring us closer to those who were quickly becoming our most valuable and courageous allies in Iraq, and the new friendships made with ten fearless men from Baghdad, Fallujah and Ramadi would end up redeeming my faith in this war.

The following April, hours before the 94th was to fly back home to the United States, we'd be extended past our yearlong combat tour to escort supply convoys into Baghdad and beyond, after the vicious insurgent uprising and the new Mahdi Army took military planners completely by surprise. Over the next three months, we'd help guide the tactical decision-making behind the business of shipping men and materials through some of the most dangerous territory on Earth. In what would turn out to be the longest 90 days of my life, the complete lack of courage on the part of our higher command, along with the military's stubbornness about changing their dangerous tactics on Iraq's unforgiving roads, would force me to make an important decision regarding a career in the military.

The brutal murder of a loved and respected Iraqi brother would bring our tour to a sorrowing end. Leaving Iraq without finding his killers is a regret I still carry.

For nearly a year and a half in Iraq, the broad policies conceived on a desk at the Pentagon or in a classroom at the Army War College in Pennsylvania came to life right in front of our squinting, dust-filled eyes. In essence, the 94th had a front row seat to some of the most significant missions—and outcomes—of Operation Iraqi Freedom. The entire time, we'd have the rare opportunity to speak with generals as they implemented their strategic visions, moving enormous legions of men, machines and materials around Iraq's biblical landscape. We, like so many other units, would negotiate a torrent of memos and policies issued by our commanders from a crumbling palace in Baghdad or canvass tent in Kuwait, meant to guide our tasks and responsibilities in this escalating insurgent conflict. We'd be given ambiguous orders from colonels and majors, putting forth their best efforts to distill from these directives a plan of action for the soldiers in their charge, fighting an often invisible enemy. Then we'd head out to some of the worst areas of Iraq to carry out our mission, cross our fingers, and watch it all unfold before us.

Over the course of our tour, I wrote back to family and friends with little journals that helped me cope with what we were dealing with in Anbar; the firsthand authenticity only a soldier on the ground could provide, and a perspective the American public hadn't seen yet. I wasn't having too much of a problem with the violence and the combat—I was expecting that much, and quite frankly, what we were seeing was *nothing* compared to what some other units were going through. However what I *wasn't* expecting was almost worse: the lack of proactive thinking by the world's best military, a hasty and often thoughtless, reactive approach to our Kafkaesque stability and support missions. A war that had begun at a time and place of our choosing was steadily sliding towards a conflict of attrition, with no tangible mission or plan. There was no aim, no specific goal—only stale reactions and archaic tactics. There was no real purpose behind the operations needed to quell the mounting threat in Anbar Province. With the military's day-to-day decisions growing more repetitive and troubling, I found myself increasingly at odds with the decisions made by our leadership. As our tour ground on, I was discovering more and more of our *leaders* were actually *managers*—at best—and were miserably failing our young men and women.

The longer we were in Iraq, the more cutting my correspondence became. As time went on, my letters grew more and more critical of tactical and operational Army policy. Frustrated with what was going on, and unable to complain to the junior troops in my platoon, friends and family back home got an earful. After we rotated back to the States and had a chance to calm down a bit, I started to revisit—through letters and notes I'd taken during my tour—what we'd gone through, and realized the concerns I had weren't minor issues. My journal entries weren't just blowing off steam. A lot of poor choices had been made. Worse yet, they were made again and again, often by people who were both professionally and morally unqualified by any reasonable person's standards.

For the fifteen months of my tour, I was steadily learning a hard, cold fact concerning our military's collective ability to fight a committed insurgency: tactics were changing, but our people weren't.

That said, this book isn't being written as a tool for me to vent a few petty gripes in a handful of otherwise irrelevant combat situations. It's not a Monday morning quarterback session where I split hairs with a few colonels or generals over their razor-thin judgment calls in fighting this war. It isn't a forum to argue a couple of pointless details from a random firefight somewhere, one whose outcome probably wouldn't have made a difference to anyone who wasn't there. In a word, it isn't "sharpshooting." I've been on the receiving end of plenty of criticism, and have learned the difference. Instead, it's a close look at how some military standards for modern warfare are failing our troops, and how a general lack of common sense is destroying our tactical advantages in this and other insurgent conflicts. A formal declaration of war on complacency and lack of preventative action, it's a just analysis of some of the United States military's antiquated and predictable ways of doing business—the conventional, one-track mindset that's still playing an unwelcomed role in unconventional warfare.

The next two hundred pages you're about to read is the story of the 94th's twenty two-month journey from citizens to soldiers and back again: a brief chronicle taking you from our stateside preparation for combat in foreign lands in the fall of 2002, to our final heart-pounding, IED-filled convoy through the Sunni Triangle in July of 2004. Far from a simple collection of war stories, it looks to serve as a learning experience; one that I hope will help both American service members *and* American citizens understand this and future conflicts—the similar if not identical campaigns we will no doubt find ourselves in again.

The stories also make a case for significantly changing the way we train both our leaders and soldiers in preparation for combat; currently a nauseating formula of antiquated garrison habits and bureaucracy that's destroying the so-called "Warrior Ethos" of the American military man and woman. They give too many enraging examples of how we're cultivating an atmosphere of hesitancy in today's military, which is compounded exponentially by the reliance on mountains of paperwork and manuals, rather than experience and decisive leadership. They painfully describe in heartbreaking detail the military's inability to learn from its own mistakes—a perilous lack of institutional memory often resulting in the senseless death of yet another service member.

The military's adherence to a status quo of inflexibility is setting up our combat troops for failure, as is a standard of over-simplicity in our training, readiness and leadership. And what's going around in low standards and complacency is coming around in a naïve view of warfare, a severe underestimation of our enemy, an eroding reputation with the average Iraqi, and lost lives.

As much as I look to expose the day-to-day problems we faced in Iraq, I try to offer just as many potential solutions. Furthermore, I actively seek to avoid the all-too convenient 20/20 hindsight when tearing apart some of the decisions made during our tour. I'm sure you've seen the observations made by "those in the know," usually involving obvious conclusions with little attention paid to what drove the decisions themselves. Instead, I chose to analyze the roots of these poor choices—uninspired leadership and their heavily flawed assumptions, the one-dimensional training and lack of focus on tactics, the over-reliance on technology and firepower, the fostering of an arrogance that can only harm our efforts militarily—and what could be done to remedy them in time.

And writing this was the most constructive way I could find to deal with the post traumatic stress all combat veterans deal with in some way. I'm blatantly critical of a lot of people (including myself) and some of the chapters of this book will want to make you smash your Kindle, Tablet or whatever you're reading this on against a wall. Good, they should. Even if you've never been in the military, you'll be able to relate to what I'm talking about. I spent the majority of my career in business, and saw just as many problems there. However, when the military has a quarter where "earnings per share don't meet analyst expectations," it doesn't mean our stock price dips; it means some good American men and women are gone from this earth forever.

In all my blustering—and I can't say this in strong enough terms—those military leaders who create so much fury and bitterness represent a very small minority of our fighting force. But it's that tiny sliver who chose to defend this country against all enemies, foreign and domestic, who deserve the blame for their decisions or worse, indecision.

Above all, writing this book is my way of praising those men and women on the ground, still very much in harm's way, fighting an adaptive and creative enemy in a house-to-house war that will undoubtedly take years to win. In a harrowing evolution of the Armed Forces, they bravely continue to refine twenty first century combat tactics in a lethal insurgent environment, no matter where they are now or where they end up. It's for those soldiers, sailors, airmen and Marines—the brave troops of the U.S. military who continue to give their lives, limbs and very sanity in this generation's world war—that this book is written.

And as you might have noticed, a portion of the proceeds from this book are funding OnBehalf.org, a nonprofit I and a few other troops from the 94th organized in 2005 for combat wounded veterans of Iraq & Afghanistan.

The good old days

I joined the Army through Siena College's Reserve Officer Training Corps (ROTC) program in Loudonville, New York, receiving my commission as a second lieutenant on June 14, 1997—ironically both my 22nd birthday and the 210th birthday of the U.S. Army. Although I was enrolled at Union College in Schenectady full time, I'd make the drive to Siena's campus three days a week, usually at 5:30 in the morning. And almost every morning without fail, I'd mutter to myself in the cold as to why I was pursuing such an affair offering no educational credit or enhancement of my struggling GPA. Union College—by the admission of its own President at the time, himself a Dartmouth ROTC graduate—did not accept ROTC credits, thanks to Union's progressive, liberal, hippie faculty. Although Union had boasted major Naval ROTC participation in the 60's, the anti-military views held by most of its Vietnam-era staff in the late 90's put the kibosh on any credit I'd receive. In the end however, I wanted more than just a diploma. Anyone with the means and a handful of drive could get a degree; I needed some life experience outside of academia, and I don't mean hitchhiking across Europe on my summers off. I made it official my junior year and became an ROTC cadet.

I opted to receive a Reserve commission because, in all honesty, I wasn't looking forward to leaving school only to end up in a stale, Godforsaken Active duty base somewhere. The few Active posts I'd seen so far were beyond depressing. During U.S. Army Airborne School at Ft. Benning, Georgia, I took a good look at the enlisted barracks and noticed they were a mess, as if they hadn't been upgraded in decades. Don't get me wrong, I could sleep in a trash bag under a cardboard box in the middle of the woods, but I couldn't believe this was the best we could offer our fighting men and women. Screw all that; I wanted to move to a big city, get a "real" job, booze it up and chase skirts. Boston it was.

I moved to Somerville, a suburb of Boston, Massachusetts, with some fraternity brothers a few months after graduation and started looking for work. Like many twenty-somethings coming out of college, I didn't really know what I wanted to do when I grew up. The U.S. Army, however, already knew what I was going to be doing for at least one weekend a month and two weeks a year, for the next eight years. I had been assigned to an Army Reserve unit at the Devens Reserve Forces Training Area, part of the 94th Regional Support Command, headquartered about an hour west of the city. I reported for my first assignment, a platoon leader for a specialized weapons unit, in the fall of 1997. Consisting of soldiers with a variety of backgrounds and technical skills, it was a unique way to enter the Reserves.

After a few years, with my career calling for a command position, I transferred to the 342nd Military Police Detachment, a unit specializing in internal military criminal investigations and the physical security of installations within the Army. The officer in charge, Lieutenant Colonel Wayne Parsons, gave me one year to obtain my MP Military Occupational Specialty, or MOS. It was a painless process involving several months of Internet tests, followed by a two-week course at the U.S. Army Military Police School at Ft. Leonard Wood, Missouri. I had already attended an Officer's Basic Course in another MOS, but two looked really good on a junior lieutenant's *Officer Evaluation Report*, the document which lists the failures and successes of one's current assignment. Considered a military "report card," it's one of the most powerful guiding factors of an officer's career, but to the surprise of too many, not the only one.

Four years into my career as a Reservist, the events of 9/11 squashed any hopes I had of serving out my eight year military obligation in a relatively peaceful way. The "one weekend a month, two weeks a year" commitment so many had grown accustomed to was over. Being 26 and pulsating with bloodlust watching New Yorkers plummet to their deaths from the World Trade Center towers, I was looking for any chance to get involved with the war in Afghanistan we all knew was coming. As a Reservist from Massachusetts, however, I figured the odds of being deployed in a combat capacity any time soon there were pretty slim. Army Rangers, Marine Recon, Navy SEALs and other Special Forces guys were already sending rounds downrange and taking care of business the old fashioned way. No mission had yet been designated for the weekend warriors; the folks with the camouflage uniforms hanging next to business suits in our closets, combat boots next to wingtips under our beds.

The mission was coming, though. Within a few months it didn't matter what patch you wore on your uniform. We'd all be in this mess together.

After the war in Afghanistan kicked off, the detachment was preparing to augment the security element at the 2002 Winter Olympic Games in Salt Lake City, Utah. If I couldn't go to war, at least the unit would be part of a real world mission we could look forward to. The past few years of filling out paperwork and running around the woods of Massachusetts with my M16, fighting the *Krasnovians*—a fictional nationality the U.S. Army often combats in its war games—was okay, but this would be a much needed marrying of our skills with the outside world.

The Olympic Games were a two-week vacation from my day job at American Express, and I had the pleasure to work with some of America's finest. The FBI, Secret Service, Utah

State Police, local Salt Lake City cops—they were all there, and did some great work. The threat to the games was very real, and we all worked together well. I spent a little time in Miami on another project that spring, came back in the fall of 2002 and found a unit that had been designated for overseas duty—the 368th Engineer Battalion, also based in Londonderry. They'd been put on some mysterious master list to deploy, but had not yet officially received their orders. Expecting one soon, I opted for a voluntary transfer and became their intelligence officer. From there, I began preparing materials for their company commanders on Iraqi military equipment, their war-fighting capabilities, and the desert environment. At about the same time I was working on these projects for the 368th, I had noticed the 94th Military Police Company, a unit that was headquartered down the hall, had already received their orders to move and needed platoon leaders.[2] *Where* they were going was the question.

My initial thought was a six-month tour in Afghanistan. The bulk of that war was already over (or so I had thought) and most of the Active duty units were being rotated out. I finished up the projects for the 368th and volunteered to lead a platoon with the 94th. As an officer who'd already "done his time" as a platoon leader and commander, I could have just as easily finished my career bouncing around New England's Reserve units from staff job to staff job, which some officers were already happily doing. But why not; an overseas deployment would no doubt add some character to my career, and a "combat patch" on my right shoulder would show the world

---

2 Each branch of the U.S. Army falls into one of three categories; *combat arms*, *combat support*, or *combat service support*. There are only three branches in the combat arms category—infantry, armor, and artillery. The MP corps falls under combat support.

I'd gone to war. Most of all, some young kids were expecting the Army to provide them with some decent (stress on *decent*) leadership. Figuring I was up for the task, after just under a month with the 368th, I requested a transfer to the 94th Military Police Company.

Just before my reassignment, I started growing a little suspicious the 94th was currently without two platoon leaders (officers, anyway), and their commander was an engineer officer. I knew of a few other MP lieutenants who hadn't been overseas and were working in meaningless staff jobs or support positions. I wondered why they hadn't volunteered to go. The troops of the 94th were looking for some leadership, and no one had jumped on it yet. It made me uneasy, and was the first real indicator not all of us were on the same page in this new wartime Army.

At the time, I thought nothing of actually going to Iraq. Maybe we'd be put on the rotation for Afghanistan, which was still pretty dangerous, but hey that's why I joined the Army. And who the hell *wouldn't* want to kill those guys? Part of me couldn't wait. But if we *did* end up in Iraq, I was convinced any actual shooting war there would be lightning fast, and few Reserve units would be involved for the first six months or so. They'd need engineers to help rebuild stuff more than they'd need military police. We might end up guarding a few humanitarian convoys or something. There's no way we'd stick around after the damage was done. Regardless, those plans were years away.

Holy living Hell. I could not have been more wrong.

CHAPTER 1

"You think of your sword and his sword and nothing else."

Eric Bana as *Prince Hector*
Troy

Like most of my generation, I like movies. A lot of Gen X-ers adore their flicks, and you'd be hard pressed to find anyone who hasn't shot a one-liner from a classic to his friend at least a few times a week. So instead of actual chapter titles like some fancy pants writer, I use movie lines to describe what I'm talking about. Most are big name classics and self-explanatory; some are not. Either way, you'll get the gist.

The 94th arrived at a bone-chilling Ft. Drum, New York, in December 2002, fully expecting to train up and deploy overseas by the end of the year. Only a few miles from Lake Ontario, most of the weapons ranges were perpetually coated in ice; the temperature on the day we qualified on our 9mm pistols was hovering around 10 degrees. The plastic pop-up targets on our M16 range were covered in driving snow, making them nearly impossible to see from just 50 yards away. Most of us had gone as far as to shed our Gore-Tex jackets for our protective chemical suits. Heavier and filled with dense charcoal fiber, they provided warmth from the face-numbing subzero winds blowing off of the lake. Our classroom instruction wasn't exactly riveting, but it was practical enough; first aid, combat tactics, and more weapons training, mostly. It could have been crocheting for all I cared at that point; it was just too goddamn cold to go outside.

It was quickly becoming clear Iraq was our most likely destination. As the prospects of war grew more certain, I began to realize how lucky I was to find myself grouped with what turned out to be a great bunch of young guys and gals. Everyone in the 94th was excited to go somewhere, but not *too* excited. There was a good vibe coming off of the group, a real level-headedness that put me at ease almost immediately. Even better, most of the senior enlisted leadership was older with substantial military and civilian experience. That just made my job ten times easier; they were seasoned professionals, not kids starting out in life.

Of course, it didn't stop me from trying to make a fake name for myself. I was throwing a lot of "I was running black ops into China before your ninth birthday" type-bullshit with some of the younger enlisted kids. They knew I was full of it, but it took the edge off and helped disarm any suspicions I was another robotic, high-strung officer. As a new lieutenant walking into a group of soldiers who'd already known each other for years, the last thing I needed was to be seen as some bonehead with shiny boots and a starched uniform, obsessed only with his own career; a standard which was quickly becoming the new normal with some officers.

Within about a week, the 94th was rumored to have a

mission securing an Army Special Forces camp in northern Iraq. The "SF" were set to train some Kurdish soldiers prior to the war's start and needed some help guarding their post. What a buzz that set off—a bunch of Reservists from New England were going behind enemy lines, earning the coveted Army Special Forces combat patch and maybe even capping some jihadist turds. We couldn't wait! Within days however, that particular mission was handed off to an Active duty unit. Too good to be true. Now, the mysterious "they" were saying pack your bags for Kuwait. "They" turned out to be Forces Command, or FORSCOM, the military brain trust that pools together combat elements and delegates their assignments.

Ft. Drum had its act together when it came to good, hands-on training, but unfortunately we wouldn't be sticking around there much longer. After about a month of some solid instruction, we were shipped off to Ft. Polk, Louisiana, and assigned to the 519th Military Police Battalion. Since most of their line (combat) units had already deployed, we'd be assisting them with *law and order* activities on the post. With "L&O" duty, we'd investigate a few fender-benders, check some locks on doors, and talk young guys out of murdering their new, promiscuous wives. Not exactly a thrilling time, but it was warmer than upstate New York, and we had it fairly easy. However, we still wanted to go somewhere and shoot stuff, preferably bad people.

This was the 94th's first real experience with the Active duty in years, and a culture shock we weren't prepared for. Within days, we were having problems with our new command, and it was there at Ft. Polk where we first began to notice the growing division between the Reserve and Active components. We got along fine with the actual combat companies of the 519th. They, too, were experiencing a similar frustration with the command

and staff sections, who appeared to be mechanically moving through this deployment as if it were just another meaningless training exercise. It didn't come as a surprise; that was all they were used to. However, as we began our inevitable march towards a real shooting war, it was becoming clearer by the day some of the Active duty staff officers were in their own little worlds. They didn't see the difference between their exercises and preparations for real combat.

When things became more serious a few weeks later, the 519th command staff started to push us around like the proverbial red headed stepchild. We were fighting for the basics—vaccinations, uniforms, training—and our equipment was being picked clean by their units who needed parts. Our 3rd platoon was barred from participating in a much needed live-fire exercise out of spite, following a small confrontation between the platoon leader, Master Sergeant Dean Miles, and a 519th staff member. To add insult to injury, we were completely ignored at a highly publicized formation just before the 519th headquarters and staff sections deployed to Kuwait. Although we were visibly the largest group there, the battalion commander, Lieutenant Colonel Paul K. Warman, had his back to us the entire time, not once acknowledging our unit as national news cameras rolled. We didn't exist. It all made sense however, after learning Warman—a last name that apparently very much belied his knowledge of military tactics—was asked to leave Bagram Air Force base in Afghanistan during his last deployment due to his incompetence.

Whatever, I didn't give a damn. He'd be out of our lives soon enough, and this certainly wasn't the first time a military unit had to deal with a shitshow commander. Aside from the childish behavior of the 519th, Ft. Polk as a post was not ready to process and deploy a Reserve unit for overseas combat. I'm not sure how the Active units fared, but no one really knew what to do with us. We all had trouble with the "usual suspects" when it came to deployment. The paperwork, equipment and medical issues were always a problem, even *after* our fights with the 519th, but the training and readiness issues—the meat and potatoes that would determine life or death overseas—were horrendously lacking.

Before I discuss some of our pre-deployment problems, I must say, in the spirit of full disclosure and complete fairness, no one knew what kind of fighting post-war Iraq would yield. Remember, this was all taking place in early 2003, a full three months before the invasion. The ambushes, IEDs and treacherous urban combat weren't fully anticipated, but the training and guidance we received during our time there—intended to ready us for an *all out ground war*—was deficient, at best.

Prior to deploying overseas, a combat unit was required to complete a Theater Specific Individual Readiness Training, or TSIRT, program. It was a checklist of activities, drafted by the Department of Defense, intended to ready troops for war. When I first heard about it, I was actually pretty excited. Finally, some *specialized* training for fighting in the deserts of Iraq. For Chrissake, the U.S. military had already been in Iraq once, and it was kind of a big deal. I was expecting some basics on our mission; enemy troop formations, the environment, weather, maps, graphs, charts, information, maybe even some lessons learned from Desert Storm. Other than steps we'd taken ourselves, we had been working blind. It would be comforting to know the Department of Defense had taken some proactive steps to ready its units. Finally, after years of near financial neglect, we'd have the full resources of the Active duty military to help. It all sounded so very impressive, complex and thorough.

It would be neither of the three, and represented the first large mistake the military was committing in getting its troops ready for war. There was a troubling absence of common sense in our approach to this conflict. The military thought it best to prepare us for combat in Iraq by showing us a video on the dangers of depleted uranium, a presentation on what sexual harassment was, and a class on suicide prevention. While important factors in a *peacetime* army, they weren't priority wartime issues. It was starting to appear the DoD was more concerned about solidifying its numbers and covering its ass than it was about troop morale and welfare.[3]

I realize a lot of the training for an overseas deployment takes place at individual Reserve (or Active) units on their own time, that it's up to leaders to draft and execute their own plans prior to war. No one's going to hold your hand as you train, and you don't need a ton of money to put together some worthwhile projects. Sometimes quite the opposite. I also need to point out the TSIRT is a Defense Department directive, not one Ft. Polk put together, and the brass at DoD is usually more concerned about hard numbers than about soldiers and their abilities. Nonetheless, the Active duty posts processing Reserve

---

3 This is obviously extremely dangerous behavior, and isn't limited to the DoD. The Federal Emergency Management Agency (FEMA) gave a similar brief to a group of over 600 firefighters just after Hurricane Katrina struck the U.S. in late summer of 2005. While New Orleans was *still burning*, these men were being lectured by FEMA reps on equal opportunity, sexual harassment and customer service in a hotel in Atlanta. The hurricane relief effort and preparation for the war in Iraq are two very different case studies, but each example highlights the dangers of setting politically correct priorities above more practical applications (Mark Thompson, *Four Places Where the System Broke Down/Why Did FEMA and its Chief, Michael Brown, Fail Their Biggest Test?*, Time Magazine, September 19, 2005).

units play a large role in readying them for combat. After all, they have the manpower, equipment, facilities and material needed to fully organize and complete the deployment process. Hell, we could even teach each other a thing or two—our platoon alone had several men with combat experience. But in our TSIRT, the combination of Department of Defense mandatory instructions and Ft. Polk's ability to carry them out fell woefully short.

Prior to the start of the TSIRT, the bulk of our training at Ft. Polk consisted of an excruciating 4-hour video force-fed to us by some fat, condescending, redneck jerk describing how to drive a car while on Ft. Polk, and how much trouble we'd get into if we broke his rules. About 20 minutes into his brief, I wanted to punch my fist straight through his face. There was also an agonizing two-hour speech from some woman about Ft. Polk's family support group. Considering no one had family in the area, which we mentioned several times, we couldn't have cared less and thought it an incredible waste of time. Combined, those two classes alone were about twice as long as our actual combat training.

We *did* have one building clearing exercise, taught by an overly conceited member of the Ft. Polk SWAT team who made sure to stop us every six seconds and tell us how much we sucked.

Ft. Polk was going through the motions and we were growing tired of it. At this point, they weren't even paying attention. The United States was headed for war, and it was more important for the powers that be on post to teach us how to drive, or show us how somebody's husband made a half-ass website about their own family support group. We didn't care about that crap. Where was the real training and preparation? Where were the shoot, move and communicate scenarios only an Active duty post could provide? Wasn't this the home of the Joint Readiness Training Center? Didn't these guys have a good plan to ready soldiers, outside of TSIRT, for an overseas deployment?

During our time at Polk, we'd heard rumors of what our role was to be in the conflict, but nothing was written in stone quite yet. Moreover, we weren't quite sure this whole war was even going to materialize. However a lot of units had already been deployed to Kuwait, including two brigades of the 3rd Infantry Division—the 3rd *ID*—one of the United States military's best trained fighting forces. It was a telling move, one that showed both allies and enemies alike the United States was serious about invading Iraq.

I was thinking, naively of course, the troop movement was being used as a threat to get Hussein to cooperate. That all changed after the Presidential Address the night of March 17, 2003. On an otherwise uneventful St. Patrick's Day, while we were enjoying one of our last beers together as a company at Ft. Polk's *Sports Depot Bar and Grill*, President George W. Bush gave Saddam and his sons 48 hours to leave Iraq, or we were coming in after him. The bar, filled with a few hundred somewhat rowdy soldiers and Reservists, fell silent. I looked around the room at the faces and saw a raw, uninhibited mix of relief, despair, fear and excitement, all at the same time. Our Commander, Captain David Bentley—the quiet kid with a heart of gold from Worcester, Massachusetts—looked unfazed. I imagine he was already planning the next steps for our unit, whatever those may be. With his short-cropped dark hair, thin build, and a permanent wad of tobacco in his lower lip, he intently stared on at the news broadcast.

Little did we know that night, American, Australian and British Special Forces units had already begun engaging in sporadic battles with Fedayeen Saddam and Iraqi commandos in the western desert, near the Jordanian and Syrian borders.

About 49 ½ hours later, forty cruise missiles made their one-way, subsonic flights from U.S. warships in the Persian Gulf and began pounding their assigned targets in Iraq. It was only a matter of time.

A few hours after the strikes began, we received our orders. We were to be included in the 101st Airborne Division's *force package*—the list of all units assigned to a specific mission. The 101st Airborne, a lethal combat outfit equal to the 3rd Infantry Division, would be one of the main forces pushing into Iraq along with the 3rd ID. I'm not sure whom the 519th MP battalion commander knew at FORSCOM, but within a day or two, he managed to get us bumped from that mission and gave it to one of his own units. We'd also come to find out it was he who had us scrubbed from the Special Forces mission in December.[4]

We waited on pins and needles as the invasion came and went. Footage of Saddam statues being toppled and cheering Iraqis were quickly replaced with casualty reports and photos of captured U.S. military servicemen. A Special Ops team had managed a successful rescue of Private Jessica Lynch about the first of an American service member since Vietnam, and the first ever of a woman. Her unit, a maintenance company attached to the 3rd ID, was ambushed in Nasiriyah after falling behind and taking a wrong turn. I couldn't help but think it might not have happened if we were assigned as their escorts.

---

4 The Special Forces mission never took place; instead, the unit headed to Hungary and trained Iraqi forces there, and actually returned to Ft. Polk before we deployed.

After four months of duty at Polk, the 94th managed to secure its deployment order. Most units of the 519th had already taken off for duty in Iraq or Afghanistan, and their headquarters section—the main source of our aggravation—was on its way to Baghdad. Within a few days, it would be our turn.

The day finally came. In the early morning darkness of April 21, 2003, five of the famous military *Bluebird* buses picked us up and shuttled us to Alexandria International Airport in the early morning darkness. Within a few hours, we boarded a civilian jumbo jet, stowed our weapons and gear, buckled up, taxied down the runway and headed off to war.

We started the 18-hour flight to the tiny nation of Kuwait, still unsure of exactly where we'd end up. Thankfully, we'd never see or work with the 519th's staff again.

We flew into Kuwait International Airport some time the next day. Within a few minutes of landing, a team of soldiers rushed onto the plane and told us the airport was under threat condition, or THREATCON, Delta.[5] They advised us to grab our gear and move with a purpose towards the tents waiting for us at nearby *Camp Wolverine*. Assuming the worst, I was expecting someone to take a shot at us as we disembarked. We unloaded our stuff onto the scorching hot tarmac without incident, found a tent and just *crashed*. I have no idea what time it was. Hell, I didn't even know what day it was. My head was pounding from

---

5 The military has five major THREATCON levels. THREATCON *Normal* was a designation used when a general threat of possible terrorist activity exists, warranting only a routine security posture. Levels would increase consistent with the perceived threat, from *Alpha* to the most extreme being *Delta*, which meant a terrorist attack was inevitable or in progress.

caffeine withdrawal but I couldn't keep my eyes open. After a few hours and more useless briefings we'd all forget in four minutes, we all piled onto more buses and started the drive to our new home in the desert, somewhere in northwestern Kuwait.

I was sitting next to my platoon sergeant, Sergeant First Class Reginald Littlefield, our backpacks firmly in our laps like little kids riding the bus to school. "Reggie", a local cop back in Maine, was a good cat. Despite his stone cold stare when he meant business, he had an infectious laugh, made even funnier by a veneered front tooth, the result of a motorcycle accident as a teenager. We didn't always see eye to eye on things, but he was a reliable soldier. He was also a world class ball buster when he wanted to be. I took out a pocket-sized manual of basic Arabic phrases from my pack and began leafing through it. Being pretty sure the bus driver was Kuwaiti native, I gave him a robust Arab greeting and a few other sure-fire conversation starters. I mean, what bus driver wouldn't want to discuss his favorite color or what where the airport was? After about a minute of shaking his head, he told me in perfect English he was from India. He went on to say I would *never* see a Kuwaiti local drive a bus—that's what the Indians and Pakistanis did. The country literally ran on immigrant labor. What a great start, I thought to myself. Then again, how the hell would I have known? I'm from a tiny town in Upstate New York with one black family.

Reggie really let me have it after that, and never let me forget it. A few weeks later, however, on a Blackhawk helicopter ride from the Jordanian border to an airbase northwest of Baghdad, I became violently airsick and threw up all over young Reginald, five or six times over the course of an hour. Along with my gloves, camouflage top and weapon, I pasted his uniform with a half-digested MRE. I figured that little incident evened up the score, but the joke was on me. Now he had something else to relentlessly make fun of me for.

Later that night the entire company arrived at *Camp Virginia*, a staging area near the Iraqi border where U.S. forces made their final preparations before entering Iraq. After our little chartered buses came to a halt, we poured off the bus onto the shadowy, blowing sand and waited for further instructions. All I could see in the open desert night were the narrow slivers of fluorescent light shooting out from the edges of tent flaps. Our equipment was unloaded into one massive, indistinguishable pile, as some major did his best to point out to us where everything was. It all looked the same to me, with neatly assembled burlap tents in every direction. While it wasn't quite pitch black yet, no one could see a damn thing, so we got a hold of the camp map, grabbed our gear, and stumbled through the wind and dirt towards our assigned tents. We were shuffling along like the sand people from *Star Wars*, getting used to the sights, smells and sounds of our new home.

Early the next day we were treated to a beautifully wicked environment with some of the bluest skies I'd ever seen. It was one of the hottest, driest and most barren places on Earth, but gorgeous in its own right. Sandstorms whipped up like clockwork each morning around 8 o' clock, with the temperature rising to well over 100 before 10 a.m. It felt like there was nothing between us and the sun. My pupils all but disappeared as the fierce rays and abrasive sand beat my skin unmercifully. However, after nature's fury was over for the day, we'd end up enjoying magnificent sunsets, a gorgeous twilight, and finally crystal-clear night skies; redeeming qualities of an otherwise brutal landscape. Still, the sand was just everywhere. Everything we ate and drank left a gritty residue on our teeth, and I could feel my enamel being buffed to a brilliant shine by the fine dirt. Every digital picture we took inside with a flash looked like it was snowing, and I was hoping the sand wasn't hiding some strange microorganism that was going to settle in my lungs, lie dormant, and then come alive to kill me in 20 years.

After the first week of taking it easy and adjusting to the heat, we learned it was now official we'd be attached to the 3rd Armored Cavalry Regiment, or the 3rd *ACR*, an Army unit equipped with tanks, Bradleys (similar to tanks but smaller) and an array of helicopters. This was the first I'd heard of them. We'd worked at Ft. Polk with the 2nd Armored Cavalry Regiment and knew the basics of their manpower and equipment, but didn't know what their mission was going to be, and subsequently, our own. After a few days, we were advised as to what the 3rd ACR's Area of Operations—the patch of real estate they'd be setting up shop in and ultimately be responsible for—would be. It pretty much included everything west of Baghdad to the borders of both Syria and Jordan.

We were to be deployed into a mammoth chunk of Iraqi desert known as the Al Anbar Province. The majority of it bypassed in the March invasion, it was now being patrolled by only a handful of soldiers. Attached to what would turn out to be the smallest major subordinate command under the newly-formed Combined Joint Task Force 7, the 94th would be venturing into this massive, sinister territory in less than a week.[6]

---

[6] In mid June 2003, *Combined Joint Task Force 7* (CJTF7) would replace the *Coalition Forces Land Component Command* (CFLCC)—the military authority under CENTCOM that executed the invasion of Iraq—soon after "significant" military action came to an end. CJTF7 would officially be dissolved into the *Multinational Corps Iraq* and *Multinational Force Iraq* on May 15, 2004.

About an hour after being advised of our assignment I returned to my tent, a huge canvass shelter with room for about 25 soldiers. I took a good look around at the neatly aligned cots. The only sounds were the metal hooks and grommets clanging with the wind, and the tent's heavy fabric sides flapping with each gust. My guys were relaxing, reading magazines and writing letters home to friends and family. I couldn't relax, not now. I'm not the type. Growing restless in my cot, I started drafting up Requests For Information, or RFIs, for our Operations Section to pass up to the 3rd ACR's people. I had a lot of questions, as did the other platoon leaders. What does our route look like? Whose Area of Operations will we be traveling through? What's the fighting like, if any? What frequencies will we be using?

I was patient with our "Ops" guys. They didn't always know who to go to for info, and some of those they talked to didn't have any answers either, but they weren't exactly going out of their way to find out. Not having trained with the line platoons, they weren't seeing the tactical aspects of the conflicts like we were. Worse, they weren't making an effort to get anything done. I wasn't expecting a ready-made Ops section who had it all figured out, but for crying out loud, go talk to people and do something. No one in our unit had a clue as to what was going on just a few hundred miles away. We needed *some* indicator as to what was going on behind this giant door before we grabbed the knob and opened it.

In one particularly unsettling circumstance, while returning home from the ranges late one night, I radioed Ops to let them know we'd arrived back on base. It was customary that units check in with the operations section upon returning to post. I called for about ten minutes, but no one responded. I thought I had the wrong frequency, but later learned that their radio had been shut off, a cardinal sin for the section that was supposed to be tracking our every move, even if just in Kuwait. It was much too early for bad habits like this. On top of it all, after a week they still didn't have a map of Iraq set up. Boxes upon boxes of maps had been sitting in the corner of their tent for days. In a matter of days, we were going to be entering one of the most dangerous countries on Earth, and we had no clue where things were or how to get there.

This was Operations 101. I was starting to lose my patience with some of my own people already, a few of which didn't have their heads in the game yet. One senior sergeant in particular would prove to be a huge disappointment, even after over a year of combat.

A few days later, the 94th received its marching orders. We were to conduct a *tactical vehicle convoy* (a.k.a. military road trip) up to a point just west of Ramadi, link up with elements of the 3rd ACR already in-country, and proceed to Al Asad Airbase—an enormous Iraqi airbase northwest of Ramadi. We broke out our relevant maps, found these locations and highlighted the routes.

We started our drive as an MP company at about 5 a.m. the same day major combat operations were said to have ended, around May 1st. All in all, 52 vehicles pushed their way over the sand onto Kuwait's main highway and started the long journey north into Iraq.

We convoyed north along the Safwan Highway, the major six-lane road leading out of Kuwait. Known in the last days of Desert Storm as the "Highway of Death," it was where most of the retreating Iraqi Army was slaughtered as they desperately tried to flee Kuwait. We saw up close the rusting metal ghosts of that last major engagement; charred tanks, military trucks, cars and even planes still littered the sides of the road. Large patches of scorched, uprooted concrete, long ago strafed with 30mm gunfire from A-10 Warthogs and Apache attack helicopters, were a welcomed site as to what kind of close air support we'd have at our fingertips if need be. We passed by all the major towns in the south, worked our way north to Baghdad, west to Fallujah and Ramadi, northwest to Hit, and finally after two days, Al Asad Airbase. A huge abandoned airfield, its barracks looked as if they had been evacuated in one hell of a hurry.

We linked up with some guys from the 3rd Infantry Division, the unit who had actually spearheaded the invasion. A few of them filled us in on the story behind the base and how it was taken. Australian and U.S. Special Forces had seized it along with some troops from the 3rd ID only days before. Being rather large (several square kilometers), it was allegedly used as a small command center for some Fedayeen in the area. The 3rd ID made short work of them, and we were sent in to set up shop for the follow-on forces. The 94th represented a handful of the first wave of fresh troops in what was now officially post-war Iraq.

Of course, being curious newcomers, we drove around Al Asad and checked out all of the vacant buildings. It was surreal. Only days before, this place had been full of Iraqi pilots and soldiers. Now, not a soul was there. Their belongings, equipment and identification cards were scattered everywhere, in some cases strewn across the floor by the hundreds. A few buildings were strictly off-limits. They were being used as casualty collection points for the dead Iraqi soldiers and/or Fedayeen who had been killed in the fighting. You could smell them as you passed by. I'll never forget that smell, ever.

The 94th Military Police Company, a handful of Reservists from New Hampshire who hadn't really expected to see much of anything, were now working with the troops who had made history: Only a few weeks before, these men & women fought and defeated the Iraqi Army in the first pre-emptive strike by the United States military. I didn't see any prisoners, and the remaining Iraqi military was nowhere to be found.

We spent two days there, exploring the landscape, sifting through some abandoned equipment, pooping into a hole in the ground and trying to make heads or tails of just what had happened in this place. In less than 72 hours, each platoon would go their separate ways.

These were the last days we'd spend together as a company for over a year.

PART 1:
White Ops

WITHIN A DAY, each platoon of the 94th was parceled out to each one of the 3rd ACR's three squadrons.[7] First platoon would be attached to 3rd Squadron, nicknamed *Thunder*. *Thunder*'s Area of Operations was to be split between Ar Rutbah, a small town near the border with Jordan, and the town of Hit (pro-

---

[7] An armored cavalry regiment (ACR) typically has 3 *cavalry squadrons* (similar in size to a brigade), an *aviation squadron* and a *support squadron*. An MP company usually has 4 platoons, and in our case one was assigned to each cavalry squadron and the support squadron. Just as the 94th was *Patriots*, each squadron of the 3rd ACR had their own names; the first was known as *Tiger* (1/3); the second, *Sabre* (2/3); and third, *Thunder* (3/3). The support squadron, known as *Muleskinner* (SPT/3), provided logistical and maintenance assistance to the other squadrons. The aviation squadron, *Longknife* (4/3), comprised of OH-58A Kiowa helicopters, provided the regiment with close air support and reconnaissance abilities. Although the 94th worked with them extensively, *Longknife* (as is usually the case with aviation assets) was not officially assigned an MP platoon.

nounced *heat*), just northwest of Ramadi. Second platoon would be fighting with 2nd Squadron, *Saber*, down in Fallujah. Third platoon would join 1st Squadron, *Tiger*, in Haditha, Al Qaim and Rawah, the major towns nearest to Iraq's northern border with Syria; and 4th platoon would stay put at Al Asad with the logistical & support squadron, *Muleskinner*. Headquarters would set up shop in Ramadi for the time being, but would ultimately end up back at Al Asad.

The nickname and radio call sign of 1st platoon was *Black Bear*, taken after the University of Maine's mascot. (Although the unit was based out of New Hampshire, first platoon trained almost exclusively in Saco, Maine). Second platoon was *Nut Crusher*, their amulet being a dead, stuffed squirrel with an acorn in its mouth, carried around fanatically by their stone-faced platoon sergeant, Sergeant First Class Roderick Burdette. Third's was *Regulator* (I have no idea where that one came from), and 4th platoon's was *Shamrock*, thanks to the overwhelming number of Irishmen, or at least soldiers with somewhat Irish-sounding last names, comprising its ranks. The 94th headquarters section's was *Patriots*, decided on at the last minute before leaving Ft. Polk.

At about 10 p.m. on the second night, I was just settling down to sleep on my little nylon and aluminum Army cot under the stars at Al Asad. We'd towed water up from Kuwait in a "water buffalo," a large cylindrical tank with a nozzle in the back for bathing and cleaning. I'd rinsed the sweat and salt from my head and brushed my teeth with a fresh bottled water, now being shipped in by the pallet. A few moments after I'd settled down to rest, the call came in: 1st platoon was to move out immediately to *Camp Eden*.

Eden was a destroyed Iraqi Army post, which was now serving as an American *Forward Operating Base*, or FOB, for

Thunder, just north of Hit. It was nearly midnight and I had no idea where we were going. After visiting the tactical operations center at Al Asad—the place where most of the regiment's leadership, radios and maps were housed—I received some directions ("drive south, you'll find it") and moved out soon after. We grabbed our gear, packed up and hauled ass through the darkness.

Relying on aging paper maps at least 20 years old, we arrived about an hour later and met up with *Thunder's* operations officer, a major who seemed to have a good idea of what was going on. We shook hands in the darkness, surrounded by bombed out concrete buildings and the remnants of a once-thriving Iraqi military post. We were seeing anti-American slogans in English (*"down wit UsA"* was my favorite), Palestinian flags and hand-painted murals of Iraqi soldiers on the concrete slabs all around us. Along with helmets and some other items, we'd find piles of gas masks and what looked like pamphlets on decontamination—not a comforting sign. Given this part of Iraq really hadn't even been cleared yet, we half expected to be barraged with chemical weapons at any second. The major said he'd been into Hit already, and other than some sporadic shootouts with a few of those black-clad Fedayeen-types, it was pretty quiet.

"Shootouts," I thought to myself. Awesome.

The rest of the regiment's intelligence section had an even more interesting assessment. According to them, the only thing the Iraqis in Hit were really worried about were soldiers invading their town and enslaving their women. Although I wasn't positive, I safely assumed this wasn't on our agenda. After some small talk, we ended our pleasantries with the major and left to bed down for the night. Using our red-lens flashlights to find our gear buried in the trucks, we set up our cots and set our watch alarms for just before 5 a.m.

I stepped off of the concrete parking area into the desert sand that was starting to engulf the camp. It was much softer and finer than what I expected, and looked like grey baby powder. After chugging some bottled water and taking a whiz, I made my way back to the trucks. The moon was on the rise, and the night was just as clear as the ones we'd seen in Kuwait. But we were in a much more unpredictable environment now. It didn't take long for me and my M16—complete with seven, 30-round magazines strapped to my vest, and an M203 40mm grenade launcher attached to its underbelly—to become inseparable. Within a day, a nylon pouch with five high explosive grenades would also be a critical part of my combat repertoire, securely fastened to my vest's side. After all, what use is a grenade launcher with no grenades? A small first aid kit, knife and pistol magazine pouches would round out my ensemble. With little room to spare, I had a place for everything and everything was in its place. Strapped on tight, I could do cartwheels and none of it was coming off.

I climbed into my sleeping bag. The pictures I'd seen of the invasion force just before we deployed started filling my thoughts, the ones of Marines trying to sleep in blinding sandstorms and soldiers in muddy foxholes. We had it pretty easy. There was some gunfire far off in the distance, a *pop pop pop* every few minutes I began hearing about an hour earlier, but I got used to it pretty quickly. The far-off sounds of automatic rifle fire were just as easily ignored in my sleep as those of honking "cah hahns" back in Boston. Surrounded by tanks on five sides, with the night air growing chillier by the minute, I drifted off to sleep.

The next day around 6 a.m., I met *Thunder's* squadron commander, a soft-spoken officer by the name of Lieutenant Colonel Hank "Butch" Kievenaar. A solid guy who looked like an age-progressed police sketch of Henry Rollins, he looked tough enough—hence the nickname—but I couldn't understand a damn word he was saying. A bit of a low-talker, the only time I could understand him without leaning in was when he became really pissed off and raised his voice to a normal, conversational volume. I greeted him with a salute and introduced myself. He seemed a little surprised I offered my hand. I figured we'd be working together for a while, so I should make a good first impression. After a brief situation report, he gave the order one squad would follow him out west to Rutbah, a good six hour drive from there, and another would stay behind with the rest of *Thunder*.

Within hours, 1st squad headed west with the Lieutenant Colonel Kievenaar and his staff. Second squad, with their very eccentric but highly effective leader, Staff Sergeant Todd Libby, had already moved out to Fallujah to briefly lend *Saber* a hand in their operations. *Saber's* new home for the next few weeks would be a very unusual outpost known as the "MEK compound." Formerly a headquarters for the *Mujahideen e-Khalq* (MEK), an Iranian-based terrorist group discovered working in and around Fallujah only days before, it was ours now.[8] *Saber*, having seized the camp and detained its members, moved in

---

[8] Advocating the overthrow of the clerical regime in Iran, the *Mujahideen e-Khalq* (MEK) was formed after the 1979 revolution, with some members relocating to Iraq with help from Hussein. Although officially designated a terrorist organization by the State Department, the MEK provided American officials with considerable intelligence regarding Iran's nuclear weapons program. The Iranians found in the Fallujah compound in late April 2003 took no action against Coalition Forces—after quietly surrendering their weapons

and set up shop. Third squad would remain in Hit, under the extraordinary leadership of Staff Sergeant Chris Henry. Despite his Coke-bottle glasses and tiny bird lips, Chris was a confident, trusted soldier who could handle whatever I threw at him. Complete with a good sense of humor and thick Maine accent, he'd be fine on his own. He wouldn't let us down.

We rolled into our new base near the western Iraqi town of Ar Rutbah, FOB *Buzz*, about seven hours later. Our austere home was a small compound built years before by the migrant workers who constructed Route 10, the major road connecting Baghdad to the western edge of Iraq. Affectionately known as *Korea Town*, it consisted of a few well-built, tiled and windowless concrete buildings. Covering the walls with maps, setting up our radios and erecting our giant antennae on its roof, we made it our base of operations within minutes. But here we were, a full three days into our travels, and our mission still wasn't clear. Neither was the 3rd ACR's.

I began to remember the great advice given to us a few nights earlier at Al Asad by our own commander, Captain Bentley, just before venturing off to our separate assignments. Dave wasn't going to win any arm-wrestling contests, but he was one of the most thoughtful, down-to-earth officers I've ever worked with. With a quiet, scholarly approach, he came down like a hammer when he needed to, and this was one of those times. Very much concerned with the fact the regiment didn't know what to do with us, he advised us to blaze our own trail. "Don't just sit there and wait for orders, be proactive," he'd said, "and *tell* them what you're there to do. Don't get pushed around."

---

and position, they were detained. It is unclear exactly what the MEK had been doing there.

It was guidance that would prove invaluable over the next 15 months.

A few hours after reaching *Buzz*, we made the short trip down the road to H3, one of the largest airbases in Iraq. After an entire afternoon of what would be best described as cautious snooping, we crossed paths with a Special Forces team that had swept into the country from the west only days before. In a spectacular tale all its own, they described how they teamed up with British and Australian Special Forces, with each unit having a specific mission, the most infamous being to find Iraq's WMD stockpiles. Most experts were convinced the stores were either buried somewhere in the sands of the enormous western desert or moved inside of neighboring Syria, but after a few days nothing had been found.

I was very curious as to what kind of fighting they'd seen, but didn't want to pry. I didn't know if they'd lost men, or what they might have gone through after what had to have been an incredibly trying ordeal. After a few basic questions about the resistance they'd run into in those first few hours, the monotone commander, John, noted the Iraqi commandos had fought very hard, and very bravely. After a couple of minutes into some very intense conversation, I found myself more than a little saddened to hear the stories of how hundreds, if not thousands, of otherwise good Iraqi soldiers had died protecting a shitbag like Saddam. They all knew what they were up against, and some had no intention of surrendering. They fought us tooth and nail until the bitter end, the same way any American soldier would have if a foreign army had invaded California or Texas. The courageous troops of the Iraqi Army who saw their final hours on the hot sands of the western desert—the true professionals who stayed in uniform and fought the Coalition beside their brothers—displayed an incredible amount of courage against a clearly superior force. In my humble opinion, those men were very worthy of the term "Soldier."

Their bottom-feeding comrades—the ones who stripped themselves of their uniforms, their equipment and their honor, only to show up weeks later with assault rifles hiding behind women and kids—were not. As time went on, the thought of killing men like these became easier to accept, and eventually welcomed.

The Special Forces guys graciously offered us some tracer rounds, powdered Gatorade drink mix and MREs—all hot commodities at this point—and literally rode off into the sunset, leaving us to assume control of H3. It didn't take too long to realize the place was a mess, littered with garbage, equipment and, worst of all, unexploded bombs. There were huge shells sitting around everywhere; some still in storage, some blown into open fields by combat, and some of ours that had been successfully dropped but hadn't gone off.

The most somber reminder of the world we were now in were the hundreds of fresh spent rifle casings everywhere, most of which I didn't even recognize. From the looks of them, they'd been fired only a few days ago. There had been a ton of bombings and fighting there, and by the looks of the munitions, not all of it was either Coalition or Iraqi. My suspicions grew as to who else had been here, on either side.

The sky was overcast, and the spring winds of the western desert were surprisingly cool, even during the day. While stepping through the remnants of a small concrete shack, I paused and took a close look at H3's devastated post-war landscape. It was deceptively calm, almost as far as the eye could see; frozen in time just as it was after the last Iraqi commando was killed. Looking back on it today, the fields of H3 were poignant symbols of what was ahead of us. Full of both obvious and hidden dangers, it represented the hesitation and ambiguity accompanying the end of a formal war and the beginning of a highly charged and troubled occupation. The uncertainty surrounding Iraq's future—and the American military's involvement—was just starting to come to life.

After the Special Forces teams moved on to their new assignments that afternoon, there were only two MP squads and a handful of soldiers from *Thunder* remaining on site at H3. More ACR elements would pour in over the next day or two.

Commensurate with Captain Dave's warning, within the first few days on the ground out west, it was evident the commanders had no idea how to use us. Even worse, it was clear from the very first hours they didn't want our advice. Fair enough, for now anyway. They had no idea who we were, and we thought the same about them. Our first job in the Ar Rutbah area while stationed at our newly commandeered village was convoy escort, as everyone from the World Food Program, the United Nations and other aid organizations flowed in over the Jordanian border in route to Baghdad's impoverished, shell-shocked masses. From *Buzz*, we were assigned to guard some of those convoys as they made their way across the open desert towards the Iraqi capital. The trip from the border to our link-up point—usually somewhere in Ramadi—was about 300 miles long, a total of about six hours through some of the most barren roads in Iraq. The four lane highway cut straight through the western desert; a wide-open, sand-covered wasteland and home to a majority of Iraq's Bedouin population. However, it was relatively safe for travel. All it was missing was a McDonald's drive-thru and a decent radio station.

One squad of MPs was to be assigned to the Jordanian border, about 50 miles from *Buzz*, their main purpose being to respond to any incidents and to help babysit the new Iraqi border guards. Each squad would rotate between escort and border duty every three days or so. The border was an easy gig, living in what can best be described as a Third World turnpike rest stop. It had been looted of all metal, wood, plastic—anything that could be sold, whether it was nailed down or not. The whole place was stripped bare. Even some of the doors were gone. But, there was hot running water—an intoxicating luxury for the grimy, sweaty soldier who'd just wrapped up an 18-hour shift in temperatures easily in the low 100's. Most of the hot water we were seeing at *Buzz* was flowing from the spout of a 5-gallon water jug, hanging in the sun from two steel beams that made up our makeshift shower point. A couple of camouflage ponchos strung up between the beams offered some privacy, but at that point we really didn't care.

Every Iraqi working at the border crossing, I'm told, evacuated the place the second they heard the invasion had begun. A bunch of state workers had either hitchhiked their way back east, or had fled into Jordan with the help of their own border guards they'd probably gotten to know pretty well. Knowing it was the one chance they had at a better life someplace where the grass was greener or sand was browner, I can only imagine the thousands of Iraqi *dinars* that exchanged hands in hundreds of back-room deals, as the border guards plotted their final escapes.

To our dismay, the ambiguity our first mission was only the beginning of what would turn out to be a rapidly growing problem during our tour in Iraq, and a greater Army-wide flaw. Most combat commanders don't know how to use their attachments effectively, or even at all. As a military police officer, I was trained pretty well on how best to serve my company and battalion commanders in a tactical environment, but I didn't always know their mission. Everyone in the platoon had proposed some good ideas. Just about every idea we tossed at the regiment's staff was immediately rejected.

"That's not your mission," they'd say.

"Then what is?" I'd insistently ask. "We're working on it" they'd reply.

I knew we were not calling the shots, but we needed to put our heads together and think about the best way to handle this. Several tons of fuel were being shipped on that road daily, in clearly and enticingly labeled tankers. There was a serious criminal element, pouncing on the opportunity vacuum created by the lack of any real law enforcement, pirating anything and everything that looked remotely expensive. Worse, we were sure foreign fighters were making their way into Iraq from Syria and Jordan the old fashioned way by simply being driven over the border. It was turning into the Wild West, and here we were, *not* talking about it.

I nominated taking a page from the American policing playbook and to at least start with patrols instead of escorts. State Troopers back in the U.S. patrolled highways, and didn't do much escorting. The ACR was still too hesitant.

Unfortunately this indecisiveness was fueling the increasingly treacherous conditions on the highway. With the absence of any effective patrolling, highway bandits and thieves were hammering civilian traffic in western Iraq day and night. It was just a matter of time. Third country national drivers from India, Pakistan, and Bangladesh—their trucks loaded with fuel, water and even cars—were being hijacked on the barren 4-lane road countless times each day. With only two squads of

MPs, *seven trucks,* and hundreds of escorts daily, we couldn't guard everyone. Our idea was to patrol the road at different times and areas, making it harder on bad guys to know where we'd be and when we'd be there. You'd at least make them think twice about any funny business, and you might even catch them once in a while.

Unfortunately, they wanted us to continue with the escorts, foolishly concentrating our assets into one area for an extended period of time. Sure we'd see a few trucks of food, fuel and supplies to Ramadi safely, but this was only about 5% of what was coming over the border. The rest were on their own, at the mercy of whatever *Mad Max* element lay in wait for them on this lonely desert highway.

This was a stretch of road nearly twice as long as the Massachusetts Turnpike. It wasn't going to work, and the U.S. Army was starting to look like an ineffective force; a lumbering, cumbersome giant, unwilling or unable to deal with the smaller biting flies swarming our road.

Our biggest "accidental clients" on the freeway between Jordan and Ramadi were Iraqi businessmen (I use that term loosely) importing stolen cars from Jordan, only to sell them in Baghdad at a fraction of their cost. They would stop near our camp and then tail our escorts when we took off. Always closing, one wide-smiled, cagey dude offered me a '99 Mercedes for $2000 within about six seconds of meeting me. If it had better armor, I would have considered it.

They loved us. Once in a while they lost a shipment or two, but our intimidating presence did help them move their products into Baghdad more easily. Wow that was quite a sight—seeing a load of cars being shipped across the western desert, some with the license plates still dangling off the back. Apparently, the guys in Jordan working the docks, not to mention the borders, were in cahoots with our little entrepreneurs. The border guards didn't give a damn about what you had, as long as it wasn't a weapon. Most of the vehicle tags were European, but some were from the United States. I remember one specifically with North Carolina plates; I'm still kicking myself for not writing down the tag. I can only imagine what the owner would say after discovering his stolen Ford Taurus was on the back of a transport truck in western Iraq.

The ACR's leadership would eventually see it our way, but the glaring fact our superiors had no idea how to use the combat support units attached to their commands was troubling. And this was just some patrols of otherwise permissive territory, not really heavy lifting in the grand scheme of things. It didn't look as if the military was cross-training its senior combat commanders on the use of their attachments. [9] I'm sure they received some basic instructions on what our mission was, but it definitely needed to be updated. Without it, a lot of good training at the attachment level was wasted, as our *own* commanders were quickly being turned into talking heads who simply echoed the orders of their superiors. Our first

---

9 Captain Bentley attended a meeting in June of 2003 at the presidential palace in Baghdad International Airport, specifically regarding the use of MP assets in Iraq. With representatives from the Coalition Provisional Authority (CPA), Combined Joint Task Force 7 (CJTF7), and 18th MP Brigade (the main MP command in Iraq) in attendance, Bentley discussed the problems with, among other things, escorts compared to patrols. In what would become monthly meetings, the subject quickly turned to the Iraqi Police Forces, or IPF, with little attention paid to the tactical role of the military police after that. Dave could see that the issues surrounding the combat use of the MP corps wasn't being seriously addressed, and soon would witness the disastrous mishandling of the training and outfitting of the IPF, discussed in a later chapter.

experience with a higher command in Iraq was, at most, disappointing. We didn't expect them to have a master plan, but this was common sense. It appeared we were simply tagging along for the awful ride.

We met some interesting characters that first week in western Iraq. Some of the infantry guys we'd been hanging around with showed us their handiwork, the result of sporadic battles near Ar Rutbah at the beginning of the invasion. One of the captains described an encounter with the Saddam Fedayeen in one of the first battles of the ground war, just after the major Iraqi units had been engaged.

Small groups of Fedayeen were driving around the edge of town in their telltale white Nissan pickup trucks, shooting at U.S. troops with .50 caliber machine guns mounted to the bed. A group of American scouts, having stealthily moved into a concealed position, had targeted a vehicle atop a small hill on the west end of town, about a ½ mile off the main highway. Barely out of the Fedayeen's line of fire, they decided it was time to try the *Javelin* missile system—one of the Army's more devastating anti-tank weapons—on a soft-skinned target like a pickup. The order to fire was given and the shoulder-fired missile was on its way. The scout spotter, peering through his binoculars, relayed to the firing team that the Fedayeen had seen the missile launch and, sensing their impending doom, darted from the truck. However, as they watched the missile start to climb sharply, they stopped in their tracks, ran back to the Nissan and continued to fire. Apparently, the Fedayeen thought it had misfired; the *Javelin* has an arced trajectory in the initial stage and climbs sharply upward, not in a straight line like a conventional missile. About six seconds later, the captain witnessed the missile's incredibly destructive power as it found its target, the blinding explosion leaving a smoking wreck and the barely recognizable remains of four men in its wake.

We got a nice tour of one site, with the remnants of a car chassis and small mounds of rocks about ten feet away. "What are the small piles of dirt there?" I asked one of the infantry officers.

"Graves," he responded nonchalantly. They couldn't have been more than a few feet wide.

The H3 base was enormous, and had been one of the largest *Ammunition Supply Points*, known as "ASPs", of the now defunct Iraqi Army. At the time, no one had heard much about the outright theft of weapons from abandoned Army posts following the invasion, but we knew some conventional munitions had been used in ambushes back near Baghdad and Fallujah, the now-infamous town that was quickly becoming a household name. My first real unnerving experience at H3 came when I walked into a massive underground room through a large metal door whose lock had clearly been cut. Stacked to the ceiling—which was easily ten feet high—were hundreds of wooden crates full of anti-tank mines. In a disturbing irony, the crates were marked in English, but had no country of production. It was a very peculiar feeling—the sheer amount of explosives in that room could level everything within a quarter-mile, and I was standing at ground zero. All I could hear was a slight ringing in my ears and soft echo of my boots as I cautiously walked across the bare concrete floor, staring at the towering columns of raw power.

A few minutes later I reported the find, along with the cut lock, to our command. Realizing these weapons could easily be taken by anyone who wanted them, I quickly pushed for patrols of H3 until our *Explosive Ordnance Disposal*, or "EOD", guys could get on it. Screw the highway for now, this stuff could kill a lot of people and it was really easy to use. Although it was a massive area, we did what we could to scare off the scores of Iraqis who had been trying to get in to steal anything they could find. Most simply wanted the metal remnants of H3's abandoned military buildings and could care less about the weapons, but some were clearly after the bombs.

We met up with our 3rd squad a few days later. They had been attached to a *Thunder* unit based out of Hit, conducting a *Traffic Control Checkpoint*, or "TCP" for short, a few hours from our post. They had their own problems back near Hit, as amateur bomb thieves were being blown to pieces almost daily by the very weapons they were looking to harvest and sell. A few from 3rd squad had the distinct pleasure of picking up and disposing of the remains of four or five unfortunate looters. Actually they weren't quite sure how many there were, since all they found intact were a few hands and a head. I thought maybe it would serve as a warning to others looking to profit off of the fall of the Iraqi Army, selling their munitions to others with more dubious plans. No such luck.

Soon after our discoveries, we were personally introduced to the courageous EOD soldiers who had the unenviable task of blowing up all of the stray, highly unstable weapons we were finding on our missions with their stockpiles of C4 explosive. With kid gloves, they'd gather up all the weapons that could be found, attach their square blocks of C4 and destroy them in a "controlled detonation." Little did we know at the time, we'd eventually become very good friends with these men over the course of our tour here.

After they had begun the demolition of most of the weapons in H3, we started again with our run-of-the-mill convoy escorts, which quickly became boring, ineffectual work. Again, it was impossible to safeguard every convoy with MPs. Over 95% were moving on their own without escort anyway. Most of the trucks we were protecting could drive much faster than we could, and would often simply abandon us when we stopped to refuel; a problem we ended by taking each driver's passport prior to every trip.

I started to push again for random patrols along our route, limiting the predictability of our movement and creating somewhat of a more secure environment along our stretch of highway. We wanted to hunt! Fuel trucks were either being hijacked by bandits or taken by drivers themselves, who could set up shop around Ramadi and make a killing selling the precious gasoline directly to patrons. The Iraqis weren't stupid; they knew the deal. There were only so many of us, and those who were available were constantly tied up with escorts. These lawless marauders had free reign over the roads in western Iraq, and the getting was good.

It was difficult, watching all of our training being wasted on driving up and down a highway, babysitting a few trucks. I started to think maybe the Iraqi Police in Rutbah could take up some of the slack, if only we could get them some guns and vehicles. I was starting to push a little harder for more patrols and less escorts. In the meantime, I began developing the rough draft of a training plan for the new Iraqi Police Force in Ar Rutbah. Although it wasn't our mission yet, I anticipated it could be shortly. Highway security would be a priority. It was a waste of military police manpower to escort anything. Any Army unit with some vehicles and a few guns could guard a couple of trucks making their way across the western desert. But it took people who had experience to work with and train the Iraqi cops.

And that's when the real fighting started between the ACR and our platoon, specifically over what our job in western Iraq was going to be. It was turning into the quintessential conventional versus unconventional showdown.

I wanted to make sure the new cops, over 100 potential allies in our war there, were trained and put to use as soon as possible, in *some* capacity where we could hold them accountable. Some even spoke English pretty well. *Thunder's* operations officer, the guy who planned the missions, didn't agree, and from then on became a huge thorn in our side when it came to actual mission development. I was starting to learn the hard way that the regiment's resource management, from the staff level, was either incredibly stubborn or just not very well thought out.

Dammit, we were just starting to get along. The operations officer was from Boston, and had a pretty good attitude about things, but from here on out, we'd start to resent each other.

During our time western Iraq, we'd gotten pretty friendly with a detachment from the Texas-based 490th Civil Affairs Battalion who was working with Rutbah's government and police. While not on patrol, we'd escort the civil affairs guys into town and either sit in on meetings with the local leadership or secure the building outside. To say that town had some personality was an understatement.

Rutbah was a fairly quiet city, with more of a reputation for sheep smuggling and car theft than any major shenanigans. It could best be compared to that bar in *Star Wars* where all the freaks from the galaxy came to hang out—a haven for shady characters, but not really of the dangerous sort. A truck stop town with a total population of about 17,000, it was an absolute pit with garbage everywhere, and reeked of smoldering diesel and decay 24/7. Most of the people in town were uneducated, having been menial city workers who relied solely on government wages for their livelihood. The government was obviously gone, so no one was getting paid. Oh, how the angry looks flew whenever we drove through town.

When sitting in some of those meetings, it was clear just how bad the mayor had it. He was willing to deal with the Americans, so he was a sellout to his fellow Iraqis. He had sheik leadership pulling him in one direction, the people of the town in another, and the Army in a third. It had to have been driving him nuts. Dressed in a cheap blue suit, his thick mane of salt-and-pepper hair slicked back, he'd nervously bounce his leg and chain smoke through each meeting, the floor around his feet littered with what looked like hundreds of crushed cigarette butts.

In these meetings we were starting to see how complex the dynamics were of restructuring post-war Iraq's government, economy and politics, and just how difficult things were going to be in getting this country on its feet. This whole "nation building" thing was becoming thornier than I'd anticipated. And this was *Rutbah,* a forgotten town in the middle of nowhere—Baghdad must have been a colossal mess in comparison.

Of course, when our Humvees and security teams set up shop outside of the mayor's office during these get-togethers, we always drew a small crowd. Sometimes I'd wander back and forth between the conferences and the growing throng of curious Iraqis outside. It was one of the benefits of being a military police platoon leader; if things got too boring at either, I could just get up and leave. Wary but outgoing enough, we'd talk with some of the kids and younger adults, pick up a little Arabic here and there and probe a select few for some info. One thing that was apparent almost immediately was the fact an Iraqi, at any age, can read you like a book. If your posture, facial expression or tone of voice indicated *any* fear, they'd screw with you. When the crowd got too large or the kids too close to our Humvees, you'd inevitably see or hear one of our soldiers become a little flustered; their voice would crack or they'd start nervously pacing back and forth. The children loved to see just how far they could push the envelope—how close they could get to the Humvee before being shooed away, daring a friend to sneak a hand inside a window, or managing to touch (or steal) our equipment. A stern voice and dead stare into their eyes let any wily ten-year old know you meant business and usually did the trick. But if you lost your cool or looked as though they were getting the better of you, they wouldn't stop. Like the mean kid in grade school, your frustration only fueled their desire to push your buttons. I jokingly tried to handcuff one of the more devious children, but his stupid wrists were too small and his dainty little hands slipped right through.

Once in a while, a few angry-looking young men in their twenties and thirties would come along and manhandle the children away from our Humvees. With the kids in tow, they'd shoot us a squinty-eyed mean face over their shoulders and disappear back into their homes. However, some would stay. They'd linger in the back of the crowd and just study us. Those were the guys I was worried about. They fit the profile of the lurking danger we couldn't quite put our finger on yet.

While we were outside playing our little staring contests, the civil affairs team was inside, trying to figure out who everyone was—who was trustworthy, who wasn't, who were in it for themselves and who might be a bit more sincerely aligned with Iraq's interests. The Ba'ath Party was everywhere, but we quickly learned membership wasn't always a bad thing. Most of Iraq's educated were forced to enter the party in order to find meaningful work. An Iraqi engineer who served as our translator for quite some time was a member, but he, like most other professionals, wasn't as interested in the fundamental cause of the Ba'athists as he was in getting a paycheck. It was like being a member of a union in the United States. However, the newly-formed *Coalition Provisional Authority* (CPA)[10] required each member of any of Iraq's governing councils to denounce the party in writing, signing their names to a form drafted by the military in English and in Arabic. It wasn't the best way to separate the good from the bad, since most of the Iraqis couldn't care less about anything they might have signed and it was hardly enforceable anyway, but it was a start.

The civil affairs team was putting some serious effort into sorting out those we could work with and trust, and those we couldn't. Plus, they were working on the more pressing economic issue of getting gasoline to the town. All legitimate shipments to their town had stopped since Baghdad fell. Businesses were at a standstill, and the guys driving the gas trucks on the highway were either taking it east where the real money was, or selling it to the highest bidder at the side of the road somewhere. No one gave a damn about Rutbah.

---

[10] The Coalition Provisional Authority was established as a transitional government following the 19 March 2003 invasion of Iraq by the United States, United Kingdom, Australia and Poland forming the Multinational Force (or 'the Coalition') aiming to oust the government of Saddam Hussein. Citing United Nations Security Council Resolution 1483 (2003), and the laws of war, the CPA vested itself with executive, legislative, and judicial authority over the Iraqi government from the period of the CPA's inception on 21 April 2003, until its dissolution on 28 June 2004. (www.wikipedia.org)

Outside of the infantry and Special Forces teams who had invaded the country weeks before, the men and women of the U.S. Army's Civil Affairs branch were the first introduction the local Iraqi leadership—and some locals—had to the United States military. Although they were a welcome sight compared to the soldiers who had knocked the shit out of the area a few weeks before, I'm sure they were being received with mixed feelings.

Adventure is dangerous. Routine is deadly.

In the last few days of May of that year, the 3rd ACR suffered its first combat casualty. Reggie quietly let me know that a staff officer was killed just south of Haditha while on a re-supply convoy from Al Asad Airbase. It wasn't in a car crash, and it wasn't from an accidental weapon discharge. It was in a well-planned ambush by people who knew what they were doing. His Humvee was struck with a rocket propelled grenade just behind where he was sitting, and its doors were no match for the 7.62mm bullets from his assailant's AK-47. He'd been shot several times and most likely died instantly.

Our intel guys said two rounds had struck his chest, but the bullets hadn't punctured the ballistic plate fastened inside his vest. For some reason, the fact that the thick, bulletproof ceramic insert actually stopped the rounds was a big surprise. I was much more concerned with how easily the Humvee's soft metal door had been compromised. The bullets sliced cleanly through the frame like a hot knife through butter.

The ambush was coordinated, and its accomplices well-skilled. However, after some investigating, I learned the convoy was leaving the base at the same time every day. It was a mistake American Forces would commit again and again in a war against a rising insurgency.[11]

At that point I decided Reggie could handle the fight in Ar Rutbah. He knew the military police mission cold, was a former infantry soldier, and usually had a better way of dealing with some of the senior officers' styles that yielded better results. I was starting to butt heads, which wasn't getting us anywhere. We had been escorting the civil affairs team into Ar Rutbah almost daily, and had a good idea of what was going on in town—how money was being spent, what the police needed, and what the mayor was trying to do. Reggie knew what to do, and would assume control of military police operations in western Iraq.

Meanwhile, our squad back east was getting hammered with missions. Three teams—nine soldiers—were constantly shepherding three separate attachments into Hit, patrolling the city and the surrounding roads, and transporting prisoners an hour north to Al Asad airbase whenever the need arose. In early June, the regiment was planning a new task, one requiring an additional MP squad. Eager for a change of pace, 1st squad and I packed up our gear, piled into our Hummers and made the mind-numbing six-hour drive from *Buzz* back to Hit, just northwest of Ramadi, the now-unofficial capital of the Al Anbar Province.

Sergeant Henry was doing great work with *Thunder*'s staff in Hit, but needed a hand in guiding the mission planning (most of *Thunder* was based in Hit, including Colonel Kievenaar). Until then, the military police had been on several meaningful missions, but most of the work was passive. They were escorting the tactical human intelligence, civil affairs, and

---

11 Major Matthew Schram; May 26, 2003

psychological operations teams into town almost every day, but had a good idea of what they were all working on. Although the squad wasn't *directly* involved with their projects yet, they were starting to get a clear, big picture view of what was going on in town, from almost every angle. I planned on coming in and tweaking things a bit; first by getting to know the team leaders of the units we were working with, and then by making a few suggestions after I knew what their major goals were. And in just a few short days, the military police would be, officially, in everyone's business.

With a little more direction and a pair of captain's bars, we started to carve out our niche in post-war Iraq. What we would learn over the next few months in what was becoming one of Al Anbar's most volatile towns would help get us through the next year in one piece.

CHAPTER 2

"The greatest trick the devil ever pulled was convincing the world he didn't exist."

Kevin Spacey as *Roger "Verbal" Kint*
The Usual Suspects

First squad and I arrived back at *Eden* from *Buzz* the first week of June 2003, a few days shy of my 28th birthday. It looked a lot different from when I left a few weeks before; rows of tanks and Bradleys lined the open lots, the roads were actually cleared of debris, and the troops had started to get comfortable in their new bunks. The guys (and one gal) looked tired and a little worse for the wear, but were in good spirits. The hum of gasoline-powered generators filled the desert air, and the living areas were progressing— improvised showers and toilets were set up, a hasty chow hall had been constructed, and the Tactical Operations Center, or "TOC", was bustling with activity. I'd just received my first package from home, featuring several pictures of Natalie, my older sister, on her wedding day. She'd met a man through work a year or so before and had exchanged vows in May of 2003. The two families had gotten together for the celebration in a small town in Maine. Everyone looked great—my parents, Mike and Tina, looked a little stressed, but appeared to be in good health. Smiling back at me in the graceful black and white photographs were the faces of Kecia and Sean, my older sister and younger brother, enjoying an increasingly rare family get-together.

This was the first time I'd received pictures of my family since arriving in Iraq. With ambushes and organized attacks on the rise, it was also the first time I began to understand there were no guarantees they'd ever see me again. Anything, and then some, could happen here. It didn't take long for that uncomfortable fact of life to settle in.

Fearful of the distraction thoughts of home would bring, I carefully packed them away in my nylon binder and zipped it up tight.

Our new mission was to assist with a five-day curfew operation in the nearby town of Hit. No one was to be on the streets between midnight and 4 in the morning. The hours were late, but it was a damn comfortable time to work. The temperatures were only in the 80's at night, much more bearable than the 120-plus daytime conditions we were seeing. Between the heat and our frenetic mission pace, the only rest we'd be getting over the next week would be from about 4 to 6:30 in the morning. By 7 a.m. it was already nearing 90 degrees and just too damn hot to sleep. It was a radical change from the pleasant weather I'd grown used to out west—the night temperature at *Buzz* usually fell into the low 50's and made for some great sleeping. Those days were over.

Things were markedly different here. Less than a mile from the Euphrates, the humidity was almost oppressive at times. I'd often wake up sticking to my canvas cot, coated in sweat and baking in the cement building we were in. Albeit protected from some punk who might try to shoot a missile or mortar at us, it was by far the most uncomfortable place I'd ever been in.

Apparently things had gotten worse over the past two weeks in Hit, and I was hearing nothing but bad news. Some townies had been taking shots at us, and appeared to be getting bolder by the hour. Sergeant Henry's squad had even driven through a hail of gunfire only days before. Too many young men were defiantly buying and selling weapons in open air markets. The mayor was crooked. A Ba'ath Party riot destroyed the police station and ran the chief out of town. The list went on and on. At one point during a confrontation, an Iraqi actually picked up the red-hot smoke grenade Staff Sergeant Henry had tossed into the crowd and threw it back at our troops. There was even a rumor that American pilot Michael Speicher was executed there after his plane was shot down during the first night of *Desert Storm*'s air campaign in January 1991.[12]

Colonel Kievenaar lost patience and decided to lock the place down. I was in complete agreement. We needed to put a cap on this nonsense, pronto. Our job, along with a small band of Iraqi policemen, was to keep people off the streets of Hit—a town of about 120,000—overnight. It was a difficult assignment at best, and the fact it was after dark made the situation that much more dangerous. While a technologically superior fighting force, the United States Army did not yet own the night, especially in an archaic town where, up until a few weeks ago, no American had ever stepped foot in.

---

12 With the assistance of migrant bedouins, Captain Speicher's body was eventually found on August 2, 2009 in Iraq's western desert. It appeared he did not survive the crash.

Before our arrival, the ACR had already been out for two nights of curfew with interesting results. They'd already been at *Eden* for a few weeks, and had engaged in sporadic firefights with some local yahoos. Many didn't fit the description of the Fedayeen and weren't the hard-core fighters they'd been expecting. Most were simply aimless young guys, terrified as to what the Americans might do. A lot of these people had been brainwashed by the Iraqi government prior to the invasion—if not for the past decade—and were convinced the Americans were there to rape, pillage and slaughter. The major fighting had ended, but some residents weren't going to chance it, and would willingly take matters into their own hands. Just about everyone, it seemed, had a gun of some kind.

On top of Hit's precariousness, I was getting nervous about the tactics being employed. On the night of my first curfew op, I was getting the low-down from Sergeant Joe Rawls, an absolutely fearless and ultra-competent team leader on Sergeant Henry's squad. An outgoing and charismatic troop, he had a sincere smile and great laugh. We got on well. But we wouldn't be laughing that night. The team rolled out of *Eden* at about 11:30, right behind one of the M1 Abrams tanks. I was in the back seat, behind the driver, Specialist Jared Brewer, a courageous young kid with a wonderful sense of humor, cool head and love for awful music. Surrounded by rolling fields, thick patches of palm trees and even a graveyard, the stretch of road between *Eden* and Hit was an ambush paradise. I was growing exponentially concerned with our speed by the nanosecond. Creeping along in our thin-skinned Humvee at barely 15 miles per hour, we had to go faster.

Seconds later, Joe spun around, faced me and in a matter-of-fact voice said, "Last night, we're driving through here and I heard this 'tink tink tink' noise on the tank. Somebody must've been shooting at us."

Jesus Christ Joe, now you tell me?! Our lights were off; blackout drive was Standard Operating Procedure, or *SOP*, at night when in tactical march. Sure, that's fine when avoiding the Soviet bombers circling above us in our old-timey war games back in the States, but certainly not here. Given our speed, and the fact the road was flanked on each side with pitch-black fields, someone who knew the area and our schedule could easily get within 50 yards of us and really do some damage with an AK-47 or RPG. Worse, he'd be long gone by the time we knew what hit us.

The ACR had insisted we travel together. *I*, however, insisted that when we pulled out of the gate from then on, the military police would move out first (at well over 15 miles an hour), scout the area out a bit and then meet up with the slower moving, heavily armored tanks up the road and guide them to their positions.

Why in the world they had us follow their tanks at such a slow speed, at night, with perfect cover for enemy fire all around us, knowing we had no real protection, I'll never know. We never made that mistake again, and it set the stage for the way we'd come to deal with the conventional approach of the regiment's leadership.

As the attacks around Hit grew, the speed and surprise of our Humvees would become priceless assets.

My first run-in with the people of Hit came about ten minutes later, just a few seconds after pulling into town. About 50 or so young men were gathered around a traffic circle in clear defiance of the curfew. "Here we go," I thought to myself.

It was the same testing of the American military we had seen so much of in Rutbah. But these guys weren't kids. On that particular night, we'd be working with a relatively new civil affairs team, one who wasn't quite sure how to handle things.

One young sergeant looked at the crowd, looked at his watch, and said to me, "Sir, these people are not in compliance!" with the straightest face and hardest tone he could muster. I looked at him and nearly laughed. So, should we shoot everyone? Throw some tear gas? Arrest hundreds of people? It was clear we were vastly outnumbered, and if we were to detain every curfew violator in the city, 90% of the town would be in handcuffs and on the ground—not a good way to win the hearts and minds fight we were so desperate to achieve. Plus, we could never pull it off anyway. We knew we couldn't control everyone in Hit, and they did too. A little diplomacy would have to do in dealing with proud, seemingly unarmed citizens looking to provoke a confrontation that had the potential of getting out of hand very quickly.

The lone translator attached to our outfit, Rafael, was a few miles away, working on a different project in another part of town. We made the call and requested his presence, but we knew it would probably be a while. We couldn't just sit there with our thumbs up our butts, so with a little conversational Arabic and a good poker face, the twenty or so MPs on the ground made a move. In the most non-threatening, casual way we could, we lowered our weapons and started walking towards the crowd. Just in case, I quietly flicked the selector switch on my M16 from "safe" to "burst. Slowly wading into the sea of clearly agitated young men, we calmly and quietly asked them in their native language to go home.

I wasn't sure if the translation was perfect—keep in mind

less than a month before I was speaking broken Arabic to a guy from India—but Rafael told me later on it was close enough.

After a few seconds, what appeared to be one of the group's organizers came up to me and said, "Okay, okay," and started to motion his friends out of the circle. About 15 minutes later, everyone was gone. It was the first in a long line of things we knew we had to do in order to gain the respect of the community, balancing authority and fairness, without sacrificing our security.

As the crowd finally broke up and meandered away, I was more than a little relieved. About two minutes later, I found myself with a few troops alone in the middle of the traffic circle. My "oh cool, we did it" moment lasted about three seconds. Wary some kind of trap might have been set—a bomb or sniper or something—I moved smartly back to the cover of my Humvee. While the first encounter went fairly well, we'd have a chance to make a name for ourselves with some real pieces of work who decided to push the envelope a little later.

The curfew was a good opportunity for us to look around town—as was the case in Rutbah, a fixed military presence was certain to draw attention from people, curfew or not. We pretty much had the place locked down with a serious amount of firepower. Of course, our saber-rattling was forcing a few who wanted to prove their own meddle out from their homes and into the heart of the town. But other than a few errant punks, we had a pretty good handle on things. Throughout the night we'd run into smaller groups of guys hanging out on the street corners or sidewalks near their houses, claiming they were *ashurta* (police) or at least the relative of a cop. It was probably true; it was beginning to appear the whole damn town was related. Like little kids in footy pajamas pleading with their parents to stay up past their bedtime, everyone we met was feeding us a reason to stay out late. No one was being divisively confrontational, but it was clear they wanted to give us a hard time.

On the third night, a couple of younger guys in particular decided they wanted to goad us on, provocatively sauntering around the traffic circle with beers in their hands, sashaying back and forth between our parked Humvees and the adjacent side streets. My patience thinning by the second, I told them to get lost. After being ignored three times, I dispatched an MP team from 1st squad, lead by Sergeant Chris Hamilton, to arrest them. Sergeant Hamilton was a stocky, pleasant guy, whose eyes completely disappeared when he smiled. But few could match his intensity when he was in the zone. He took his team over, rifles at the ready, yelling "Kif! Kif!" ("Stop! Stop!") and threw them both to the ground. We were being diplomatic, but there was a limit. We still had a big stick and would use it if necessary. They were hauled off to the police station and later released with a warning: stop screwing around or you'll end up in *our* police station, and that place is far more unpleasant than the one in Hit.

The same night, in another part of town, two teams from our 3rd squad ran into a smaller band of rascals who were giving us even more trouble. One young Iraqi would brazenly turn his back and fold his arms, even after the stern commands given by one of our team leaders, Sergeant Scott Couture. A Maine State Marine Patrolman with a love of mixed drinks and public nudity, Scott had the charm and boyish good looks that made you want to pinch his cheeks and give his hair a tussle when you met him. However he could flip the switch from cool to lethal in about a half a second, and he was scary smart. He'd picked up a ton of functional Arabic in no time, and tonight was the first real test. Politely but firmly, he advised these guys to go home. After three warnings, Scott had had enough, and with the fourth calmly loaded a less-than-lethal "beanbag" round into his M203 grenade launcher.

The beanbag was a dense, spongy projectile that wouldn't kill someone, but would definitely get their attention. It was kind of like a big paintball bullet, and trust me, the term "beanbag" belies the power of these things. Just imagine your friend swinging an actual beanbag into your back at about 100 miles per hour.

"This is the last time I'm going to tell you, go home now," Scott said in Arabic, leveling his weapon at the Iraqi, now only about ten yards away. Again, the turning and folding of the arms. POP! Direct hit. Scott shot him square in the ass. The crowd scattered as the young man screamed, *"Fuck you, American!"* at the gathering of hysterically-laughing soldiers. Clutching his buns, he managed to hobble away after a few moments.

We actually ran into that same guy the next night, sitting quietly (and no doubt painfully) on the steps to his home. *"Maku mooshkillah, mistah."* "No problem here, mister." Good answer! Now go tell your friends about us.

Few of them gave us trouble from then on that night. However the curfew put us in direct contact with some people who were the driving force behind what was becoming a growing resistance to our involvement in one of Iraq's most peculiar cities.

On the fourth night of our lockdown, we met a group of guys in what our intelligence team professionally and officially labeled as the "not-so-good" part of town. Holed up on a critical piece of property near the only bridge over the Euphrates River within 30 miles, it was simply known then as

Checkpoint 11. They were sitting near one of the three satellite police stations, on the edge of a four-road intersection, minding their own business. They, too, said they were cops. (We wouldn't know anyhow, since no one had any uniforms or ID). Unarmed and not causing any trouble—other than being out past midnight—they sat quietly in the still, humid night air, a dense cloud of cigarette smoke slowly swirling around their heads, their faces barely illuminated by the streetlight above. Again, knowing full well we couldn't enforce a 100% curfew, we stopped to see what they were up to. It was a good chance to start talking to these guys in a forum we controlled. Plus, I'd much rather head into Hit with a tank company and talk with people under curfew at 2 a.m., rather than drive into town at high noon with just our three little paper-thin Humvees.

They invited us to sit down for a more down-to-earth discussion of what was going on in their little chunk of Iraq. Interested but still skeptical, we took a seat for a while, smoked some crappy Iraqi cigarettes and shot the shit about how they felt about us being in their fair city. They were personable and pleasant enough, but offered no real insight or information. We calmly tried to explain our position; we clearly weren't there to shut the place down or "take over" outright, but rather get rid of a few bad apples who were making trouble for their somewhat quiet town. After an hour or so, we parted ways peacefully and resumed our patrol.

We met the main bad apple the next night. We called him "Charlie," a local resistance leader who was one of the main religious figures in Hit. Charlie was about 40 years old, and a smaller, balding guy with a bushy, black beard. Wrapped in a dingy white *dishdasha* (similar to a robe), he looked like a deranged professor from some awful comic book. He had a friendly enough demeanor, accompanied by a genuine smile, but refused to shake my hand when I introduced myself. This would repeat itself with other religious leaders who didn't like Americans in their Iraqi neighborhoods. According to some sketchy intelligence (at that point anyway), he was most likely bringing in weapons and putting together a roster of resistance sympathizers—as well as Coalition supporters—in town. He was a terror Project Manager if I'd ever seen one. At the time, he was on the *gray list*, a catalog of folks who were suspected of being up to no good, but would require more surveillance and analysis as time went on. The *black list* guys were the ones we knew were rotten and would pick up on sight.[13]

Charlie was hanging out at Checkpoint 11, along with everyone we'd met the night before. Surprisingly, not one of them shook our hands, offered us a cigarette, or even talked to us. To prove to myself I wasn't being paranoid, I took a friendly seat down next to three or four of them. Within five seconds, they got up to leave and moved to another spot. Clearly, Charlie's presence was having a profound effect on the fellows we'd fraternized with the night before.

We weren't stupid. The men gathered the previous night were probing us as well, maybe for the insurgency or simply out of sheer curiosity. We weren't going to show all of our cards to a bunch of people we didn't know, *especially* in this part of town. They gave us a lot more information than we bargained for that night by such a drastic turnaround in behavior when this guy showed up. Old Man Charles had some influence, and they were clearly made anxious by his presence. I looked over

---

13 The gray and black lists were actively being compiled by the hour by the tactical human intelligence team, a military intelligence (MI) unit responsible for making head or tails of the town's main players, and determining the overall threat situation.

at the man who offered me a cigarette the night before. He shot me a quick smile and a wink, and then quietly stepped aside. He barely moved for the rest of our time there.

By that time, Rafael, our translator and a Lebanese native, was on the scene. A tall, handsome dude with a patient way about him, he immediately made note of the fact, in both English and Arabic, that Charlie's unwillingness to shake our hands was not a practice of a good Muslim. A true Muslim, according to the Koran, offered his hand in peace to anyone. According to Rafael, this lack of even the most basic of civil contact showed us Charlie would have just as much liked to see us dead. I wasn't looking to start any trouble, but Rafael's mentioning of this to Charlie started a mild argument between him and the others.

Rafael clearly had no qualms about confronting other Muslims over their differing interpretations of the Koran. He began quarreling with Charlie in his own language, defending both the American point of view of this war and his personal values as a Muslim. Fascinated with this exchange, but wanting to guide the conversation a bit, I tugged at Rafael's shirt like a little kid every few seconds and asked him to tell me what he was saying. Rafael would turn to me once every minute or so and give me the run down in English. Without getting too specific, he gave us all reason to believe Charlie was personally tailoring Islam to his own liking and interests. Not interested in a heavy religious debate at 2 in the morning, I started to level with Charlie, telling him we didn't want to make trouble in his town or "impose our will" on anyone here. At the time, we simply were looking for those select few who were up to no good.

Charlie went on with the stock rhetoric we'd heard all too often; President Bush was the devil; we were invaders; we were after their oil, etcetera. I assured him if we were invaders, we wouldn't be sitting here having a friendly debate: this place would be locked down and occupied 24 hours a day. Compared to other towns in the province, Hit was fairly docile and, for the exception of some patrolling, the residents were left alone. After all, most of them had been convinced the Americans were coming to take their women. Although we were *technically* the aggressors here, we didn't exactly fit the barbaric profile they were expecting, and were making real efforts to respect their religion, families and businesses. I considered it fair enough, but I had to remind myself that I wasn't arguing with an American.

All the while during our conversation, Charlie never raised his voice and always kept a smile on his face. If I had known then what I came to know two months later, I probably would have shot him dead on the spot and left him for the rats.

We talked for over an hour, with Rafael often going on his own, quiet tangents for several minutes at a time. As a Muslim working for the U.S. Army, he actually was more of an enemy than I was. He repeatedly challenge Charlie on his interpretation of the Koran (I understood that much anyway), a work each had intimate knowledge of. Towards the end, both were growing visibly upset. Others in the crowd were joining in the debate, which was becoming more and more heated with each passing second.

This was not a good place to be, especially at night. Although we had the forces all over the city, we were sitting ducks for anyone who wanted to take some shots at us from the maze of dark buildings and tight alleyways flanking Checkpoint 11. After the third or fourth finger was pointed into an opponent's face in anger, I decided it was time to end our conversation and bring Charlie "downtown" to the police station. He was on the gray list, and that was good enough for me. Charlie refused to get into our Humvee, so we compromised; he would drive himself to the police station with the MPs in escort. He had shown us enough courtesy that evening. We would show him the same.

We arrived at the police station a few minutes later, and the uneasy looks on the faces of the police told us instantly they knew who he was. He was released within minutes.

Here's what I didn't understand: we passed the details of the conversation up the chain immediately, and let our staff know this guy wasn't a big fan of having U.S. troops in his backyard. He was clearly up to something, and his influence was suspicious to say the least. For some reason, however, the powers that be decided Charlie would be a "useful asset" in assisting with our curfew efforts. He was actually allowed to drive around town and tell the few remaining people staying out late to go back to their homes.

But that wasn't all he was doing. With an all-access backstage pass from the ACR's staff, he was quietly making notes of our positions.

Charlie was hastily enlisted by the regiment to give them a hand, seen as a new friend who would make their jobs of controlling the town much easier. The leadership saw him as a pretty helpful guy who had some sway that could take some stress off of their frustrating task. To us, in contrast, he was a dangerous man who was exercising his influence with the people of Hit. People were clearly afraid of him. This guy had some power, but no one wanted to talk.

Charlie's "help" in taming the locals came with a price. The very next night, three rocket propelled grenades were fired at one of our stationary tanks, set up near the eastern edge of the city. The distinctive, "thump whoosh" of the RPG being fired could be heard for blocks.[14] The rounds missed their targets and exploded harmlessly, but almost instantly our names came over the radio. With a brief situation report, the military police along with ground troops were given orders to start canvassing the neighborhood in search of the triggermen.

Thunder's aviation element, *Pegasus*, hovering almost silently above in their tiny Kiowa helicopters, directed us to the suspect's location with their cool infrared laser pointers. Visible only through our night vision devices, it was a great way to guide us through this dark, sketchy neighborhood.[15] On their mark, I took two teams and darted into the dimly lit area. Sergeant Henry and I, on foot in front of the Humvees, would fire a few parachute illumination rounds once in a while, trying to drive anyone on foot to the ACR's waiting units.[16] Within a few moments, one of *Thunder's* teams had completely surrounded a nearby mosque, after a sympathetic local pointed out he'd seen someone running towards it. Seconds later they

---

14 The RPG is a simple shoulder-fired weapon whose main projectile, an oversized grenade, has a range of about a ¼ of a mile and can be used against personnel or vehicles. Their ease of use, range, effectiveness and portability make them a formidable weapon of the insurgency.

15 Each of the ACR's *troops* (used here to indicate a company-sized element within an ACR, not an individual soldier) was labeled by a letter of the alphabet, and assumed a name that began with that letter; we worked with "K" troop, a.k.a *Killer*; "M" troop, a.k.a. *Mad Dog*, among others. "P" troop referred to *Pegasus*, the 3rd ACR's aviation detachment.

16 The 40mm parachute illumination round could be fired from our M203 grenade launchers into the air about a hundred meters. They'd explode and float to the ground, attached to a small plastic parachute. As it made its way back to Earth, it would glow brightly for about 30 seconds, illuminating an area a couple of hundred yards long.

stormed in, but only after the Iraqi Police had joined them—no American was to go into a mosque without an Iraqi officer. They eventually found a guy hiding in the very top, in the minaret, and brought him out. He was detained immediately and brought back to *Eden* for questioning.

As a precaution, we stayed in town until just after dawn the next morning. Three MP teams had set up a hasty perimeter along one of the main streets in the neighborhood closest to the police station. The Humvees were parked in a mildly conspicuous place, and teams of two or three MPs fanned out on foot. With a good line of site to the other men, I and another soldier took up a concealed position about a block away, hidden in an alley between two concrete houses.

There, we waited. Eager to draw any potential gunmen closer to our Humvees, we froze in place. After a few hours of crouching patiently, the first hints of sunrise brought the call to prayer echoing through the town.[17] After a very tense few hours sitting motionless next to a lattice-enclosed porch, I almost shot some poor guy coming out of his house to pray when his screen door slammed shut. About ten minutes later, after the loudspeakers fell silent, he went back inside. He never saw us. All of the hide and seek I played as a kid was paying off.

I motioned our crew to move back to the Humvee. After carefully covering each other's movements towards the trucks, we jumped in and the three teams sped out of town, back to *Eden* for a few hours rest.

The entire curfew operation was quite a learning experience, one that would help us in understanding the dynamics of our enemy in Hit. It was a unique opportunity to pick the

---

17 Those of the Islamic faith perform their call to prayer, or *Salah*, five times per day, the first being just before sunrise.

brains of some of the town's more unsavory characters, after the drunks had long passed out and amateur night was over. The young, hardheaded idiots had made their stand and had their fun, no doubt running back to their friends and families with heroic tales of how they'd boldly resisted the American invaders. However, it was the quiet ones who would end up posing the greatest threat to our mission.

It was always the quiet ones.

Charlie would be #1 on the ACR's black list in a matter of days. The intelligence rolling in pinned him as a major recruiter, planner and operative with more than a few of the more violent groups in town, including one with loose ties to Al Qaeda. Quickly making a name for himself, he now had a reputation as a serious resistance fighter and was growing in popularity. Although not everyone in Hit was anti-American, Charlie's raw bravado appealed to many; a trait almost every Iraqi universally respected, easily trumping any goodwill we'd created in the past month.

Hours after Charlie made our naughty list, our bosses decided it was time to pick him up. Colonel Kievenaar, in an understandable effort to better establish ties with the police department, requested they be the ones to detain him and turn him over. He wasn't being arrested, just brought in for questioning. If not, the U.S. Army would be forced to enter the town and get him themselves—a plan that would no doubt piss a lot of people off, and once again make us and the Iraqi Police Force fairly unpopular.

In a panic, the police stalled. Charlie was tipped off and he disappeared.

Fortunately, for the next few nights, things stayed relatively calm and the curfew was lifted. Not only was the past week an excellent exercise in joint-operations with the Hit police, it gave us a glimpse of the more human side of the quieter Iraqi populace, as older men and children brought us water, juice and fruit on several occasions. We weren't supposed to take it, but we did anyway. Fruit wasn't exactly abundant in Iraq, so we grabbed what we could. We always had candy with us, and I'm sure the kids knew it. We still heard random AK fire in the distance each night, but it wasn't close enough to make us nervous.

We had to keep in mind this city was almost 2000 years old, and had a way of life that I still, to this day, couldn't even begin to comprehend. And although this town was *ancient*, the culture clash was not as pronounced as I thought it would be. I was learning that American and Iraqi men were strikingly similar, and the guys I had the chance to talk with were no exception. The eye contact, body language, "razzing" and general interaction was teaching me that people were fundamentally the same in their behavior, no matter where they were on Earth. But a few sticking points—pride, politics, religion and women—were the major divergent factors on this part of the planet, which would come to influence our role in this war soon enough.

The baptism by fire we experienced that first week in Hit was a stunning introduction to a town we'd get to know intimately over the next five months. For the rest of the summer, Hit would prove to be a surprising source of actionable intelligence, genuine compassion, immense frustration, and ultimately terrifying close quarter combat.

CHAPTER 3

"This shit's chess! It ain't checkers!"

Denzel Washington as *Alonzo Harris*
Training Day

Things were more political in Hit than out west, and a lot of Iraqis were trying to put others out of business by gaining favor with us. In almost every initial encounter with someone, be it a sheik, policemen, farmer or craftsmen, they'd without fail bring up the fact someone they knew was up to no good and needed to be arrested. We could see what they were trying to do and weren't going to be playing those games. We weren't born yesterday. We might be shot dead today, but we sure as hell weren't born yesterday. In the end, nonetheless, we gave everyone an equal chance to prove himself (within reason), and some even ended up giving us some truthful, accurate information.

After the curfew had ended, the platoon medic, Sergeant John Bachman, and I decided to stay on with 3rd squad, sending 1st squad back to Rutbah without us. We were now officially part of what had affectionately known as "The Hit Squad." John was a postal worker from South Boston and an absolute pleasure to have around. A combat vet from Grenada and Panama, he was a valuable—albeit eccentric—source of humor, virtue and good old-fashioned life experience. He'd often, much to our Active duty counterparts' dismay, grow his mustache far beyond the Army standard, and his uniform didn't exactly fit the image of a poster-boy soldier. Nonetheless, this wasn't a beauty contest, and experienced soldiers like John were worth their weight in gold. Besides, the Special Force guys in Afghanistan were sporting full beards by then. I cut him a little slack and gave him some space.

John was a very senior E5 (sergeant). He should've been made an E6 (staff sergeant), years before. After asking him what the deal was, he went on to explain an unfortunate incident between him and a major in his command during the invasion of Panama. He became so enraged with a staff officer after a botched firefight he punched him in the face after it was all over. He feared a promotion packet would no doubt cause the incident to surface again. I told John that the Army had lost my medical paperwork five times in the past two years. I wouldn't worry about any 25 year-old fistfights resurfacing.

That's something that always concerned me; how the U.S. Army was literally *obsessed* with paperwork, but was still so fucking bad at it. I saw the same in my civilian careers; where administrative rules, regulations and personnel that were intended to make a situation simpler and more organized took on a life of their own and in turn—like some monotonous, sentient robot—destroyed the system it was programmed to serve.

FOB *Eden*'s development was coming along slowly but surely. Being an abandoned Iraqi Army training camp, most of its crude one- and two-story concrete buildings were partially destroyed. Those that hadn't been bombed out were crumbling around the edges. Its wiring, windows and amenities had been looted and were long gone. After claiming the first floor of a building near one of the diesel-powered generators, we managed to procure some window screen material from a merchant in town. Stretched between the huge gaping squares in the concrete walls, the mesh drastically cut down the number of bugs flying through our hooch, most of which were becoming incredibly annoying. Sleeping with the heat was hard enough; something gnawing at every square inch of your flesh every ten seconds made it that much worse. We were soaking our cots each night with a blend of Army-issue bug juice and *Skin-So-Soft* insect spray (compliments of some school kids in California), but nothing was totally effective in our war for a decent night's rest. A few of the guys built a makeshift fridge out of plastic and Styrofoam, and, coupled with a few massive blocks of ice we'd picked up from the local vendors for $1 USD, we managed to keep it stocked with cold water and soda. That was a big help, and a *force multiplier* (morale builder) in itself. Ahhh…the joy a cold Pepsi would bring after a hot 6-hour patrol.

Once in a while we'd have some mortars or rockets come crashing in at night, but nothing was hitting even close to us. Later on they'd get a little more intense, and we'd eventually be tasked to figure out where they were coming from. In our investigations, we began to notice that the lights of a mosque across the river appeared to turn off just prior to a mortar attack on our base. On one June evening, immediately following a near direct-hit on our post, we zipped across the river, searched the place and questioned its parishioners, but came away with nothing. For all I know, we had it all wrong; they might've been secretly trying to warn us of an impending barrage. We didn't know who to trust at that point.

Not too long after John and I moved in, 3rd squad joined elements of *Thunder* for a week-long patrol of Euphrates River valley north of Hit, searching the tons of little towns and villages dotting the valley. Acting as scouts with *Thunder*, we slogged our way over every dirt path, muddy river bank and patch of tall reeds in search of contraband weapons, hideaways or wanted men. Marching up the fertile lands lining the river, we'd come upon houses and small neighborhoods, greet the people and start asking questions. Most of the villagers we talked with were scared to death of us, but we did our best to put their minds at ease. Of course, it didn't stop us from searching their houses.

One in particular would pose quite the tactical challenge. It was a maze-like, farm-style compound, with living areas for both people and animals intermixed. It was like some bizarre Iraqi petting zoo. A few of our guys walked into a small storage room, kicked over a few bales of hay and found a decent-sized stockpile of AK47s, about 50 of them. Right across from that room was another door, but it had been locked from the inside. Sergeants Scott Couture and Joe Rawls decided to break it down, just in case.

With Sergeant Rawls providing cover with his M16, Sergeant Couture broke the lock with a swift kick. The door flung open and banged against the inner wall of the room with a loud, reverberating thud. Inside were three very attractive Iraqi women in their late teens, all dressed in black, huddled in the corner. Frozen at the sight of these alien beings with jet-black guns and funny looking dark glasses, they began to scream as soon as Couture's foot crossed the door's threshold. Scott, who'd picked up an impressive knowledge of Arabic by this point, lowered his weapon and softly calmed the girls down. After a brief search of the room and finding nothing, he headed for the door. He turned around, only to have the screaming start up again, almost in unison. As he stepped past the door, the women fell silent. In a comical but highly insensitive gesture, he'd turn to face the women again, placing one foot into the room as if he was about to re-enter. The screams started up. He'd step out and again it stopped instantly. He did this a few times with his foot and got the same on-off reaction. After a few seconds, he smiled, said good-bye, and closed the door behind him.

The rest of the farm compound was searched with some eyebrow-raising finds. It was soon discovered this house was holding more than a few AKs and frightened women—within a few moments we'd discovered a small inventory of artillery shells. Stacked nearby were rods of propellant; highly flammable sticks of a solid combustible material, used in the primers of Iraqi rockets. Propellant wasn't really a weapon by itself, but combined with the fire of an explosion, it could cause some serious burns.

The men of the house were quickly rounded up and questioned. It came as no surprise none of them knew where this stuff came from or how it got here; just more shrugging shoulders and blank stares at the ground. And as per the usual, no one actually lived here or knew where the owner was. It was odd; every male in this farmhouse was either a young kid of about 12 or 13, or scraggly, unkempt older men in their fifties.

These guys weren't weapons dealers, and for all I knew they were telling the truth about babysitting the compound, but a frightening picture was starting to develop. Iraq was full of weapons, and I mean jam-packed, much more than we anticipated. When the invasion began, the first Iraqi soldiers to beat feet were the guys guarding the tons of guns and explosives in these local depots. With these soldiers running as far and as fast as they could, opportunist swept in and started grabbing anything and everything they were able to either carry or toss in the back of their trucks. Unfortunately these guns weren't collector's items; they were being sold to—or seized by—the insurgency.

This was more than we expected to find, and now we needed to make an example of someone. Just to teach them a lesson, we told the occupants our EOD attachment was going to blow up the explosives right there in their back yard.

We cleared the house, including the hot, screaming Iraqi chicks. The EOD chaps dug a small hole in the sand, put the shells and propellant inside and set their charges. While all of this was going on, we noticed there was a makeshift animal pen, full of sheep and chickens, not too far from the detonation site. Playing a shepherd with a heart of gold, I took a few troops to help gather up the animals and get them out of harm's way. As the pen's doors swung open, a few stray sheep tried to make a run for it, but they just weren't quick enough for the fast and wily soldiers of the U.S. Army. They were safely corralled into one of the farmhouse sheds.

We took shelter behind our trucks and Humvees. The EOD attachment advised us there would be a ten-second countdown to the explosion, broadcast over the Humvee radios loud and clear. Eager for some up-close action footage, I readied my Olympus digital camera. Man, this was going to be good. I was about a hundred yards away with a direct line of sight to the charges. It was a little too close to be completely safe, but the combat photographer in me simply couldn't resist. Besides, I was bundled up pretty well with ballistic equipment, and was willing to take the chance to capture some awesome footage to send back home (as if my friends and family weren't already worried enough).

While waiting for the countdown, I started joking with some *Thunder* troops about what these old men were doing with the animals in this place. Mid-sentence, I turned back to look at the stockpile just as the charges were detonated. Caught completely off guard, the resulting concussion knocked me square on my ass. It felt like someone punched me in the chest. Choking dirt and dust engulfed us immediately, so thick it blotted out the sun's rays for a full five seconds. Small bits of shrapnel and rocks started to rain down on my helmet.

Squinting and spitting small bits of dirt, dust and metal from my mouth, I yelled "What the hell was that?!" into the radio. No answer.

The EOD team had counted down on the wrong radio frequency. They were chatting it up on their own internal channel, and no one else could hear them. After a quick check, I learned everyone was fine. But I was pissed! What a video that would have been. A minute or so later, one of the staffers pulled his vehicle around the corner from the other side of the house. The windshield of his Humvee had been completely shattered by the explosion. Apparently, he was a little too close as well. At least the livestock were safe, as I watched the animal pen burst into flames and burn to the ground in a matter of seconds. "Shwew," I thought. I didn't want the ghosts of some murdered sheep haunting me for the rest of my time here.

In a few days, the actual owner of the house would come to our post, seeking payment for his destroyed property. He was promptly arrested. As we suspected, he had been looting the local depots in the middle of the night like a kid in an unguarded candy store.

We got a good look at the entire Euphrates River Valley on that mission, including the great Haditha Dam. Overlooking a huge reservoir of water endlessly feeding into the Euphrates, it was a picturesque view of what could have been a page torn out of a travel brochure for a tropical getaway—beautiful blue water caressing gorgeous sandy beaches, surrounded by tall, majestic palm trees. On the other side, however, there were burned out tanks and trucks littering the sides of the road. On our search through the small towns lining the river, we continued to run into some folks in the valley who had probably never seen an American before, especially a soldier. The looks on people's faces were priceless; it was as though we were from outer space. As far as they were concerned, we probably were.

A few days later, 3rd squad was "on point," out in front of *Thunder's* elements about a mile or so. In the driveway of yet another small, neatly manicured house was a shiny white SUV, the trademark car of the old Ba'ath Party leadership. This guy was definitely a somebody. Wasting no time, the home was surrounded and our men performed a "tactical entry" (kicked the door down with weapons at the ready). Calmly sitting on the couch inside was a healthy older man in his forties. Our own Sergeant Eric Giles, a very intelligent, bespectacled, good-natured non-commissioned officer, noticed a picture hanging on the wall of Saddam Hussein shaking a man's hand. The man in the photo looked an awful lot like the guy sitting on the couch.

With a "what took you so long?" look on his face, he surrendered willingly. Within minutes he confessed to our interpreter that he was formerly an Iraqi Army General, the commander of a tank division. Interrogations by the regiment's intelligence cell—now in full swing at Al Asad airbase—would later show he had been in contact with Saddam within the past month. The cell didn't go into further details on how they'd found out, but at this point I didn't care. The time for polite conversation with the growing insurgency was over.

After plodding through some of the most austere, remote villages on this planet, our weeklong mission was to culminate at an abandoned airfield near Haditha. This was where our first joint mission with *Task Force 20*, the super-secret U.S. paramilitary group headed by the CIA and supported by the National Security Agency, would take place. We had been briefed about a week before this mission kicked off that this small airfield was allegedly a base for a band of well-trained Fedayeen warriors, working out of an underground complex. The whole thing seemed a little far-fetched at the time. We had a platoon in Haditha, and they hadn't seen any patterns even remotely indicating something big was going on there. It all seemed too good to be true.

It was. We arrived at the airfield a few days later only to find a few surprised farmers and four empty sheds. That's it. One old man had an antique shotgun that he used to scare off wild dogs. We were a little disappointed about not being able to have our shoot-out at the OK Corral with a bunch of Fedayeen die-hards in black pajamas, but none of us were even remotely surprised.

I remember thinking the story made no sense to begin with. It seemed a little too diabolical, that a secret band of resistance fighters was organizing a massive underground training camp right under the nose of the U.S. military. Maybe it was a ploy to give the troops on the ground a little more purpose, more of a wartime objective, rather than rummage through a few farmhouses in search of weapons or people who may or may not have existed. Maybe it was a simple oversight. Maybe they just wanted so badly for it to be true. Or maybe it was someone who didn't really know too much about what was going on in post-war Iraq calling the shots.

At about the same time, I'd heard from our intelligence reports that a huge convoy of Iraqis was bombed near the Syrian border. Unfortunately, what was thought to be a group of Saddam's bodyguards trying to flee into Syria, ended up being an outlaw ring of sheep smugglers. Again, the work of Task Force 20, intercepting what they thought to be the cell phone calls of some Saddam loyalists.

These were the first big tests of the might of strategic American defense technology in the search for Hussein and his rebel army. Intelligence agencies back in the U.S. were depending on state-of-the-art electronics and satellites to find people in a Third World nation who knew exactly how to avoid it. Our experiences thus far in Iraq were demonstrating the limitations of our capabilities, and were showing our puppet masters that things weren't as simple as they'd once thought. The only way we were going to get who we wanted was either for the Iraqi locals to come forward, or through some good old-fashioned police work. Our efforts in Hit and Ramadi—as well as what would be the case with Uday and Qusay later on—were proving that.

Since the curfew, other than a few random attacks, Hit had quieted down considerably. With this welcomed break in violence, we started working with some of the other elements of the ACR that we were beginning to get to know better. For example, the psychological operations team leader, a tall and lanky guy with a slight southern drawl, would come over to hang out with us almost every evening. We were pretty popular with our new fridge, plus we often had at least a few female soldiers hanging out with us. *Every* night was Ladies' Night in Iraq.

The good sergeant filled us in on how their narratives were born; the ones being played to the locals over large loudspeakers attached to their Humvees. They'd draft them, Kievenaar would approve them, and *voila*—they'd be translated, recorded, and broadcast to the people of Hit. Up until then they had consisted mostly of, "This is curfew. Please go home. Thanks for your cooperation." Basic stuff. We were concerned his team wasn't being employed as a real *psychological* operation. They were being used as stereo equipment to play a few messages. We coyly asked if we could help write a few. He said yes.

Given how much time we'd spent on the streets of Hit, we started drafting up our own scripts with our own unique spin. There were no more demands being made, no more meaningless, ignorable announcements. We would be more to the point. "We're here to help. We're working to improve security, electricity and water issues, not to interfere with everyone's life" type-stuff. In short, we began leveling with the town.

Our efforts paid off in just a few short weeks.

Around the end of June, the Iraqi Police Force received their first issue of what was to be their standard uniform. Consisting of the older U.S. Air Force "dress blues," the dark navy slacks and light blue button-down shirts actually looked pretty sharp. Wow, did they love them, and so did we. *Any* kind of uniform for these guys was a huge relief. We had, on several occasions already, targeted plain clothes police officers walking around Hit with AK47s, nearly shooting a few on sight. One afternoon, while patrolling through Hit, we'd noticed a younger man in black pants and a red shirt toting an AK on the sidewalk. We stopped our Humvee so suddenly that a young Iraqi kid, riding too close to our Humvee on his bicycle behind us, came crashing into the back of our truck. Our weapons drawn, we leapt over the tailgating bike-rider, grabbed the AK out of the man's hand and demanded identification. With our M16s firmly pointed at this kid's face, a uniformed cop came running up to us in a panic a few seconds later, vouching for his fellow officer. *This is getting complicated,* I thought to myself, as the two flustered, breathless policemen bounded away towards their station.

Once they were outfitted and began taking shape as a visible, organized force, I decided it was time to start training these guys to be real cops. I drafted up a quick outline and went to Colonel Kievenaar with the plan. I had Scott, Chris and Specialist Harlan Adams—all with law enforcement experience in Maine and New Hampshire—work on the specifics of what we should be teaching our newest allies. We weren't going to start with anything super fancy, just give them an idea of how the American model worked—due process, patrolling, the role of the police in the community, officers and their responsibilities, why it's not good to beat confessions out of bound prisoners, things like that. Most already had AK47s and even a few vehicles, and we'd given them the nice, new white Nissan SUVs we'd confiscated from the old Ba'ath Party officials who had been arrested.

The "Hit Police Academy" had begun.

Over the next week or so, the planning was going well, but we were having trouble getting resources and equipment from Ramadi. Baghdad was priority for everything, but we were building a good reputation with the chief, the officers, and the people in town. Even the mayor kind of liked us. It was all falling into place. The police seemed somewhat eager to go back to work, the mayor was on board with our suggestions, and we had a plan in place to make Hit a model town in Anbar Province.

On an exceptionally hot afternoon in late June of 2003, we headed out with some Humvees and a few Bradleys to the first ever police-training event for the Hit Police Department, to be held at a soccer field on the north side of town. The field was easily defendable, with open terrain on three sides, and was just out of small arms range of the closest buildings. The edge of a massive palm tree grove wasn't too far away, but we had enough men and guns to deal with anything that came up.

As we were driving on the main road towards Hit, the lead vehicle made a sudden left turn into the sand. The Humvee, under the direction of *Killer* Troop's commander, Captain Dave Rozelle, had decided to take a shortcut to the soccer field, one that took us onto a narrow dirt road. I had no idea why this path was there in the first place, and at the time thought it had been made by some of the farmers in town. The route was more secure than trudging through the town's busy streets, which were lined with 5- and 6-story buildings on both sides and deep alleys all around, but I was immediately concerned with the decision to take this sandy shortcut, and mentioned it to my driver. We were the third Humvee back, with Sergeant Giles leading the team and Specialist Jeremiah Ayotte in the turret. Ayotte always meant business, and his demeanor showed it. He looked like a younger version of Eminem with glasses, but with a slightly less pissed-off look on his face.

Wait, why were we taking this route again? There was an asphalt road just up the highway a bit that also led to the field; one that skirted a row of new houses in a more peaceful part of town. It was in a "nice" neighborhood, wasn't taken too often, and had open desert on three sides. It was a route my men and I preferred when traveling to the satellite police station on the northern edge of town, one I found easily defendable and tactically sound. Best of all, it was made of concrete, not loose dirt.

As an MP officer who's been trained on the 1990's "Bosnian scenario" many, many times, I had it *pounded* into my head that anything off of the asphalt road was mined. Never, ever, take the dirt. This wasn't Bosnia, but the visceral reaction was still there; stay on the road when you had the option. Unfortunately, it wasn't strong enough for me to hop on the radio and say something. I'd come to regret it in a few seconds.

The explosion sent sand and rocks 50 feet into the air and would blow the right front end off of Captain Rozelle's Humvee, along with most of his right foot. I was just taking a sip of soda when the blast rocked our Humvee. I briefly stared in amazement at the narrow plume of dirt that had violently erupted in front of me. It was my first real, up-close encounter with the extraordinary violence the insurgency was capable of.

After a good three seconds of complete, heart-pounding confusion, we composed ourselves as quickly as we could. I dropped my soda into my lap and took the safety off my weapon.

Specialist Ayotte yelled down from the turret, "What do I do?!"

Sergeant Giles came back a second later with an authoritative "Charge your weapon!"

It was impressive. Giles had a clear head and knew how to handle his young team. I still had soda in my mouth. Specialist Ayotte was a MK19 ("Mark 19") gunner, commanding an absolutely terrifying machine that could hurl 40mm high explosive grenades over a mile. Before Sergeant Giles even finished his sentence, Ayotte had his weapon charged and was ready to go to work.

Thinking the worst case scenario—an ambush—we dismounted our vehicles and were ready to start returning fire. With dirt and chunks of sand still raining down on us, I dashed to the nearest large rock, crouched behind it and stared down the barrel of my M16 for targets. I was scanning the nearby homes and palm trees, the image made wavy from the intense heat radiating off of the sand. My rifle was getting heavy, and my vision narrowed a bit. Ready or not, this was how it was going to be.

About 30 seconds later, the radio traffic confirmed the lead Humvee had hit a land mine.

From where I was now, I could see the Humvee resting in the crater the blast had made, sunk in a few feet at the front passenger-side wheel. In arguably the longest 120 seconds of his life, *Killer* Troop's First Sergeant, a slim, tough bastard by the name of John McNichols, inched his way on foot from his truck through the sandy trail to the crippled Humvee. After a few minutes of clattering equipment and muffled voices, I noticed McNichols and a few others carrying someone out on an olive drab nylon stretcher. It was Rozelle. They carefully made their way back to the medical evacuation (MEDEVAC) truck that had been called in. Hastily tied down to the stretcher, Rozelle's limp body jolted side to side with each step of his rescue team. From what I could see, his right boot was shredded and soaked in blood. Just then I also noticed a few of the men helping to carry him were the other occupants in the Captain's Humvee. They were banged up and in shock, but otherwise okay. Exhaling deeply, I made my way back to my own Humvee, with my guys still covering the palm grove.[18]

Ten minutes later, after the dust literally settled and the

---

18 Captain Rozelle would end up losing his right foot. First Sergeant

ringing in our ears faded, it dawned on us—where the hell were the police? We were enraged. No one was at our chosen training site. Someone had set us up, had noted our training area, and was ready for us.

Thankfully, we'd soon learn it was all a huge mistake. A few police had heard the explosion and came running to see what was going on. They'd gathered at another smaller soccer field, not too far away. You could see the looks of relief wash over our guys. There was no conspiracy, no inside job—just a few words lost in translation.

The EOD guys arrived on the scene about an hour later, called up from Ramadi. Without the benefit of metal detectors, they got down on their hands and knees and poked through the sand with a metal stick about a foot and a half long, carefully probing for anything that might be considered a mine or a bomb. They didn't yet have those huge green blast suits, instead donning flak jackets and Kevlar helmets like the rest of us. Safely behind my Humvee, I watched the EOD team do its work. I remember thinking if another one of those mines went off, the only thing left of that guy would be the helmet, and we'd find it about two hundred yards away in a ditch. Maybe a few shreds of the vest, too. Maybe.

They found two more mines within a half hour. Jesus H. Christmas, those guys had balls.

They were Italian-made anti-tank mines, and from what the EOD guys said, they were set up by someone who knew what he was doing. They had been buried upside down, increasing the surface area by which they could be detonated, and in a way that forced the majority of the blast upward. I

McNichols would earn a Bronze Star with Valor ("V") Device for his heroic actions.

didn't understand the physics of it all, but EOD was convinced we were no longer working with amateurs. The guys in Rozelle's Humvee were fortunate; the explosion appeared to have had been restricted by something that sent the main charge nearly straight up. If it had spread, it would've killed everyone inside. An antitank mine contains about 12 pounds of high explosives—less than a pound can easily blow a man to bits.

We had gravely underestimated the capabilities of Hit's budding insurgent element, but had also committed a cardinal sin. I learned from my troops a little later, the ones who had been in Hit since mid May, that the ACR tanks had been using the *same* path at the *same* time to the *same* place each night during curfew the week before. They had fallen into a routine—by far, the most powerful ally of the insurgency.

Up until then, land mines were fairly rare, but they would grow in popularity, especially around where we were. Along with the now-infamous 155mm artillery round—the weapon of choice for the dreaded *Improvised Explosive Device*, or IED—they were being used in just about any sandy area the Americans had been seen driving on. When looking at our operation in retrospect, the regiment was doing the right thing in trying to mitigate the likelihood of an ambush. The open desert made any would-be attacker a perfect target. We had tremendous firepower and maneuverability, and there were few escape routes—one of the most important factors when our enemy chose an ambush site. But we had committed a major tactical oversight—repetitive, foreseeable behavior—long before the mine detonated.

Attacks in Iraq during the spring and summer of 2003 were on the rise. Although nowhere near as sophisticated or eventful as they would be the following year, the use of mines would become common, especially in the sandy areas around Hit.[19]

I was uncomfortable with our chosen route, but had fallen into a classic trap of "going with the flow" against my better judgment. My instinct was telling me something was wrong, but like a jackass I kept my mouth shut. We've all felt it at one time or another, that follower mentality when with a group of people, the one that makes you say, "Where are we going?" after a few minutes of chit-chatting and walking aimlessly down a city street with your friends. It's like you're all sharing one brain; the more people you have, the less brain there is to go around. Everyone else just assumes someone knows exactly what's going on. We all should have known better than this. Especially me.

No one could have predicted the mine, but it was the circumstances surrounding the explosion that troubled me most. The shortcut, the sand, the over-dependence on armor, the routine use of the path—they were all factors in a system that would lead to something giving way. With a cunning insurgency on the rise, it was just a matter of time.

From then on, if I felt uneasy about any decision that was being made by anyone, regardless of rank or role, I said something. I did my best not to second-guess anyone in my own

---

19 In the summer of 2003, Camp *Eden* was abandoned as most of *Thunder* redeployed to Ramadi. Within a few months, the military decided to retake *Eden* in an effort to set up an IPF training facility. Over the course of a week or so, a few military vehicles would reconnaissance the area, driving in and out of the former post, before any major units were to move back in. About two weeks later, a team of Army Rangers, part of *Eden*'s recon team riding in a confiscated SUV, would strike a land mine buried in the dirt at the end of the vacant camp's entryway. All four were killed.

unit, but I made myself a major pain in the ass to a lot of people. Better me than something else, like an exploding piece of foreign military hardware.

The officer who lost his foot, Dave Rozelle, returned home that summer and began his long recovery. As of the date of this book, Dave received a prosthetic foot, was designated "fit for duty" by the Army, and again received a company command. He and his troops headed back to Iraq in the spring of 2005. His book, *Back in Action*, documents his journey.[20] Dave was, and still is, a strong and principled leader, one that my men and I respect enormously.

Unfortunately, mistakes like these were being made repeatedly in Iraq. Even to this day, years after the invasion, there is still an institutional amnesia within the military. With new tactics and technology being employed to fight the insurgent threat, we're still ignoring the mindset that gets people killed. In late 2003, an M1 tank in northern Iraq was completely destroyed by an IED buried in the sand on an overused route, killing the crew inside. Later on in early 2004, over 50 insurgents engaged an all-too routine patrol in Baqubah, a troublesome town northeast of Baghdad. That was one of the most audacious and well-planned attacks to date. Both were horrible events, but events we should have seen coming a mile away and made efforts to avoid.

The presence of such a large number of insurgents during the patrol in Baqubah tells me the enemy probably knew our patrol schedule better than our own planners did, and the attack on the M1 stemmed from the deeply rooted belief of most people that these tanks are indestructible. In the

---

20 Captain David Rozelle, *Back in Action* (Washington, D.C.: Regnery, 2005). Buy this book, it's incredible.

conventional sense, they nearly are; in a head to head fight, they can withstand a lot of firepower and destroy just about anything. With few conventional enemies, the tank is one of the toughest, most powerful and most sophisticated weapons on the modern battlefield. The problem is this isn't a modern battlefield anymore. There are few head to head fights, and the tactics are often anything but conventional. If you're driving a tank on a route every day that's left unguarded for eight hours at a time, all it takes is an insurgent with the right amount of explosives and an hour or so to bury them—not a difficult task when most of these fighters have nothing but weapons and time.

Both incidents were the result of three fundamental flaws; routine behavior, overconfidence in our equipment, and underestimating our enemy's abilities. In succumbing to all three, Coalition Forces made it that much easier for the insurgency to plan against us.

You can do everything right in war and still be a casualty. A lot of these incidents *can't* be avoided. The U.S. military can't defend every inch of territory it patrols and vise-versa. But a blind reliance on big weapons, vehicles and technology will eventually lead to disaster; as will the belief that our enemy plans his fights word for word out of some 50-year-old Soviet combat manual. It's going to take more than the revolutionary advances in thermal imagery, ammunition and armor to defend against the unconventional means of our insurgent foe. Don't get me wrong; they'll definitely help, but in the end, soldiers from both sides end up relying not on machines, but on common sense and adaptability.

That said, playing into the enemy's hands by committing these mistakes is insane. Patrolling the same route at the same time of day, failing to secure main routes and relying solely on firepower to win engagements is deadly thinking in post-war Iraq, or post-war *anywhere*. These insurgents mean business, and to think you'll have the upper hand in any fight they're permitted to coordinate is foolish.

The enemy *always* gets a vote.

I would often tell my guys that when the first bullet or RPG is fired in an ambush, someone's plan is in effect—and it's clearly not yours. This was turning into a defensive war, a war of attrition, and our enemy now had the advantage. There were so few times we had that "clear shot" or knew exactly who the enemy was. The improvised explosive devices and ambush trends in Iraq were multiplying in the summer of 2003, and there we were, in our thin-skinned Humvees. We didn't have up-armored trucks or tanks. We didn't even have the Interceptor Body Armor yet, the vests with those ceramic bulletproof plates in the front and back. However what we *did* have was a good understanding of how our enemy worked. That was more critical than any piece of equipment we'd ever receive (although the vests and armor plating were eagerly welcomed). Our small band of brothers, along with a few sisters, was beginning to adjust our tactics and take back the advantage in a war being fought against an unconventional opponent.

The reports coming out of Baghdad in the summer of 2003 were bursting with instances of coordinated hit and run attacks on U.S. patrols. Too often, they were taking place along the same stretches of highway the military was using as major travel routes. Those oversights, specifically the failure to protect our main supply routes, would open up a mother lode of problems for us the following spring.

The land mine gave us an opportunity to reach out to the

citizens of Hit for information. Within a day, we'd write up a draft script for a PSYOPS broadcast. We couldn't just ignore the progress we'd made in town and start tearing the place up over one isolated (yet devastating) incident. I'm sure a select few in the city wanted us out, and had no problems using land mines and RPGs to do it. A majority, however, were fairly indifferent to, and maybe even supportive of, our presence. Our message was clear, in both our broadcast and when talking with those in town: "Is this how you want to live? Kids play soccer on the outskirts of town all of the time, and it could have been a father of six who hit that mine. Are you going to stand for this? Are you going to let your friends and family die because of these people?" Give us information. Talk to us.

There were plenty of Iraqis in Hit who wouldn't think of taking up arms against us, but if some insurgent planted a mine that happened to kill an American, so be it. On the other hand, we were sure some Iraqis knew what was going on and maybe even wanted to help, not so much to aid *our* cause, but to keep their own families safe.

A handful of people reluctantly came to us with details after the broadcast. However, after visiting our base for the second or third time, they'd abruptly cut off all contact. A few of them quietly let us know they'd been threatened. The resistance was forcing those Coalition sympathizers in town into some kind of involuntary insurgent conspiracy: *we'll tell you where the mines are buried, but go to the Americans, and we'll kill your son.*

We wanted people to know that we knew the situation, and we weren't the type to punish the town for the actions of a few. This group of soldiers was going to put in the effort to find ways to distinguish between the two. After all, our intelligence operations cell had intercepted several conversations coming out of Hit, indicating a fair amount of support of our patrols and curfews.

Despite the threats, information on what was going on started flowing into our camp from those brave enough to come forward, including members of the police department who feared speaking out in public.

The intelligence picture was becoming clearer.

Outside of the combat operations were other critical efforts by the U.S. Army in Hit, branches that helped put it all in perspective. Here's how two of the most important attachments—the civil affairs and tactical human intelligence teams—were working things out in Hit.

The civil affairs team openly talked to the tribal sheiks, police and government leadership in their assigned section of Anbar on a near-daily basis, doing their best to prioritize the millions of U.S. dollars now flooding into Iraq to support local projects—new youth centers, hospital reconstruction, outfitting the police force, water purification, sanitation, electricity, agricultural programs and so on. They were the check-writers of the U.S. Army, the quarterbacks that held the purse strings, and the faces behind American money. They weren't all-powerful, but they had a fair degree of discretion over the way their budget was spent. As was the case in Rutbah, they often had to figure out who was trustworthy and who had other intentions, before handing over a blank check. As you can imagine, almost everyone wanted a meeting with the civil affairs team.

The human intelligence cells were a little more behind the scenes in their work. Their job was to quietly develop informants, figure out what the threat structure looked like, and fill in the blanks as to how our enemy was operating in our sleepy little valley. One of the toughest parts was finding out who the major players were in the neighborhood and who was responsible for what. With innocents, informants and suspects—all with similar names and varying degrees of integrity—it was a tall order. For instance, it was soon discovered that two Imams were offering their mosques for recruiting fighters and planning attacks, and a handful of businessmen were financing the purchase of weapons and vehicles through another merchant near Ramadi. Less wealthy men, usually drunks, convicts or pissed off unemployed government workers who needed some quick cash, would actually serve as the trigger men. The intelligence teams had to figure it all out, and get a name, description and address for each one. Once in a while, they'd strike gold and find out what type of car the person drove, which they'd of course pass up to us. Their due diligence resulted in critical information that drove our operations, and every piece counted in countering an insurgency that was quickly catching fire.

At this point, the impression was, while there were a lot of wannabe tough guys in Hit, few were willing to do the rebellion's dirty work. A lot of Iraqis were talking shit about picking up arms against the Americans, but few were actually doing so. Trying to weed through the background noise and pinpoint our targets was a difficult task. Putting it all together took time, patience and a hell of a lot of effort. The military police started to fill in the gaps where we could, through our own informants and people we'd quietly met with in town. However the tactical human intelligence teams were the backbone behind figuring out the *who, what, when, where, why* and *how* of the budding insurgency.

Our biggest enemies at that point were the planning cells in the city; the rabble-rousers who were stirring up a small hornet's nest with provocative flyers and blistering rhetoric. There had been a lot of leaflets handed around the city; the first were crude, handwritten letters critical of the invasion. Then a few more popped up promoting some kind of resistance. Finally, professional-looking pamphlets pushing for all out jihad against the infidels made their way onto the streets. While none of the protests had yet resulted in their intended effect, the nationalistic language of some religious leaders was undoubtedly starting to influence the young men in town, and for those who really didn't care about the cause, there was money to be made.

This wasn't exactly a sophisticated lethal network, but it was beginning to resemble a campaign template that was creeping up in other towns around Iraq. As time passed, Hit became more of a planning center for operations in Fallujah and Ramadi, where anti-Coalition elements could draw on a more abundant supply of idealistic, unemployed young men, willing to put their money where their mouths were and take up arms directly against us.

It was going to take some serious work with the people of Hit to let them know we were still on their side. A tragic accident in July of 2003 was the first in a series of events that would either make or break our tenuous relationship with its citizens.

It was a warm, clear night, around ten. We had set up a traffic control checkpoint about a mile away from *Eden*, just north of Hit. The TCPs usually consisted of two massive M1 tanks sitting in the middle of the road, and at night, surrounded by 20 or so of those fluorescent green "snap and shake" chemical lights. It wasn't a good setup. Everyone was concentrated in one place and there was usually little or no warning for Iraqi drivers, especially after dark. Even worse, the Iraqis didn't exactly drive what we'd call "safe" cars, the most common being a beat up, rusted out, late 1980's Nissan pickup truck that had to be hot-wired to start. They weren't very dependable, especially if you had to slam on the brakes.

We had just come in from a patrol, having passed through the checkpoint a few minutes before, and started to wind down from the day's work. Our austere camp had little in the way of entertainment options. This was months before the Internet would become available, and there was only one barely reliable satellite phone on post that could be used by soldiers to call home. One of our guys had a laptop with a DVD player, so we popped in a movie and sat down to tune out for a while. I looked around. Everyone had taken his gear off, but everyone still had boots on. We just knew better.

About 15 minutes later, the radio came alive with agitated-sounding voices. There had been an attack, and some Iraqis had been killed. Our field phone rang with its telltale crackle. Sergeant Henry picked it up: Shots fired at the TCP, get moving NOW.

We were on the scene in less than ten minutes. Pulling off the road just shy of the first tank, I hopped out of the Humvee and made my way towards the bright lights of the trucks. Everyone was moving in slow motion, apparently in shock over what happened. Walking closer, I saw the car. An older model sedan, its windshield had disintegrated from gunfire and the entire interior was covered in splattered blood. Nearby, I noticed a younger man moaning in pain and gripping his leg being comforted by a handful of soldiers. Not far away from him, another group of soldiers was huddled around a man lying motionless on the ground between two Humvees. It was *Thunder's* medics, fervently working on what appeared to be an older man in a white *dishdasha*. Illuminated by both trucks' headlights, I could see his chest was covered in blood.

After a few minutes of trying to stabilize him, there was nothing else they could do. The medics slowly stood up, gathered their gear, and walked away without a sound. A minute later, another young soldier casually covered the man's body with a nylon poncho liner.

Within minutes, the police quietly told us the driver was a teacher and the principal of Hit's elementary school. Their somber, monotone voices explained to our interpreter that he was a well respected leader and a good man. My heart sank. My own father was a teacher. A few of the police began to tear up and walked off. A handful of soldiers grew visibly emotional. This shouldn't have happened. We had the best intentions with our checkpoints, but instead we watched helplessly as an innocent man bled to death on the side of a filthy Iraqi highway. Loading his remains into one of our Humvees, we discreetly took his body to the Hit hospital and returned to *Eden*.

Later than night, I found out what really happened from one of *Thunder's* gunners. Apparently, this poor guy and his buddy (another teacher) had been speeding down the road and simply couldn't see the dimmed lights of *Thunder's* trucks, or the tiny chemical lights through their dusty, half-shattered windshield until they were about 25 yards away. The unsuspecting driver understandably slammed on his shoddy brakes and the car swerved toward the soldier stopping traffic. The gunner on the tank manning the machine gun, thinking it was an attack, riddled the car with 7.62mm rounds in a burst from his M240B rifle, killing the driver and maiming his friend.

We were sure Hit was going to be out of control the next day, and waited on pins and needles for the protest we all knew was coming. Early the next morning, we wrote up a message for PSYOPS, one outlining the safest way to approaching our stationary checkpoints. However, we had a message for *Thunder*, too: these TCPs were a fucking disaster and needed to change. It was only a matter of time before this happened again.

That afternoon, we headed out to the streets to express our sympathy to the people we met. We were sweating bullets, and had no idea what to expect. We knew we had to exercise a little damage control, but I didn't want to be torn to shreds by an angry crowd, either. It was a dangerous, but necessary, step. We had to let people know we were sincerely sorry, and from now on, checkpoints would be clearly identified.

During the summer of 2003, the military police were often the interface between the people of Anbar and the United States Army. It wasn't exactly an enviable position. We had little control over other Army operations in town (which we were working on) but still had to deal with the fallout of any mistakes made as a result. The staff creating these problems rarely had to calm an Iraqi policeman whose friend had been killed, comfort a hysterical woman who couldn't find food for her baby, deal with kids throwing rocks at our gunners because we'd cut their electricity, or duke it out with the brother of a slain man who'd decided to pick up an AK after a few beers and take some shots at us in anger. The teacher's death was surely going to be one of those times.

It never came. There were no protests, no riots, nothing. When we talked with Hit's police chief later that day, he told us not to worry about it. *Insh'allah*—his death was the will of God and would be understood. I didn't think we'd be let off of the hook so easily, but most people we talked to later on said the same. It was surreal. Death just wasn't a big deal here.

Insh'allah was a term that would come to upset me greatly over the next year, as it was often used as a blanket expression by the Iraqis to describe otherwise avoidable situations, circumstances that would end up in the deaths of hundreds of good

Iraqi Police and government officials. It's like an American saying, "whatever happens, happens." Except when we say it, it's usually about stuff we can't control. However, in Iraq, some locals were taking unneeded chances in very manageable environments, putting their fates blindly in *Allah's* hands. Insurgents would prey on this widely held belief, as thousands of Iraqis failed to take even basic security precautions when going about their everyday lives. The assassinations of people who took the same route to work each day, at the same time in the same car, often unarmed, grew in popularity over the next 12 months. It saddened and frustrated me to no end. It still does.

Our first order of business was changing the way *Thunder* was conducting its TCPs. An overly-conventional approach to say the very least, it just wasn't well thought out. Tactically, they weren't very practical and, even worse, not very effective. Any would-be insurgent scout, probing the local roads, could easily phone a friend who might be in the area to let them know the Americans had set up a *noktah tefteesh*. Sure, once in a while you'd pick someone up out of sheer luck (which did happen), but hiding a tank in the road at night was neither safe nor useful, especially when manned with understandably trigger-jumpy soldiers who'd lost friends in earlier checkpoint attacks. It was a disaster waiting to happen, and unfortunately it came to be, as a few of us watched an innocent man shot full of holes bleed out before our eyes that night. Was it technically justifiable? Yes. But was it avoidable? Hell yes it was. These checkpoints were setting everyone up, both the American soldiers and average Iraqi, for failure. It was a thoughtless, reactive approach to a complex problem. The ACR was "checking the box" and we all knew it.

Soon after the shooting, the regiment took our advice and

put a little more thought on how to best employ these things. After about an hour or so of manning a TCP, they'd break it down and move it to a different part of the road about five or ten miles away. A good start, but their tactics were still all too conspicuous. During any given checkpoint mission, there would often be lines of 20 or more cars in both directions waiting to be searched. We had the idea to at least position spotters a few hundred yards on either side, to either respond to any problems in and around the checkpoint, or chase down anyone who turned their car around to avoid it. We figured we'd at least have "eyes on" the awaiting traffic to pursue those looking to hightail it out of there. Obviously, anyone who stayed in line either had nothing to hide or was going to use it as an opportunity to attack a stationary American target—another fundamental problem with this conventional approach. We weren't looking for escaped convicts in disguises here; some of these drivers had guns and maybe even a car full of explosives. We knew there had to be a better way.

Two days after the unfortunate death of the school principal, I went to Colonel Kievenaar with an idea. We wanted to introduce a different technique. With armor support at the ready—pre-positioned outside of the gates to respond any problems—the MPs and other regiment elements, roaming the highways in Humvees, would patrol at different times and set up shop in different places. In what would come to be known as "snap TCPs" a few months later, we were looking to create mobile checkpoints. In addition to our flexibility, we'd be more selective in our searches. First we'd stop every pick-up truck, the next day every taxi, then every late model luxury car, and so on. When working in pairs, we'd have spotter teams hidden from view and surveying traffic. They'd select a target vehicle and radio it to the other teams a half a mile or so away. That team would pull out into the street, intercept the car and search it. If there was a problem, both the spotter team and armor support could spring into action within seconds. But the two main points were to keep our enemy off kilter *and* offer a safer alternative to the soldiers working in fixed checkpoints. It wasn't a perfect situation by any means, but at least we'd take back some of the initiative and surprise, two things our enemy was using against us almost daily.

The ACR continued with their dangerous, static approach, but did like the idea of having us close by. And what the ACR lacked in ingenuity, they made up for in sheer effort and manpower. A few weeks following the shooting, one of their night checkpoints yielded quite a payload. It wasn't exactly a snap TCP, but they'd learned that moving around more was a more fruitful plan. I was with two teams about a half mile from the TCP one night, manning one of our "spotter" positions when the call came in: four young men had just been stopped driving a huge dump truck filled with RPG launchers and grenades. By the time we got there thirty seconds later, they were zip-tied and lying face down on the dirt.

The EOD team estimated there were about 500 RPG shells in the bed. The passengers were taken prisoner and the truck was "blown in place" the next morning in a devastating controlled explosion felt by Army units stationed almost ten miles away.

Like they say, even a broken clock is right twice a day.

We kept pushing for the mobile TCPs, but the staff wouldn't budge. The military police should simply lay low and "stand by to stand by." In other words, sit there and be ready to handcuff any troublemakers. But the staff rarely went out on missions. The guys with their boots on the asphalt—the soldiers who actually ran these checkpoints—liked both the idea of having the overwatch positions close by, and having us patrol the roads more often. We were already supplementing their TCPs when we could, and logging some serious hours on the roads around Hit. The ACR's staff gave us a little room to breathe, and we immediately started making arrangements with the checkpoint commanders. While it wasn't the "snap TCPs" we were hoping for—which were coming soon—it was a step in the right direction.

About a month later, our model proved successful. One of *Thunder's* mobile TCPs nabbed a Fedayeen General just outside of Hit. They stopped in his car on a narrow road that paralleled the main highway, and after a brief interrogation at Al Asad, he folded like a cheap lawn chair. In a stunning confession, he admitted to being a deputy commander of the local insurgency, and an organizer of Hit's planning cells. In the hours that followed, he went on to give us an incredible amount of information about the financing, training, and operations behind the growing insurgency in Ramadi and Hit, most of it still classified.

There was an interesting angle to our work in this area. For some reason, even though we were out and about in town more often, it was the regiment in their tanks who were shot at most of the time. This easily could be explained away as a (somewhat) fortunate byproduct of our tactics. Some of the other units we worked with saw it as a result of how we dealt with the town as a whole, lending to our theory that we weren't up against serious hard-core fighters, but rather a bunch of defiant local yahoos looking to make trouble and even impress a gal or two. On top of our good fortune, the civil affairs teams, to my knowledge, were *never* attacked in our area, even though they rode around in their signature un-armored, canvas-sided

Humvees. As a matter of fact, over the next few months in town, residents began to approach us with a huge smile, a thumbs-up and an enthusiastic "Palacios!," the last name of the civil affairs team leader. The impact of Captain Palacios and his team was so incredible on the citizens of the area that it was widely believed some were actually standing up to these local hoodlums and shaming them out of the community.

But sometimes shame didn't work. A few months later, while preparing for a night mission into Hit, a *Pegasus* Troop pilot radioed back to the TOC that their Kiowa helicopter was taking small arms fire from a couple of men in the nearby town of Zuwayah, just across the bridge from Checkpoint 11. We asked them if they were positive they were being engaged— Iraqis would often fire their AKs into the air to celebrate a wedding, ring in the weekend, or after they've had a few too many. After about 20 seconds of silence, Pegasus advised us they were *clearly* being shot at and, knowing we sometimes had people in the area on foot, asked us to clear them to return fire. The company commander and I were looking over a map when the call came in. I looked at him and let him know that my guys were off the road. He didn't have any units out, either. Being kind of a character, Captain Steve Williams, the commander of "M" Troop (*Mad Dog*), radioed *Pegasus* and said in his best tough-guy voice, "Clear to engage."

Ten minutes later it was all over. A Hellfire missile killed one guy, but another survived, dropping his weapon and running into an abandoned building. Apparently upset at the attention this young man had brought to their quiet suburban town, a group of angry Zuwayans pulled the man out of the building and beat him to death. To my knowledge, his body was never found.

That was the last incident we ever had in Zuwayah the

entire time we were there. Given the brutal effectiveness of their Neighborhood Watch Program, I wasn't surprised.

Zuwayah was nearly perfect. All of the houses were well maintained, there was virtually no crime, and the people never gave us a problem. *Everyone* had money. We were pretty close with the sheik that ran it, Abdul Razzak, as well as his sons, Moaayed and Hekmit, whom we'd visit on occasion at their lavish estates. Although we enjoyed the relationship we had with the town and its tribal leadership, we were skeptical of the lack of violence and abundance of wealth. Zuwayah would be an intelligence target from here on, and would wind up offering us some interesting views of Iraq's tribal structure.

We never felt threatened in Zuwayah, and we'd only been experiencing light, random attacks on our patrols around Hit. I was beginning to think the Sheik and his sons might've had something to do with our good luck.

CHAPTER 4

"Once that first bullet goes past your head, politics and all that shit, just goes right out the window."

Eric Bana as *Hoot*
Black Hawk Down

In late June of 2003, the civil affairs team started working more closely with some of the local sheiks, which meant more off-post adventures for us. As part of their escort, we were always involved in the meetings in some way. We now had a good idea of what the community was looking to do, and what we were dealing with in terms of local politics and leadership—who was *really* in charge. It turned out the sheiks really did run the show. Iraqis didn't always respect authority, but wow did they respect their elders—as long as they were Iraqi. The growing introduction of foreign fighters would add an extra layer of mud to all of this in a few months, but in the meantime, there was a pecking order of sorts when it came to Iraq's tribes. There was a lot of paranoia in Iraq as to America's "end game," but it appeared as if its people were starting to trust us more. There were endless community projects to fund, and several new friendships were being made. The Americans were beginning to better understand Anbar's tribal mechanics.

Best of all, our small gang of MPs was starting to "get it" more. With the intelligence team giving us access to their informants—particularly to their knowledge of threats in Hit and in the smaller towns dotting the valley—our squads had a good springboard to start running our own missions, even quarterbacking other projects between attachments.

When the majority of *Thunder* was reassigned to Ramadi in mid July 2003, we convinced the operations officer, Major James Gallivan, that we were fairly well entrenched in the communities around Hit, and that we should stay close to continue our work. Gallivan, who looked like a slimmer version of Dylan McDermott, was a cool customer. He agreed.

Gallivan would prove to be a tremendous asset, and was the exception to the rule when it came to the frustrating dysfunction permeating the ACR's staff. *Thunder*'s command agreed as well and attached us to *Mad Dog* (M) Troop, a good bunch of armor soldiers, who also stayed behind.

We moved into an abandoned train station in Mohamadi, dubbed Camp *Mad Dog*, just northwest of Ramadi. Out of *Thunder*'s direct influence, we made it our home. We jerry-rigged our own shower from a big 50-gallon water drum on the roof of the train trestle, slept out on the platform and best of all, planned our own missions. We were now on our own, just the way we wanted it. Better yet, Hit was doing all right. Having handed most of the basic security work to the local cops, we weren't patrolling in the city all that often. Things were generally quiet, tactically anyway. With most of the intelligence and civil affairs assets having been moved to Ramadi, we gladly took up the slack for them in what was quickly becoming our backyard.

By then, our informant network was in full swing. We had guys coming out of the woodwork left, right and center. Most were twenty-something men with permanent 5 o'clock shadows, cheap pleather jackets and 1980's Western style jeans. A handful were either concerned with wayward older brothers who'd joined the insurgency, or simply dishing on a bad dude everyone in town hated anyway. However, some had much more critical intelligence to offer.

They'd walk up to our gate, hands in the air and jackets open, having either hiked in from town or secretly hitched a ride from sympathetic friend. After a thorough search from our gate guards, they'd make the walk up to our station and ask for the *ashurta jaysh,* the military police.

A handful spoke passable English. Few laughed at our lame attempt at jokes. Most were well-groomed and intelligent. But *all* of them were cool, and I mean a degree of calm I had never seen back home. They had an unattached, almost dispassionate way about them. Their faces—aged too soon by the emotional toll this conflict was taking—reminded me of a boxer's calm gaze as he made his way to the ring with his entourage before a prize fight. Within minutes of our first ever meeting, I realized they had to be; they were from tiny villages where everyone knew each other. Most of these young informants lived two houses down from known insurgents, men who wouldn't hesitate to kill them if they even suspected our new friend was talking to the Americans. They just couldn't afford to look rattled, and a "1000 yard stare" usually did the trick.

We kept up our meetings with the Hit and Mohamadi police. They'd usually pop in to our post unannounced, Seinfeld-style, but often with chicken, lamb or dates in hand.

We'd spend a few minutes practicing our Arabic, but after a few moments of struggling with even the basics, we brought in our interpreter and got down to business. The theme of each meeting was almost always the same; the cops wanted more guns, trucks, uniforms, and sunglasses. They loved their sunglasses; a luxury in Iraq, they usually indicated power and prestige. We'd sit in Hit's air conditioned police station, drinking pineapple juice out of little 8 oz cans, doing our best to make heads or tails of how things worked in this mysterious town.

The intelligence they provided in return was usually something we already knew. There *had* to be more going on. It was just too quiet. The police brass in both towns was capable enough, worked hard and appeared honest, but I got the uneasy feeling there was a lot they weren't telling us.

Every so often we'd cruise into town and check out their stations, carefully positioning our vehicles outside for a little added security. As was the case in Rutbah, our presence always attracted attention. Impromptu mini-soccer games would spring up between our guards and little kids from the neighborhood. They were at most ten years old, and even though half of these kids were wearing sandals, they were running circles around our men. Man, they were quick. I was all for a little hearts and minds winning, but when visiting Hit, I'd insist the gunners at least stay in their turrets with their game faces on.[21]

During our field trips into Hit, we quickly noticed that we rarely saw any adult women. I wasn't sure if it was tradition,

---

21 After we returned home, a few of the 94th's staff put together a massive collection of every picture the company took while in Iraq. In an unsettling review of these photos, a la the last scene of *The Hangover*, I cringed to see pictures of riots, known ambush areas and Humvees with empty turrets pulling security. Jesus, guys.

or if their protective fathers or husbands just kept them out of sight. However, we'd sometimes bump into a group of them during our foot patrols, and let me tell you some were just beautiful. We were making small talk with one (made smaller by the fact we didn't speak Arabic well at all), a police officer's wife I dubbed "the Iraqi Christy Turlington," when she hurried off with a smile when some young men approached. Drop dead gorgeous. And in that particular section of Hit, it wasn't a figurative term. We knew the neighborhood next door was probably crawling with guys itching to kill us, and we were almost *always* within small arms range of at least one of them.

Over time we began to see we shared a very common threat with the Iraqi police. Insurgents weren't shooting at just us anymore; attacks on local police and their stations were on the rise. The men of Mohamadi's police force were go-getters, eager and bursting with courage, but were young and had a lot to learn about the way the local insurgency was conducting its business. Mohamadi was still a quiet, sleepy town, but the spillover from the latent angst in Hit and Ramadi was making its way onto its streets.

Thanks to our shadow network of informants, Hit was becoming an intelligence goldmine, but there was still plenty of trouble of the conventional sort. The roads around the area were getting hot, and the use of explosive devices was on the rise. Consisting of large 155mm artillery shells buried or hidden on the side of the road, they'd be detonated by wire via a car battery, cell phone or even a pager. Once in a while they'd be "daisy-chained" together, four or five in a row, exploding simultaneously as a convoy passed by. After four shells exploded nearly in unison as one of our own convoys drove through Mohamadi a few months later, we'd put that particular stretch of road under surveillance. Insurgents were often reusing the holes created by other IEDs and worse yet, that specific IED site was less than a quarter mile from the Mohamadi police station. We definitely had some work to do.[22]

We were finding quite a few of these new roadside bombs. Every platoon in the company noted their use was becoming much more prevalent. For the most part, they were buried in the sand. Freshly unearthed dirt was a dead giveaway, as was anything that looked like it had been staged near the road (including dead dogs). One of our units had found a 155mm shell near Hit, having been exposed by the previous detonation of another round concealed next to it. It had been clearly rigged with wire to some kind of computer modem. The turret gunners of 4th platoon, the literal eyes and ears of the convoys between Baghdad and Haditha in the summer of 2003, had became infamous for their ability to discover them, which was happening on nearly every mission. Understandably, the units at Al Asad planning a convoy were either clamoring to sign on 4th platoon as their escorts or, believing them to be bad luck, wanting *nothing* to do with them. Almost overnight, these things were just everywhere.

We'd continue to discover quite a few in and around Hit. As first responders of sorts, we'd secure the scene until explosives personnel could arrive to disarm them. Our platoon had become very friendly with the EOD teams; with so much work, we were getting to know each other well. Obviously we didn't want our new friends be blown to kibbles and bits, so we suggested we'd simply blast anything even remotely suspect with

---

[22] That IED explosion injured Erik Karlon, a staff sergeant and squad leader with 4th platoon, nearly blinding him. Another shell, concealed in the dirt, blew up as soldiers from 4th patrolled around the area by foot, barely missing two. Erik has almost fully recovered.

our MK19 grenade launchers. They calmly advised against it, saying it usually wouldn't destroy the explosives, and just made them that much more unstable and difficult to disarm. Given they'd gone to school for about a year to learn how to do this stuff, I readily took their word for it.

In yet another disturbing trend in the province, intelligence was noting the use of diversionary devices in ambushes. A conspicuously-placed IED would lure our EOD teams closer, only for them to be killed by a secondary device buried nearby. It had happened in Fallujah twice already, and it was only a matter of time before our local insurgent teams picked up on it. The EOD teams—already concerned with cutting red, blue and green wires and such—had enough problems to deal with. From now on, when possible, we'd make a thorough sweep for additional IEDs, and push our security perimeter out to keep an eye on anyone who might have been watching our ordnance guys from afar. By this time we could tell the difference between curious Joe Iraqi and those other, more suspicious characters eyeing our every move, lingering just out of range. And if they had a cell phone, forget it; they were getting grabbed and questioned. Those particular missions were highly unsettling tasks, at best, and they were happening more and more often.

There was also a lot of talk that Saddam and other *High Value Targets* were traveling the routes between Haditha, Ramadi and the Jordanian border. There were even rumors that Hussein was living with the former mayor of Hit, now living in Haditha (the house was later raided with no trace). On one afternoon during an operation in Ramadi, we were radioed to lend a hand with the apprehension of some who were believed to be suspects on the "55 Most Wanted" list.

Before we knew what was happening, our three Humvees

were rocketing down the local highway. A late-model luxury car had allegedly zoomed around a checkpoint and was heading out of Ramadi at high speed towards the Jordanian border. A Kiowa helicopter team was dispatched from Ramadi to track it. At a top speed of around 150 mph, it didn't take long for the pilots to catch up. A few moments later, the car came crashing to the side of the road, its back driver's side tire shredded by the Kiowa's .50 caliber machine gun.

We caught up to them a few minutes later. Leaping out of our still-moving Humvees we surrounded the car, our M16s intently aimed at the doors and trunk. As we got closer, we noticed a man was tending to a woman in the passenger seat, with specks of blood and broken glass littering the asphalt. Medics from the checkpoint unit in pursuit started treating her. The woman had been shot in the leg, a 5.56mm round piercing her thigh.

It was a man and his wife driving to Jordan. They weren't suspects, fugitives or on anyone's watch list. Neither was the car. Apparently some wires had been crossed, but no one had any idea how it started. We questioned the driver, who spoke perfect English, about his involvement. Apparently, he was a businessman on his way to Jordan. We did a cursory search of his car and found nothing.

He abruptly changed his tire, threw his tools in the trunk and slammed it shut. He came up to Scott and me and angrily told us he was headed straight into Amman, finding the nearest Al Jazeera cameraman and telling him the story of the trigger-happy American Army. We apologized again. He jumped into his car and sped off into the western desert toward Jordan.

These were the mistaken identity incidents I knew were happening all too frequently, but also knew couldn't be avoided. Nothing was that black and white in Iraq.

Then I thought, why would that guy go to Jordan? He could have found an Al Jazeera cameraman on any street corner in Baghdad, so I was told, anyway. We'd pulled their "news teams" over a few times already in our checkpoints, and whenever we did, we grew very suspicious—those guys didn't randomly show up in search of the latest news, it was usually just prior to something big going down. In some kind of sick arrangement, someone had usually tipped them off beforehand.

On July 23, 2003, Captain Joshua Byers, the company commander of *Fox* Troop, 2nd Squadron, 3rd Armored Cavalry Regiment, was killed by an IED in Ramadi. His driver, Specialist Tim Buskell, was formerly a soldier in our own Army Reserve unit years before. Tim was spared; his body only slightly pocked with shrapnel from an explosion that killed a man sitting two feet to his right.

Within a week, the U.S. military would know who was responsible for it, and where they lived.

Third squad and I were up at the train station when the call came in from Captain Andrew Watson, the new commander of *Killer* troop; our unit had been personally requested for a joint operation with Special Forces Operational Detachment Alpha, in a mission to capture or kill the IED team that had taken Captain Byers' life. In what would be considered one of the most successful joint operations of the past six months—involving the massive conventional machinery of the ACR and the quiet intensity of the "SF"—the small Army Reserve unit from New Hampshire would find itself right in the middle of it.

The Alpha detachment had been quietly working in Ramadi for some time, and had developed an impressive network of informants. They were working out of a small complex of buildings just across the Euphrates from the 82nd Airborne's headquarters, *Champion Main*; the tiny, walled-in compound featuring several of the former dictator's once-luxurious palaces. It was one of the strangest feelings driving by their post. We all knew who was there, but we never saw a soul. They managed to keep a low profile for a little while, but within a few weeks of moving in, our common enemy knew who—and where—they were. Public enemy number one within days, their small compound became the focus of more and more attacks. Peppered with mortars nearly every night, most would splash harmlessly into the warm water of the Euphrates. However, perhaps after drawing the short straw, some foolish insurgents would attempt to approach the lair on foot, only to be cut to ribbons by deftly-camouflaged men, lying in wait nearby.

They were dangerously efficient in their work, and their covert activities were the stuff of legend. On one occasion it almost proved deadly in a near-miss, friendly fire incident. Members of our own 3rd platoon, responsible for gate security at *Champion*, had fired a few warning shots at what turned out to be Alpha's SUV as it silently crept up the road towards the camp with its lights off late one night. A few soldiers from Alpha calmly exited their vehicle with their hands up and shouted, "Don't shoot, we're Special Forces." After reaching the gate—a little relieved no doubt—they explained to our troops that they were sick of their rations and wanted to hit the "midnight chow" on *Champion* for a tastier meal. I didn't think the Army's chow was to die for, but apparently for some, it was.

Alpha had a good relationship with the premier "spooks"

in the region, the long-range surveillance (LRS) team.[23] These were the men of Special Forces who could infiltrate an area undetected, gather intelligence using a unique blend of camouflage and stealth, and then disappear into the shadows of Iraq's alleyways. After Alpha had a solid lead on the IED team, LRS went to work. Perfecting their camouflage and carrying only what they absolutely needed, they slipped off to locate their target. Before long, they'd quietly make their way into Ramadi, find their objective, and settle in. Blending into Ramadi's ruthless backstreets, they took up positions just outside the main target's home and tracked his every move. Within 72 hours, the LRS team had identified the entire IED team, and had learned the patterns of the eight-man enemy force.

They were extremely effective at their task, and impressive doesn't even begin to describe it. While I can't go any further regarding how they managed to move into place, the LRS team settled within about 100 yards of our insurgent enemy and stayed there for days, perfectly invisible to the community around them. Their years of working together—from their unique, coded hand signals refined over months of training, to the way each man could recognize another in the pitch black darkness through night vision goggles simply by the way he crawled, walked or ran—was about to pay off in a big way.

Alpha team had been tipped off as to the identities of the IED team by their Iraqi informant, thanks to an age-old human defect—vanity. While the men who killed Captain Byers were very good at concealing explosives, they were horrible at keeping their mouths shut, and their swollen egos would lead us right to them. Over the past few days, most couldn't help but

---

23 The term "spook" generically refers to anyone in the intelligence business, or special operations soldiers who carry out highly sensitive missions.

brag to their families, neighbors and guys at the local barber shop about what they had done to the young Army officer. Unfortunately for them, Alpha detachment's informant was all ears.

Over a few days leading up to the raid, the LRS team observed that the "leader" would stop outside his house and fire his AK twice just before daybreak; the signal for his little piss ant minions to gather. After about six minutes, they'd all eventually make their way to the leader's house and shuffle off to another hideout, no doubt to organize their lethal to-do list and plan more attacks against us.

After the pattern seemed consistent, Alpha devised the capture plans. While it was formally a Special Forces mission, they needed the hardware of the regiment to secure their target area, a fairly unstable section of Ramadi.

The night before, Captain Watson, a very intelligent and inspiring leader with a knack for motivational speaking, briefed us on the operation. He was a little concerned about the way the regiment had been reconnoitering this particular area of Ramadi, that so many fly-bys from *Pegasus* might have spooked them into hiding. However, Alpha's informant carefully let us know they hadn't moved, and was confident our targets would still be there by the time our raid kicked off the next day.

The mission was straight forward enough. Around daybreak, after the IED team had gathered and headed inside, the LRS team would quietly slip away. Moments later, Alpha's SUV would casually make its way towards the IED team leader's house. Having driven through this area before, the SUV shouldn't look too out of place. Their informant, concealed in the backseat in sunglasses, Kevlar helmet and a bulletproof vest, would point out the target house and verify the LRS team had the correct spot. Once the house was positively identified, a small, plastic chemical light would be tossed on its front lawn. When the signal was given, the operation would begin and we'd go to work.

We'd heard stories about soldiers from the Alpha detachment searching and clearing houses by themselves, a task usually reserved for a squad of 8 to 12 men. While we wanted to detain this IED team alive, it was clear Alpha would shred anyone in their way who put up any kind of resistance. And after what we'd been through over the last few months, so would we.

That being said, these were the offensive missions that made us all feel like soldiers. If we were to die the next day, it wouldn't be from an explosion of an invisible IED while patrolling a forgettable piece of dirt, buried by faceless men we'd never meet. It would be close up and very personal, surrounded by acrid smoke, noise, and a hot pile of spent 5.56mm shells in all-out combat, with the clear intention of capturing or killing our sworn enemy. We'd see their faces, and they'd see ours.

After the brief, 2nd platoon and our squad rehearsed a few times and then bedded down for the night. It was already about midnight, and we were to spring into action well before dawn. At that time, *Rifles West* was an absolute hellhole, filled with bugs, fleas, dust and the putrid stench of burning garbage. The engineered murals of Hussein hoisting the Palestinian flag or surrounded by smiling little children, served as a constant reminder of why we were there.

I spent most of the night staring into the star-filled Iraqi sky from the top of my Humvee, unable to sleep due to the relentless attack on my bare skin by the legions of invisible insects. After about a total of 45 minutes of rest, my watch beeped and I got up to prepare myself and my men for the pre-dawn raid.

Most were already up and about, joking with their friends in the dark about nonsense, the way soldiers do before such a serious mission. Although we'd have a tremendous tactical advantage with our Bradleys, tanks and Humvees, all it took was one stray bullet or RPG to end it all. Hell, there's always the possibility of getting killed accidentally by one of your own guys.

These raids were often lopsided, with American firepower easily having the upper hand, but in Iraq none of that mattered anymore. Our enemy was very cunning and had found ways to combat the conventional powers of the United States military. Worse, they had no respect for life, and would gladly sacrifice themselves or others if it meant taking a few of us with them.

We milled about the darkness, focused on the task at hand, but well aware this could be our last day on Earth. It's a feeling I can't describe, but know all too well. Most combat veterans do. Then I started thinking, if I was hit by an RPG and blew up, would I even feel it? Or if I was killed, would I even know I was dead? What, if anything, was waiting for me on the other side?

Okay, enough of blowing my own mind. It was time. We slowly rolled out into position just shy of our target neighborhood, the only sound being the soft crunch of loose dirt under our tires and the rough idling of our Humvee engines. Keeping our distance, we crept up to our avenue of approach, ready to storm in when the signal was given. The radio was quietly echoing Alpha's every move as they drove through the pre-dawn light towards the house. After a few minutes, just before daybreak, the chemical light was tossed. Our radio exploded with shouts of "*GO! GO! GO!*"

We were taking the corners of the mixed dirt and asphalt

roads so sharply we were briefly up on two wheels. Swiftly cutting around the tanks that were moving into position, it was barely light enough to see as we came on the scene about 20 seconds later. Just as we had stopped, BOOM! Alpha had kicked the door in and deployed a "flash-bang" device to disorient anyone inside. Despite its fun-loving name, the concussive blast and blinding light from one of these potent gadgets could fuck you up in a hurry. No one wanted to be on the business end of one of those little canisters.

Our Humvees came to a sliding halt. Dashing towards the small rock fence in front of us, our squad took up position just outside the target house, rifles sweeping for targets. If anyone inside wanted a fight, it was going to happen now. While scanning every window and rooftop, a few older men wandered outside. Seeing they were unarmed, I angrily motioned them back with a wave of my left hand. For Chrissake, only an Iraqi would come outside in a dangerous neighborhood after an explosion. Better yet, a little girl, maybe about 4 or 5, was right behind them, staring in wide-eyed amazement at the Army men who'd blazed into their neighborhood.

We were in a tight spot. Our Humvees were bullet magnets, and the best cover we had in front of us was a waist-high stone fence. From the map recon the night before, I thought we'd have more room, but there was only so much you could get from a map. The main road was very narrow, with houses only a few yards away on either side. We couldn't move. If anyone popped out of one of these windows with an AK, it was just a matter of who could fire first.

Within seconds, Special Forces had a few men in cuffs and face down in the dirt. Man, they were quick. But where were the rest? Seconds later, a firm voice came over the radio, warning everyone a handful of men fitting their profile had scurried towards another house at the opening of the raid. Adjacent to a thick patch of tall reeds, it looked abandoned. Special Forces and a handful of *Killer's* men assaulted the house, as our squad shifted position to the edge of the neighborhood. The second place was searched and cleared. No one was inside.

Second platoon, setting up a perimeter behind the row of houses, shouted over the radio: *"Watch your six!! They're in the reeds!!"*

The tempo of this operation was growing exponentially by the second, and we were closing distance with our own men. In giving chase, we looked like chickens excitedly running around a farm yard. Worse, the reeds were ten feet high and *thick*. We weren't sure where these guys disappeared to, or what they were carrying in the way of weapons. At that point, we didn't care. We'd pinned down this gang of thugs and were ready to kill them if they didn't give up. After a few seconds, crouching behind a solid wall of men with guns at the ready, the interpreter began shouting into the thicket. "We have the place surrounded and are prepared to fire. Come out now or you're dead!"

Most of the people in the area knew how Alpha detachment worked, and realized this wasn't an idle threat. Almost on cue, a few darted out of the reeds and bounded away towards the road, unarmed as far as we could tell. A few troops from 2nd platoon gave chase, closed in and violently tackled them onto the hard-packed dirt path.

After we had a few more in custody, the units collapsed back on to our designated rally point. Two of 94th's MP teams were still out chasing a couple of men who were thought to be part of the IED team, but returned empty handed. Those on the run had melted away into the landscape, as was often the case in that conflict.

The operation ended without a shot fired. After all was said and done, we'd nabbed the punk who had actually detonated the IED that killed Byers, and captured all but three of the eight men of his ruthless crew. A couple of other younger Iraqis were detained out of an abundance of caution, but would end up being released after a few minutes of questioning. Wrong place, wrong time.

Ten minutes later we gathered once again at the rally point, doing our best to stay vigilant despite our adrenaline crash. Our cuffed enemies were now kneeling pathetically at our feet, whimpering softly, their clothes torn and stained. Although a professional soldier in the U.S. military, I began to understand the feelings of retribution that sometimes overwhelm soldiers who have insurgent killers in their possession. Honestly I don't know how I would have reacted if they had taken the life of someone I knew. I didn't know Captain Byers personally, and for all I knew I was staring at a man who had taken away the father of two small children, the husband of a crippled wife, or the son of a proud father, only to brag about it afterwards like an amateur football player wildly celebrating a fucking touchdown. Staring at a wretched member of a cowardly army, I now understood how a soldier could take a man's life without remorse. It put some serious hate in my heart; a hate that would stay tucked away somewhere in my head for the rest of my days. Human life wasn't worth as much as I once thought it was.

The intelligence reports up to that point were filled with heartbreaking statistics of IEDs killing soldiers and Marines in Iraq, their assailants being anonymous, invisible men who would often vanish into thin air, living to fight another day.

This was one time they wouldn't.

Around Hit, we were leveraging our informants and police connections, and doing our best to stay on top of any potential problems. Everyone in Hit knew who the cops were, and they didn't really try to hide their association with us. We'd have meetings every few days, their telltale old trucks rattling up the road to our camp. On occasion, we'd sneak to the city's edge at night and meet with a handful of trusted Iraqis who were giving us the straight dope on the latest gossip in town. They'd hop into the back of our Humvees, light up a cigarette of course, and offer up some details. We'd run it past the police a few days later for their take, and grab someone if we had to.

Our units were actually getting more information by staying out of Hit than when we were patrolling. Not only could we take a breather from our nonstop operations there, it allowed us to tackle some of the bigger, more pressing tactical problems beginning to plague Ramadi. There were still a lot of weapons and bad guys zipping along the highways between the two cities, and still only a handful of troops to deal with them. We had some serious work to do. The roads between Hit and Ramadi weren't just our main supply routes—they were the insurgency's, too. Convinced we had Hit under control, we started to focus more on the roads. With an unpredictable and unrelenting patrol schedule between us and *Mad Dog*, the word was getting out—the U.S. military was getting better, faster and smarter.

Back at the train station, we were also beginning to enjoy some of the creature comforts we'd put together. Scott had bought a nice gas range and a few pots and pans from the local shop; perfect for cooking up those Ramen Noodles some gracious folks back in New Hampshire had sent us. Our cooler was replenished every few days with fresh ice, and we kept up our soda runs, purchased from local merchants. Until then, I'd never had a Coke with Arabic writing on it. We even had some rudimentary weights for lifting (mostly spare parts from the tank garage) and a decent chin-up bar. The steel 50-gallon drum of water on the station's concrete roof, heated by the sun's intense rays all day, served as a makeshift shower point. Hoisting nine or ten 5-gallon water jugs about 25 feet from the platform to the roof every few days was a pretty good workout in itself. With a small rubber hose about 15 feet long lowered down onto the platform, those showers were a sanity-saver after being caked in grime and sweat for three straight days. They were even better than recalling the sight of our favorite female soldier back at *Eden*—a beautiful nurse with huge fake tits—who'd carry those very cold blocks of ice against her skin-tight t-shirt into our hooch every few days or so. We missed her company, but otherwise had it made.

Then everything got complicated.

The Siege

The big show came on August 9, 2003, testing all we'd learned about urban combat tactics, what our teams had put together, our relationship with the Iraqi Police Force, and our tenuous rapport with the people of Hit. The curtain would go up around 2 p.m.

The temperature at 8 a.m. was already hovering at around 80 degrees. By noon it was capping out at a blistering 120, made worse by the black asphalt oozing under our boots. Lieutenant Colonel Kievenaar was scheduled to attend a well-publicized meeting with the Hit police chief later that afternoon, along with the mayor and sheiks from around Ramadi.

Tied up with an informant at the train station for the morning, I assigned our three military police teams to *Mad Dog*'s gun trucks as an extra, mobile security force for the Colonel and his posse. All they needed to do today, I thought, was look tough and discourage any troublemakers. This would be an easy gig and wouldn't require a lot of heavy lifting. Besides, who on Earth would start shit with all of these soldiers there?

Famous last words. No one had a clue as to what was about to happen.

Our Humvees rolled into position just outside of the Hit police station, carefully tucked away on its western edge. Given the station's accessibility from the road, we preferred to flank the station rather than post ourselves on the main road right out in front. With no real cover for nearly a block in either direction, any would-be guard standing post was simply an easy target and nothing more.

Major Gallivan, along with a handful of *Thunder's* staff, had joined us for the conference, and had pulled their vehicle within the police station compound. Surrounded by a concrete wall about eight feet high, they sat motionless in the shade of their Humvee, patiently waiting for the meeting to end. It was too hot to move, let alone breathe, in the searing afternoon sun.

Initially, things went about as well as they could go. The police, sheiks and Americans were, at least on the surface, on the same page with one another. Monitoring the radio back at the train station, I was pleased to hear it. *Wow, actual progress*, I remember thinking.

The town was quiet, with only a handful of diehard kids roaming the streets and playing soccer on the sidewalks. Most were hidden away in their houses, sitting in front of fans and air conditioners, hoping they'd be spared from yet another unpredictable power outage. Everything was fine. Growing bored and tired, the security teams manning the Humvees outside began talking and joking quietly.

Out of the corner of his eye, one soldier noticed two men dart from the main road into the large apartment complex directly across the street. Two seconds earlier, a few feet away in the yard, neither Major Gallivan nor his driver heard the two grenades hit the ground behind them.

The yard was rocked by a loud explosion. Before our guys could even process what was happening, a second blast, on the heels of the first, rang out in the yard. It was now abundantly clear: the Hit police station was under attack.

The first explosion had hurled shrapnel into the ass of Major Gallivan's driver, a young specialist with the ACR. Shards of metal from the second burst sliced their way into Gallivan's throat so deep, small bubbles were being formed in the wound every time he inhaled.[24] Using their vehicles and the station's wall as cover, the security team leapt into action and started looking for targets. Within a few seconds, a handful of troops from Kievenaar's security team rushed across the street and assaulted the apartment complex, looking for the men responsible. It was a huge building with a ton of apartments, and these guys could be anywhere. It was the worst game of hide and seek imaginable.

Scott, followed by two of Hit's finest, dashed to the station's

---

[24] The specialist's "million dollar wound" was painful, but he would eventually recover. Gallivan would eventually be OK too, and returned to duty a few weeks later. He came back from a military hospital in Germany with a large, menacing scar across his neck, which he often used as leverage with the timid Iraqi Police.

roof for a more commanding (but unprotected) view of the street. Carefully peering over the side, neither Scott nor the Iraqi police saw a soul. What they *did* see however was a Vietnam-era Mk 2 grenade sitting on the sidewalk beneath them. Apparently dropped by the two men in a nervous rush to deliver their payload, Scott couldn't tell if the pin had been pulled or not. Seeing an opportunity to bypass EOD, he took matters into his own hands and advised his team to cover him. Like a predictable—but still super cool—scene out of any given B-list action movie, he was going to shoot this grenade and blow it up. With an Iraqi policeman curiously gazing over his shoulder, Scott carefully aimed his M16 and fired, barely missing it as the first bullet ricocheted off the sidewalk. The second shot connected and the decades-old grenade exploded into a cloud of gray smoke and concrete powder.

Within minutes, gunfire started erupting all over town. Things had escalated quickly, and the call was made to 2nd platoon's *Nut Crushers* for help. Throwing on all my gear—and I mean all of it—I hitched a ride with one of their teams on their way from Ramadi to give us and the local cops some extra firepower.

It didn't take long for the situation to get out of hand. The small confrontation that began with a few grenades was turning into sporadic firefights around the city. In the 20-minute drive up the road into Hit from our post, we could hear the battles developing over the radio, but we were still unclear as to who was doing the shooting.

Rumors spread quickly that a band of Fedayeen were responsible for this mess, with several thought to have taken up position in the apartment building across from the station, the same complex our own troops had rushed into moments before. The word traveled through the ranks of Hit's police department like wildfire, and in true Iraqi fashion, every cop outside nervously swung his weapon towards the boxy concrete building and started wildly firing into it. Just our luck; along with our own men now clearing its stairwells, there were fifty innocent families inside.

Then I heard the radio transmission no one wants to hear; someone inside had been shot, and they thought it was one of our guys.

In Hit, Scott Couture, Chris Henry, Captain Palacios and a handful of *Thunder's* soldiers heard it, too. Under a hail of gunfire, they rushed into the apartment building in search of the troops who had gone in just minutes before to secure it. Staying as low as they could, doing their best to avoid the shattering glass and AK rounds clacking into the concrete all around them, they ran up the stairs ready to find their men and kill anyone who got in their way.[25]

Before I knew it, 2nd platoon and I were in Hit with bullets flying everywhere. We roared up to the police station, bounced out of our Humvees, took cover behind its engine, and started looking for people to shoot.

From our intelligence collection over the past few months, we were learning Hit was becoming more and more radioactive. The human intel guys in Ramadi had even told us Hit was hanging on by a thread. We didn't think things were quite that

---

25 The report was of an Iraqi who had been shot in the leg. Seven young men were detained near the roof, claiming they had nothing to do with the attacks on the police station. No weapons were found and the building was secured. No U.S. soldiers had been hurt. The building was pock marked by thousands of rounds, its façade shredded by the force of the bullets. A number of soldiers, including Scott and Chris, received the Bronze Star with "V" Device for their actions.

bad, but with the deteriorating situation with the mayor, internal conflicts within the police, the growing division between those who supported us and those who didn't; things were simply too unstable. Each day, the teeter totter would tilt a little towards war, and then a little towards peace, but at the end of the day it would usually find its balance.

Not today. We just didn't think any of this would happen with us around. In retrospect though, it made perfect sense. We were experiencing the proverbial calm before the storm.

At the time, this was our best guess as to what was going on in Hit: The mayor was from a tribe based outside of the town, who had a serious beef with some of the families in Hit, as well as with another tribe just across the river near Zuwayah. The town didn't like the mayor and the mayor didn't trust the police. The mayor was the nephew of the region's most powerful sheik (Abdul Razzak, in Zuwayah), who was cooperative with the Americans, but had a checkered past with all three. At that point, we were pretty sure the Sheik helped hide Saddam after Baghdad fell in April. His own tribe was split down the middle, the result of a feud caused by the death of one of their own at the hands of Saddam.[26]

Regardless of the decades-old bickering, any significant,

---

[26] With the death of an Iraqi comes retribution—an eye for an eye. However, this can be "waived" with a cash payment to the family of the slain. Saddam had killed a key member of the large, well-respected Albu Nimr tribe in the 1980's, and in an effort to avoid trouble, paid the tribe millions of dollars. One half of the tribe accepted the payment. One half, considerably slighted at the other's willingness to accept the cash, angrily split off. Since then, the two halves had been at war with each other, with one openly defiant to Saddam's regime. The man who headed the division against Hussein was running for political office in the Ramadi area the summer after Saddam's fall.

heavy-handed U.S. military involvement would serve to ruin just about everything we'd worked to build since May. It would appear we were beginning to take sides in an already extraordinarily complex political environment. Some Fedayeen decided to bring the U.S. in by paying a couple of thugs to throw some grenades at us, knowing what our response would be—a total lockdown of the town and an eventual division between us and the police.

It worked. Colonel Kievenaar took charge and set up tanks and Humvees at different points in the city in a reasonable effort to better control things. He wasn't about to go crashing through the whole town, but he had to do something. It was quite a sight, seeing that guy walk down the middle of the street with a 9mm in his hand, totally unfazed by the gunfire snapping around him. That took some serious balls and set the stage for the fortitude this man would need in this urban shootout. His efforts were in vain however, and only served to rile things up further.

Most of the shots being fired at the police station (which most of us were gathered around) were coming from a part of town near the river about 300 yards away, near Checkpoint 11—Charlie's territory. We could hear the bullets crack over our heads every few seconds, but couldn't see exactly where they were coming from. Crouched behind the front end of my Humvee, I carefully peered around the corner of the hood to find a target. Staring down the barrel of my M16, I started to scan for muzzle flashes, silently praying it wouldn't be the last thing I ever saw.

On top of it all, there were several small pockets of houses between them and us, including a school. We were pretty sure the kids hadn't been back since the invasion, so it was considered a "free-fire" zone. The police, who had taken up position on top of the roof of the station just behind me, were now firing madly into the part of Hit near Checkpoint 11. It was the exact same place we had our conversation with Charlie during the curfew only a few months ago. Specialist Adams then spoke up. "Sir, there's smoke pouring out of the top of the mosque. Can I engage?" The constant stream of radio chatter let everyone know the regiment had moved a tank into the area. Fearful they might have sent troops inside, we held off from peppering the mosque with our SAW machine gun; a fully automatic, belt-fed 5.56mm rifle with a range of about 700 yards. A few seconds later, the tank crew that had maneuvered into Checkpoint 11 came over the radio; they were taking fire from a group of men across the river, near Zuwayah. I had no idea who they were or why they had decided to join in. They might have been, like us, shooting at the thugs we'd dubbed "Charlie's Angels," but thought it a good opportunity to take some shots at us, too. At that point, no one knew what the hell was going on.

After about a minute of the random volley of shots, menacing gunfire ripped through the thick afternoon air. Everyone instinctively ducked in unison. It was our tanks with their 7.62mm co-axial machine guns letting loose. The staccato bursts from the ferocious killing machine bounced through the alleys and off of the hot stone buildings, its terrifying sound amplified with every echo. My eardrums pulsed with each fired round. To hear these guns in training was one thing—to hear them fired at another human being in anger is an entirely different experience. Everything fell silent.

It didn't last long. The shooting from the Iraqis on both sides started so intensely again it sounded like fireworks. Again, the bullets began zipping over our heads. I still couldn't see the gunmen.

This was turning into a very serious firefight, one that might force us into an all-out gun battle in one of the most ruthless areas of Hit. Part of me was relieved. We were finally going to settle things, once and for all. Hit's insurgency was getting out of hand and needed to be put down. But there was a lot of real estate between our position and theirs, with plenty of women, kids, good guys and bad guys all over the place. Getting there would be half the battle; flushing out our enemy would mean a house-to-house search of almost every building in easily one of Anbar's worst neighborhoods.

I had control of both my squad and the squad from 2nd platoon that had raced from Ramadi to join us. I was with Joe Rawls' team across the street from the police station, anticipating an eventual direct engagement from an area to the south of us. On the edge of an open field about a hundred yards long, there was a row of buildings, including the school, and several small alleys to shoot from. Anyone who wanted to start taking shots at us could fire a few rounds and then easily melt back into the town. Scott and Sergeant Henry's teams had taken up position at the traffic rotary about 100 yards away to the east—the site of the gathering on my first night of curfew, known as Checkpoint 2—with more of a direct view of our attackers. Charlie's men were also firing from "the ruins," a group of ancient stone structures sitting high on top of a hill near the bridge. I had one team from 2nd platoon stand fast with me and the other two take up position at the main entrance to the city behind us. I didn't want any surprises sneaking up on our 6 o' clock.

Before I'd even joined the Army, I had heard the officers of the Armored Cavalry were a little on the "cowboy" side. For crying out loud, Stetsons and spurs are an authorized part of their uniform. Their tactics were plain and simple, and they usually depended on their big guns and intimidating machines to win fights. The troops of the 94th working with outdated equipment didn't have that luxury. However, we were under their tactical command, and their true colors were starting to shine through.

Little did I know at the time, I was about a minute away from disobeying my first combat order. In the middle of all this, Colonel Kievenaar ordered my MPs to charge down to Checkpoint 11 to "start arresting agitators." Come on, agitators? First, this wasn't a European soccer riot, it was a firefight. Second, we wouldn't be arresting anyone: we'd be firing two shots to the chest and one to the head of anyone who leveled a weapon at us.

After receiving his order, I contacted my men on our private internal channel and let them know the plan, one I clearly didn't approve of. I told them to stay put for a second until the situation at Checkpoint 11 was under better tactical control.

The soldiers in the tank down by the river radioed that the real trouble was now coming from across the river, not from Checkpoint 11. But they were inside a damn tank, well protected from just about any threat. They hadn't even seen the men firing at us from the ruins just above them, and were unaware their position—surrounded by tall buildings and alleys—was a perfect area for an ambush, especially on a thin-skinned Humvee.

If Kievenaar's orders were to be carried out, my troops were to drive straight into a potential death trap. The road leading down to the bridge was flanked by the massive, vertical hill housing the ruins. Enemy gunmen firing from an elevated position would slaughter our guys with ease as they drove down the narrow street. They wouldn't have cover from the group of guys across the river, or from the men raining bullets down on top of them from the ruins. I knew enough about Hit at that point to know this was a mistake. We knew who worked in this seedy part of town, and we knew what it looked like down there. Other than the tank, there was no cover if things got sticky. Our mortal enemy at this point, Charlie, owned that part of Hit. His minions no doubt knew the town inside and out. On the other hand, this was Kievenaar's first time in the city in about a month; we'd spent more time in Hit the week before than he'd spent there in the past twelve.

After about 20 seconds of running through some options in my head, I went back to my guys on the radio channel and got a hold of Sergeant Henry. It was his call. I told him what I knew, but that he probably had a better idea of what was going on than I did. I didn't want anyone getting sucked into an ambush because of a hasty tactical move. Noticing a new surge of activity in the ruins, Sergeant Henry decided to sit tight and continue to punish the buildings with M16 and SAW fire. A few moments later, he'd end up striking one of the gunmen square in the chest, sending his lifeless body to the ground.

Sergeant Henry later told me the gunman couldn't have been more than 14 years old. Combat in Iraq was rarely black and white, and this was one of those times. Whether shot by a man, woman or child, AK bullets were all the same and could kill you just as fast as they were fired.

With the cover provided by a Bradley fighting vehicle and an almost direct line of sight to the gunmen firing at us, the MPs at Checkpoint 2 had an ideal spot to shoot from. Within seconds of putting the radio down *Pegasus* arrived on the scene, darting past us no more than 50 yards off of the ground. The sudden roar of their engines and clatter of their rotors cutting through the blue sky was a startling but welcomed sound. They were smaller, two-man helicopters, but at such close range, they'd get your attention. Skimming across Hit's skyline, newly armed with Hellfire missiles and .50 caliber machine guns, they were ready to do some serious, precision damage. It was quite the combat contrast: this advanced weapon of warfare zipping over a city that was probably around when Jesus was a teenager.

Relaying every message to *Pegasus* through the main channel would waste precious time. Having worked so closely with them over the past few months, and since we both shared a disdain for the slow-moving regimental "switchboard," we'd made sure we each had the other's internal frequency. This would be one time we needed to be in direct communication with each other, and there's no better tactical dream team than a ground unit with some kind of close air support on speed dial. Within a few seconds, they calmly told us they were taking heavy fire from both the ruins and the mosque at Checkpoint 11. The ruins housed plenty of civilians, and the mosque was a very narrow target. If *Pegasus* fired on and missed either one, they were sure to hit innocent people. So instead, they hovered in place, leaned out of their doors, carefully aimed their M4 rifles, and started taking shots. The courage of these men was simply relentless.

Less than a minute later, however, some of my worst fears were confirmed. *Pegasus* was reporting groups of men were seen loading rocket propelled grenades from the mosque into a pickup truck.

This was just perfect: the whole damn city's going to be overrun in a few minutes with dozens of guys with rocket propelled grenades. The *Pegasus* choppers, floating statically just beyond the rooftops, were easy targets for an RPG round. If they were hit, we were looking at a potential mini-*Black Hawk Down* situation, if they even survived the initial crash.

Pegasus couldn't fire on the truck itself because of its proximity to residential areas; the result of a direct hit on so many explosives could easily kill anyone within half a city block. The truck started to drive off, picking up speed and cutting through Hit's narrow streets. They tried to follow it, but with so much action, they'd eventually lose it as it drove into the city. All they could say was it was traveling to the east. Given there were pickups all over the place, it only added to the confusion of the situation.

Elements from 2nd platoon were re-positioned a few blocks away to intercept the rogue truck's movement. If they were making a run at the police station, *Nut Crusher* would eventually find them. Unfortunately, the truck disappeared.

Seconds later, another pickup truck overflowing with hooting and hollering guys with AKs raced up to the police station just behind me. Almost in unison and completely surprised, a handful of us swung around and leveled our weapons at the group. Wide eyed and stunned, I took aim and clicked my M16's selector switch to its three-round burst setting. If I didn't know what "spray and pray" was yet, I was about to find out. They were 50 feet away, and it was too late to find cover. I shouldered my M16 and had the fattest guy in the front—wearing a red & white checkered *shemagh*—in my front site post. Cheering and pumping his AK in the air with one hand, it was just a matter of time before he saw me. We were about a half a second away from this devolving into a Quentin Tarantino-themed shootout where everyone was going to take a bullet and die at the same time.

Just then, an Iraqi policeman to my right jumped in front of me and screamed, "*LA! LA! LA! ASHURTA! ASHURTA!*" and motioned to me to lower my weapon. The men in the truck were Iraqi police reservists.

Barely exhaling, with my finger still super-glued to the trigger, it took me a few seconds to drop the pitch of my rifle. However, one thing immediately crossed my mind—hanging out with the local cops and learning the language had paid off. It probably saved my life and at least a handful of theirs.

That situation would set the bar for what the definition of "complicated" would be for the rest of my life.

Sergeant Henry and his squad were now engaging insurgents in both the ruins and then the mosque itself. The fact it was a mosque meant absolutely nothing to us. Muslim mosque, Catholic church, Jewish synagogue, Jehovah's Witness Kingdom Hall—if you shot at us from it, we were giving you lead and plenty of it. And if anyone reading this thinks otherwise, I invite you to get shot at by someone from a mosque and see how you feel. If the Iraqis didn't respect where they worshipped, then neither would we. Scott told me later he'd even taken it a step further and started shooting at the loudspeakers on the minarets. According to our translators, the Imams inside had begun broadcasting the call for their fellow countrymen to pick up arms against the Americans.

After that shootout, I'm sure the electricians in Hit were tested as to their full knowledge of exterior sound systems. Scott is a *really* good shot.

To say the least, this situation was a complete mess, and I believe the professional term for it was "a clusterfuck." But we knew enough to know, at this point, that we were being drawn into a very personal, age-old civil war. It was obviously much clearer in retrospect, and we later, *kind of*, had idea of what happened. The group of bad guys at Checkpoint 11—Charlie's Angels—who just happened to be firing at us, was also firing at the police. Charlie's Angels had a problem with the police working with the Americans, as well as the fact that the police belonged to a different tribe, one who had been in a semi-permanent conflict with theirs for generations. The Angels were also being shot at by another group of bandits from across the river, men believed to belong to the *same tribe*. Fractured long ago by some internal dispute, splinter groups were now engaged in a fierce battle among themselves for supremacy. Supremacy of what, I haven't a clue. The police, most of whom came from a tribe with a reputation for diplomacy and peacekeeping, didn't have much fighting experience and were firing randomly at the Angels and the guys across the river. The guys across the river had a beef with the police as well, so they shot at us, too. Simple, right?

And given the antiquated grenades, it made more sense our would-be assailants were most likely just a couple of amateurs paid by some thug (probably Charlie) to light the fuse on Hit's smoldering powder keg. The U.S. Army was in town, in full-force for a critical meeting no less, and someone was certain to take advantage of it. In retrospect, I don't think they were looking for some final confrontation, but rather the chance to influence the more impressionable Iraqis, and shatter the fragile bonds we'd made with those who tacitly supported us. It was their big chance to once and for all discredit the U.S. military's presence in Hit, and for those still on the fence, in Iraq.

This might give you an idea of just how complex the tribal and political situation had become following the fall of Saddam, the one guy who kept this Pandora's Box of chaos under a very tight and brutal lid for decades. It all went much, much deeper than Sunni, Shi'ite and Kurd.

Later that afternoon the mayor, in some mini-coup attempt to seize power, tried to send us across the river to take care of business. Nice try, Mr. Mayor, but we were not there to settle old family scores. We'd been sucked into this squabble far enough. We'd defend the police and ourselves, but we weren't anyone's hired guns, and we certainly didn't report to you.

During the chaos of that day, we did have a few unlikely surprises. It was becoming more evident the town's population was split. At one point in the fighting, from among the homes the shooters were using as cover, a woman emerged and began to point out the positions of the gunmen. Risking her own life, but seemingly with little to lose, she wandered out of her house and motioned to where they were hiding. She was one of the reasons why we weren't about to start randomly firing into the area with anything larger than our M16s, even though *Pegasus*, with their devastating arsenal of Hellfire missiles, could have ended the fighting in a matter of seconds. Honestly, if it were Fallujah, we probably wouldn't have hesitated. However we were walking a finer line with Hit, and any large-scale attack with total disregard for civilian life would have ruined all of our efforts there. Our cautious ways were paying off, and that woman was living proof of it. I just hoped she stayed living: bullets were making holes in the stone less than a few feet from her.

Near Checkpoint 2, an older man slowly shuffled out from his home, defying the gunfire, and offered our men some tea, carefully carrying it on a small silver tray. Absolutely surreal.

The fire from the police station was becoming incredibly random. Eventually, the lack of discipline was putting everyone's lives in danger. Calls were coming in from Checkpoint 2 that the Iraqi police were firing so close to their position, that several of our own men had considered engaging them as well. "*Stop those goddamn cops from shooting!!!*" someone shouted over the radio. The transmission was so loud the handset vibrated against the steel frame of the Humvee.

I heard that message loud and clear. I ran over to the station and yelled up to a young soldier on the roof. "Tell those cops to cease fire!" He looked at me with his eyes wide open, staring. I yelled again, with no response. He was frozen, his head resting on the edge of the roof. For a second I thought he was dead, until his eyes rolled to his left. I turned to a soldier standing next to me and asked, "Whoa, do you know him? Is he okay?" Another soldier assured me, "I'll take care of it, sir," and ran into the police station. Seconds later, the shooting stopped, and the young soldier regained his composure. I'll never forget the look on that young kid's face. If I didn't know what mortal fear looked like before, I knew it then.

The fighting went well into the night, the sporadic crack of AK fire reminding us our work wasn't done. The tracer rounds raced over our heads like shooting stars, their bright pink trails burning out above the city in an otherwise spectacular show. The MPs and regiment elements collapsed their units back on to the police station around dark and planned for raids later that night. It was tense; by then most of the city was covered in pitch black darkness, and there were still people everywhere. Pushing out our perimeter, we set up shop on a roof with a few other troops near the police station, waiting, ready to pick off anyone trying to sneak up on us in the dark.

At around 8 pm, our intel guys advised the command of their assessment: they were fairly sure of who started this fight and, better yet, where they were hiding out. They didn't have all the details, but it was good enough for us. After about an hour of planning, we rolled through the dimly lit town, quickly set up a perimeter, raided a house and grabbed two suspects without incident. They fit the description and the demographic; well groomed young men with money. In an archaic town nearly two centuries old, they weren't from around there. At 3 a.m. we hit another one and grabbed three more. At 9:30 the next morning we jumped a mosque near the entrance to town, thought to be a recovery area for fighters. Unfortunately, no one was home.

Roughly twenty-four hours later, the siege of Hit had ended, with scores of Iraqis dead and a handful of Americans wounded. Later we learned one of the dead Hit policeman was the victim of a tribal revenge killing that occurred just before the melee. The attack on the police that day was probably spillover from the shooting, and a couple of people decided to take advantage of the fact we were in town—right place, right time. All it took was a grenade or two to kick it off.

When all was said and done, we'd end up detaining over 20 people. Later that week we'd be blamed for the death of a small child in the fighting, struck down by a stray round. Heartbreaking, but we were pretty sure it was an AK bullet that killed him. On top of it all, the Iraqi police—men we were risking life, limb and reputation to protect and train—came dangerously close to gunning down American troops on several occasions with their gunfire, some of which was probably intentional.

We were starting to see a pattern emerge with the Iraqi people. At this particular phase of the war, the U.S. military was for some reason very sensitive to the religious foundations in Iraq. For instance, no soldier was permitted to enter a mosque without a member of the police force. I found out the hard way when I had climbed into a mosque back at *Eden*, which was *on our own post,* only to be warned by an officer I was violating policy. You'd be in some hot water if you even opened fire *near* a mosque. The military was literally bending over backwards to appease the populace at large. If they'd only seen us a few weeks earlier, pounding away at that mosque in Hit with our M16s.

But where was the Iraqi outrage? For some reason, when a mosque was used to store weapons or, much worse, as a shelter from which to shoot at U.S. troops, the Iraqis didn't hold their own people accountable. When Americans returned fire on, or attempted to enter a mosque, however, the locals in town would go *nuts*.[27]

It was becoming a disturbing trend throughout our tour in Iraq, the convenience in which the Iraqi people would selectively wield their own religion. And this wasn't limited to Anbar of course; it was quickly becoming the norm around the world. The U.S. would continue to respect the mosques as long as they weren't being used in a military capacity. Obviously, the resistance groups caught on to our restrictions and immediately took advantage, but few average Iraqis ever made mention of their disdain of the use of mosques by the insurgency, the police, their local leadership, or us.

If it wasn't the convenient use of Islam, it was a brand of selective complacency that troubled us. If we had learned one thing so far, it was that every Iraqi in this area of the country knew one another, and knew what was going on in each other's lives. It wasn't like in the United States, where you might not know half the people in your own apartment building; there were no "anonymous citizens" in this part of Al Anbar.

---

27 Luckily, few had complained about our assault on Charlie's mosque on August 9th. Allegedly, Hit's populace respected our firm stance, and most believed Charlie was getting what he deserved.

A few weeks later, after a raid in Aqabah (a town south of Hit) to capture a well-known weapons dealer, our Bradleys and Abrams tanks tore up a guy's private property pretty badly. He approached us afterwards and demanded compensation for the destruction we had inflicted on his homestead. However, we'd found out only hours earlier he had prior knowledge of his neighbor's activities. He wasn't directly involved with the trafficking weapons, but he definitely knew what was going on next door.

This man was knowingly living next to one of the province's biggest explosives dealers, one who was actively and openly selling munitions to our enemy, but he nonetheless insisted on financial restitution for the property we'd destroyed. He decided to keep his mouth shut, and simply assume the Americans would shoulder the financial responsibility for any losses if and when we made our move.

We weren't asking the average Iraqi to take up arms and fight these men themselves. Some of these guys were dangerous. We were also well aware of the fact there was a fair amount of shadow support for the insurgency. But for Chrissake, don't indignantly demand cash and apologies from a military that was forced to act. Some of these men had known all along about the weapons and what his neighbor was up to, but decided to quietly lie low until we stormed the neighborhood. Obviously, in this particular operation, we had troops and vehicles everywhere. The Bradley and Abrams tracks tore up some land, damaging his irrigation pipe and other items on this man's property. Yet somehow, according to him, the blame falls entirely on us. He came to us kicking and screaming about his water pipe a few hours later. I asked the interpreter to explain our situation, and to tell him what goes around comes around—an Iraqi lesson on instant karma. He wasn't getting a dime, and he was lucky we didn't detain him.

Over the next month, the give and take we expected from the Iraqis, in an effort to bring our intervention in town to a minimum, was slowly disintegrating. Some Iraqis couldn't (or perhaps didn't want to) believe we were trying to remove hardliners from the towns while doing our best to stay out of regular people's business. Locals were choosing to ignore the root cause of American interference. The result was un-needed damage to property and eventually civilian deaths. Again, it was just a matter of time.

Since the siege, there was an understandable friction between Hit's leadership and the U.S. military. While we were adamant about not punishing the entire town for the actions of a few, the regiment in its "carrot and stick" game shut down all funding to the city just when they needed the cash, the vehicles, and the support the most. We gave our assessment to Colonel Kievenaar about the real causes behind what had happened, but in his eyes it was a police failure, so he pulled the plug on the training program.

We were livid. The harsh approach would only serve to alienate those who were working with us. Ten MPs were again dealing with the fallout from a major decision made by a squadron commander.

The Iraqis who were on the fence as to what to think about us just had their minds made up for them. A few of the police we talked to understood it wasn't our call, and knew we were still standing up for their cause. In an act of contrition a few weeks later, the ACR would ask the Hit Police to turn over some known *mujahideen* and Ba'ath Party operatives in town.

Walking their own fine line, caught between a city that didn't trust them *and* a regiment that didn't believe them, they stalled. The fugitives were tipped off and ran, but most were eventually tracked down with help from one of our informants.

One of those fugitives happened to be Charlie; the bearded, jovial scumbag we met a few chapters ago. And in an instance of perfect irony, less than two weeks after our shootout, a brave Iraqi policeman came forward and pointed out Charlie's house in Ramadi to us. The resulting raid to grab him was somewhat of a success, although the result was not intended. As Charlie approached his hideout, he literally stumbled onto the units looking to detain him. The soldiers surrounding his place quickly recognized him from his picture, but as they closed in, he made a break for it and ran to his car. From what I heard, he retrieved a weapon and was shot dead by a soldier from a Florida National Guard unit, stationed in Ramadi. "Good riddance," I remember thinking. The boys from the Sunshine State just did the province a huge favor. However Hit, once more, was a dangerous place for us to be. We were again dealing with the fallout from an operation we had no control over, but given the circumstances, we were more than ok with.

Charlie's death was a big deal to the Iraqis in Hit—all of them. It was rumored he was murdered, simply grabbed in a raid by the ruthless Americans and shot to death in cold blood. While untrue, conspiracy-prone Iraqis often believed what they wanted to believe. Although not the most popular or well-liked guy in town, he was *respected*, and the fact he died fighting American "oppression" made him a hero. We'd inadvertently created a martyr, but we didn't have a choice.

A few weeks after Charlie's little accident, during a patrol through Hit, we crossed the bridge into Zuwayah, near his old stomping grounds. It was around noon, and the call to prayer had begun over the speakers on the mosque, the one that had been the target of our gunfire in August. The Imam on the microphone was wailing passionately. I didn't know what he was saying, but it didn't sound good. This was the first time we'd passed through this part of Hit since the siege, and if looks could kill, we would have been dead a thousand times over. We zipped over the bridge and continued our patrol into Zuwayah. But there was still a big problem. The bridge in Hit was the only place to cross the river within about 30 miles, and the Iraqis in that part of town knew it. We'd be coming back sooner or later.

It was a safe bet to assume we'd be all shot to shit when we rolled back through on our return to base. We thought about simply heading to Ramadi, crossing that bridge instead, and making our way back north to *Mad Dog* along the main road, but we weren't about to be bullied off of our patrol. Just before the bridge, both Scott and Chris came over the radio, noting they were picking up chatter on *Pegasus*'s internal frequency. Lucky for us, they were doing some reconnaissance work nearby. After a quick situation report, they agreed to escort us over the bridge back into Hit.

With the Kiowas hovering only a few meters above the buildings, we made our way across the bridge and into the traffic circle at Checkpoint 11. Whether it was the sound of the helicopters or the anticipation of an impending ambush, the Iraqis milling about the open area disappeared in one hell of a hurry. Anyone who's been to Iraq knows when people in town start to scatter, something's about to go down. The hair on the back of your neck stands straight up, your eyes widen and your "pucker factor" increases twenty-fold. I leveled my M16 out of the window and took the safety off of my loaded M203 grenade launcher, just in case. We carefully made our way around the hills that housed the ruins, past the alleys and all the shady characters still staring us down. *Pegasus* had a close eye on the ruins—the maze of ancient, crumbling buildings that offered the ideal perch for gunmen looking to rain bullets down on top of us—and our own gunners were prepared to engage anyone who stepped out of the shadows with an RPG or AK. With our chopper escort came a lot more confidence, so we slowed our pace a little. We weren't about to give the impression we were running scared.

What a site that was—*Pegasus*, the petrol-fueled angels on our shoulders, hovering right above us with their .50 calibers, Hellfire missiles and M4s at the ready. Other than a thin layer of plastic and about a ½ inch of government-funded aluminum and fiberglass—all made by the lowest bidder—I'm convinced they were the only things standing between 3rd squad and certain death that afternoon.

After a few weeks, when all of the "tough guy" talk had died down from Hit's drama queens, our relationship with the local cops began to improve. We were starting to understand the more complicated politics of the valley, and began getting an idea of just how fragile everything was. In retrospect, it was a good thing the people of Hit were divided, because as a result our support base was growing again.

Some of the more emotional police officers had begun to pop into our post more frequently, pleading for more help. Panicked, they claimed Hit was on the brink of disaster, the *mujahideen* were planning a big offensive, the Ba'ath leadership were acting up again, blah, blah, blah. We were understanding enough, but growing very impatient with the way they were—or weren't—handling things.

For some reason, the cops thought their hands were tied. They often knew *exactly* who these people were *and* where they lived. This was a war; if you knew who was responsible for the attacks, which by this time had involved *several* on the police, what were you waiting for? They were telling us that masked men had actually had the balls to come to the *station* to threaten them. We let them know in no uncertain terms they didn't need our permission to start knocking people off. We backed it up by saying if anyone came to a police station in the United States and threatened a cop's life, that man wasn't going home. But this wasn't the States. I just didn't get it.

The bad guys were starting to feel their wild oats again, and the police were getting a little jumpy. A tribe known for peacekeeping, they were in over their heads when push came to shove. Fed up with the bullshit these people were causing, and the fear they were trying to spread through town, we decided on some unorthodox behavior. Everyone had seen our weapons up close during the siege, but no one knew what they were capable of. Not yet, anyway.

On a crystal clear night a few days later, we slowly made our way to an open field just southwest of the city. It was about midnight, and there were still people milling about in town—this city *never* slept. As the three Humvees approached Hit, we cut our lights and slowly, steadily made our way to the southwestern edge of town. We pulled off to the shoulder on the main road, staggering ourselves about 200 meters away from each other, the only sounds being the hum of our diesel engines and the slow grind of our tires on the cracked asphalt. Every weapon we had was set up and loaded. A quick call back to *Mad Dog's* TOC confirmed we were the only units operating in the area.

The city was awash in an eerie yellow glow from the

decrepit streetlights lining the town, but the open desert to the west of Hit was perfectly dark. We'd worked this piece of property before; it was a good staging area where troops could be dropped off to stealthily approach the city by foot, under the cover of night. Making our way to the edge of town, we could set up shop in a concealed area and observe what was going on there in relative secrecy.

We weren't looking for secrecy tonight. The acoustics of the land assured any noise made from the highway would bounce through the alleys, off the buildings and into the windows of just about every home in Hit. It was time to begin our "demonstration."

Almost simultaneously, the 40mm incandescent parachute rounds were fired from our grenade launchers and screamed into the night sky. Exploding with a loud "pop," the entire western edge of Hit lit up like a Christmas tree. After we figured we had everyone's attention, we turned our weapons towards the open desert. Then the real fireworks began.

In a spectacular exhibition of military firepower, every weapon we had came alive in a deafening display of lethal elegance. For two minutes straight, bullets from our M16s and SAW machine guns raced into the darkness, the tracer rounds leaving a ghostly, glowing red trail. The booms of our M203 high explosive rounds bounced off of every concrete and metal structure within two miles, the vibrations finding their way to the hills on the other side of the river and back again—offering a sobering reminder to our critics down near Checkpoint 11 of our capabilities. More flares went up in unison, this time a little deeper into the city.

Our display would end with the introduction of our belt-fed, MK19 automatic grenade launcher—a mysterious weapon whose power, until that night, the Iraqis had not yet been witness to. Spitting out its 40mm high explosive munitions with an earsplitting thud at a rate of nearly four per second, the concussions rocked the 1-¼ ton Humvee back and forth on its axles. The violence of the high-speed blasts was chilling as the grenades chewed up the earth less than a hundred yards from us.

In a hazy cloud of gun smoke and a sea of spent shells, we jumped into our Humvees and raced back to camp.

This would be the simplest, most direct message we'd send in months: keep it up and we're going to kill you. We'd do our part in rebuilding this new Iraq, but there was a limit to our patience.

The next day, reports came flooding in. Everyone in town heard it and most of them knew who it was. I wanted to make sure anyone planning attacks against us—or the police—knew what kind of hardware they'd be up against. *And that was just ten of us.* For the most part, it worked. Hit calmed down considerably, as the growing resistance started to understand their little symbolic "victories" and empty threats made against us or the police meant nothing. The quiet, tolerant American Army was ready to kill, and could do so relatively quickly. With the intelligence we had on people in town, it would simply be a matter of time before we found out who was behind any attacks—or threats.

The people of Hit knew we were getting smarter. We were taking time to separate the good guys from the bad, and were gaining ground.[28] Instead of working with the often-stubborn

---

[28] Our success was in no small part due to the tireless efforts of the 323rd Military Intelligence Battalion, Staff Sergeant Richard Eaton, specifically. Unfortunately, Staff Sergeant Eaton died of pulmonary edema in his sleep in Ramadi, August 12, 2003.

conventional regiment elements, we started developing our own tactical signature. The mobile traffic control checkpoints were stepped up considerably, with tangible results.

However we knew full well this war wasn't going to be won with a few status quo TCPs and some escorts. With a list of target vehicles, some state-of-the-art night vision equipment, a few high explosive rounds, ten well-oiled machine guns and a burning desire to become a little more predatory, we'd set out to fight our own proactive guerrilla war. The staff of the regiment had checked the box long enough, and we were ready to do things our own way. It was time to perform.

Our first goal was to re-establish a standard of unpredictability; random patrols at random times on random routes became the norm. With only three vehicles, we did our best. We had other projects going on, but this was the meat and potatoes of our existence. It was working. Within days we had apprehended a black list resident during one of our TCPs on a back road, one often neglected by the ACR during its operations. Within days of shipping him off to the military intelligence interrogators at Al Asad, it was reported through ACR channels that he admitted to being a former Iraqi Army General and Fedayeen leader—by far one of the most powerful insurgent collaborators in the valley.

During another midnight patrol, barreling down the road with our lights off during the full moon (for added psychological effect, of course), we ran across a vehicle fitting the description of a big-time weapons dealer in town. The tip came from an informant whom we'd met during our patrolling; another benefit of frequent face-to-face contact with locals. I was driving at the time and didn't really notice it, but Scott recognized the car immediately. We radioed ahead to our lead vehicle to stop in the road and cautiously intercept the jet-black truck.

He and his passenger reluctantly pulled to the shoulder and were carefully searched. While we had the technology, we didn't always own the night. It was still a very dangerous time to work.

Within seconds, the other two teams caught up and surrounded the tiny black pickup. A loaded AK magazine was sitting on the dash, but no AK. "No weapon, no weapon," the two men pleaded with their hands held high above them. More than a little skeptical, we weren't exactly ready to take them at their word. Scott sent his team back down the road. Less than two minutes later, they found an AK on the shoulder about 300 yards away, right where we'd passed them.

We were furious. The locals had been warned not to travel with AKs in their vehicles, and these guys had just lied to our faces. True, it was better than shooting at our faces, but we were still angry. We took them back to *Mad Dog* and interrogated them on and off the entire night. No one was sleeping until they told us what they were up to.

We soon discovered the intel team had a rap sheet on one of them a mile long, one that included serious activity in Mosul. According to them, the driver was a major suspect in importing weapons along the desert road between Hit and northern Iraq. Among some of the items in his inventory were Katyusha rockets, similar to those being sporadically fired at Camp *Mad Dog* from some unknown location. We had no idea who his passenger was. He didn't look as though he was from this part of Iraq. As a matter of fact, he didn't even look Iraqi.

At one point during the interrogations the next morning, our interpreter pointed out something interesting. It was another Koran reference. Both men had been brought together for the questioning, and the ringleader told his passenger something along the lines of "Allah will forgive your lies if it's meant to save your life." [29]

After that little piece of information, I knew I could never trust an Iraqi under questioning again. I started wondering if all the intelligence we'd gathered so far on other interrogations was bullshit, too.

They might lie to us, knowing we probably couldn't do anything about it; but if they didn't care about what we'd do to them, maybe they'd decide to take other people's opinions more seriously, namely their fellow Iraqis. Maybe it was our turn to lie.

I had the interpreter let this guy know that if he didn't want to cooperate with us, we'd make it look as though he was anyway, and in a big way. If he didn't play ball, we had no qualms with taking him straight into the middle of town, dropping him off, stuffing an American $20 into his shirt pocket, giving him a big kiss and thanking him for his info. If there was one thing the insurgency hated more than an American G.I., it was an Iraqi snitch. Although we never had to take such a drastic measure, it was a useful ploy, one that helped us gather a lot more intelligence on some of the usual suspects in town. No one was really afraid of us yet, but maybe they were afraid of someone else. This guy was running weapons for the insurgency, for crying out loud. His capture was sure to shake *somebody* up, and giving the impression he was singing like a bird would no doubt be a death sentence for him, his family, and even some of his friends.

Within a day he'd end up being released. Set free from captivity back into the wild with a huge figurative tag in his

---

[29] Known as Al-taqiyya, it's seen as a concealment of a truth, not an abandonment of that truth, if the lie benefits Islam.

ear compliments of the 323rd MI Battalion, he'd go on to help us track down the major players. Thanks to the dirt our new friend dug up for us, more pieces started to fall into place.

Over the course of the next three months, we sent quite a few prisoners up to Al Asad as part of our solo ventures. The staff back in Ramadi was *really* impressed with our results. Hey MPs, your numbers are up this week!

Hey chief, go screw yourself! This wasn't a goddamn sales meeting, and we were definitely not looking to impress anyone. We were putting some effort into finding the right people and some great information was pouring in. The numbers weren't a coincidence, and they certainly weren't the main goal.

However there was still a serious problem with the way the ACR was dealing with its prisoners; one that was a widespread practice in Iraq, and one we were guilty of as well. After an incident, IED or raid, most military units would simply round up people who might have been involved somehow, and ship them off to Al Asad or Abu Ghraib to be processed. Worse, few were following up on their prisoners to find out where and how they fit into the grand scheme. The ACR was practicing a similar "out of sight, out of mind" policy. It was just easier that way.

You might've seen the pictures and stories on the news regarding the scores of suspects detained during raids in Iraq. With no real information on who's good, bad or indifferent, it's just too easy to take a bunch of people who *may* have been involved with something and cart them off to these processing centers. The last thing these detaining units were going to do after a 20-hour day was to pick through their detainees one by one with a fine-toothed comb. "Flex-cuff" them, throw a bag over their heads, and herd them onto a truck. Who gave a damn where they went? It was understandably just the way things were, and we sometimes did it ourselves. Once in a while it *was* necessary: Iraqis in the same tribe or family, who might not have been *directly* involved, could still have information. After all, as was the case in Hit, Iraqis almost always knew what was happening in their neighborhoods. However, more often than not, it only served to clog these detention centers even further, taking away from the much more critical task of gathering intelligence—critical information that could save lives and maybe even help win this war.

While there was never a directive issued encouraging capturing units to work their own angles, we took care in following up with prisoner interrogations. In the late summer of 2003, it was starting to pay off. I can't begin to tell you how much a simple conversation with the interrogators at Al Asad tightened up our intelligence picture, improved our morale and increased our effectiveness. Some of the info they gave us was very useful in shaking up an Iraqi prisoner. The "How do you know that?" look that came across their faces in some of our own future interrogations was priceless, especially with the men who didn't think the U.S. military knew where they lived, who their girlfriends or mistresses were, their loose friendships with known bad guys, or the fact they were gay. A few well-timed drops of a name, fact or photograph worked wonders.

In most cases, when we detained an Iraqi for something quite serious, like planning or participating in an attack on a patrol or convoy, it was obviously in our own best interest to find out more about what they knew. Why wouldn't anyone on the roads do the same? Without fail, they almost always had a tidbit of information that helped fill in a gap somewhere—a name, car, vehicle, a town, *something* we could work with. Those bits and pieces added up, and helped identify specific dangers in Hit and Ramadi, as well as general threat trends in both the province and the rest of Iraq.

However the sheer volume of prisoners flowing into interrogation cells at Al Asad was often overwhelming, sometimes more than 50 per day. Of course, the Coalition Provisional Authority had strict paperwork guidelines accompanying a detention, and the more people the interrogators had to process, the more they had to focus on their paperwork. It obviously took a toll on the resources available for interrogations, and subsequently intelligence began to suffer.

The soldiers at Al Asad knew it, too. After a while, they created their own system of categorizing prisoners, one used to rate their potential intelligence value. The *CAT 1* guys were the ones caught with the smoking gun, whereas a *CAT 4* guy was someone who might've been caught stealing military equipment. In an attempt to bring some humor to their plight, the interrogators went on to invent a fictitious new category, *CAT 5—poor bastards who were at the wrong place at the wrong time*. Needless to say, the detainees fitting that category were growing exponentially by the day. As long as it helped triage the prisoners coming in, I'm sure they didn't care. Whatever field expedient measure they needed to take to ensure things were done right was ok in my book, too.

As the processing points started filling up, the line between detention facility and interrogation center started to blur. Al Asad wasn't intended to be a common jail, but with all of the small-time *Ali Babas* (thieves) being sent there, it was turning into one. The same goes for Abu Ghraib. Unfortunately, the line was smudged enough and mistakes were made, and Americans watched in horror as the pictures of naked and dead detainees went public in April of 2004.

Not too long after, four interrogators we'd worked with at Al Asad would end up being indicted by the military for the alleged murder of a prisoner in their care.

I can't defend the guilty soldiers. If there's anything I've learned in the military, it's the simple truth you're responsible for your own actions. However, instead of placing the blame on them alone, which is all too often the case in today's military, I'm looking to expose some of the circumstances behind the problems of detainee processing, both those in the facilities themselves and out in the field. It's a common practice in the military to spend countless hours on ways to punish soldiers for violations, but to invest very few in preventing those regrettable situations in the first place.

The most fundamental issue behind the overcrowding problem in our detention centers is what we've come to know as the *weapon of mass detention*. In a war where the enemy is slow to understand American justice and the bad guys blend in perfectly, it forces us to sometimes pick up everyone within sight for questioning after an incident. Units have to be a little more selective when sending prisoners to the big house, which means more effort has to be put in at their respective headquarters. The 94th was lucky; we were good friends with the intelligence guys attached to the ACR, and could call them up when we had a major haul. They'd do the initial interrogation and then decide which ones should be sent on for further review, rather than simply ship everyone off en masse.

Every unit should have a detachment, even if it's a handful of soldiers cross-trained on interrogations, that can help determine if a detainee is a real somebody, a common criminal, the town drunk, or just guy out for a walk who happened to fall ass-backwards into the local insurgency's latest caper.

Second, there's little active effort between capturing units and intelligence cells in the field. The old doctrine regarding POWs is *"the five S's"*—secure, safeguard, segregate, silence and speed to the rear. But it's just that: old. This war didn't exactly fit the mold of our conventional Soviet battlefield. In Iraq, it didn't matter if you were an infantry, MP, chemical or finance soldier: if you were involved in a prisoner's capture, you needed to follow up on it. The guys doing the interrogating didn't always know what *you* were looking for, and the odds are they were only focused on finding the big fish. Your involvement could mean the difference, producing that one flash-in-the-pan piece of intel that could spell life or death for one of our own down the road. It often all came full circle, if you put the time in. There were only so many bad guys in Iraq.

The third was an institutional problem within the military—the lack of any meaningful training or real supervision. As was the case of Abu Ghraib, soldiers were left high and dry by the stagnant mechanics of their own leadership. I'm well aware the average soldier doesn't need a manual to tell him not to beat a prisoner to within an inch of his life or attach electrical wires to his penis, but a breakdown in guidance eventually leads to a breakdown in discipline. The disastrous inevitability that was the Abu Ghraib prison scandal was being put into motion long before the 800th MP Brigade—the military police command that eventually oversaw all prison facilities in Iraq—even entered the country.

The 800th's lack of common sense set their own troops up for failure, as the reliance on hundreds of obscure Army regulations and useless manuals again regrettably took the place of tangible supervision. This unit might have been "paper-ready" to handle the mission (remember our TSIRT checklist?), but were in no way realistically prepared. An investigation went on to prove the 800th wasn't trained on even the basics of prisoner detention prior to the war. Standard Operating Procedures on handling enemy prisoners of war hadn't even been *reviewed*. After taking the mission, those at the lowest levels simply went along with what others were doing. According to a separate investigation following the scandal, After Action Reviews—vital military reports intended to spotlight the pros and cons surrounding a serious incident, after the fact—were rarely conducted. And in those cases, if any lessons were formally learned from such mistakes, they were being rubber stamped by the general in charge, General Janis Karpinski. Even fewer were actually pushed down to the units actually guarding prisoners. It was a paperwork shuffle that ended up giving this nation's military a huge black eye. It couldn't have come at a worse time; our street cred as MPs was evaporating by the minute because of the idiots at Abu Ghraib.

The fourth and final sticking point with me, along the training and supervision lines, is the lack of accountability by leadership. Abu Ghraib just gave a face to what is happening all too often in the military at large. In a changing battlefield like the one we experienced in Iraq, especially when it came to intelligence and the treatment of prisoners, constant adjustments had to be made. In the case with Abu Ghraib, no follow-up was initiated by commanders to see if the corrective action ordered had actually been taken. They just went ahead and signed off on it, as if a piece of paper could somehow make things magically happen. They checked the box and passed the buck. Well, the buck stopped with the officers and enlisted soldiers who were working the midnight shift in Iraq's most notorious prison.

Ask anyone in the military about the huge cork boards back at their unit, filled with memo after memo detailing every obscure Army policy; from the definition of sexual harassment to where to toss your cigarette butts. While their conspicuous posting is "required" by command, they're not a substitute for accountability, training or supervision. Most of the time, these official-looking, one-page letters are barely referred to, or not even read. You could tack a winning lottery ticket to one of these memos and the odds are no one would ever find it.

Hiding behind posted pieces of paper—whether an SOP, policy guideline or official memo—is a tactic of weak leadership. Period. It's a despicable cover-your-ass-tool for the looming disciplinary problems that are bound to come up. And when the shit finally hits the fan, no one is going to care how loud you're yelling "I told you so" while holding one of these useless pieces of paper. Go lead your people instead.

That being said, I'm sure Abu Ghraib had a memo pinned to the wall somewhere that beating a prisoner was wrong.

Do I blame General Janis Karpinski for Abu Ghraib? Yes, but not entirely. A great deal of blame falls directly on the MI detachment (elements of the 205th MI Brigade) working at Abu Ghraib, and their ridiculous, frenzied interrogation practices. However, it almost upset me more to see General Karpinski go through the motions and place the blame on others, than to see those pictures of a leash around a prisoner's neck. Trustworthy soldiers can't be everywhere all of the time, and you're not going to stop every instance of Enemy Prisoner of War abuse. But the circumstances surrounding the Abu Ghraib scandal were willfully ignored, and the 800th's internal problems clearly too widespread.[30]

---

30 *The Taguba Report*, ordered by Lt. Gen. Ricardo Sanchez, then-commander of Combined Joint Task Force 7 and the senior U.S. military official in Iraq, prepared by Major General Antonio M. Taguba, following the allegations of human rights abuses at the prison. The report was part of an *Article 15-6*

In her defense, in a final irony that perfectly defines the degree of disconnect between U.S. Army leadership and their own chains of command: General Karpinski was first notified she'd been relieved of her position by a journalist, not by any military authority.[31]

Camp *Mad Dog* was well guarded and a tough target. It was about 150 meters off of the road and surrounded by miles of desert on three sides. There were gunners on the roof as well as on the train platform, and the only real security problem we had was when actual trains would roll by; while we owned the station, we didn't own the tracks. That was a pretty odd sight; watching a train full of curious Iraqis slowly chug past us, the windows of which were full of either smiling faces and friendly waves, or middle fingers and the bottoms of shoes.

We were still very accessible; people in Hit, Mohamadi and Ramadi knew who and where we were, and would often stop by to ask questions about family members who'd been detained. We had a small guard shack down near the road, serving as our access control point. They'd radio our Tactical Operations Center with the names of Iraqis looking to pay us a visit, search them, and send them up. We were the closest and most approachable post around, and had been informally decreed the least abrasive interface between the Iraqi people and the U.S. military in Anbar. The men of *Mad Dog* Troop

---

investigation, an inquiry usually initiated by a commander (at any level) when a military service member is suspected of wrong-doing (courtesy of The Agonist, www.agonist.org)

31 Debra Dickinson, *Was Abu Ghraib Her Fault?*, Elle Magazine, November 2005, p. 250

were the consummate professionals—cautious and aware, but super cool and very receptive.

Our time at the train station was actually enjoyable, at least in comparison to some other areas we'd bunked at around the province. Having moved around so much with our different missions, we'd already spent a few days in just about every major post in Al Anbar. We still did plenty of dangerous stuff, but at the end of the day we were coming home to our own place and running our own show. It was our little and much needed "man cave." With a little more breathing room, we were allowed to do things that probably would have been frowned upon by the bureaucracy of a major military post. One example: the way we dealt with the tactical challenge of having an open stretch of road about a mile long in front of our camp.

Forever wary of either an attack of the conventional sort or suicide car bomber, Captain Williams took some proactive steps. Steve gave the word to his men at the gates to engage, with warning shots, those cars that slowed or stopped near our eccentric home. And oh how they did. We'd be going about our business during the day, only to be startled by gunfire as the gate guards blasted a few shots at some poor Iraqi driver who'd pulled to the side of the road. Most of the time, it was a guy whose only crime was having a shitty car that happened to break down within sight of us. It got so bad that Steve had to finally put a leash on *Mad Dog's* gate guards, who were firing at just about everyone with car trouble. You should've seen the look of some of those drivers, filling their radiators or changing a tire like a NASCAR pit stop crewmember as bullets streaked over their heads. We'd drive over to check them out, and usually ended up apologizing to a frazzled, 60-year old Iraqi fruit salesman on his way to market. Most understood the difficult position we were in, and some even got a laugh out of it; probably out of sheer joy they hadn't been blown away.

Our post did catch the attention of some people, and we soon became the target for the infamous 107mm *Katyusha* rocket—a favorite weapon of Palestinian terrorist groups for years. Although an unguided, somewhat inaccurate self-propelled munition, the Katyusha's 14 pounds of high explosive in its warhead was capable of causing some serious damage upon impact, to include liquefying a person's internal organs if they happened to be in range.

It's quite an experience to be on the business end of a rocket attack. On five separate and horrifying occasions, the rockets streaked into our camp and exploded with a thunderous crash. I'll never forget the sound of those things screaming in, the deafening explosion booming off of the walls of our makeshift compound. The closest of the five landed about 300 yards north of our camp, but with the echo they always sounded like they hit much, much closer.

With a range of over five miles, they could have been fired from anywhere. Soldiers who had any type of artillery experience would eventually comb the impact site for clues, and usually were only able to provide a rough direction from which they were fired. Their detonations left a crater a few feet deep and an oblique ring of scorched sand about ten meters wide, with a lopsided circle of displaced earth ballooning out from the point of impact. But as I said, this place was open desert for miles in every direction, and they could have been launched from any one of the thousands of hilltops, valleys or isolated trails surrounding the camp. For all I know they were mobile and being launched from the back of a truck.

The third attack—ironically launched on September 11th of that year—landed within 50 yards of a convoy making its way southeast from Al Asad, along the road just outside of our camp. There were no injuries, but I'm sure it scared the holy hell out of the troops in the first few vehicles. I was looking out at the convoy from our "front porch" and saw the explosion firsthand. I didn't even see the rocket, and assumed it had to have been an IED. But how could that have happened? And why wasn't it buried closer to the road? Plus, our 24/7 gate guards were only a few hundred yards away and surely would have seen *something*.

Of course it turned out not to be an IED but in fact a rocket; one that managed to strike within a few yards of a military convoy. It was much too close to be a lucky shot; somebody watching the road further north must have called the "rocket men" and informed them of the large, slow-moving target of opportunity.

After the first two attacks we started to feel a little helpless, and we couldn't get our hands on the *counter battery radar* from Ramadi (the "counter-bat" equipment could pinpoint the origin of a fired mortar or rocket—it was real cool stuff we'd get to know better after our transfer there). But we couldn't just sit there and do nothing. Immediately following the third impact, I sent our three MP teams to where we began to speculate the rockets were being launched. I stayed behind, climbing one of the fifteen 60-foot observation towers lining the stretch of track near the station, with a radio and a pair of binoculars. With a commanding 15-mile view of the flat, gaping terrain, I thought I might be able to talk my guys towards a potential firing site.

It was around sunset, which made it near impossible to see anything on the horizon. The blinding ocean of sand and sun were bleaching out everything west of the camp, beyond a few hundred yards or so. It would be dark in about an hour, and the terrain would soon bleed together into one shapeless, muddled black and brown glob. The wind picked up, and the towers began to slowly sway in unison. Armed with an M16, a radio, binoculars, and a pair of night vision goggles, I strapped myself onto the small three-foot platform with some rope. If I was going to die in Iraq, it wouldn't be from a fall off of some stupid tower.

About 45 minutes later, the sky turned twilight gray and our three teams—two miles away and barely visible at that point—were quickly swallowed up by the darkening landscape. I radioed my guys to strap their infrared strobe lights to their helmets and click them on. Small canisters a few inches wide, the strobes emitted an infrared pulse every few seconds that could only be seen with night vision devices. There were few if any landmarks we could both identify at that point, and with the night rushing in, this would be the only indicator of where they were. Within a few seconds, success: their pulsing green lights began to dot the horizon.

They scoured Mohamadi's back roads for about two hours, but found no trace of anyone or anything resembling a launch device.

The only thing I saw in three separate trips to the tower's perch was *that* first night, and it happened to be a suspicious white SUV speeding across the desert floor about five miles away, just to the west of us. Well out of range of our MP teams, it disappeared into the heat waves vibrating off the orange desert floor and into a setting sun. A white SUV, in our experiences, meant either a Ba'ath Party official or Iraqi police officer.

A few days later, while again patrolling the area where we thought the artillery was being fired from, we saw three young men walking on the train tracks, about five miles north of our post. We yelled for them to come nearer, but they refused.

After firing a few warning shots, they scattered and bounded away from us. Oh you bastards, we got you now!

All three teams tore off in our Humvees and bounced violently across the rutty desert floor in a slow-motion pursuit of our rocket men. We soon passed a small concrete pit with burn marks all around it, which suspiciously resembled the black residue from an expended artillery shell. The guys were still on the run, heading toward a nearby village directly behind the Mohamadi police station. I radioed for the trucks to stop and took a few guys in on foot, chasing after our alleged assailants. We found one pathetically and comically trying to hide under a small bush, and the others eventually tired out and stopped running. With their hands up, they were searched, cuffed, brought back to *Mad Dog* and questioned.

Our interpreter said they insisted they weren't the attackers, but instead some kind of "metal workers." Yeah whatever, I'd heard this story before; it was a term used by looters stealing abandoned military ammunition, allegedly for the brass (selling brass was big business for poor Iraqis looking to make a buck). We questioned them thoroughly the entire night, and after judging that neither of the three had any information, let them go.

A week or so later, a single train car came cranking up to our camp and stopped on the tracks right in front of the platform. Obviously suspicious, we had the men get out, searched them and the car, and asked them why they'd stopped. The conductors said there was a problem with the tracks up ahead, and they couldn't proceed just yet because work was being done. They also said the problem hadn't yet been completely fixed because someone had shot at the track repairmen a few days before.

Sorry guys, our bad.

The little Iraqi train engineers turned out to be nice older fellows. We had some tea, got a tour of the train, and after an hour or so they went on their way.

We asked the chief of the Mohamadi Police to pass on our apologies to the residents of the small village behind their station, and for the workers involved. The black residue I'd seen was charred garbage from a local burn pit. Some things you just can't learn in ROTC.

After the first two attacks, I noticed something peculiar; a small white car passing by our camp very slowly. My gut said it was a "spotter," looking to assess where the round struck, any damage it caused, and to gauge our response. The guys at the main gate got the go-ahead to disable any vehicle fitting the description after a rocket attack, but they never showed up again. Maybe the word got out our gate guards were shooting at any slow poke that happened to putter by.

Our big chance came on the fifth and final attack, which happened to coincide with a "fly-by" from our *Pegasus* friends, on their way to Al Asad. Their timing couldn't have been more perfect. It was customary for them to give us a holler when in our area, and after a few minutes of idle chitchat over the radio on this particular day, BOOM! A rocket blew up about 600 yards away to the north, close to the other impact sites. I sent them down Route *Uranium*, the narrow back road behind our camp that paralleled the main highway, in search of our assailants. After about a half hour of scouring the rolling dunes, they found nothing. No one. The rockets had either been fired automatically from some kind of stand-alone launcher, or we were just looking in the wrong place.

In all, five rockets would scream harmlessly into the hot Iraqi sand. We never found out who was behind it, or from where they were fired.

With all of the people we were detaining, there were sure to be some questions from their families and friends. Four or five people stopped by each week, sometimes a few times a day, looking for someone the Americans had taken. Most were fathers trying to explain how stupid their sons were, that our prisoners weren't capable of such a crime. Amazing—we had captured people caught *red handed*, but their families simply refused to believe they were guilty. That's why there were reports on the news of so many civilian casualties after a Coalition raid or air strike—a mom or dad sees their "innocent" son dead in the rubble of a destroyed building, totally blind to the fact junior was working with the insurgency.

Either way, they wanted to know how they were being treated, or if they could be seen. I didn't have too many answers. Most of the time there were either no records of the men being detained, or it was a completely different command that made the arrest. However, for the men we personally picked up, I always had something to say. We didn't arrest just anyone, and I always made a point to explain our case to the families who came by to inquire as to their whereabouts. Most would bring us letters proclaiming the good standing and innocence of those arrested, signed by all of the prominent sheiks in the area. I quickly got used to seeing these things, and they alway started with "In the Name of Allah, Most Gracious, Most Merciful" or something along those lines, in big letters on the top of the page. Funny, how Allah was so gracious in some people's eyes, but for others, sanctioned the killing of prisoners, aid workers and innocent children.

One in particular, a former Iraqi Army general and a wanted man on the black list, was a respected man who had more than a few visitors. A couple were even high-ranking police officers. After a brief meeting with a few of them debating the general's guilt or innocence, I gave them the straight scoop: within hours of his detention, he'd broken down and admitted to being the main financier of the local insurgency, complete with details. They looked at me as if I had three heads. I wasn't sure if they were going through the motions or sincerely didn't have a clue. Regardless, we made it a policy from then on to not argue with every Mohammed, Tariq and Duraid regarding the case being made for someone's arrest. We were trying to maintain some degree of operational security. More importantly, we were sick of explaining the rationale behind every damn arrest we made. We were frustrated, but sometimes the friends and family of our prisoners would inadvertently offer up information we were looking for—the benefits of a friendly interrogation.

After a few months of playing ambassador, amidst the aggravation that comes with searing heat and no sleep, we were fed up with explaining to every Iraqi visitor their detained brother or best buddy was up to no good. Scott had a morbidly brilliant idea—instead of fighting with every fourth cousin who came to the defense of one of our prisoners, we'd start telling anyone who showed up that we'd found their family member or friend guilty, and as punishment, the Americans had eaten them.

If anyone asked if his or her father were well, we should say, "Yes, *well done*, just off the grill in fact." Or, when asking, "Is my friend good?" we should reply, "Good? They're great, absolutely delicious with hummus." "My father has a good heart," they would say. We should remark, "It was exceptional, actually."

We were making this up as we went along, allowing ourselves to be entertained by the dark humor that came with the unnatural stresses of this conflict. Keep in mind this was before the Abu Ghraib scandal, and we never actually said this stuff to anyone. But it did cross our minds much too often. As if the Iraqis didn't think we were animals already. My God, the sick and twisted shit that goes through one's head when at war.

Our sincere style with the Iraqi people was again starting to generate some very real results. On yet another sweltering afternoon, a young man from the small nearby town of Aqabah arrived at our front gate in a taxi. A smaller guy in his early 20's with a stone face, he came to us bearing some disturbing intelligence about what was going on in his neighborhood.

The Mohamadi police had weeks ago advised us that Aqabah was once a seething hub of contraband explosives under Saddam. After seeing some of the scars of the residents—a majority of whom had missing fingers and limbs—it started to make sense. Since the invasion, there hadn't been a ton of activity, but there was no doubt the town still had a lively black market for these goods. Given their history, they were most likely now quietly selling their stores to the highest bidder. We'd been through Aqabah a few times, but since it was so quiet and no intelligence pointed to any major players living there, we didn't really think much of it.

That would all change this afternoon. According to our newest informant, his neighbor had some serious artillery buried in his back yard, and knew of another spot where over 100 land mines were being hoarded. He also had the name of the suspect, where he lived, and knew for a fact he was preparing to sell them.

This was too heavy to ignore. We drafted up the order for a reconnaissance that day. Our informant had cooked up a cover story for his family of spending the evening at a friend's house, so we had him bunk with us for the night. After watching *A Night at the Roxbury* with some of the younger enlisted kids, he bedded down next to our Tactical Operations Center, which was well lit and manned 24 hours a day. We still had to be careful; we just didn't know who this guy was.

The following morning he'd be questioned by our intel team and ended up drawing a map showing us exactly where things were—both in his neighbor's house and the open field where the mines were allegedly buried. The next day, X marked the spot, indeed. With some support from the ACR, we surrounded the open field and started to dig. Within minutes we found plenty—hundreds of pounds of anti-tank charges, artillery rounds, and bullets. Later the same day, covered up with jackets and disguised in the back of a Humvee, our boy led us to another alleged cache of explosives, not far away from the first. After a few minutes of searching, guess what we found: on the surface alone were well over a hundred loose and scattered land mines. Reporting our newest find, our troops stopped digging, softly stepped backwards, and evacuated the field in record time.

Our EOD team was called in immediately and within hours their C4 charges were set. The blast area was cleared in all directions for nearly a quarter of a mile. I was back at *Mad Dog* over three miles away, enjoying the privacy of a newly installed Porto-Potty. Anticipating the low rumble from what was supposed to be a routine explosion, I was literally scared shitless when the concussion of the massive charge hit the plastic walls of my new office like a baseball bat a few seconds later. The subsequent controlled detonation was much more powerful than expected, so much so it convinced the explosive disposal team it was too large for hundred mines—by their estimate, there were well over a thousand buried there, along with who knows what else.

There was no doubting our informant now. He again pointed out who'd been stockpiling this stuff, as well as the names of a few bandits involved with importing it into Aqabah. There was little doubt they were most likely behind selling them, too. We need to grab these guys *now*, but the ACR staff had different ideas. Instead of making an immediate arrest, they went with their signature tactic—a heavy, visible recon effort over three days, followed by an all out raid.

Later that week, we stormed the house. Our guilty party—most likely tipped off by the tanks, Humvees and Kiowas circling the house every hour for the last 72 hours—had fled. Out of an abundance of caution, we grabbed a few people for questioning. Maybe they could give our intel team *something* on the men we were looking for, where these bombs were coming from, and most importantly, who was buying them.

Our most recent spy casually walked by the MP and EOD teams with a few friends as the arrests were being made. Staring in the opposite direction, I did my best to telepathically relay my sincere gratitude for his courage. I and the others ignored him as he walked on, smoking and joking with his buddies.

A few days before, as his story started to jive with our intelligence estimates, we tried to give him some cash for his troubles. He politely refused. I was ready to hand him $100, but all he wanted was enough bus fare to get to his family up north, what amounted to about $10 USD. Through an interpreter, he told us if we wanted any concrete, useful information from anyone, we shouldn't pay a dime. He was probably right. We'd tried that before in Hit and it only lead to trouble. It was becoming clear the Iraqis would tell us anything we wanted to hear for a few bucks.

I'm sure he didn't want to be caught with any American bills so soon after a raid either, one that was much too detailed not to be the result of a tip. Maybe for him, the desire to rid his town of known troublemakers, and subsequently Americans, was the driving force behind his willingness to come forward. Either way, he single-handedly saved the lives and limbs of countless troops in Al Anbar Province that week.

We never saw him again.

By late August, 2003, the war in our fair valley was at its quietest. The weather had begun to cool, and we were enjoying more and more down time with the local cops. On a remarkably perfect evening, the squad had a friendly dinner with some new Iraqi friends on the banks overlooking the Euphrates River, on the stone patio of one of the elegant compounds belonging to the wealthy local sheik, Abdul Razzak. The Sheik's sons, Hekmit and Mooyed, and nephew, Laith, were our hosts. They were grilling chicken purchased in Fallujah, which I was told was the "chicken Mecca" of the Middle East. Praying silently they weren't poisoned, I grabbed a few pieces and chowed down. Marinated in some vinegar, lemon and exotic spices, it was by far the best chicken I've ever had, and you couldn't beat the venue.

Laith was a Captain with the Mohamadi police station, and a charismatic, lead-from-the-front kind of guy. The son of a modest sheik from the valley around Ramadi, he was making quite a name for himself with the Americans for his courage. Laith was putting in the time to help us out, often in defiance of the intimidating phone calls and chickenshit, second-hand threats by local thugs. He didn't always have a solution, but he had some influence over the cops in his charge, and that was enough. Admittedly, when I first met him, he struck me as kind of a player; another chubby guy in a pleather jacket with a nice smile, nodding away and telling us what we wanted to hear. However after some of the positions he put himself in, I grew to trust him completely. The more he stopped by the station (which was just about every day at this point) the more I got to liking him. A semi-permanent fixture at the plastic table near our TOC, he was quickly becoming one of our own.

After a few drinks—technically illegal, but we'd earned it—some of the squad had stripped down to their boxers, walked down the marble steps to the waterfront and went for a refreshing swim. A couple of others were enjoying some chicken and champagne near the house. Laith and I soon found ourselves alone on the patio near the riverbank. A little drunk off of the three or four Carlsbergs he'd pounded back, Laith started to open up to me about his family. His beautiful little 5-year-old son, who reminded me a great deal of my own nephew, Sam, back in Boston, had tagged along with Laith on visits to our post on several occasions. Even Laith's dad had spent a lot of time with us.

Laith was a big smoker, but for some reason he was scared to death his father would find out. It was very amusing, to finish up an hour of talking with Laith about bad guy X, informant Y, or dangerous mission Z, only for him to leave the station pleading with me not to tell Pop about his secret habit.

Being 27 and a typical guy, he enjoyed a lot of the same things we did. After investigating an ambush, IED attack or crooked cop, he liked to spend a few evenings each week with us watching movies at the train station, filling in the gaps in his broken English with lines from such classics as *Old School* and *Ocean's Eleven*. We'd sit out back near the train tracks in a couple of cheap lawn chairs, usually held together by duct tape, and just talk. He was never short of words, yet was careful how he chose them. We'd talk over our futures; how he'd like to see America some day after this was all over, and how he'd be more than welcome to stay with me when he did. I told him I'd be open to hiding him in my basement if he managed to get to the United States on a visa. On some nights, before I even knew it, three or four hours had passed, and we'd smoked an entire pack of cigarettes. With more in common than I originally realized, those twilight talks with our new friend were some of the most memorable of my life.

Laith made a very good point one night, an obvious one I couldn't believe I didn't see before. Bottom line; no one became rich in Iraq without Saddam's permission. The richer the sheik was, the more likely he'd dealt with Hussein. In this case, it was true; Abdul Razzak had quite a history—he'd made millions importing weapons from Jordan for the Iraqi Army, a claim later validated by the tons of weapons crates we'd find bearing Jordanian marks in almost every village around the valley. Laith went on to say, in his trademark attempt at English, that the reputation of both him and his father with the people of the area was exceptional. That was very true; his neighbors thought highly of them both. Laith said, in his own words, that he and his father weren't "high rollers" (a term I think he picked up from *Ocean's Eleven*) and hadn't achieved the wealth and status of Abdul Razzak because they hadn't played ball with Hussein.

They were a respected family around Hit and Mohamadi, but their support of the Americans was attracting the attention of Sunni militants.

I remember that all-you-can-eat chicken night so vividly. Laith had let me use his Thuraya satellite phone, purchased for him by the civil affairs team for emergency calls. I called

Kate, my girlfriend, back in the States, who just happened to be having lunch with my sister, Natalie, in Chicago. What luck. However the conversation was cut short as I got word from Staff Sergeant Henry that an IED had just exploded near one of *Mad Dog*'s tanks during a patrol, about five miles away. A gunner was injured, and they thought the triggerman might have run into Mohamadi. It was time to go back to work. By far, it was one of the most unusual phone calls of my life.

It was followed by one of the most unusual patrols of my life, given half of my squad was now shitfaced. Although crossing the median several times, each truck made it safely to our target area. Having found no one even remotely fitting the description of an insurgent in Mohamadi, and given we weren't exactly "fit to fight" anyway, we headed back to camp and slept it off.

We were starting to make some decent, fruitful ties with the police, bonds we hoped to see set the example for U.S. military-Iraqi Police relations in Al Anbar. As far as I was concerned, the better they learned their jobs, the faster we could pass the torch and expedite our own departure. They'd already established a decent, Western-style judicial system, had their own informants, set up several well-managed traffic checkpoints, and even found IEDs buried near the road, no doubt meant for a passing American or Iraqi Police vehicle.

Soon after our tour was over, we'd come to learn some were killed trying to disarm an IED near their station. Leaving those guys behind at the end of our time there would prove more difficult and emotional than I'd anticipated.

"The commander in the field is always right and the rear echelon is wrong, unless proved otherwise."

-Colin Powell

For better or worse, the 94th was quickly making a name for itself as a bunch of tough nuts. We already had a pretty good relationship with the *Pegasus* pilots, as well as a few other attachments. All of us had a common obstacle—the ACR's infamous Tactical Operations Center, tracking and coordinating our every move from their little concrete hut back on base.

On one wonderfully boring night in August 2003, we'd learn just how bad things were back at the ACR's TOC, both administratively and operationally.

I and the squad leaders were wrapping up another Battle Update Brief, or BUB, with our commanders, which yet again contained no useful, actionable information. The intelligence officer stood up in front of the group of commanders, read his news, and...that's all. "This is what happened today in Fallujah, Ramadi, Baghdad." Okay, soooooo.....what does that mean? Where's the analysis? Anyone could simply read what happened. What are the trends? What should we be watching out for? Intel at that point was just spitting back at us the news of the day—I could get the same report from Fox News in two hours. There wasn't even a basic attempt to find recognizable patterns in the chaos around us. There were tons of statistics, but no one was processing them. No one was breaking down a complex situation into concrete intelligence. What the fuck were you doing in your tent all day, besides devising the next spirit-crushing way to waste our time, or worse, get us killed? Strike one.

After two painful hours of my life I could never get back,

the BUB finally wrapped up. I'd noticed it was getting late, about 10 p.m., and we were scheduled for a late-night patrol near Hit. As we drove out of the compound, we flipped over to the *Pegasus* internal frequency to see what they were up to. Almost immediately the radio came alive with heated voices— they were taking heavy ground fire from someone in a car just off post, three minutes away.

Champion Main had its own Quick Reaction Force, or QRF, ready to respond. We didn't really have to do anything, but this was *Pegasus* for crying out loud! They'd saved our asses more than a few times, and it was the least we could do for them. Picking up the radio, I reluctantly called back to the TOC and let them know we'd take it from there. I could almost hear my driver, Specialist Alan Givetz, roll his eyes. "Jesus, Mike," he grumbled under his breath.

The TOC was usually manned with a staff officer and an enlisted soldier, usually a sergeant. I completely avoided them whenever possible. A few had been in active combat and knew the deal; maneuver units didn't always have the time to give every detail, or to answer every question. However, the majority had yet to be in *holy shit I might die* combat and therefore were a liability. Like a blind announcer forcing ballplayers to give a real-time, play-by-play account of their own game, they just served as another layer of mud that slowed things down in an engagement. Strike two.

In addition, without tactical experience and an understanding of the ground truth, there was a good possibility we'd end up pawns in their own little war game. And on top of it all, if *one* shot was fired, they'd run straight to their favorite, stock tactic—send in a bunch of tanks. Like clockwork, it was one we'd been involved in countless times over the past five months, and a reactive, conventional approach that rarely yielded results. It only served to spin people up unnecessarily. The tanks would show up an hour after it was all over, and we'd end up sitting with them, staring into a palm thatch until 4 in the morning, our enemy long gone. Strike three.

I'd had enough of playing by the insurgency's rules. Right, wrong or indifferent, we were going in now.

The two radios in my Humvee were now set to both *Pegasus'* and our own internal frequency. From now on, they were the only two that mattered. Speeding through Ramadi's backstreets, the pilots eventually led us to a raised road about 10 feet above a small neighborhood, with a row of about eight houses on one side and a few more on the other. A unit had already responded, a bunch of PSYOPS guys. I remember asking myself, *how in the world did they get here before us?* To no one's surprise, they'd been dispatched by the TOC. Why, I'm not sure.

A sharp bunch of folks, yes, but this wasn't exactly their bag, baby. They were milling around on the elevated road, standing dangerously close together, silhouetted by their own Humvee headlights and those of the local traffic they'd stopped. The lieutenant in charge of the scene was standing directly in front of his own truck, weapon slung, with a line of Iraqi drivers building behind him. I yelled to the guy to get out of the road, and I had the Humvee drivers turn their lights off.

Pegasus was on the horn a few seconds later. They were so close at one point it was difficult to hear their voices over the sounds of their Kiowas circling above us. Their pilots had a bead on a couple of houses where the shooters might be hiding, tucked off to the side of the dimly lit neighborhood. For all I knew, they were six feet away; with my eyes having been bombarded with the light from the Humvees, I couldn't see a damn thing. From the top of the road, I could barely make out the rusty old porch lamps from the homes just a few steps away, and the flashing taillights from the wrecked Iraqi taxi-cab that had crashed over the side of the road. In a pointless attempt to outrun *Pegasus*, they'd careened down the embankment and straight into a small cluster of palm trees.

Wonderful. This was Ramadi, at night, with shots fired. While good people and extremely competent, PSYOPS wasn't equipped for something like this and it showed. I told them to stay put, cover us, and for Chrissake, not to stand in front of any headlights!

The squad and I moved off of the shoulder, made our way down the steep hill flanking the road, and set out towards the dark row of houses. The rocky decline was made even worse by the fact our eyes hadn't yet adjusted from the glare of the Humvee headlamps. Again, within a few seconds, I couldn't see my hand in front of my face. We didn't have time. I retrieved the night vision goggles (NVGs) from the pack on my thigh and put them on. With a faint clicking noise they came to life, my eyes now awash in a gravelly black and green hue of indistinguishable shapes and stationary objects. While certainly not perfect, it was better than stumbling down a hill in near-complete darkness.

As we moved closer to the stone buildings, the coarse rattling of Humvee and Kiowa engines quickly gave way to the sounds of excited barking dogs and hurried Iraqi voices inside. Sweeping our M16s back and forth between the crude, one-story houses and pitch black palm groves, we did our best not to tumble down the steep bank. The taxi's doors were wide open, but no one was inside. With a quick search of the palms, we closed in on the first house.

By the time the MP team arrived at the door, it was already open. Inside stood a middle aged man and his family, understandably scared shitless as to what was going on. Adding to the frustration, and as per the usual, every one of his neighbors had decided to come out and see what was happening, nearly at the same time. With weapons drawn, we searched each house on the block, one by one.

Our teams were poised to enter the last house when *Pegasus* radioed they had seen a group of men running toward it a few moments earlier. Unsure if they were hidden nearby, I asked them to waive off for a second. I'd since lost all depth perception with the NVGs, and with so much background clutter and light, everything started to look the same. Was that a person or a fence post? Shit, I couldn't tell. While a critical piece of combat equipment, night vision wasn't always practical. I took them off and let my eyes adjust for a few seconds. We were starting to gaggle up again, silhouetting ourselves against the bare walls of the last house. Spreading out, I went to the radio. "Stand by, I'm putting up a flare."

My casual use of the flares had become legendary with my men. A few even jokingly asked me later on what had taken me so long to use one. Depending on the mission, I always had either an illuminating parachute or high explosive round chambered in my grenade launcher. While I was pretty sure a parachute round was loaded, I double checked just in case, and for good reason. Weeks earlier, while peeling out of Ramadi at high speed one night, we thought we'd shed some light on a potential ambush area on the outskirts of town. Instead of an illumination round, Scott had mistakenly fired a high explosive grenade straight into the air from our moving Humvee. After about five seconds of no pop and no light, we looked at each other in mild panic. The low boom of a single explosion rang out about ten seconds later, barely 200 yards away. Thankfully, it had landed in an open patch of desert.

With a loud snap, I fired off the 40mm illuminating projectile from my M203 into the night sky. My men were right—I loved those things. Along with the obvious benefit of light, they usually flushed panicky runaways out of their hiding places, and with our targets cornered, it was now or never. The shot went up right over the last house, exploded, and slowly drifted back to Earth, flooding the area around the last house with a bright, flickering, white-hot glow. A *Pegasus* pilot came over the radio a few seconds later: "*Cooool.*"

Ignoring the hissing sounds of the burning shell floating high above us, I leveled my weapon at the palms surrounding the houses. Firmly behind whatever cover we could find, no one moved. A week before, a unit had raided a house in Ramadi and a soldier was shot in the face as he stood outside, guarding the troops that had gone in. I didn't want any of my soldiers, or me, for that matter, taking a bullet we should have seen coming. It was time to go in, and go in quickly. Speed and surprise mattered in a conflict like this. It always does.

As the curious occupants opened the door, the team of waiting soldiers rushed in. The house was searched without incident, and we pulled away five suspects. No weapons were found; they'd probably tossed them from the car into the tall reeds lining the winding dirt roads snaking around this part of Ramadi. But they fit the description, and at the time, it was good enough for me. See what I mean about the detention problem? We were often guilty of it, too. However these prisoners would end up in the "pre-interrogation" cell that had been set up in Ramadi, a very smart use of the regiment's intelligence detachment.

In this case, another QRF wasn't required. *Pegasus* was above us and PSYOPS had our backs. The regiment's TOC had been effectively removed from this engagement. I would radio them if I had a second—or if Kievenaar got on the horn and gave me a hard time, which he sometimes did—but I usually had a driver monitor their frequency for anything important. Sometimes they were just little too insistent on getting information, like little kids at the movies asking their mom and dad, "Hey what's going on?" or "Who's that guy?" I could understand their frustration, and I know their intentions were noble, but it was clearly way too much of a distraction. When you're trying to talk to your own men sneaking through someone's yard, or to a pilot who may see a guy behind a tree with an AK, the last thing you need is some dude chirping away on the radio. Don't call us. We'll call you.

We sped home and resumed our patrol a few hours later, having tightened our bond with *Pegasus* and no doubt driven the wedge a little further between us and the TOC's staff. Who the hell knew what they would have had us do if I picked up the radio and followed their every order. In my opinion, they'd taken the well-beaten path of least resistance and unnecessary danger many times before, and I made a command decision they wouldn't be involved unless absolutely necessary. While in the field, they worked for us: we didn't work for them.

Our unsurprising QRF strategies would go on to fuel enemy attacks. After catching on to our repetitive and predictable behavior, the insurgency would often "stage" incidents in an attempt to draw the QRF into coordinated ambushes.

I was so proud of my soldiers and of our service in securing this new Iraq. The 94th was, as were others, making do in a situation that was changing by the hour, and Captain Bentley's "just do it" advice months earlier was paying off. First platoon had worked with almost every major combat asset the regiment had, and was doing some damage in our assigned sector of Anbar. Second platoon was relentless in its patrolling of a main supply route in Ramadi, making it safe for military travel and putting the hurt on the local insurgents prowling the roads. Third platoon was up north in the town of Haditha, conducting raids nearly every night and taking a lot of bad dudes off the streets for good. Fourth platoon was protecting shipments of men, material and supplies between Al Asad and Baghdad, often driving thousands of miles per week.

By no means did we have it all figured out, but we were making quite a name for ourselves. Attacks were down, convoys were hit less frequently, and we were sending a message to the bad guys that we were ready, able and very much willing to close with and destroy them. The 94th wasn't going through the motions or simply checking the box. Best of all, we were learning to fight our own fears of the unknown with information. It made us all much more comfortable with this treacherous environment, and our confidence in dealing with a dizzying assortment of lethal dangers soared. If we were to die here today, it wouldn't be in a morbid panic, surrounded by the unknown. It would be in a place that was quickly becoming our home. It sounds weird to you I'm sure, but in an unforgiving country short on tomorrows, it was oddly comforting.

We'd go on to keep up a very unpredictable, random schedule of patrols, traffic control checkpoints and visits to the police stations, one that kept anyone watching us guessing. Once in a while we'd even put on one of our infamous late night small arms demonstrations on the edge of Hit and Ramadi, just to let people know we were still out there. We'd rarely do the same thing in the same place at the same time twice. It meant a lot of missed meals, screwed up sleeping habits and pooping behind bushes at 3 a.m. whilst cradling your

M16, but it worked. In keeping things impulsive, even a little disorganized, we were becoming hard targets. And around Hit, we were becoming a class of insurgents ourselves against those who would do us harm.

Fortunately for us, in the fall of 2003, Hit was in a state of transition more than it was in a state of unrest. The chief of police was looking to become the mayor, the former having decided he'd had enough and jetted off to live with family in the UK. He was a nephew of the sheik; quite powerful but still in a very tough position. Complete with a small army of bodyguards, he was being pulled in four different directions by the sheik, the police, the military, and the people of Hit. There was clearly too much history at odds with these new demands, and exemplified the problems Iraq, in general, had in setting up functional independent local governments. At about the same time that summer, the Tribal Council in Ramadi started work on an Iraqi Charter and was having similar problems. However it was the only hope the Americans had in giving the local towns the power they need to run their own show in relative peace.

Over the course of five short months, we'd built up a network of informants, developed a police force that was standing up on its own two feet, and learned more about Iraq and this war than most units would learn in a year. In my opinion, the successes we had with our small campaigns were the result of an almost obsessive involvement and hyper-awareness of our surroundings, one which would continue to plague thousands of troops in the form of post traumatic stress disorder for years following the war, myself included. However, the extra time we were putting in was paying off huge—our arrest of two former Iraqi Army Generals, a Fedayeen colonel and tens of other known loyalists was draining the insurgency's morale. Confiscating a ton of guns and explosives didn't hurt either.

While not always super-efficient, and by no means diplomatic, the platoon was forever looking for a better way to do things. First platoon—comprised of soldiers who were law students, corrections officers, cops, mailmen and carpenters in their civilian lives, led by a financial advisor with absolutely no combat experience—was quickly learning the ins and outs of guerrilla warfare. A small element of a no-name Reserve unit, hailing from a tiny town in New Hampshire, was slowly putting it all together; and then, with the help of some very talented and dedicated men and women, putting it all to work.

CHAPTER 5

"Everyone thinks they're gonna get the chance to punch some Nazi in the face at Normandy."

Owen Wilson as Lieutenant Chris Burnett,
Behind Enemy Lines

After enjoying some significant successes with our own missions, we were about to be reminded we were still under the beck and call of the ACR. In late September of 2003, only two weeks before our alleged rotation back to the States, we'd fall victim to a pointless exercise in conventional warfare. It involved another 94th platoon that was working at *Rifles West* with *Sabre*, one of *Thunder*'s sister squadrons in the ACR.

First Lieutenant Chris Lee, the leader of 2nd platoon, had been working the heavily traveled Route 10 around Ramadi for just about as long as we'd been in Hit. He had an ambitious and fruitful plan of patrolling the road 24 hours a day with three, eight-hour shifts. Chris was a workhorse, and so was his platoon. It was a challenging plan geared towards results, and it was working. In their entire time there, no IEDs had been emplaced. NONE. They had learned every inch of ground on their route, every crack in the road, every trouble spot, every vendor, every piece of trash on the shoulder. We, too, had learned our area of Hit well, down to the last pothole.

However, in order to "develop our leadership abilities," the ACR wanted to swap our two platoons. Wait, what? *Say again, over?* My inner John McEnroe came out when talking with one of the operations officers: "You CANNOT be serious!"

I just didn't believe it. It was an unreasonable, irresponsible decision with no practical worth. Plain insanity. The fact two platoons were being forced to "switch" assignments so hastily was just fucking nuts. Our respective missions weren't warm body jobs, like gate or guard tower duty. We were literally entrenched. To switch two units at this stage of the game, each with developed expertise in its own area, was indicative of the problems behind the Army's inability to control its tactical environments throughout Iraq. It was relying on academic solutions the military had grown accustomed to, not the reality on the ground. In addition, the high soldier turnover in Iraqi cities since the fall of Baghdad was counterproductive to both the Iraqis' progression and our own. A solid presence indicated we were both taking our responsibilities seriously and were putting in the time to separate the good guys from the bad. Obviously, the ACR leadership had no idea what we had been up to over the past six months, even after reporting our results every day to their commanders in our Battle Update Briefs.

Even *worse*, this was to come less than two weeks before we were expected to leave theater. Beyond naïve and potentially lethal, it was a foolish move. In the end, we had no choice. First and 2nd squads would be pulled out of Rutbah to join us, our new responsibility being the security of the main highway in Ramadi. Second platoon would send elements to Rutbah, and the rest went to Al Asad with the task of securing the roads between Ramadi and Hit, our former backyard.

While it almost came as a breath of fresh air to our guys out west, the rest of us in Ramadi knew better. Our soldiers in Rutbah wanted to get to where the real fighting was and were looking forward to their new mission. Rutbah was a joke, and Lieutenant Lee's platoon in Ramadi was seeing a lot of action. They wanted the big missions, the firefights, the detentions. But they didn't know the situation in Ramadi, or the difficulties within the ACR's staff, the way we did.

While Lee's platoon was enjoying some cooperation with the ACR elements around Ramadi, including joint patrols with their tanks and Bradleys, the big guns were now being pulled for a different assignment. That meant 1st and 2nd squads would be thrown into a horrendous situation, patrolling 30 miles of road with three thin-skinned vehicles, supplemented with little to no air or armor support. Driving around in a feeble attempt to patrol an area that had the potential of getting out of control, we'd be easy targets for the insurgents in the surrounding towns. It was a tactical nightmare and would only serve to corrode our force protection efforts in both areas.

It was a bad situation I wasn't at all comfortable with, let alone even capable of fixing in the three weeks before our anticipated redeployment. Even the ACR's operation officer admitted the switch was "unnecessary," and that our situation was a "big shit sandwich we all had to take a bite out of."

However this wasn't some unavoidable situation, as the

major would have led me to believe. It was the result of over-conventional, impractical thinking, the kind that was gift-wrapping victories and FedEx'ing them to our enemy. First and 2nd platoons were seeing better results than anyone could have possibly expected in their respective areas. If it wasn't broke, don't fix it. On top of it all, the 82nd Airborne and 1st Infantry Division were now in Iraq, and we'd already conducted a "Relief in Place" with both of them. They now knew the area, had state-of-the-art technology, drove brand new five-ton "up armored" Humvees and enjoyed plenty of organic air support. With fresh troops and equipment ready to take over, we'd be best finishing up our business where we were and getting the hell out of Dodge.

After pleading with Colonel Kievenaar, even going as far as to type up a formal memo to the regiment commander, we were forced to swap assignments.

In the resulting switch with 2nd platoon and the Relief in Place with the new Active units, I was a little concerned with what I was hearing. Knowing that the newer troops—even members of my own platoon from out west—hadn't yet experienced the true joys of post-war Ramadi, I did my best to hit the brakes on some of their unrealistic expectations. I didn't want people to fall victim to a condition I've dubbed as *tactical masturbation*, a distorted perception of war I was beginning to see a lot of in some younger troops throughout the Army. This wasn't Hollywood. The odds of your coming across some insurgent planting an IED, setting your crosshairs on his head and blowing him away were a million to one. Nothing was that simple in Iraq, *especially* when it came to actual combat. Nothing.

This was an unconventional war, one where we were at a

tremendous tactical disadvantage. The more a soldier stuck to naïve, even fantasy-like beliefs of what war was like, the more the mission was certain to frustrate him beyond words and eventually lead to mistakes; another unfortunate byproduct of the U.S. military's linear, one-dimensional approach to combat training.

I didn't have all the answers, nor did I pretend to, but I felt obligated to offer up any information that might help someone out. We'd been there for six months and had seen quite a bit. Most of the captains and lieutenants I had the pleasure of talking with were very attentive and asked a lot of questions about what we were doing. A few had even heard about us and wanted to know what we were up to.

However, there were problems brewing within the platoon, too. I asked one of my sergeants, soon after we assumed the patrols, what his plan was in the event of an IED attack. I was looking for a little common sense, but instead he gave me the worst possible answer; "Light 'em up and kill 'em all." Clearly the wrong response, but it was one I expected from someone who hadn't witnessed firsthand just how bad things were becoming. The more likely outcome was confusion in its purest form—surrounded by dirt, shrapnel, and concrete, everyone's probably going to be deaf with no idea of what's happening. And that was before the bullets came. You needed to expect the worst and have a plan of how to get out in one piece, if only something basic everyone could remember (my favorite being floor it and drive fast, just get out of the kill zone). "Lighting people up" wasn't going to work. We knew it, and so did our enemy sneaking around Ramadi's shadowy palm groves and lethal backstreets.

The squad who'd been in Hit, while it hadn't yet experienced everything the insurgency had to offer, *had* been through enough to know being proactive worked. We were being put on the defensive more and more, and had to start thinking about what was going on. No one, especially the military police on the roads, could simply hop into a Humvee, drive around and hope for the best anymore. And if something *did* happen, we couldn't just go through the motions the way we'd done back in the States. While important, our training didn't quite prepare us for this, because back then we had no idea what to expect. Now we did. This war was the real deal, and it was going down on the roads all around us.

I wanted them to get used to the way things were done. Care had to be taken to recognize the danger areas that were becoming a problem. There were rules to learn: Don't be afraid to "recon by fire" into the tall reeds near a road's edge if you suspected an attack. Put up some illumination rounds over known ambush points (clearly one of my favorites). Dismount once in a while and go in on foot, staying off the edges of the roads. Have some static overwatch set up to cover the units that were moving. Learn what these insurgents consider an ideal target and avoid becoming one. Patrol some nights for five hours and then switch it up. Scare people off that road at night. Use the intelligence and be unpredictable. Think like an insurgent. Ammo is cheap, lives aren't!

Hit and Ramadi were two very different towns, but avoiding common mistakes and sticking to some fundamentals was always a good idea, no matter where you were in Iraq.

Fortunately, Lieutenant Lee's platoon had taken *very* detailed notes as to where the trouble areas were. Some attacks were occurring in the same places, which was a huge concern for me. But just as our own repetitive behavior was fueling the insurgency's tactics, their own habits would help ours. I was a big proponent of putting my troops in our enemy's shoes. In my opinion they were scavengers, waiting for us to predictably come down the road into their trap. There was a good chance our foes were jumpy and scared. Most of them weren't likely professionally trained operators. Some flares or gunfire might make them lose their nerve. It wasn't foolproof and hardly conventional, but it least it made you feel more like a soldier and less like a sitting duck. No one was afraid of a Humvee driving around. For Chrissake, these people have shot at tanks with AK47s, and a few had blown themselves up in the name of Allah. They were learning our limitations and reactions. We were just being too predictable, both before and after their attacks. A "show of force" by driving around wasn't a show of force.

"We're hit…we're hit bad."

The transition went smoothly enough at first. Second squad traded their quiet, cozy life in the suburbs of Rutbah for a spacious, sun-drenched apartment at *Rifles West* in the big city of Ramadi. Well, replace the word "sun-drenched" with "mortared," and "apartment" with "concrete shack."

Rifles West was slowly being settled, but still looked like a map from a first-person shooter video game like *Call of Duty*; rows of three-story stone buildings with no windows or doors, covered in Arabic graffiti and reeking of dog piss. Other than the occasional rocket or mortar it was fairly safe, had a decent chow hall, and even a small PX. First and 2nd squads, occasionally subsidized with a team from 3rd squad, grabbed a floor of one of the larger abandoned buildings and set up shop. Within a few days, they managed to procure some wood from the Active duty maintenance guys, some desk lamps, and even a handful of air conditioning units. The carpenters and electricians from our platoon went to work, and had a ball making it their home. With the help from a huge gas-powered generator parked right outside, the dank concrete walls came alive with lamplight and fresh, cool air being blown in by the AC units, now firmly secured to the crumbling window frames with custom wooden mounts.

However Ramadi was still no joke, and the learning curve on the road would be a steep one. Ramadi was a lot bigger than Hit, and almost every night there were AK tracer rounds bolting into the night sky from just outside the gates. Lousy neighborhoods were intermixed with friendly ones, and the line between the two was very blurred. The regimental staff bureaucracy we'd avoided for so long was now looking over our shoulders, 24/7. The mosques were much more active in Ramadi, complete with the passionate, unsettling cries of their Imams over the loudspeakers at all hours. And on top of what the insurgency might have in store for us, Ramadi had a growing Special Forces and "Other Government Agency" presence, whose men were operating in our area. The number of friendly-fire incidents was steadily on the rise in Iraq, and this place was crawling with Rangers, SEALs, SF, and probably CIA guys. Given the nature of their activities, it wasn't always practical to "deconflict" with their operations when conducting ours. We just didn't know where they were, or what they were up to.

We'd soon find out firsthand what Ramadi's rebel army was capable of. On an unseasonably warm night, just a few weeks after we took over the mission, 2nd squad was patrolling the troubled stretch of highway that cut through Ramadi, about two miles from *Rifles West*. Specialist Chris Kotch, a young, towheaded kid from Maine with a sharp wit and thoughtful approach to everything, was manning the turret of his team's Humvee, scanning the nearby houses. The team leader,

Sergeant Curtis Mills, was seated in the passenger's seat. A bigger fellow, Mills was level-headed and hilarious—a great and welcomed combination. He could punch a hole in the anxiety that often accompanied missions like this.

The first two trucks were about a quarter mile in front of Mills and his team. From Kotch's perch, all looked clear. What he couldn't see were the insurgents hiding in the tall reeds flanking the highway, preparing to ambush the patrol.

The IED violently exploded less than twenty feet from their vehicle. The remote detonation of the 155mm artillery shell—buried in the sand and housing over 30 pounds of high explosive—sent a concussive blast of metal shards tearing into Mills' leg and shoulder, instantly breaking the bones in both. Exposed from the chest up, Kotch was struck in the neck with a searing chunk of jagged metal from the IED, cutting through the air at nearly 1600 feet per second. Blown back by the shockwave, he fell into the Humvee. Seconds after the insurgent team detonated the IED, AK rounds poured from the reeds.

Specialist Kotch miraculously regained his composure and returned fire, but his breathing was growing labored and his eyesight was dimming by the second. Kotch didn't know it at the time, but his carotid artery had been severed in the explosion.

Sergeant Mills, despite a compound fracture to his shoulder and substantial injuries to his leg, kept his composure and managed to find the radio's microphone with his uninjured arm. He radioed the front Humvee with the situation: "We're hit, we're hit bad. Contact right." Without missing a beat, Mills dropped the radio to the floor, grabbed his M16 and started squeezing off shots from over his badly wounded shoulder.

By the time the other two teams heard Mills' shaken voice come over the radio, they were nearly a half a mile in front of them. Taking up position on a nearby overpass, they covered the team's movements, but with no line of site to the insurgent team, had no clear shot. The Humvee, although hammered by the explosion, managed to keep pace and limp its way out of the kill zone to the relative safety of the waiting teams. Mills, with the entire right side of his body absorbing the blast, was bleeding badly and Kotch—still manning his turret—was quickly losing consciousness. After shooting their way out of the kill zone, the team's driver, Specialist Rick DiTrapano—a former Marine, Desert Storm veteran and all-around badass cop back in Massachusetts—made the call back to the TOC with the air MEDEVAC request. His own face bleeding and peppered with bits of shrapnel, Rick knew Kotch and Mills might not have much time left, and rushed to help to patch them up.

The TOC denied the MEDEVAC. The area was still considered too hot, and the teams couldn't secure a landing zone. Nine men, two of them gravely injured, would have to make due. In a moment of sheer bravery, common sense and outrage, Rick and his crew radioed back they were inbound to *Rifles West* with two injured soldiers: Get the helicopters ready for an incoming MEDEVAC now. If the Black Hawks couldn't get to them, they'd get them to the choppers. With wounds this severe, they'd have to be rushed to the medical team at Al Asad Airbase if they stood a chance, and that was at least a half hour away by air.

Without a MEDEVAC and a Quick Reaction Force that clearly wasn't quick enough, the teams realized the only way back to *Rifle's West* was on the highway. They were going to have to make their way through the kill zone again.

Kotch and Mills were loaded into one of the lead Humvees, and a young specialist by the name of Steve Thibeault took Kotch's place behind the SAW. With their precious cargo clinging to life, the three teams quickly steeled themselves for the all-out dash back down the highway. In a violent barrage of gunfire from both sides, the MPs rocketed back through the kill zone, pounding the dark patch of reeds with SAW and MK19 fire as it continued to spit AK bullets. DiTrapano's Humvee, visibly scarred and slowed by the IED, was losing ground fast. Falling further back from the two lead trucks, now in a desperate rush to get Mills and Kotch to the ACR's medics, DiTrapano and Thibeault crawled their way through the kill zone. The insurgent team, seeing their crippled target straying from the herd, detonated a second IED just as they passed, its violent charge barely missing their vehicle.

The entire engagement lasted less than twenty minutes.

Both men made their flights and would eventually recover, although Kotch technically *died twice* from blood loss on his chopper ride to the combat support hospital at Al Asad. Today, Mills usually needs a cane to get around, but after seeing the golf ball-sized dent in his bulletproof Kevlar helmet from the impact of the shrapnel, he's thanking his lucky stars. All the men involved did some true blue heroic work that night, and later received awards for their quick thinking and courage. Although the teams didn't receive the level of the award they were nominated for, the men were more than satisfied knowing both of their friends would live to see their families again.[32]

---

32 They were each put in for a Silver Stars with "V" Device, but each award would be downgraded by the 82nd Airborne Division to Army Commendation medals (ARCOM) without the "V" device. Obviously, both injured men would receive Purple Hearts.

While all of this was going on, our own 3rd platoon had heard the whole thing develop on the radio as they were guarding the gates of *Champion Main* only a few miles away. (They were on rotation with 2nd platoon). Knowing that our guys returned fire and probably hit some of their assailants, they went on to stop an Iraqi ambulance before it sped past their position on the way to the hospital with the wounded moments later. They detained the injured Iraqis, treated them and sent them to the detention center. Thanks to the sharp thinking of 3rd platoon, four of the injured insurgents would go straight to Abu Ghraib. The 94th would have the last word that night.

Helplessly, I heard the entire event unfold on the radio, 20 miles away at Camp *Mad Dog*. I will forever feel horrible for not being there. And I will never ever fucking forgive the ACR for making such a haphazard choice and putting us in such a shitty position. But we dealt with it—another experience that intensified our commitment to doing things our own way.

Obviously I can't blame the ACR staff entirely for what happened, but I can't help but think it might have been avoided if we weren't so casually switched with another platoon who knew the area cold. Would the attack have happened to 2nd platoon if they had been there instead? I'll never know, but one thing was clear; it was a stupid decision that took away our advantage, and handed our enemy an easy victory. And on top of a poor tactical decision, it was a tremendous morale killer. We were losing faith in our leadership. After all, I had to remind myself who we were working with; just days earlier, I'd read a report describing how an IED, concealed in the chassis of a destroyed Iraqi tank sitting idle on the side of the road, had exploded and wounded a soldier on a foot patrol. It was a perfect place to hide an IED. The tank had been sitting there for *months*, and only *after* the explosion was it cleared and moved.

A few days later, I went to speak with Major Gallivan, the ACRs operations officer, in search of an explanation as to why our patrols weren't being provided with the tank support they needed. I'd pleaded countless times before that armor assets needed to be pre-positioned outside of the gates in overwatch. They were useless parked on the post, and that piece of highway was a constant problem. Our Humvees, although poorly armored, were much faster than the tanks and at least made for harder targets. But we wanted tanks readily available to help us pin down and kill any insurgents on the spot, rather than "come to the rescue" from a dead standstill on post several miles away, a half hour after the battle had ended—and that's assuming they knew where we were. I was sick of the reactive tactics of the ACR and wanted more cooperation, and was quite upset when I entered Gallivan's room.

After my ranting and raving over how the ACR continually dropped the ball, Gallivan lost his cool and put me in my place. What I didn't know was that a soldier from *Thunder* was fatally wounded by an IED during a patrol the night before.[33] As tank gunner, similar to our own Humvee gunners, he was standing behind his weapon—a machine gun mounted to the tank's exterior—his upper body exposed to the serrated metal of an exploding artillery round. In one of the most disturbing tones I've ever heard, the major told me he had just finished scraping pieces of skull and brain off of his boots. He didn't need this shit, and certainly not now.

---

33 Staff Sergeant Frederick L. Miller Jr.; September 20, 2003

I didn't utter a word. I just didn't know what to say. A few seconds later, in a feeble effort to speak, I could barely whisper an apology. Gallivan was a patient guy; very thoughtful and logical in the way he handled things. This was the first I'd seen him really get angry, and on top of the shock and anger from the death of one of his own, I could sense he was starting to feel the unrealistic pressure from his commanders. Gallivan had arrived a little late in the game, sometime in June, replacing the original operations officer who'd been rotated back to the States. I had the feeling he was a little tired of the standard, predictable approach of the ACR as well, but unlike the captains of the 94th, *he* was in a good position to do something about it.

After his temper cooled, we started talking man to man. He went on to describe how he felt, years before, when he lost his first soldier—how he remembered just where he was when it happened, how he could still hear his voice on quiet nights, and how he knew the face of the dead soldier better than he knew his own wife's. I prayed I would never know that feeling.

Gallivan was understandably irate with my hotheaded approach, but recognized and appreciated at least some of the effort I was putting in. It wasn't just my guys out there, but good decisions would be of tremendous benefit to anyone working Ramadi's roads after dark. After several minutes of discussing the best practices of protecting our men and women, he agreed to provide an armor escort for our next patrol, scheduled for 6 a.m. the next day. The tanks would be ready and waiting, and would roll out with our guys. They'd set up in an overwatch position, on an overpass a mile or so from the stretch of road the insurgency was increasingly laying claim to.

I apologized again, and said a prayer for both Sergeant Miller and his family on my way out.

The next day, the tanks were nowhere to be found. Apparently, there was a communication mix-up, and the armor unit never got the word of our patrol—another lesson learned. From now on, I'd coordinate things myself, and then notify the staff of my plans afterward. I'd check in with the ACR to make sure I wouldn't be stepping on someone's toes or compromising other missions, but that was the extent of it. It was becoming clearer this was the only way to get things done in such a fast-paced conflict. From now on, I'd be looking for forgiveness, not permission.

Two days after the IED attack on 2nd squad, I took the squad down to Ramadi for a patrol with our fellow soldiers from 1st and 2nd squads. There we were, just before dark, seven teams roaming through this problem neighborhood right around where the IED had gone off. We could tell right away this wasn't going to be an ordinary patrol, and frankly we didn't want it to be. With the sunlight slowly draining away, we pulled to the shoulder of the eastbound carriage lane and went in to question literally everyone within view about the IED. A couple of younger guys, at first curious as to why we stopped, got spooked and ran when we approached them. Sergeant Couture, his patience understandably gone by this point, sent a well-placed M16 round cracking into the wall of the concrete house they had just sprinted past. Knowing we meant business, the men froze in their tracks with their hands in the air. A little startled by the shot (Scott was behind me and had fired just a few yards over my right shoulder), I aimed my weapon and motioned them to the ground. While we questioned our newest catch, 2nd squad hiked to the mosque a few blocks away to find out what the Imam knew; they always had their fingers on the pulse of the neighborhood.

Just as we suspected, none of the men questioned knew anything, neither at the mosque nor back near the road. Moreover, the guys at the mosque wouldn't even shake our hands—we knew what that meant. Being with the group closer the road, I was keeping in touch with 2nd squad via our bright yellow hand-held Motorola radios. The squad wasn't getting anywhere with the Imam, so I pulled them back. As they made their way from the mosque, some asshole just couldn't resist picking up his AK and taking a few shots at us. He wasn't very close, but definitely within range. Convinced this part of town was rotten (that was the intel assessment, too), and fearing Kotch might already be dead from his wounds, I restrained myself from jumping behind the MK19 and leveling everything between the shooter and us. Instead, as the AK fire grew more intense, I looked over at Sergeant Bachman and told him to put a five-round burst from the MK19 into a stretch of sand near a row of houses. The small crowd that was starting to gather ducked and scattered at the sounds of the ear-splitting explosions, less than 100 yards away. Out of range of any bystanders, the shells struck harmlessly into the open patch of land, but we'd made our point to the shooter, who was no doubt close by.

The MK19 is a very loud, fast and intimidating weapon. As was the case during our midnight patrol in Hit, a careful demonstration at the right time could prove useful, and if this guy wanted to whip it out tonight, so would we. Our message was perfectly clear: If you wanted a fight tonight, you got it. And if you fired your weapon again, you'd better kill us. All of us. Otherwise, whoever's left is going to send you straight to your 72 virgins. Just show us a muzzle flash, and in about three seconds you'll be wowing those bitches in paradise with the story of how you took on the American infidels.

The AK firing stopped.

CHAPTER 6

He's got a two-day head start on you, which is more than he needs. Brody's got friends in every town and village from here to the Sudan. He speaks a dozen languages, knows every local custom. He'll blend in. Disappear. You'll never see him again. With any luck, he's got the Grail already."

Harrison Ford as *Indiana Jones*
Indiana Jones and the Last Crusade

I love these references, and it won't be the last for Indiana Jones. If you don't know this particular one, see the flick. It boils down to Indiana throwing a bunch of bullshit at the Nazis in an attempt to throw them off the path of his clearly inept friend, Marcus. We, in a small way, try do the same, with our own disinformation campaign.

The Iraqis we'd talked to gave us some interesting insight as to how they perceived the American soldier. I had to keep in mind these people had been insulated from any kind of technology besides the gasoline engine, light bulb and electric motor for the past 50 years, and tended to be quite superstitious. Wow, they had overactive imaginations. Here are just a couple of examples, the ones we both made fun of *and* exploited.

First, they thought our military sunglasses had magical x-ray powers. Once in a while the kids would want to look through them, thinking they'd be looking through walls or people's clothing. The second superstition: we took pills to help keep us cool. There was no way we could operate in that uniform and all that gear without some kind of medication. Third, (easily my personal favorite): the intimidating "red dot" laser pointers attached to our 9mms caused impotence. The fourth: our Humvees were protected by some kind of force field that could deflect rocket propelled grenades. That one, I really drilled home to people—we'd have our interpreter talk up stories about how our Humvees could block incoming RPG rounds, how our "radar systems" could help us find the shooter, or how we'd have to cut our conversations short to go "charge up our shields" or some such nonsense. The reality was most of the Iraqis were either terrible shots, had no idea how to arm a grenade round, or both. But what the hell, the more their imagination was left to wander, the better. And the more we reinforced our capabilities—imagined or not—the more it might have chipped away at the confidence of the resistance. It was worth a shot, and we'd use everything in our arsenal to our advantage.

Sergeant Eric Giles, who later in the tour would travel with a plastic pink flamingo (don't ask), would tell the small Iraqi children it was an "evil genie who possessed terrible, untold powers." Hook, line and sinker.

"TOP...MEN"

Again with Indiana Jones. At the end of *Raiders of the Lost Ark*, Indy defeats the Nazis and delivers the Ark of the Covenant to a bunch of Army intelligence guys. They're sitting around a table discussing it, with Indy insistent it be studied more carefully so as to understand its mysterious abilities. When asked who'd be working on it, the Army brass assured him "top men" were on the project. Indy demands that he be told who they were. The response again was an indignant *"TOP...MEN,"* complete with theatrical pause and an icy stare. At the very end of the film as the credits role, an old man wheels the Ark, now sealed in a plain wooden crate, into a huge warehouse filled with thousands other just like it. The Ark—with all of its destructive capabilities and awe-inspiring power, a supernatural wonder men had killed and died for—was just another box. And the people responsible for it? Top men.

We were about to find out what our own "top men" were up to, and exactly what their vision was for winning this war.

So there we were, at the end of September 2003, waiting for our redeployment orders home. We all gathered again at Al Asad, with the exception of a few squads who were still out on missions, some as far south as the Iraqi-Saudi border. From a historical standpoint, no combat deployment had lasted longer than 8 or 9 months, especially for the Reserve component. We'd done our unofficial six-month rotation and were ready to un-ass the country.

Most of us had seen some action, more than we expected. A few lovely young ladies in 3rd platoon had gunned down some Iraqi men who had tried to ram their checkpoint with a car near Haditha. Another young specialist shot and killed a man in Fallujah who was firing at their position. A squad from

2nd platoon in Ramadi got into a major firefight during an ambush on one of their night patrols. A soldier from 4th actually had videotape of an IED exploding *right next to his vehicle* as they drove into eastern Baghdad. A sergeant from 3rd platoon defused a pretty tense situation with a handshake after his squad stared down a Syrian border patrol at gunpoint near Al Qaim. Third squad and myself had our own little 24-hour gangbusters melee about a month prior, along with an IED that banged up two of our men pretty badly. A couple of our troops even had their pictures in Maxim magazine, and some of 3rd platoon's soldiers had their photo in Newsweek, thanks to the embedded reporter who was traveling with them. We'd gone to war, and it was time to move out. Mission accomplished. Let's get the hell out of here.

But it wasn't quite that simple. A few weeks before moving up to Al Asad, a rumor was floating around all units in Iraq would serve a full year boots on the ground, or BOG; another painfully stupid acronym devised by men at the Department of Defense or Pentagon, who most likely never saw a day of combat in their lives, much less an actual pair of boots. This sexy new buzz-term was a good indicator our fate was drawing nigh.

Within a few days of ending our missions in Hit and Ramadi and reporting to Al Asad, we learned our fears were confirmed: All major units and their attachments were to be extended an additional six months in Iraq. Every soldier who'd finished this marathon was told to turn around, head back, and run the whole damn thing all over again.

In retrospect, operationally, it was the right move, but at the time it was a real sucker punch. After a few days of sulking about, after all of the turmoil surrounding the decision had died down, we realized it was for the best. There was no shortage of work to be done, and we had seen the negative effects of high troop turnover on the areas we were working in—to swap out now would mean a lot of our work would be for nothing, and probably get people killed.

It was quickly becoming apparent the Army's role in Iraq wasn't a simple "show of force," or to hold some real estate in the Middle East. We were there to build and train their police, their government, to expand our informant base, to investigate more leads. Technically, despite what the brass back home said of our mission, it was nation building. Of course, we weren't thrilled with the prospect of another six months, but at least we had enough to do to keep us busy for quite some time.

After all was said and done, though, I still had a bitter taste in my mouth. It wasn't the extension I resented; it was the way we found out about it. The 94th headquarters element at Al Asad had heard the then-rumor from concerned family members and spouses in the family support group back in New Hampshire. Our troops were picking up the phone and calling home only to hear their wives or husbands in a panic on the other end, sick with worry about the decision to extend tours in Iraq. This was a solid two weeks before *anyone* in our chain of command confirmed it for us. It wasn't the ACR's fault that we weren't informed—it went much higher than that.

The *official* extension memo finally came down about a week later from Lieutenant General Ricardo Sanchez, then the Commander of Combined Joint Task Force 7 (the fancy name for Coalition Forces) in Iraq. It could not have been more apathetic or uninspiring. To sum it up, it was one of those "tough luck, sucks to be you" letters. Barely a half page in length, it wasn't what I was expecting from a commanding general. In my humble opinion as a soldier, half of a general's job is keeping troops motivated and informed. Having a tactical genius would be nice, but having a man who kept our energy up was critical. This was not to be the case either way. Much would be written on the general following the war, very little of it praising his abilities.[34] Consider this book one such instance.

The military had a unique opportunity to use this extension not only to increase troop morale, but map out a real strategy for the armed forces on the ground. They blew it. It came and went with barely a word. I made the best out of it with my guys, even when some of it wasn't exactly sincere. Sure, there would be a few in the company who would be bitter about it for days on end, but we couldn't let the complaints start to define our overseas service. Once that started, it would be tough to reign in. For the most part, we dealt with it. We didn't have a mission yet, but we kept sharp. Our gear and weapons were packed and ready to be shipped off to any city in Iraq the U.S. Army wanted to send us to.

Unfortunately, there was no plan, on any command level. In my opinion, it was "top men" like General Sanchez who were shelving the might and potential of the United States military. Over the next week, while dealing with the reality of another six months of war, I couldn't help but notice there was no vision for how this conflict was being fought. We were gathering a lot of intelligence; information we were certain ultrasmart guys and gals in a think tank somewhere in Baghdad or Washington were processing. However it appeared no real goals were being set, no real big picture plan was in place. The mission statements for the combat units we were working with were still too obvious and vague, like "find and destroy anti-Coalition fighters in our sector." Well, no shit. Any crackpot could have scratched that on the back of a cocktail napkin. I'm

---

34 "General Failure" by Thomas E. Ricks, *The Atlantic*, November 2012, was probably the best one

all for keeping it simple, but how was it going to take place? What would it look like? No one was tying it all together. We were looking for a little cohesive guidance from our general, something that said we have a thoughtful plan for dealing with the growing insurgency in our Area of Operations, especially after learning we were to continue our dangerous work in the volatile Anbar Province.

It wasn't to be. Supporting the day-to-day activities of the military—moving food, supplies and personnel around—was the mission. Take this truck and escort it from here to there. Half of these things were filled with junk food and soda for the PX. It felt like we were just waiting for the next attack. It was a hyper-reactive posture that was becoming a growing trend since the invasion. Too few resources were being focused on dissecting and actually destroying our enemy, and time was a luxury we clearly didn't have. I saw it almost every day at our meetings, those "Battle Update Briefs" I discussed earlier. It was becoming painfully clearer I might meet my Creator on any given mission, which now was the noble duty of escorting Mountain Dew to some thirsty troops who missed the sugary, uber-caffeinated taste of home.

I was growing impatient with our new circumstances. It came as no surprise in the fall of 2003 that the guys working on the roads had a vested interest in this information. The MPs, the transportation folks, and the combat units were the ones dealing with the ambushes and IEDs most often—the biggest killers in Iraq by far. Over the next nine months, we'd spend countless hours learning the newer enemy tactics and procedures, usually by seeking out and speaking to other commanders. With a little due diligence, we'd tie it together ourselves.

To add insult to injury, about two weeks after our extension, one of our medics actually received a rubber-stamped

"Welcome Home" letter from the deputy commander of our entire Reserve unit—one of our own top men back stateside—thanking him for his service in Iraq. His parents back in Massachusetts, who weren't sure to laugh or cry about it, had mailed it to him at Al Asad. It was promptly posted on our company board.

If it wasn't clear before, it was now: we were officially on our own.

CHAPTER 7

"I want to see plenty of beach between men. Five men is a juicy opportunity; one man is a waste of ammo."

Tom Sizemore as *Sergeant Mike Horvath*
Saving Private Ryan

Here's another movie reference that applied very well to the tactical situation in Iraq, and it accents a core fundamental. In the opening scenes of *Saving Private Ryan*, Sergeant Horvath tells his men, moments before storming Omaha Beach, to separate as quickly as possible after charging off of the landing craft. The German fighters would be shooting at the largest and most profitable target, looking to do the most damage.

The same was true of our enemy here, or anywhere for that matter. The insurgents in Iraq were risking their lives to emplace these IEDs and start these ambushes—not everyone was looking to become a martyr. They were looking for American trucks traveling together in a tight bunch as to maximize damage and send as many people into disarray as possible. They were looking for gunners in their turrets not paying much attention. They were looking for people asleep at the wheel. They were looking to kill as many of us as they could in the least amount of time. They were looking for their ideal target.

There was no one magical answer or tactic that was going to insure our success, but using common sense was critical. Through our investigations of these ambushes, we developed an understanding of our enemy's capabilities and adapted our tactical posture accordingly. Much of the success we and other units were experiencing was owed to a due diligence of the insurgency's techniques, and not the busy work I'd been witness to by the "scholars" back on post. Instead of a thoughtful analysis of the changing situation on the roads of Anbar, we were seeing more and more effort being put into worthless pursuits. Some officers were losing sleep trying to find color printers, which no doubt made their empty presentations more impressive in the eyes of their leadership—ridiculous First World problems in America's newest Third World war.

We were slowly building an informal database of information, and in talking with soldiers in other units, we were learning more about what *they'd* seen. The more we knew about our environment and our enemy, the better off everyone would be. The war was going to be won one sector at a time, one town at a time, one street at a time. One decision at a time.

Pretty soon we started coming up with some rock solid info—how IEDs were being emplaced (usually a four-step process), how far off of the road an average ambush was, the most typical areas in which they occurred, how insurgents were getting to and from these places, the morale of the fighters in town, the weapons they were using, how money was coming in, who was moving the weapons, and so forth. But most importantly, we began to talk with convoy commanders who had actually been ambushed, learning from their experiences, taking notes and passing information along to other units.

Even after the biggest intelligence payoff since the war started—the capture of Saddam in December of 2003—no one thought it would signal the end of the resistance. Maybe of our time in Iraq, but not the insurgency. This fight wasn't going to end so easily, as we'd come to find out in spades the following April. If we wanted to win, it was going to require an all-out effort from every unit, every platoon and every soldier. If you weren't getting involved with every aspect of what was going on, you were going to miss something that would prove critical to your own survival and the defeat of our enemy. A soldier's job in the Army wasn't going to be as simple as driving a truck, shooting a gun or walking a patrol anymore. While these were all required tasks, they were the tip of the iceberg. Every troop had to be alert to how the war was shaping itself.

Just about the time we were learning of our six-month extension, we were beginning to realize the Iraqi fighters, the former regime sympathizers then-Secretary of Defense Donald Rumsfeld labeled "dead enders," weren't waning in number or lethality. Quite the opposite, in fact. The dreaded IEDs were becoming a serious concern, and the frequency of ambushes was climbing sharply. While we appreciated Mr. Rumsfeld's attempt at cheering us up a bit, it didn't help much. No one there bought into the spin he was putting on this conflict, no matter how much we all wanted to believe it. We just wanted him to stop giving empty, rambling press briefings and start getting us better equipment.

Regardless of what was being said at the Pentagon or White House, we had to adjust our tactics. This much was clear. Being on the road more often meant more danger, but it was also giving us a better awareness of newer trends being employed by our cunning, adaptable foe.

That being said, I'm willing to accept tactical risk. A certain degree is very much necessary, and I understand death and injury are inherent to conflict. As I've said before and will say often throughout this book, you can do everything "right" and still become a casualty. Sometimes it truly comes down to fate, but that's not to say you throw everything to chance, which was being done much, much too often. In my opinion, to not do all in your power, to not be resourceful, to not put forth a proactive effort every day was simply ludicrous, if not criminal. Yes, there were ambushes, shootings and IEDs where we worked. You couldn't possibly predict and prevent every attack. However, there wasn't a night (or day) that went by when I and a lot of other troops couldn't sleep, knowing we hadn't done all we could to keep up with our enemy, complete our mission, and safeguard our men and women.

We were seeing, from our own research, that the guys not putting too much effort into their jobs were the ones getting shot at more often. Here's a perfect example. Fourth platoon of the 94th was attached to the *Muleskinners*, the regiment's logistical troops based at Al Asad Airbase, early on in the deployment. Known as "loggies," their main mission was ferrying supplies back and forth between operating bases, which usually meant a lot of convoys. Fourth platoon was assigned as their escorts, and not the fun, pay-by-the-hour-bachelor-party kind. They were the serious, keep-you-from-getting-shot-or-blown-up kind.

After talking with the troops of 4th platoon, I was starting to learn the loggies weren't taking anything seriously. I even had a staff sergeant from 4th, Dwayne Eidens, stop by *Eden* one afternoon, desperately looking to me for help. Dwayne was an outstanding non-commissioned officer, but had run into some serious trouble. He was in the middle of convoying down from Al Asad to Ramadi, and the convoy commander, a Sergeant First Class, clearly wasn't taking any sensible precautions. At his wit's end, Dwayne was pleading with me to give him a hand; "Sir, you've got to help me with this knucklehead." We ended up working things out on the spot with the indolent convoy commander, for the time being, anyway, but the problems continued.

From what I'd seen and heard from the troops in 4th platoon, the vehicles were never properly maintained or prepared, troops were rarely ready on time, and the convoy commanders were sidelining reasonable attention and care; not at all a comforting fact for the military police assigned to protect them. Their convoys were often ambushed in the same places on the road and at the same time of day on their way to the post near Haditha. And yet, these lethal events were all chalked up as "just a part of war" by an unsettling number of leaders there. This, I never understood. It wasn't a part of war; it was rotten planning. In fact, it wasn't even planning; it was gambling, and again, not the fun bachelor party kind. The main mission for these guys wasn't movement to contact or patrolling. It was getting from point A to point B with their cargo safely. They weren't even checking their trucks, for Chrissake.

On one occasion while at the gate at *Eden*, I saw a soldier in the passenger seat of a fuel truck—a pretty large and sought-after target by the insurgency—drive by with his white-socked feet hanging out of the window. I should have shot them off myself.

This nonchalant approach to life wasn't restricted to the loggies. Since we were always shuttling back and forth between Al Asad and Ramadi, contractors would often seek us out, looking to hitch a ride. I remember escorting a couple of guys from Halliburton, who would often ride in their dark SUVs between our Humvees, wearing their little blue vests and black ballistic helmets. They weren't armed, and most looked as though they hadn't seen a gym in years. One came up to me after our safety brief, looking for a radio. They didn't have any Army communications equipment, so I gave him one of our little portable Motorolas. He shook my hand and thanked us for the escort. Then he said something I'll never forget.

"Man, every time I ride with you guys, it's so boring. Nothing ever happens."

Oh, well I'm so sorry to have disappointed you! That's right, you fucking idiot. This wasn't a guided tour of the African safari. This was war, with a thousand ways to take your life. Every day, there were new, creative ideas on how to kill you being born right here in Iraq. The military police weren't here to show you some action; we were here to keep you from getting forced off the road by a bunch of insurgents who'd happily slit your throat and laugh while they were doing it.

I sincerely hoped his tour would be as boring as it had been, but it wouldn't. A few months later, four contractors from Blackwater were brutalized and killed following an ambush; their battered corpses burned and strung up from a bridge in Fallujah. Hundreds of other contractors would be massacred in similar ambushes, rocket attacks, or worse, taken hostage; their headless, half-decomposed bodies found weeks later in a shallow desert grave, dressed in orange jumpsuits. A handful are yet to be found, and most likely never will be.

Just after the extension, about a week before our (unknown at the time) reassignment to Ramadi, I had the displeasure of working with these loggie jackasses and their staff for about a week. While learning what was to be my new job—escorting these posers around—I was introduced to a couple of staff officers who were running the show. One had been responsible for, among other things, belittling a fellow MP officer and platoon leader, ridiculing his suggestions and giving him a hard time on a daily basis. First Lieutenant Jim Sacchetti was 4th platoon's leader and, albeit kind of a strange bird, was a competent officer and a good friend. He was making the case for military police patrols over escorts (sound familiar?) between Al Asad and Haditha, their usual destination, and getting nowhere. Those in charge "knew what they were doing." They had it made, living it up at Al Asad, at that time arguably one of the safest bases in Iraq; a growing relaxation that was throwing a wrench into their tactical works. They didn't realize the comfort of their daily lives in no way, shape or form translated to better conditions outside the wire, and the more they withdrew from reality, the worse it got.

While making the rounds at their offices, I stopped at the intelligence officer's desk to see what kind of show they were running. In my humble opinion, it was beyond disappointing. I asked to see a list of major engagements from the last 30 days. She did produce a nice-looking chart, in color of course, complete with grid coordinates and details. A good start, I thought, but when I crossed-checked some of the ambush sites against each other, I found several had occurred in the same place, sometimes at the *exact* same 10-digit grid coordinate. When I reported my findings back to her, she looked at me as though I had a huge goiter on my neck. To my knowledge, *Pegasus* hadn't been made aware of it, and neither did Al Asad's QRF. Jesus, was anyone paying any attention up there? A major from their unit had been one of the first combat casualties of the ACR, and it seemed no one had learned from it. But, to her credit, the chart looked really sharp.

I'd met two other staffers that day, a major and a lieutenant colonel. One was best known for sitting at his desk, devising a convoluted "Bible" on force protection measures for Al Asad. (Force protection is both the fine art and exact science of keeping everyone on a military post safe.) Unfortunately, they'd gotten so wrapped up in its details it failed to have any real, practical worth. After meeting them and having nothing to lose, I briefly insisted I was not as easy to deal with as my counterpart, whom most of the staff had enjoyed using as a punching bag for the past five months. They'd picked on Jim a lot. He was a good guy who was just doing his job; keeping their men, and ours, from being killed. God for-fucking-bid they did the same.

In addition, if the MPs were going to be responsible for the security of the convoy, they were going to be *in charge* of security for the convoy, to include the decision not to move until we checked all vehicles, weapons, personnel and equipment. As is often the case with any conflict, it was clearly coming down to a battle of wills—who wants it more. It was as simple as that. And in this case, the MPs wanted it more.

It was also a recurring theme throughout our tour so far: we were responsible for our own safety and security. We had a mission to accomplish, but no idiotic oversight was going to cost us our lives. It meant a lot more work on our part, but it's better than saying, "I told you so" over the chaotic gunfire of an ambush, or after the eulogy of yet another dead soldier or Marine.

The major and lieutenant colonel were nice enough guys, but nowhere near in touch with the reality outside the gates of Al Asad. To them, everything was academic. Later in the week, I met with one of them again to talk over some of his proposed ideas. I wanted to discuss the real problem; the disturbing fact that convoy commanders were putting their people at serious risk. He wanted to talk more about one of our new, additional jobs—gate security. What MPs were available to do this, I didn't know. We were tapped out with the escorts every day. However from then on, we'd be part of the team checking people in and out of Al Asad, and maybe even patrol on post a little.

However, instead of polishing up on the tactical know-how of a mission—the checklists, guidelines and overall common sense measures intended to ensure a safe convoy through the unforgiving badlands of Al Anbar—I'd be handed the force protection manual for Al Asad Airbase. A *book* of rules and regulations the staff had been working on for so long, it discussed, in agonizing detail, such critical issues as the "host nation access" arrangement, which consisted of a colorful and complex badge system for the Iraqi workers on and around post.

Fine, whatever, I thought. The next was vehicle speed limits, complete with signs posted in both English and Arabic. Okay, barely relevant. And of course, we couldn't forget the procedures regarding the omnipresent *clearing barrels*, the large 55-gallon steel drums filled with sand designed to catch any accidental misfires when you cleared your weapon of chambered rounds before you entered post. It was becoming glaringly apparent priorities weren't being set.

I was getting annoyed with their "let's build a little town" SimCity bullshit. The fight was out there, not in here. The convoy preparation checklists were a total mess, and their supervision and enforcement were even worse. They were leaving that post every day on their way to some very dangerous places on extremely dicey roads, and for some reason, their staff was working overtime with their color printers and laminating machines, devising absurd rules few were following anyway, and even fewer would enforce. There was a huge master list of safety concerns involving the convoys, but instead of looking at the problems facing their soldiers on the roads, they focused on the more insignificant nuisances around Al Asad. If none of them were following even basic safety precautions on the highways between Haditha and Ramadi, it was very unlikely their soldiers would give a shit about the color of the badge an Iraqi worker was or wasn't wearing on post.

A similar lack of common sense would prove disastrous at Abu Ghraib prison in a few short months. It wouldn't matter how many memos, guidelines or regulations were being written if there were no actual practical, reasonable applications. Leaders out of touch with reality simply aren't leaders.

A week after our meeting, sometime in early October of 2003, my platoon would be reassigned to our new mission in Ramadi. The loggies would go on to face countless ambushes due to their negligence. To our last day assigned to them, they were never attacked while with an MP escort.

The operational tempo of the military police was at an all-time high in the fall of 2003, meaning we had a greater degree of involvement with missions in comparison to other branches of the Army. On one hand, it was welcome. Because we were working with just about everyone, we knew what every Army element was doing and how everything was coming together. We were still pretty close with the civil affairs team in Ramadi, and the intel guys were uncovering quite a bit in the province. It gave us an excellent operational perspective that, in turn, rewarded us with a greater competence in our own tactical decision-making, which we'd of course pass on to other units. In other words, it was better to be busy and independent, rather than be less involved and simply take your chances.

Being more active usually meant being exposed to more of the conventional dangers "outside the wire," but hey, that's why I joined the Army.

However, our missions were taking their toll on our equipment and often my patience. It used to burn me up to see *rows* of Bradleys and Abrams tanks sitting dormant inside our posts, non-mission capable because of some obscure problem, after we wrapped up yet another five-hour mission with an 18 year-old broke dick Humvee. Surely these machines could be used in *some* capacity. The fact was we were being hit less often than anyone, and it wasn't for a lack of activity. Although we were growing more upset at the fact we had no higher MP command to assist us with the issues we were having, the self-reliance we were learning would prove to be a life-saving quality in the months ahead.

Captain Michael J. Gifford

PART 2:
Operators and Administrators

IN OCTOBER OF 2003, 1st platoon was officially reassigned to the 82nd Airborne's new police-training academy in Ramadi. Because of the experiences and successes we had in Mohamadi and Hit, and the progress we'd made in getting the Iraqi Police some attention, we'd be attached to the 82nd's Provost Marshal's Office (part of the 82nd MP's headquarters element), tasked with the mission of training the police officers of Al Anbar Province, the most unstable and dangerous in Iraq, outside of Baghdad. And even that was debatable.

Almost overnight, our mission and mindset changed. It would be a marked difference from the first six months we'd spent in the most austere conditions imaginable and on the roads almost constantly. For the next six months, we'd be entirely *garrisoned*, meaning we'd be living on post and working in a fairly safe and well-defended area. The patrolling, escorts and raids were over. We were now tasked with teaching the new police how to do it. We'd be sharing *Junction*

City—formerly known as *Rifles West*, the home of 2nd platoon and several 3rd ACR elements—with the 1st Infantry Division, known as *The Big Red One*, from Fort Riley, Kansas.

When we arrived, we set up shop in yet another vacated concrete building and, with the help of some engineers, custom built the place as best we could, complete with wooden doors, window frames and even some crude furniture. The academy construction itself was getting underway, being built by some contracted Iraqi laborers. The civil affairs team, looking to Iraqi companies for help in the new projects, was hiring them through postings at the governor's office in Ramadi. It was a good way to pump some cash into the local economy and take the stress off the military engineers who were usually tasked with such missions. To our surprise, we'd be working with another MP platoon from the Arizona National Guard, the 855th Military Police Company. We hit it off almost immediately and, with the exception of a couple of bad eggs, we'd get along with them swimmingly for the next half-year.

Just before the first class, around the last week of October, we sat down and decided on the academy's content—the 855th had been working at the academy in Mosul for a while, and had a good idea how to run things from an administrative point of view. Most of us from our platoon had selected, trained, and worked along with the Iraqi Police in Hit and Rutbah since June, and knew what would be effective in the way of actual instruction. From there, we hammered out a pretty good outline, touching on the basics of Western policing (community interaction, human rights, due process, ethics) as well as what would best be described as paramilitary classes (building clearing, weapons training). The next day, the instructors, consisting of the enlisted men and women in each platoon, got to work on their lessons. Within a week, we had a working schedule and were ready to go.

The days of not knowing what the next hour would bring were over. Back in June, if we were going to be tasked with a mission, we'd be lucky to know about it five minutes in advance. Now, we had set weekly class schedules. While at Camp *Mad Dog*, we were planning and running our own missions, but we were constantly distracted by several outside factors that disrupted our police training plans; an informant would show up unannounced, the police would stop in to visit, there'd be an attack near us, and so on. Now we had all the time in the world to devote to the Iraqi Police Force of the entire Anbar Province.

It would come at a price.

With the new schedule, things were a little less exciting, which was both a good and bad thing. On one hand, our exposure to the conventional hazards had decreased literally tenfold. For the past six months, we'd been working twenty-hour days with constant missions checking every house, shack, palm grove and chicken coop between Ramadi and Al Asad. Frankly, I was looking for a break. Besides, we were the ones that initially spearheaded the police training effort with the ACR around the province, and to see some familiar faces from Ramadi and Hit come through our new academy added to our credibility with the Iraqi Police. In the process, however, a lot of our guys were becoming too complacent, myself included.

We'd still head north to Al Asad once a week or so, which by comparison to other routes was fairly safe, and we were sending a few teams through the congested streets of Ramadi to *Champion Main* every day. While the movement helped keep the tactical edge with our troops, the missions to *Champion* were routine, which was a huge concern. On top of our somewhat foreseeable departures, the roads were narrow, surrounded by tall reeds and piled high with debris. Once in a while we'd venture out at night when the roads were clearer, but with the dark came more obvious tactical headaches. The streets of Ramadi were dangerous enough during the day, let alone midnight. As soon as we left post, shady characters zipping about on motorcycles would probe our patrols and the small *combat outposts* in town. They'd often venture a little too close for comfort, so as soon as we could see literally the whites of their eyes, we'd pull out our 9mm pistols—newly equipped with those intimidating, impotence-inducing red aiming lasers—and "paint" the head or chest of any bozo out for a midnight recon. The red beams, cutting through the darkness and centered on someone's torso, usually stopped any would-be evildoer dead in his tracks. It was an effective, non-lethal way to confront what was most likely an unarmed threat, and it I felt good to quietly rattle our enemy once in a while. I felt like "The Terminator," or at least like that Predator thing, sans its cool thermal imagery.

I didn't like guys on motorcycles in Iraq. Sometimes, while on patrol in Hit, surly-looking teenagers would fly up to our Humvees on mopeds, and it wasn't out of curiosity. A few months prior while escorting the civil affairs team, I'd seen a guy on a motorbike close distance on our truck and start following us. Sitting in the back of their truck, facing the rear, I stared at him intently as he drove up within about twenty yards of us. His face was concealed in a red and white-checkered *shemagh*, a favorite of the Sunnis in the area. He stared at me and repeatedly made a slashing motion across his neck. If he hadn't had a small child riding with him, desperately clutching his waste from behind, I would've put a three round burst into his chest and left him to rot in the middle of the road. If I saw any threatening gestures like that in Ramadi, weapon or not, I honestly wouldn't have thought about it twice. Every weapon I had was locked, loaded and ready to go. And have I mentioned I didn't like Iraqi guys on motorcycles?

We'd noticed Ramadi had quieted down considerably in the later part of 2003, in no small part because of the 124th Infantry Regiment, an Army National Guard unit from Florida. They were combing the city; patrolling, responding to attacks, raiding nearby hotspots, and fine-tuning the Iraqi Police Force, 24/7. A great bunch of guys, I'd forgotten they were the guys who blasted "Charlie" a few months ago. Now I really liked them.

Their commander, Lieutenant Colonel Hector Mirabile, was the subject of a November 2003 *Wall Street Journal* article outlining how he managed to pacify Ramadi.[35] Basically, he was using good diplomacy with the sheiks. While looking for some input from their operations cell for ideas on how to better train the police at the academy, I had a chance to talk to their operations officer, a major from Pembroke Pines. Half of the units were either local cops or state troopers back in the Sunshine State. Half of the 94th were cops too, so I understood how well-suited we were for the mission. The major went on to explain just how they'd made it happen; organizing the Ramadi police into different units, holding their hands through advanced patrolling techniques, and teaching them to deal with the average Iraqi on the street. Even an internal affairs branch was in its infant stages. With the introduction of our academy, some badass AK-47s, a handful of bulletproof vests and—coming

---

35 Yaroslav Trofimov, *To Find Peace in Sunni Triangle, Talk to the Sheiks*, The Wall Street Journal, November 5, 2003

soon—the coveted Glock 9mm pistols issued to their graduates, these rookies should be in good shape.

With the town relatively under control, our enemy had taken up positions just outside of the city. The mortar attacks began to step up considerably but hadn't, to date, managed to cause any serious damage, with the exception of a Katyusha rocket blowing up a bulldozer at *Junction City* a few weeks before our arrival. However, the insurgency's use of another kind of missile would soon cost the lives of several American servicemen.

On November 2, 2003, a shoulder-launched, man-portable air defense system (MANPAD) missile struck one of two Chinook transport helicopters as they lumbered across the sky near Fallujah, killing 16 soldiers on board as it crashed into the Iraqi countryside. They were heading to Baghdad International Airport, filled with troops eager to take some leave and begin their R&R. In a day or so, they would have been on a commercial flight destined for either Qatar (home to one of the military's regional vacation spots), or to a major airport back in the United States.

The 94th had a few soldiers currently on leave, with three scheduled for this particular rotation. Little did I know, they were scheduled to fly to Bagdad Airport that day, and had boarded the Chinooks at Al Asad that morning. Literally seconds after I realized we had troops on those helicopters, we received a call from our headquarters advising no one from the 94th was injured—all three were on the first Chinook, a hundred or so yards in front of the destroyed chopper. In the end, the only casualty from our unit that day would be a decent night's sleep for those three soldiers for the rest of their lives.

For better or for worse, their helicopter landed safely near the wreck a few moments later, its distraught occupants rushing to the downed craft in a desperate search for survivors. One of the fatalities was a soldier who had been fighting tooth and nail *not* to go on leave, understandably concerned a vacation would be too distracting. Relenting only a few days before, he boarded the doomed Chinook that morning.

After a couple of days, the military found out exactly what had happened. The first Chinook was equipped with *countermeasures*—small infrared flares that are fired off in the event of an attack, intended to thwart heat-seeking, surface-to-air missiles. According to the reports, they were released soon after the first missile was fired. It's believed that the second helicopter's countermeasures either malfunctioned or weren't activated. In any event, they don't always work perfectly, especially against the smaller, man-portable missile systems.

It was also discovered the Chinooks were flying on a route regularly used to shuttle soldiers from points northwest into Baghdad, directly over the farmlands on the outskirts of Fallujah. Avoidable, routine behavior again cost the lives of several American soldiers.

The use of MANPADS by the insurgency was a rarely used tactic up to this point. Most were sticking to mortars; a cheap, concealable and relatively easy-to-use munition that could be fired from just about anywhere. And the fact that no one knew where the MANPADS were coming from was troubling. But our new hosts, the 1st Infantry Division, had some artillery assets of their own, and were ready to start using them.

Up until now, American artillery had been limited—the Army couldn't start launching shells into the congested areas around Ramadi. However, the field artillery unit attached to the division had some real cool stuff, and was about to up the ante in our deadly game. More specifically, they were set to unleash one of the most lethal technologies available to the

United States military—counter battery radar, or *counter bat* as it's often called. Shockingly quick and accurate, this technology allows an artilleryman to track a projectile as it passes through its radar net and, judging by its arc and speed, pinpoint from where it was fired—within three meters—in just a few seconds. The troops working the radar receive the coordinates from a computer, relay them to their howitzers or mortar men, and they, in turn, send rounds downrange to the fired round's point of origin. With most of the enemy's attacks at night, we often drifted off to sleep to the sounds of artillery barraging our enemy. It used to scare the hell out of the police at the academy, but I really loved that sound.

The counter bat radar struck hard and fast. There were even urban legends of hitting Iraqis who were firing from the backs of trucks on the highway. God, I would have loved to see the last looks on those guys' faces. They thought they could just fire a shell at us, hop into their truck and speed away safely into the night. Instead they'd jump in their pickup, check their mirrors, use their turn signal, hit the gas, blow up and die.

Hail, hail, Artillery! Your Allah isn't so Akbar now, is he.

The division was incredibly accurate with both its 125mm mortars and 155mm howitzers. In a wonderfully accurate partnership between technology and good old-fashioned firepower, the radar was really giving our enemy a hard time. Even better, the success of the patrols and raids was forcing the insurgents out of town, mortars in tow, right into the hands of our waiting artillery.

The 155mm artillery shell is one of the most potent, destructive munitions of the U.S. Army, if not the world. In December of 2003, the division shot *16* of the high explosive rounds at an insurgent hideout about ten miles from post within 90 seconds. What an onslaught. We were at the academy late that night, listening to the rounds streak over our heads, only to hear the low "boom" a few moments later as they struck their targets. The next day, those doing the battle damage assessment of the artillery attack reported there wasn't much left to assess, just a few destroyed trucks and small buildings, the rest shredded to micro-bits by the lethal barrage of incoming shells.

On my down time, out of sheer curiosity and a healthy dose of boredom, I wandered around and visited the different units around the post every week or so. It was one of the privileges of being an officer; I could pretty much go wherever I'd like without a permission slip or hall pass. One such outfit was the Air Force's detachment working near the 1st Infantry Division's Tactical Operation Center. Their officers were nice enough, but understandably pretty tight-lipped about their missions. Air Force spotters were on the ground guiding bombs into some of the hottest areas around us. They'd recently hit an ammunition supply point not too far from *Junction City* being looted of some heavy weapons and artillery rounds, the main component of the deadly improvised explosive device. The units who conducted the damage assessment from the most recent counteroffensive found a couple of smoking shoes and some random chunks of flesh. In addition, the shock effect of an F16 screaming over town at two in the morning a few hundred feet off the ground had a unique impact all its own.

While all this was going on, the EOD units were still busy cleaning up another ammunition supply point about 20 miles away. Their 5000 pound "shots" (controlled C4 detonations) could be seen, heard and felt from *Junction City*, complete with their signature mushroom cloud, low rumble and shockwave that usually blew our loosely hinged doors open a couple of inches. We'd visited their TOC in Ramadi a few times while working in Hit, trying to get some more attention paid to a small ammunition depot near *Eden*. Explosions had been rocking the place on and off for a day or two at a time, as looters coming to pick up bombs and mines would inadvertently set a few off, killing themselves in the process. Our 3rd squad had already responded to a few incidents and cleaned up plenty of stray body parts. Unfortunately the blasts were knocking live rounds across the Euphrates, over a quarter mile away, a few of which we'd find in the high grass along the river during our patrols.

However, the EOD teams had their hands full. Showing us a large map of the Al Anbar Province, they went on to point out just how busy they were. Scattered over the 10' x 6' map were hundreds of colored thumbtacks, each one representing an active ammunition supply point. There were so many tacks, the disposal guys were running out of space on the map, not to mention tacks. Iraq was literally chock full o' weapons—counting the tacks at eye level on the map, there were over 100 abandoned ammunition depots between Ramadi and Rutbah alone.

So many things were blowing up in Ramadi during the fall of 2003 that we could usually tell what kind of explosion it was right off the bat. Incoming mortar rounds were sporadic and usually had a telltale "thud," depending on where they landed. The IEDs echoed off of the city buildings, their muffled "booms" having a distinctive wavelength. The American 120mm mortars made a unique "popping" noise, and our howitzers were plain damn loud. Unfortunately, the sound of a car bomb would soon find its place in our audio inventory.

The 82nd Airborne's headquarters at *Champion Main* was just across the river from us, as the crow flies not even 400 meters. Formerly a complex of Saddam's palaces, it was now jam-packed with hundreds of U.S. troops and tons of senior officers. Quite a bit smaller than *Junction City*, which was much more spread out in comparison, it was the perfect target for insurgents looking to do maximum damage and was mortared almost every day.

I walking towards our makeshift laundry room one afternoon back at *Junction City,* getting ready to greet Sergeant Bachman who was walking towards me. His face said it all. He'd seen the massive fireball erupt from the *Champion Main* compound behind me, a second before the noise hit us. The thunderous explosion rocked our camp. I instinctively ducked my head and spun around. Wide-eyed and stunned, I saw the balloon of thick black smoke rising into the gray afternoon sky about 300 meters away. It was much too big of a blast to be a mortar, and much too close to be EOD's work. I figured it was another IED on the back roads snaking between *Champion* and *Junction City.* After seeing smoke continue to pour from the general direction of our helipad, I thought it might have been a chopper crash. However, after verifying it was neither, it was becoming painfully clearer something had gone wrong at *Champion.*

I jumped into my Humvee parked nearby, turned on the radio and got on *Devil X-Ray's* frequency—the call sign for the 1st Brigade Combat Team, the element of the 1st Infantry Division that was stationed at *Junction City.* I had a growing knot in my stomach something happened at *Champion's* main gate. With such tight security, no one would be able to smuggle that much explosive into the post without being caught, so they probably just blew it up right there. The gate was usually filled with soldiers, contractors and laborers lined up for inspection, looking to enter the post. Third platoon of the 94th was working the gates at *Champion.*

My hands started to shake. Those car bombs could easily shred anyone within 50 yards, and we had men all over the place. Sergeant Littlefield and two teams from our platoon, along with one team from the 855th, were there with the 82nd's sergeant major, whom they'd escorted to *Champion* just a few hours before.

After ten minutes of desperately trying to get a hold of anyone in our unit, radio traffic confirmed a civilian truck had exploded about 50 yards inside the gate. The first report said it was an accident; an acetylene tank had blown up. It just didn't occur to anyone, myself included, that it had been a car bomb. That only happened in Baghdad. Ramadi for the most part wasn't that bad. *It had to have been an accident.* A few minutes later, reality set in: someone had managed to get a truck loaded with explosives past the guards into the compound and detonate it, in an attempt to kill as many people as possible.

I was nervously switching back and forth between our own internal frequency and that of the 855th. No one was responding. It was roughly 1:30 p.m., the time the sergeant major's transportation detail would usually leave *Champion* on their way back to *Junction City*, exiting through the gate closest to the explosion. No one from Black Bear or *Predator*—the 855th's call sign—was answering. I was sweating bullets and feared the worst.

After about 30 minutes of being glued to the radio, I made a call to our company headquarters at Al Asad to see if they'd heard anything. Third platoon had already called and informed them of what had happened, and let them know none of their guys were hurt—a tremendous relief. I still couldn't get a hold of Reggie, but figured he was with 3rd platoon, hanging out in their air-conditioned hooch. With that news, I felt a little more optimistic about the condition of my men. As the MEDEVAC helicopters starting flying by, the casualty reports came rolling in. Within a half hour, four soldiers were still missing. Thirty minutes after that, all but one had been accounted for, and they were ok.

Within two hours, we'd learn a specialist with a communications unit attached to the 82nd was killed.[36] Seven others were slightly injured.

The specialist who lost his life in the blast was an escort for the truck; each time an Iraqi vehicle came onto the post, a soldier would ride along to make sure they didn't poke around anywhere they didn't belong.

The truck was detonated less than 50 yards from one of Qusay's old palaces which, by the grace of God, happened to be one of the most sparsely populated sections of the post. There were only a few concrete buildings and an open lawn area, which served as the compound's helicopter landing pad. Another 150 meters up the road and they would have destroyed the mess hall. One man was dead. It easily could have been 100. I imagine the insurgents in the truck jumped the gun and decided to blow it up as soon as they could.

Reggie arrived shortly after and told me all about it. They were running late that day. If they had been on time, they would have been rolling right past that truck when it went off. The Army's notorious inability to stay on schedule had just saved seven lives. If I hadn't believed in pure luck before, I did then.

Our guys were some of the first on the scene after the explosion. Specialist Adams talked to a soldier who had witnessed the entire thing, who actually saw the escort desperately trying in a heartbreaking effort to get out of the truck right before it exploded. He knew what was about to happen, but it

---

36 Specialist Marshall L. Edgerton, December 11, 2003.

was just too late. I can't imagine a faster way to go, but knowing what was coming had to have been the worst possible feeling. Sitting in a truck with a bunch of Iraqis on a heavily guarded post, fairly confident you were safe, your job simply to keep these idiots from going anywhere they shouldn't. Then you hear those assholes shouting "Allah Akbar," knowing it was all about to end. I don't even like to think about what was going through his mind in those last few seconds.

Not much was left of anyone with the exception of a few items. The soldier's torso, with the body armor vest still attached, was blown clear over the gates to the compound, into the vehicle search area. Shrapnel from the explosion pocked the entire side of a nearby building, and the charred remains of the truck's chassis were sitting in a small crater. It was filled in within a few days, with a small white cross posted into the grass near the site.

An EOD investigation later revealed several 155mm artillery rounds, each layered in plastic explosive, had been carefully embedded in the truck's gas tank. There was no way they would've been found in the gate inspection; we just didn't have the technology yet to do so.

I found out later the truck was owned by a man who had done some electronic work on both our post and at *Champion*, installing everything from satellite dishes to washing machines. I guess he was pretty well known with some of the guys in both places. The 82nd grabbed him in a raid soon after, and with any luck, pushed him out of a moving helicopter somewhere over the western desert.

A few days later, I began thinking about the giant "x-ray machine" I'd seen collecting dust and rainwater at Ft. Polk's back gate months before—one capable of scanning a car or truck for explosives. It had sat relatively unused for weeks at a time outside of that docile, backwoods post. As if anyone would attack a fucking useless place like Ft. Polk.

We really could have used it there.

Group shot following one fun obstacle course; Ft. Polk, Louisiana, April 2003 (top from left to right, SSG Scott Durst, SPC Chris Kotch, SPC Ben Dexter, SSG Todd Libby and SPC Rick DiTrapano; bottom left to right, SPC Travis Frost, LT Mike Gifford, SGT Kevin Chabot, SPC Steve Thibeault)

SPC Rick DiTrapano and SSG Scott Durst letting Saddam know just how they feel (*Al Asad Airbase, May 2003*)

Incoming sandstorm; *near Rutbah, May 2003*

Local Iraqi giving Saddam the bottom of his shoe; *near Ramadi, June 2003*

H3 Airfield (SGT John Bachman, LT Mike Gifford, SFC Reggie Littlefield); *Western Iraq, May 2003*

Controlled detonation; *somewhere in the western desert, July 2003*

Captain Michael J. Gifford

A photo of a single fluorescent bulb through night vision goggles; *Forward Operating Base Buzz, Western Iraq, July 2003*

A tad too close to a controlled detonation; *near Haditha, August 2003*

A few soldiers from 3rd platoon atop an abandoned Iraqi jet; *Al Asad Airbase, August 2003*

Prisoner transfer to the ACR's detention center; *Al Asad Airbase, August 2003*

After a brief but intense thunderstorm; *near Hit, August 2003*

Remnants of a 107mm Katyusha rocket attack; *Hit, September 2003*

Iraqi Police Forces (IPF) room-clearing training; *Ramadi, October 2003*

Captain Michael J. Gifford

IPF training; *Ramadi, October 2003*
Myself and Captain Laith Faaris, following his graduation from

the Anbar Police Academy; *Ramadi, November 2003*

An M109A6 155mm Paladin Howitzer through binoculars, sending rounds downrange at enemy mortar positions; *Ramadi, December 2003*

IPF securing a scene following an ambush; *near Ramadi, December 2003*

Soldiers from 3rd platoon raiding a suspected insurgent hideout; *Haditha, December 2003*

Myself and SPC Denise Moquin with Ukrainian troops, following a convoy escort; *Combat Support Center Scania, April 2003*

Myself, Todd Libby and Vince Vaughn, who toured with the USO; *Camp Udari/Buehring, Kuwait, June 2004*

CHAPTER 8

"Believe what you want. These walls are funny. First you hate 'em, then you get used to 'em. After long enough, you get so you depend on 'em. That's 'institutionalized.'"

Morgan Freeman as *Ellis Boyd "Red" Redding*
The Shawshank Redemption

The 82nd came down hard on 3rd platoon for missing the explosives. With the investigation still pending, a colonel from one of their units ripped into 3rd platoon and berated the Army Reserves for their incompetence. Third platoon's leader, Master Sergeant Dean Miles, was fairly strong willed and hadn't made many friends over at *Champion*, but knew his shit inside and out, and didn't pull any punches; a refreshing contrast to some of the politicians you find so many of in the service. He didn't take that kind of criticism very well, and I don't blame him. After a few days, the 82nd's search team came forward, admitting that it was they who'd checked the truck, missed the explosives, and allowed it onto the post. It must have been pretty difficult, but it was the right thing to do, and I admired them for it.

As for the colonel's stinging accusations? Nothing. Not even an apology from a man who was just propagating more of that "us versus them" bullshit between the Active duty and Reserves. This little twit, who'd made a comfortable nest inside a lush compound (by comparison to some other posts), had no appreciation of the efforts of troops who were working more than 12 hours a day, in one of the most hazardous jobs in Iraq, keeping him and others like him on post relatively safe from harm. He, like so many other idiots, would arrive from the States to a secure post, strike a pose with his M16 for photos in front of bombed buildings—as though he had something to do with it—and second-guess every decision made by his attachments.

Our time with the Active duty component across the river was getting tense as well. I can tell you without hesitation—from direct experience—that most of the 1st Infantry Division's and 82nd's staff were so hung up on the reputation of their own units, riding the coattails of the brave soldiers who had served years ago (or were serving now), they weren't taking time to understand this guerrilla war we were fighting. They were the big guns in charge, and that was that. Instead of following in the traditions of great soldiering, displayed by so many of their courageous young troops each day on the streets of Ramadi, the senior command hit the ground running in the wrong direction.

Day in and day out, we were being forced to deal with middle-aged asshole command sergeant majors or lieutenant colonels, who'd arrived just weeks before to ready-made billets, showers and hot chow. There was just something about those two ranks I didn't like. Quick to play the tough guy card, they thought it their sole purpose in life to dwell on the most remote, insignificant details of military life. Blind to the bombs going off all around them, I witnessed on a handful of occasions their complete disregard for the conflict at large. One in particular found it necessary to publicly humiliate some poor 18 year-old kid for an errant bootlace that had come undone. Piles of concrete and trash lined the dangerous streets all around us, but a tiny flashlight hanging from someone's uniform top was a major tactical problem to another such "leader." And, according to yet another, an unauthorized brimmed hat would no doubt spell disaster for the war effort. God forbid they'd put some sincere thought into better ways to pursue the war outside—*or at*—the gates. A courageous young man at *Champion* was dead, literally blown in half, and this was the best they could come up with. This was their well thought-out response, the result of years of military training.

I could understand their frustration, assuming that's why they were acting this way. But that aside, they'd only been there since September and had *no idea* how much worse it could—and would—get. I was beginning to long for the days with the ACR, where at least the staff understood leadership was often letting other leaders do their jobs, not micromanaging each detail or getting hung up on how someone walked, drove a Humvee or wore his uniform. That was a huge morale booster in itself.

However it was this lack of priority thinking that was getting kids killed, frustrating people, and, in my opinion, losing wars. Although the junior officers and enlisted of the 1st Infantry Division were very competent with their tactics, the attitudes of their senior representation were infuriating, even shameful at times. The captains, lieutenants and junior enlisted soldiers were busy off post, taking the fight to the enemy and knocking it out of the park during the fall of 2003. Everyone else who stayed behind was justifying his existence by giving others a hard time. It was almost as if that's all they knew how to do. Your tax dollars hard at work.

I'll give you one of the more mutual examples. As a military police officer, not specifically assigned to patrolling but still concerned about the roads just off post, I had *thrice* recommended the engineers clear them of debris that could possibly be used to hide an IED. We had done so with a stretch of road around southern Hit back in July and, using an engineer unit's bulldozer, found three bombs in less than two hours. Iraq's roads were often lined on both sides with either trash, vegetation or piles of rocks—usually all three. Those around *Junction City* and *Champion Main* were no exception. The narrow streets winding around our post had all sorts of that shit along the shoulders, often piling as high as a Humvee door. My guys were on these roads every day between there and *Champion* (as were other soldiers), shuttling the sergeant major back and forth to his meetings. Each time I went to the engineer section or 1st Infantry Division staff, I was told there were other priority missions for those big clearing machines, tasks assigned by the senior officers.

And those priority missions? Building someone's fucking driveway on post, or moving gravel around to make the parking lots look prettier. Seriously, gravel was being put in so we would, without a shadow of a doubt, know where to park our Humvees. And dust was blowing all over the place, getting into people's eyes and stuff. Something had to be done!

Der Kommissar's in town

Someone please tell me, when did we win the war and move to this type of thinking? The 94th was spending 16 hours at the police academy each day, pounding away on cadets for information about what was going on in their towns in an effort to keep our soldiers safe. First platoon was taking patrols out, well beyond our assigned duties, doing our damnedest to find potential ambush and IED sites so they could be cleared. We were giving reports to our tactical intelligence people working out of Ramadi, providing them with information that was filling in the gaps in their investigations. The combat units of the 3rd Brigade Combat Team of the 1st Infantry Division were patrolling Ramadi and working the city, with impressive, tangible results. Every few nights I'd tune in to their radio frequency to see what they were up to: those guys had their tactical shit together and were making a difference.

And yet I had a lieutenant colonel, literally sit and stare at me all through dinner one night because I had neglected to wear a Kevlar helmet for the ½ mile Humvee drive from the academy to the mess hall. Sure technically it was a mistake, but not one warranting such a childish, idiotic response. Here's what went down: There were two of us, myself and a lieutenant from the 855th, who were trying to get to the mess hall before it closed. We were working late and, not wanting to miss chow, took off in a Humvee without wearing a Kevlar. (It's Army regulation to wear your Kevlar helmet while driving in a military vehicle, whether on or off post.) The mess hall would have closed in the ten minutes or so it would have taken to head back to our barracks and pick up our helmets. (We'd both walked to the academy earlier.) And once the mess hall closed, that was it. They literally locked the doors and wouldn't let anyone in.

As we pulled into the lot he marched up, stopped us both, and read us the riot act. I mean he *really* nailed us. Busted. Point taken. Roger that, sir, it won't happen again. But it wasn't over yet. He intentionally waited for us to finish our meal, glaring in our direction the entire time. *The entire time.* I don't think he even ate anything. As we got up to leave, he stormed up, stepped in front of us, wagged his stupid bony finger in our faces and said, "I'm watching you, and you'd better be walking."

This was the first time in my military career I really, truly wanted to hit someone. It took every fiber of my worldly being not to remove my 9mm Beretta from its nylon holster, hold it edgewise, and pistol-whip this clown right across his stupid, weathered face.

This guy didn't have a goddamn clue as to what was going on. He just didn't get it. A simple "put your Kevlar on" would have sufficed. But no. Instead, we were to walk home in the dark; surely a much safer way to go on a post filled with ankle-spraining ditches, wild dogs, and incoming mortar and rocket rounds. And of course, who could forget the sergeant major who was caught driving around like a lunatic two nights before, trying to run over a few of the wild dogs littering our post. The guy nearly clipped one of my troops on his way to the shower point with his Humvee, in a maniacal attempt to murder a few stray pooches.

What bothered me most was the fact this lieutenant colonel was an engineer, apparently with nothing better to do—a habit formed by years of paperwork, inane assignments and garrison duty—than to harass us. We were at war now. People were dying all around us, *every day,* and not from milling about post without a helmet. It was just a matter of time before a soldier, maybe one in my own platoon, would end up paying the price for this man's utter incompetence.

It still angers me to this day, old men and their fucking egos, their toxic bile corroding the morale of America's finest hard-charging young men and women. We weren't on Forts Bragg, Benning or Stewart anymore—we were at war in Iraq. We were all wearing the same uniforms, driving the same trucks, carrying the same weapons and, to our detriment, dealing with the same poisonous attitudes we'd imported along with them.

These aren't just a couple of anecdotal examples. That same month, another dim, foolish man who should've known better—a command sergeant major with the 101st Airborne—would end up ordering his young driver to take him into downtown Mosul in a civilian car, alone. I have no idea what would necessitate such a reckless decision, and never found out why. Within minutes, they'd be sprayed with bullets, mutilated with concrete bricks and dragged through the streets. For some reason, this command sergeant major was hailed as a hero for giving his life for his country. I wonder if the parents of his 26 year-old driver felt the same way.

All of this was stemming from one major problem, one which will forever plague military leadership at war overseas—the need to return to the stable, reliable garrison environment they all know and love. Too many are in a big damn rush to get as comfortable as possible, to have that warm blanket of a familiar environment draped over them, where their orders are rarely challenged and even worse, well thought out. Oblivious to the hazards of post-war Iraq, their complacency and inflexibility grew with each passing day on a relatively safe post. Out of sight, out of mind.

That is, until, they left the wire. No matter who they were, what their rank was, or what they did on the inside, it was all waiting for them on the streets of Iraq. The insurgency was an equal opportunity killer, and business was booming.

I guess it was simply human nature. The 94th was undoubtedly enjoying the creature comforts that came with living on a huge, well-stocked post, but at least we had our heads in the right place. There was more to living in Iraq than avoiding the occasional mortar round on the way to breakfast, but for some, this was the only threat. They'd cross their fingers and hope they didn't become a statistic.

Not one of these men or women had learned a lesson from what had happened here just weeks before. For troops driving into Ramadi from the northwest, there was a left-hand turn off of the four-lane highway onto a long dirt road that delivered you to *Junction City*'s main gate. At the intersection of this turnoff was a pile of loose concrete and asphalt, about five feet wide and a foot tall. I'd been seeing this pile get larger and larger over the past three weeks or so. Wanting it cleared, I'd bring it up almost every time I met with the staff. Hundreds of soldiers passed by it daily. We were driving by it ourselves every afternoon on the way to our meetings, often within the same hour, earlier that summer. We tried to keep our travel time somewhat unpredictable, but we had to get to these meetings. There was only so much you could do as a "non-resident" to influence the times they took place. The *first* morning at *Junction City* I was abruptly woken by large explosion at about 5:30. An IED had detonated at the intersection at the end of the turnoff, hidden in the concrete rubble near the front gate. One soldier was fatally wounded. The Humvee was towed back inside shortly after, completely shredded on one side. That was the second time I'd seen a Humvee smashed by an IED up close. I didn't want to see a third.

There was another, similar spot we'd seen just outside of *Junction City* that had been a cause for concern about a month earlier. It was a 25-yard dirt path that cut from the carriage lane to the main highway near a volatile Ramadi neighborhood, flanked on both sides with ominous-looking piles of trash, weeds and dirt. For some reason, soldiers driving in the area had made it a shortcut from the carriage road to the freeway, even though the actual on-ramp was only a hundred yards away and clear as a bell. The shortcut would save someone *maybe* eight seconds, tops. It was clearly being used regularly, as the tracks in the sand were well defined. I didn't understand why people were taking the risk. The ramp was much safer— wider, made of asphalt, and clear of debris—and it was just a few seconds away. A few weeks after the attack at the gate, two IEDs exploded nearly simultaneously from the pile of vegetation and garbage lining the dirt shortcut, ironically ripping into a 94th MP vehicle, being driven at the time by a few of our maintenance guys from Al Asad in Ramadi on a supply run. Fortunately, no one was seriously hurt. I screamed at our guys afterward, asking them why on *God's green Earth* they thought it best to cut through a death trap like that to save a few seconds. For Chrissake, the damn on-ramp was right there, less than a hundred yards away! Their answer? "We don't live around here." It looked well traveled so they just assumed it was safe. Later on, one even told me he was thinking that this was a perfect place to hide an IED, just before nearly losing his right arm from the resulting explosions of the well-camouflaged artillery shells.

Again, that path of least resistance was just too tempting, and like Murphy's Law states, "the easy way is always mined."

Although I wasn't responsible for the physical security on and around the post, I was definitely concerned as an officer, an MP and an at-risk resident of Ramadi's most notorious U.S. Army post. Afterwards, I couldn't help but feel at least partly to blame for both. I still do. I should have grabbed a damn shovel and cleared the rubble near the front gate myself. I should have gone to the engineers a *fourth* time and insisted they at least block the shortcut, a clearly dangerous path too many people made a habit of taking on a regular basis, often by those from out of town. I should have blocked off the route with yellow police tape. I should have...

But why was it up to us to do this? It was evident the idle hands of a peacetime force were destroying our wartime focus. It was becoming too difficult for those in charge at *Junction City* to make a tough decision in the absence of a book telling them what to do. Were the people actually in charge of post security, or the safety of the main roads around the area, punished after these incidents? Not to my knowledge, and it figured. Few were held responsible in the military unless there was a violation of some specific, clear-cut Army regulation or Standard Operating Procedure, both of which were growing exponentially by the day it seemed. The military introduced literally hundreds of new disciplinary measures each year to deal with every stupid, petty, inconsequential violation that had been, or might be, committed. But when someone was injured or killed in war, rarely was anyone held accountable, and worse, few learned from it.

If it sounds like I'm ranting, being too harsh, or too critical, ask any parent, spouse, or sibling who's lost a loved one in combat. They—as well as the young kids military leaders were charged with protecting—deserved better.

At this point in the war, the U.S. Army was proving itself to be an organization that had perfected the art of assigning blame for meaningless oversights, and was miserably defective in both taking preventative action and learning from its own mistakes. Instead of using rational thinking to deal with smaller problems before they became major issues, we "drove on" until something tragic eventually happened. Rather than draw on any of the brutal lessons we'd learned, we were burying our reports and investigations in a neglected heap of useless paperwork. Or worse yet, ignoring their root causes and chalking it all up to being "a part of war." Again, with this bullshit term! In the winter of 2003, that was quickly becoming the Army's stock explanation for everything bad that was happening in Iraq. Too many mistakes—the result of poor planning—were being swept under the rug and explained away as inevitabilities of conflict. In the meantime, the military cranked out regulation after regulation in search of some imaginary, universal Army solution that was supposed to be the magic answer for every tactical or disciplinary problem—a perfect substitute for proactive behavior, supervision, and common sense. I've dubbed that one *the paper unicorn*. It just doesn't exist. So the military should stop looking for it.

I was regrettably learning that paper and bad habits, not leadership, all too often drove the U.S. military—even at war.

Some things *were* unavoidable in warfare. You couldn't stop every IED, ambush, or car bomb, but not putting in common-sensical effort was criminal. People in the civilian world are fired everyday for much, much less. In this case, the officer in charge of security should have been relieved, at the least. If no one was in charge of security, the post commander should have been. I remember telling my soldiers I'd resign if that happened on my watch. Only *after* the IED at the front gate did the post commander decide to set up a concrete fighting position at the end of the drive, near the road. The reactive thinking was getting worse and worse. And we were wondering why we were always one step behind the insurgency.

I often wondered if the little finger-wagging lieutenant colonel had actually checked into these tactical errors. He was an engineer and should've been chomping at the bit to take care of some of those threats. Later that month, *his* boss, a "full bird" colonel, ripped into me one afternoon when he *thought* he saw me get out of a Humvee without a Kevlar on. (I had taken it off just before opening the door, I swear!) Jesus, you'd thought I'd given him the finger and told him to go to Hell. He seemed to recognize me immediately and almost looked like he was waiting for me to screw up. For a minute straight, he went up one side of me and down the other. I was, and I quote, "that problem captain" on post, the Reservist with the 94th patch. I was famous! Ironic that in my left hand was yet another list of 10-digit grid coordinates of potential IED sites, the ones that my platoon had risked their lives to find in our searches around Ramadi in our precious down time. I handed it to him and walked off. Forgive me for trying to set the example in a more practical way.

Another arrogant old man who had the balls to face me, but not the balls to face our enemy. Enjoy your dinner, Colonel.

There should have been no, "That's not my problem" in Iraq, no "That's not my lane." Complacency was everyone's problem, and by not overlapping our duties we were letting the enemy win time and time again. It wasn't our "job" to point out these potential trouble spots, but in the general interest of safety, we went out of our way to do so. We weren't working the customer service desk at Sears, and this certainly wasn't a training exercise. *This was war.* And if you're going to go to war, GO TO WAR. There's no half-assing it. And despite being assigned to the academy, we were still MPs and genuinely concerned about mobility support; I wanted to make sure these hazardous areas around our camp were identified and cleared. Force protection is everyone's concern.

And why make it easier for the insurgency? What would it have taken to clear that debris at the end of our walk? To block off the entrance to that shortcut? To push our perimeter out a bit more? To do something other than push dirt around our shitty post? The explosion in that rubble at the end of our road was yet another justification a good offense makes the best defense—a reminder that the more we crawled into our hiding places in Iraq, the more bold and creative our enemy became, until he was in our back yard, and literally in our driveway.

By this time, all of us were getting sick of having our lives in the wrinkled, bony hands of *Junction City*'s brass, the ones who were standing right in the middle of the tracks but couldn't hear the train until it was three feet away. I was really getting uncomfortable. In the coming days, the ranks of these men and women quickly disappeared. The only thing I saw was if they "got it" or not, and by this time I could size up just about anyone in ten seconds or less. The formalities I'd once taken great pride in stateside—a sharp salute, uniform appearance or adherence to a strict, time-honored tradition of military bearing—were fading fast, replaced by a general distrust of anyone I found even remotely suspect.

Just a few months ago, when we were working on the roads, we had a lot more control over the way we did things. Here, while with a worthy mission of training the Iraqi Police Force, we were at the mercy of leaders who just "didn't want to deal with it." That's an actual quote from a sniveling major who'd been forced to deploy, kicking and screaming with his unit, his main task in Iraq to walk around *Junction City* and tell soldiers how they're bunks should be organized. We called him the "Feng Shui" major behind his back, and I imagine a few times to his face. Again, a great many brave men and women were traveling off post, into Ramadi, every day. But the ones who stayed behind were getting tougher to deal with. There were simply too many of them, and they all had some serious rank.

There was a hard truth I was beginning to learn. There are two types of people in the military, if not life: *administrators* and *operators*. Administrators made themselves look busy. Operators got shit done.

There will always be more administrators than operators. Always. Like a mold, administrators crawl their way into even the most remote and confined spaces of a conflict, their nauseating spores poisoning the morale of those men and women who simply want to win a war. Unable or unwilling to affect any meaningful change on their own, they sit on the sidelines and tear down those soldiers who make the decisions no one else wants to make, and do things few others have the nerve to do. They hide behind paper, check the box, and blame others when things ultimately go wrong. They're the gatekeepers to a useless world, their sole purpose to refuse essential challenges, dwell on the unimportant, and enforce inconsequential policy—most likely devised and perpetuated by yet another member of their despicable, loathsome kind.

At least they were letting us run the academy without giving us too much flak. It was like our own little town, the tree house or pillow fort we'd run to when Dad yelled at us. Amazing—seven months earlier, with temperatures easily topping 120 degrees, scrounging through the MRE box for some breakfast and being bitten relentlessly by invisible bugs each night, things were so much easier. Don't get me wrong, those conditions were atrocious, but we had room to move, breath, and be a little more pragmatic with how we did things. We were soldiers with missions who were doing the best we could with what we had. The simplicity made it so much easier to focus on and deal with the situation at hand.

Now we had air conditioning, hot water, a fully-staffed chow hall and a decent place to live. It came with a high price tag. The meaningless hassle from the staff members of our Active counterparts, who I'd come to dub "Inactive duty" officers, was starting to wear on my patience.

What we put up with for God and Country.

The Unsung Heroes

Our time at the Security College was one of the most interesting and rewarding times of my life, and not simply because of the experiences with the Iraqi Police. Living with us were ten residential interpreters—*real live, English-speaking Iraqis*—who had given us unbelievable insight into just about every aspect of life there. They were well educated, outgoing and, quite simply, very cool young guys. We couldn't have done what we did at the academy without them, and their dedication was put to the test more than a few times.

While I could easily write a book solely on our experiences and interaction with them while stationed in Ramadi, I have to make any discussions about them rather short. Some are still working as interpreters for American interests in Iraq, putting themselves and their families at great risk. Due to my great respect and love for these men, I'm omitting specific information about their jobs, where they lived, what they're currently doing, or even what they look like.

Unfortunately, we lost three soon after we left Iraq, murdered by the insurgency. I have an email from one, sent years ago, still saved in my inbox. I plan to be buried with it.

A sincere "thank you" to those young Iraqi men serving as both police and interpreters, the unheralded champions of Iraq's freedom you may never meet or hear about in the news.

Our new translators were all men ranging from their late 20's to late 40's who'd answered the advertisement posted in the U.S. Army "want ads" on the community board in front of Ramadi's main government office. A few questions, a quick background check and boom, you're hired. We were over the moon that anyone had the balls to actually take this job.

They were a mix of Shi'ites and Sunnis from Baghdad, Fallujah and Ramadi, hired to work on the post as interpreters for the academy. Living in a small concrete one-room hut near the MP compound five days a week, they were just as social as any of us, and were inquisitive as to these Army guys they were now working for. After a few weeks of getting to know them, I found myself wandering over to their barracks every few nights, only to run into a few other troops from my platoon with the same idea, smoking and joking straight through the night to the wee hours of the morn. With every visit, a thick, acrid cloud of cigarette smoke smacked me in the face when the heavy wooden door to their hooch flung open. Man, they loved their cigs; some nights you could even see smoke wafting out from between the cracks in the makeshift wooden windows.

All of them had their own reasons for working there. While the pay was good, they were looking for jobs with the new government and maybe even a shot of working in America. However, there was another common thread that brought them there—pride. They shared a hatred for the insurgency and what it was doing to their beloved country. For the educated Shi'ites, recalling their treatment under the Hussein regime, it was profoundly more personal. For their own protection, and for that of their families, they made up stories about where they were spending the week. Most had computer backgrounds and told people they were traveling on business: they didn't dare breathe a word to anyone they were working with the Americans. They couldn't. They had to be award-winning actors at a moment's notice, often surviving on their wits alone. If anyone asked, they had to have a good back story ready to go, right on the spot. Some told Mom they'd found a job in Jordan. Others told Dad they were helping to fix a friend's apartment, damaged by American bombs. For those who hitched a ride to our post, they'd get picked up in secret places and later dropped off several blocks from their houses, safeguarding their precious lie and enlisting only their most trusted friends to assist in their life-saving deception.

Despite the double lives they were leading, and the certain death it would bring if the wrong people ever found out, they were very laid back. In fact, they were defiantly so. In the first few weeks of their employment they would diligently continue their work unfazed, despite receiving threats from neighbors who suspected their involvement with our academy. A handful of nosy assholes back on the block just weren't buying their stories and suspected something was going on. One such punk actually tossed a grenade into the back yard of one of our best guys. Understandably fearing the worst for his family, he left the academy soon after.

Unfortunately, most developed a routine pattern of

entering and leaving the post, often in the same car. I prodded them to come to work a day early, at night, through a different entrance, a different route, anything that would throw off a potential ambush, kidnapping or outright murder. But just in case, as soon as we knew we could trust them, they each got an AK-47 with as many rounds as they could carry, along with an ID card allowing them to do so. With the checkpoints between there and Baghdad, they were certain to run into some American soldiers along the way. I gave specific instructions on how to approach the military so they wouldn't end up shot full of holes, as well as giving their names and pictures to the Coalition units currently patrolling the dangerous route between our posts in Ramadi and Baghdad.

Within the first few weeks, I began to appreciate just how much danger these men were in. They made us very much aware the only thing worse than an infidel on Muslim soil was a Muslim who cooperated with the invaders. And our interpreters weren't just "cooperating" with us; they were living, laughing, eating and joking with us five days a week. If they weren't the biggest targets in Iraq at the time, I don't know who would be. If the insurgency got their hands on these new friends of ours, they were doomed. Having betrayed some arbitrary inner circle of Islam, they were now more wanted than the occupiers themselves (who, I'm sure, were a close second). Intelligence reports were showing the trend of attacks on *soft targets*—the Iraqi police and laborers working for the Coalition—were beginning to grow. A few translators had already been killed in Baghdad, literally hunted down in the street by insurgent thugs.

I was starting to wonder if these unspoken Islamic accords might render our $25 million rewards for bin Laden and Zarqawi useless. In July of 2003, however, the $30 million bounty for Uday and Qusay's demise was paid out to a brave Iraqi gent, ironically a distant relative of Saddam. Driven by a lingering bitterness between him and Hussein, his motivation stemmed, surprisingly, from an old family dispute.[37] Maybe there was hope.

After a few weeks of getting to know each other, we found ourselves talking about everything—the new government, the occupation, the people, their friends and family, other soldiers, the Iraqi police, Saddam, music, cigarettes, sexy whiskey, women; everything. The very fine line between our cultures quickly disappeared, and we found ourselves in conversations identical to any we'd have with good friends back in the States. Most were laced, however, with the absolute fear the country had of its former dictator. One interpreter explained the dread of reprisal by Saddam was so strong that his father *still* wouldn't talk about him without checking his backyard for spies, even *after* his December 2003 capture. Amazingly, another translator refused to believe Qusay was dead. "Uday's definitely gone, but I think Qusay's still around," he'd say. The

---

37 Sheik Nawaf al-Zaydan, a contractor who'd gained Saddam's favor and grown wealthy under the dictator, went to the Americans in July of 2003 and informed U.S. forces that the Hussein brothers were living with him in his palatial Mosul home. It's believed that the betrayal was because of a longtime grudge held against the Hussein family (al-Zaydan's brother, Sadan, was jailed for mouthing off about being distant cousins with Saddam). The Hussein brothers were killed in a raid by the 101st Airborne and elements of Task Force 20, on July 22, 2003. Perhaps sensing impending treachery, one of Uday's final comments to his friends was, "This time I think the Americans are serious. Bush is not like Clinton. I think this is the end." (Source: Olga Craig, *Two Aces Net $30 Million Reward*, London Sunday Telegraph, July 27, 2003; courtesy of The Washington Times, copyright 2003, News World Communications, Inc., www.washingtontimes.com)

newly released photos of Saddam's dead sons—clobbered by troops from the Army's 101st Airborne and a special ops task force—were pasted all over the news, but they weren't enough for him. "Doctored," he'd confidently reply, without hesitation. The paranoia was deeper than I had ever imagined, even throughout the younger, more educated generation.

And although they were very sophisticated and well-informed, it was amusing, even comical at times, to listen to their tales of Iraqi folklore and superstition—about how there were "magic men" in their towns who could strike down any living thing with one furtive glance or wave of the hand. Or about how people would give their children very plain names or not wash their cars for months on end, because somehow an exotic name or glittery automobile would attract bad luck and evil spirits. I can't even begin to tell you how many bought into ridiculous conspiracy theories. Some were absolutely convinced Israel orchestrated the 9/11 attacks to draw the United States into a war with the Arabs. Or that Arabs weren't even *involved* in the physical attacks themselves, mirroring a popular trend in the Islamic world.[38] They had a whacky urban legend for every complex situation in the Middle East. Even after Saddam's capture, they'd go on to believe some of the rumors on Al Jazeera Television, claiming it was all a hoax. The DNA, the pictures, the story; all of it was phony.

Some even believed the gossip on the street that the U.S. had made a deal with Saddam to put him back in power—obviously untrue, but an effective scare tactic for the impressionable

---

38 Andrea Stone, *Many in Islamic world doubt Arabs behind 9/11*, USA Today, February 27, 2002 (taken from Gallup Poll, *Anti-US Sentiment in the Muslim World*, released February 26, 2002), www.usatoday.com

citizenry who might now be looking to throw their support behind the Coalition.

I told them Saddam was dragged out of a hole muttering "don't shoot" to his captors, looking like a pathetic whipped mule, holding a pistol he said he would use to fight the Americans to the death. My brother, Sean, would note in a letter soon after that Saddam was "incapable of using a pistol against anyone other than a bound prisoner." He was, at the time, the Free World's most wanted man for his crimes against humanity. I assured them the United States had no interest in his taking power again in any capacity. He wasn't coming back.

They still weren't satisfied. These guys were really smart, but still bought into this conspiracy garbage. I was starting to understand why we were having such a hard time convincing the average Iraqi we were here to help him. All of these plots and schemes, the method by which most Iraqis made sense of the world around them, were so well entrenched. After all the crap that's been shoved into their heads about Americans over the past 20 years, no wonder they didn't trust us.

Later on, they told me *Saddam* in Arabic means *the one who confronts*. Ironic.

We'd heard horror stories on the news about Saddam before, but to hear them from some of these guys was simply shocking. Again, I'm not sure if these were just myths, or maybe bedtime stories to scare little Iraqi kids, but a few in particular stuck with me. One concerned an attempt on Saddam's life years ago by his own doctor. As he was preparing to inject Saddam with some kind of mysterious poison, the doctor was understandably nervous. Sensing something was wrong, Saddam grabbed his hand, discovered the plot, and had him killed. According to another, a member of his security force was believed a spy, so he was thrown into a cage with two live tigers. After an hour, the tigers hadn't killed him. That meant, apparently, he was innocent, so he was released. They also mentioned Saddam not only didn't sleep in the same place two nights in a row, but he had *every* palace around Iraq cook a dinner for him each night, so no one knew for sure where he'd end up. That one I believed.

However, they had some very good ideas on how to handle the Iraqi Army early on, one of which ended up being adopted. They insisted it would be best if Iraqi soldiers were taken from one part of the country and sent to work in an entirely different area. While not that practical for the police to do, the Army could be organized in such a way. "But what about the Iraqi government?" I asked. They insisted we take 15 or 20 educated people they could trust to rebuild Iraq. I didn't think that was so easy. I mean, whom could we trust? We didn't know anyone yet, and were simply working with people who were well known and apparently well liked. It was an effort the civil affairs team was working on around the clock, just as they had been in Rutbah on a smaller scale six months before. Our interpreters explained how the wealthier and better-known people in town had at one time supported Saddam. These men simply couldn't be trusted. Remembering my conversation with Captain Laith a few months before, it started to make sense.

Our interpreters said we needed to find educated people with influence, not cash. I half-jokingly explained we needed the same thing in America; easier said than done. They noted the doctors, lawyers, the technical people of Iraq who stood up to Saddam, were the people we should be working with. The wealthy sheiks or businessmen who were telling the Americans what they wanted to hear, those who achieved their status by playing ball with Saddam in pre-war Iraq, couldn't be depended on.

Our interpreters were some of the bravest people I'd met yet. They started off as a group of guys I was skeptical of, but turned out to be ones I'd gladly end up putting my career on the line for.

The sergeant major with us at the academy saw things differently.

Sergeant Major Matt Demmit of the 82nd was a shining beacon of narrow-minded thinking. While a very good diplomat, it was clear he didn't want to be there. In my opinion, and in the opinion of several others, he was stuck babysitting a bunch of Reservists with the wearisome job of training a few police. On top of that, he didn't care much for the involvement of officers in everyday business. The platoon leader of the 855th, a very charming and well-spoken guy by the name of Travis Horner, had the same impression. The sergeant major always had a "whatever you say" look on his face when he talked with us, one we found very condescending and thoroughly annoying.

More importantly, he was starting to mirror an attitude that really bothered me; that the lives of the Iraqis we were working with were not as important as our own.

"Why do you want to give those guys guns, sir?" was a sarcastic question I'd heard more than a few times from him.

Well here's my answer: Because on any given day, they had it ten times worse than any of us. Here were men who were threatened repeatedly, who didn't have Humvees, tanks or body armor to shield them, and they were working for an army that didn't want to lift a finger to protect their interests, doing a job that would help to determine the timeline of when American soldiers would be able to leave Iraq. That's why.

I wasn't about to go handing out guns to just anyone, but I was getting annoyed that this man was not willing to take a risk to help these guys out. Most of the platoon, at that point, trusted them with their lives. He saw them as just another bunch of Iraqis. It was the same arrogant savior attitude I saw on the streets with some of the younger troops back in Hit and out west—*I'm an American and you're some dirt poor Iraqi who's not really worth it and doesn't know any better.* Some were the greatest men I'd ever have the privilege of working with, and made the fight for a free Iraq very much worth the sacrifice.

While I wasn't technically permitted to give them guns from the *academy*, we did have a ten-foot long metal CONEX full of confiscated weapons on post, captured by the 855th when they came into the country. They were all ours. And besides, who was going to tell me no? The captain from the 82nd Airborne, they guy who allegedly fucking ran this place, hadn't even bothered to stop by yet. Lieutenant Horner liked the idea of arming them and gave me the key. The interpreters could at least, now, defend themselves. I wasn't about to be responsible for the deaths of eight good men I wouldn't help for fear of getting in trouble. We'd already managed to round up some spare bulletproof vests they could wear when driving back and forth between Baghdad and Ramadi. And now with these 7.62mm boom sticks, they'd at least have a fighting chance if the shit hit the fan.

A few months later, the same issue would come up with the Glock pistols the new police were receiving. Our interpreters made a good case for why they should also be carrying them, as well. Yes, they were cool and could command some respect, but they were concealable. These guys couldn't just walk around the market or visit a friend carrying an AK. And for crying out loud, they were teaching the classes and on the range with us, so there were no illusions about their abilities to use them. By that time, they had demonstrated they were responsible, and a small, personal weapon would undoubtedly make their lives much less stressful. Now, they could at least give insurgents a run for their money if they were hassled. Although a little 9mm couldn't fend off a group of assailants who meant business, it would provide a little more confidence when going about their lives at home, and might even mean the difference between life and death. Keep in mind, some of these guys were being approached in broad daylight in the streets and threatened. But more importantly, it showed we gave a damn about their lives and service. They were worth it.

"No deal," the sergeant major said, "They have to be police." I pleaded: certainly we could spare eight Glocks for the lifeblood of this academy. I mean, it wasn't like people were lining up to work there. As a matter of fact, one the men from Fallujah, Sam, had his house bombed by the insurgency only days before, shaking him up pretty badly. His entire family was under suspicion because of his perceived involvement with the Americans, and his name was already being whispered around a few mosques in Fallujah.[39]

This was the danger our interpreters willingly placed themselves in each day.

But still no Glocks. "Fine," I said. I made a call to our old friends back in Hit and cashed in some favors. The Hit Police

---

39 Sam would end up quitting, but would occasionally return to the academy over the next four months with solid intelligence on what was going on around Fallujah—what was being said in the shops, cafes and mosques there—adding to our understanding of the dangers there considerably. They were places no American had ever penetrated. On one of his visits, I gave him a letter explaining his involvement with the academy and my contact information, in case he ever wanted to approach the Americans with intelligence after we'd left. As a security precaution, his name wasn't on it.

Department agreed to hire them as police consultants (using fake names, of course). They were now officially police officers and would get their weapons. They had American-issued permits to carry in case they were stopped by any of our forces. Needless to say I was very much more concerned about other Iraqis who would ask them why they had an American weapon in their possession. The stock answer to anyone giving them the third degree about where they picked it up? Tell them you bought it from a shady Iraqi police officer looking to make a quick buck. And then to tell them to mind their own fucking business.

By that time, the sergeant major didn't really care. He was too busy disciplining one of our soldiers who had become too close to a female troop with the 855th. Ironically she happened to be a gal that the sergeant major had developed a little crush on. Thanks for keeping your head in the game, sergeant minor.

Most of the translators we worked with survived their tours at the academy and eventually moved on after we left. I'm still in touch with most of them today. Unfortunately, like I said before, a few of them were discovered by insurgents soon after and killed.

Those interpreters were portraits of raw bravado, so desperately required from each Iraqi to put an end to this spineless, scavenging threat to their new nation. Godspeed guys, and thanks for your service. I hope you're well and safe, wherever you ended up.

One of the benefits of my new position at the police academy was nearly direct and confidential access to what was going on in police stations around Iraq, most of which had never been (or would ever be) visited by Americans. The new cadets who came through each month proved to be a tremendous source of intelligence.

In one of my first talks with a new class, I asked them what they thought was the biggest problem in the Iraqi Police Force in Al Anbar Province. The answer, unequivocally, was nepotism, or *mahgsobeeya*. Those who were "hired" by the chief's friend or family were arbitrarily given higher ranks than those who attended a formal school. The police who were hired legitimately obviously feared retribution if they were to complain about their treatment, and were understandably frustrated. This wasn't the first time I'd heard this. That's just how it worked in Iraq.

We saw the example firsthand in Hit in the summer of 2003, where the mayor (prior to his departure to the U.K.) appointed an uncle, Yassim, to the position of colonel—one of the highest ranks in the police department. For some reason, Yassim insisted on being the liaison only between the Americans and the Hit police. Shady, to say the least. Yassim had no prior experience as a police *or* military officer, and was kind of a jackass—self-indulgent, egotistical and petty. Absolutely no sense of humor, either. The tension in the department was starting to climb sharply.

One of the main guys we'd been working with before Yassim's introduction, Safi, was an English-speaking officer and had served as our interpreter before the Army had provided one. A lieutenant colonel with the police and former Iraqi Army officer who'd trained at the Sandhurst Royal Military Academy in England, he was intelligent, helpful and sincere. However he was caught in the middle of a turf war between Hit's police chief, Hamid Abdullah, and Yassim. One of the few Iraqi police officers who spoke English, he was often dispatched to Camp *Mad Dog* and *Junction City* with requests or information. Having little choice but to following Yassim's orders, which were usually given behind Chief Abdullah's back, he pissed off the chief in a big way. But what could Safi do? Yassim was his superior officer, appointed by the mayor, no less. Safi made the best of it, and we continued to work with him. We'd see Safi again at the academy in March of 2004 where he'd do extremely well. Unfortunately, it was the last time we'd see him alive.[40]

We'd heard someone had tried to kill Yassim with a homemade bomb a few weeks prior to taking our assignment at the academy, and he ended up losing his leg in the explosion. The class I was talking to had a few Hit police officers in it, and when I mentioned Yassim's name, one made a subtle slashing motion over his right thigh. I obviously explained to the class this was not a useful approach. As per the usual, no cadets from Hit had any information on what happened.

I went on to explain that it was going to take time to root out the nepotism plaguing their government and police—another common detriment of a dictatorship. Over the past six months, as a result of hanging around so many meetings between Iraqi leadership and our civil affair teams, I was also learning almost every major position of authority in Iraq was achieved by either violence, bribery or the returning of a favor. That was it. The entire regime was almost by definition an Iraqi Mafioso. If you knew somebody, had a good name and some tough guys behind you, you'd find a good job somewhere.

But the cops had some input of their own regarding the model American workplace. This country wasn't about fair

---

40 A man fitting Safi's description was found murdered in Fallujah in the spring of 2004, just before our redeployment to Kuwait. The name on the intelligence report was misspelled, and I never had a chance to verify it with the Hit police; but the 94th believed that it was, in fact, Safi.

treatment and just practices; anyone with an AK and enough balls could take whatever he wanted. Our interpreters had said so, too. It was another reminder we weren't dealing with Americans, but it appeared sometimes our procedures were based on that very assumption.

The majority of police were pissed the Americans were working with the same crooks that ran the place before we invaded. I did my best to fill them in on what we were up to, and the fact that Americans were quickly learning who was full of shit and who was genuinely looking out for Iraq's interests. We hadn't known anyone and had to start somewhere. Finding the dirty police officers was a priority.

Using Saddam's capture as leverage, I let the class know we'd found Hussein hiding in a hole in the ground on a farm in the middle of nowhere. That being said, we'd be sure to find a few crooked cops in a police station right under our noses. That got their attention.

Knowing these guys couldn't always talk to their Iraqi bosses, we told them they could always bypass their chiefs and speak directly to us, even after they'd left the academy. Names could be passed up anonymously (and often covertly) to me or any other soldier, and from there, onto either the civil affairs group or to our intelligence people. If they couldn't trust those in their own department, they'd at least be able to contact one of us. I imagined some of the complaints I'd be hearing were clearly driven by vengeance, but some might prove to be legitimate, especially if we started to see a pattern. What the hell, I thought. It was a start. And the more we talked to some of the guys, the more we'd get an idea of their point of view.

No one was really willing to come forward right away, but after a few weeks a lot of information began flowing in, and the intelligence was often corroborated by police from other towns and in other academy classes. That's exactly what we were looking for. And with the growing popularity of our school—especially after word got out about the brand-new Glock 9mm pistols being issued to its graduates—a lot of police were lining up to get in.

After about a month, we'd already built a formidable *people of interest* list—the names of dirty cops that kept coming up in our conversations with cadets; the cops we needed to talk to who might be involved in some shifty stuff. Through our own investigations, we were collecting information that was making cases—well beyond a reasonable doubt—against a few key police officers who were clearly up to no good. But to get to the bottom of it, we had to talk to them ASAP. However, just as we put the wheels in motion to head into each police station, guns drawn, and round these guys up the hard way, we found out we wouldn't have to. Most were coming to us in the next wave of academy classes.

The Al Anbar Security College was becoming quite a success and attracting a lot of attention. New graduates of the three-week program were being taught the basics of police work, giving them more confidence when venturing out of their stations and hitting the streets around the province. While some classes weren't exactly realistic given the situation in Iraq (reacting to a domestic dispute, for example), some were. Best of all, the cops were getting better. Our building clearing and self-defense classes were going very well; police who couldn't hold a rifle correctly in the morning were taking a room by force like pros that afternoon. A guy who couldn't win a thumb-wrestling match yesterday could now toss a guy twice his size to the ground today. It was very exciting to see how much progress these guys had made. They were taking things seriously, and better yet, they knew we were serious about helping them.

We all did what we could to lend a hand. On top of the new pistols, we'd given out the premium AK-47 rounds seized during the initial invasion months ago, instead of issuing the crappy Iraqi-made bullets the Coalition Provisional Authority was providing. While a nice gesture to the Iraqi companies making the ammunition, they simply didn't work. Some would even blow up in the breach, jamming the weapon and sometimes actually injuring the shooter. The round would become stuck inside the barrel, rendering the AK totally combat ineffective. We'd go through each bullet by hand, thousands of them, tossing out the duds and loading the rest into quality AK magazines. While the better performing students got more, we found enough for just about everyone.

Unfortunately, however, old habits were dying hard. Higher-ranking Iraqi policemen were confiscating some of the ammunition, along with the Glocks, when the cadets returned to their stations. The worst instance of betrayal came on February 14, 2004, when the Fallujah police station was hammered in one of the most coordinated and sophisticated insurgent attacks in the past six months. Over 20 police were killed; many of whose weapons didn't work. Just after the attack, highly charged accusations started making their way back to us from our Fallujah cadets that the department had been seriously compromised. According to them, a handful of senior police officers were taking the quality ammunition and selling it, presumably to arms dealers or directly to the insurgency. The substandard Iraqi-made bullets were then issued to the police, causing many of their weapons to fail when they needed them the most.

What began as a minor problem was now a major issue.

Fortunately, a lot of cadets were giving up the names of a few officers in the Fallujah department who were actively sabotaging our efforts. One name that repeatedly surfaced was the officer in charge of the arms room, a captain. The other was the chief himself, who was suspiciously late the day of the attack. According to the cops who worked the gate at the station, he'd always arrive within a few minutes of a certain time. But that day, he was conspicuously behind schedule. The academy was now dealing with a criminal conspiracy, one of many to follow, that indicated how much work the Iraqi Police needed.

At about the same time, just after a class had graduated, one of the 855th MP's caught a police cadet taking pictures of a few of his classmates who were having *their* pictures taken with American soldiers. Apparently he intended to use these photographs of these new Iraqi police officers—smiling and shaking hands with the Americans—either to threaten those who had become friendly with the Coalition, use it for personal gain, or get someone killed. One of these photographs in the hands of the insurgency could mean a death sentence to a cop, who'd be seen as an American collaborator.

The Fallujah Police Department wasn't the only institution that had been compromised: Spies had infiltrated our academy.

I was frustrated. Frankly, after hearing about some brave Iraqis died in Fallujah trying to fight off a wave of insurgents with weapons that didn't work, I was enraged. I decided to issue out a warning, albeit in anger, to each police station: anyone who illegally confiscated a weapon from a former cadet would be imprisoned. Period. The ammunition was for "police personal" use, meaning the policeman could, and should, take it home. Any attempt to take it was unlawful, and police could respond with deadly force. No more bullies at the stations. Too many good men had been killed at the hands of their so-called "leadership." At least now they'd have Americans standing firmly behind them, soldiers who'd gladly choke the living hell out of anyone who would dare put these new cops in more danger than they were in already.

Eventually, it was decided that any cadet who exhibited behavior that could be construed as a threat against a classmate would head straight to the interrogation cell at *Junction City*, innocently referred to as the *J.C. Bed & Breakfast*. We'd see just how tough they were after going a few days without sleeping. Unfortunately, it didn't take long to fill up.

Our academy had stumbled onto an immensely complicated affair, one that was fueling our local intelligence cell. It wasn't about a few crooked cops anymore; it was about serious pro-insurgent activity. At that time in Iraq, so little was known about the police, but we knew for sure not all were working for the greater good. Some stations *must* have worked out deals with the insurgency; the results of threats, trades, cold hard cash, or all three. There was talk that a few stations around the province were paying up so as not to be attacked—the insurgency was shaking down the new stations for protection money. Given the fact we were supporting these stations financially, it was a chilling thought we may have been indirectly funding terrorists through the very police we were training to stop them.

Our interpreter, Joe, pointed this out pretty well within weeks of the academy opening its doors. After we had decided to purchase supplies we needed through a Ramadi police officer (one of the full-time administers was a colonel in the Ramadi station), he casually mentioned the prices for some of the goods were inflated a bit. Not really concerned about a couple of bucks here or there, I wasn't too alarmed. It was the price of doing business. However, Joe went on to explain the lack of attacks on the Ramadi police station weren't because of good training. The insurgency was probably making money off of the new academy.

That made sense, but it was difficult to prove. Our interpreters, like many Iraqi men, were a little conspiracy-prone anyway. However, giving it its due diligence, I passed it up to tactical intelligence and suggested the 82nd be extra-cautious when reviewing financial activity within the police. If these guys were cooking the books, we'd have to get on top of things ASAP.

At this point, we were putting together weekly reports for the tactical intelligence teams, comprised of info straight out of the mouths of cadets courageous enough to come forward. They'd come see us after dark with the latest gossip, dressed in baggy clothes and hooded sweatshirts, doing their best to be inconspicuous. We'd meet them in the small office behind our command center during lunch, pretending to be on a smoke break. Like mischievous kids in grade school, they'd secretly pass notes in class, but ones intended for the instructors. Others defiantly started mouthing off in front of everyone and began naming names, sometimes of the very men sitting beside them. One thing was painfully clear; the situation in Anbar's police stations was like a real-life police drama.

In the weeks following the incident at the Fallujah station, more information started flowing in. In trying to get these guys to open up a bit, I brought the attack up in just about every class. I wanted them to see it as an example of what would happen if people chose to turn a blind eye to the crimes they were witnessing in their own departments. It worked. Again, more chatter of that dirty captain, stealing rounds and selling them.

By that time, I knew we had to pick him up. There were too many stories, often from different classes, about him. The story of the "stolen rounds" could easily be a cover for any cop who was selling bullets and looking for a scapegoat, but now it looked as if there was some concrete testimony against this guy. However, a handful of men from the Fallujah station went on to explain the captain took part in the February 14th attack, noting he had picked up arms and fought alongside the police. Some of us started thinking maybe he *was* a victim. Perhaps caught in the middle, he was being threatened by insurgents to hand over his rounds. And that's the story I expected to hear from him when we eventually spoke—it would have been the easiest way out. Either way, we needed to pay him a visit ASAP to sort this shit out.

After a few painful minutes of discussing the details of the attack with the latest class, Naquib, a cop from Fallujah, had heard enough. He was only about 5 foot 6 inches, but when he leapt to his feet and spoke, he was the biggest guy in the room. With a stern voice, he began to tell me and the entire class of cops the story of how so many of his friends were killed in the attack and, sobbing heavily, he cried out that he was tired of the corruption. Our interpreters, staring on in disbelief, relayed the English translation every few seconds. Nequib took his seat a few minutes later, asked for some paper and a pen, and started writing feverishly.

For the rest of the class, Nequib wrote down everything he knew and then publicly handed his notes over to me. Most of his fellow cops looked shell-shocked—they couldn't believe what just happened. Others were clearly moved by his bravery. But a few clearly looked pissed and scared, as if their cover was blown.

We couldn't read Arabic worth a damn, but we could read

people's faces very, very well. We added those angry cadets to our list.

Over the next few weeks, even after leaving the academy, Naquib returned with information regarding the inner-workings of the Fallujah police department, including dirt on their now-infamous internal affairs division. Thought to be responsible for ridding the station of corrupt cops, they were allegedly identifying those who were advocates of the Coalition. The information he provided convinced us we needed to detain both Fallujah's police chief and the bullet-selling captain, and gave us more insight into the attack itself—how foreign fighters were involved, where they took the bodies of their dead, where they lived and planned, their contacts at the police stations, the true conspiracies behind it all. When asked how he was getting all of this, he smiled and said in his best English, "I pretend I'm not listening." Apparently, a lot of people in town were talking about it.

Naquib was murdered that March just before we left for Kuwait, his hands chopped off and his tongue cut out of his mouth. While I encouraged people to come forward with information, I didn't want to get anyone killed. There were more covert ways of passing information to the Americans, ways that wouldn't attract attention. But Naquib had balls. He stood in a room full of cops, knowing a handful were conspirators or insurgents themselves, and let the truth be told. He gave us a ton of intelligence—information that led to the arrest of several Iraqis who were supporting the increasingly cunning rebel insurgency. Before we took off, I left word with the Marines who replaced us in Anbar of the folks who were probably responsible. With any luck, they went into Fallujah and fucking buried the guys who did it.

Nequib's death was a consequence of this war I never

thought I'd experience, and one I couldn't possibly myself prepare for. I still have trouble dealing with it. I asked those guys to talk to us, and because of it, one of the most daring and fearless men I ever had the honor of knowing was murdered. I'll carry that guilt for the rest of my life, but I'll never in a million years forget his courage.

About halfway through the academy, the Coalition Provisional Authority had the insane idea of rounding up a bunch of Iraqi Police officers—ones who hadn't even been through our training yet—for a new, two-day Advanced Weapons Integration Program, or "AWIP." Every Iraqi cop who completed the 48-hour course would also receive a brand new Glock 9mm. In the mad rush to get cops trained, the CPA had forfeited the one incentive for Iraqi police to attend the academy for real instruction—the ultimate status symbol among Iraqi law enforcement.

    I had to remind myself just how helpful the CPA had been so far in post-war Iraq. In July of 2003, they came out with a formal memo regarding the vital issue of how much window tint the Iraqis could legally have on their cars. In August, another looked to halt the movement of "contraband gold bars," no doubt gold stolen from Kuwait during the Gulf War, being secretly shipped out of Iraq by Saddam's underlings into Jordan.

    The "gold" was brass that had been stripped from abandoned Iraqi Army posts and melted down into square slabs to be sold to factories in Jordan. If they were reading our reports, they'd know that. And for crying out loud, after being shot at so many times, no one gave a damn about how much tint some Iraqi had on his 1989 Olds Cutlass. The last move they made was actually their best—turning over sovereignty to Iraq two days earlier than expected in June of 2004. It was a smart decision, and would serve to weaken at least *some* of the intended symbolism behind any attacks made by the insurgency to mark the occasion. It was the only way the door wouldn't hit them on the ass on their way out.

At the academy level however, we were starting to understand the degree of the CPA's incompetence. They had *no* prioritizing ability regarding the establishment of the Iraqi Police Force, or concern for it outside of Baghdad. They were funneling tons of money and support to "Task Force Baghdad," the military group formed to train Baghdad's police units, at the expense of the rest of the country.

Even before the academy stood up in October of 2003, Captain Bentley was having serious problems making heads or tails of the CPA-led police training process, as it dragged its feet on just about everything. Instead of focusing on the broader issues of how to train, arm and employ these police in some capacity, the CPA was coming up with memo after memo regarding what the uniforms and badges should look like, and *constantly* revising their training plan. Every two weeks over the summer of 2003, the whole system was again turned upside down. Meanwhile, the insurgency was eating our lunch for us.

Hung up on insignificant factors that simply weren't important yet, we were suffocating—and losing the confidence of—the IPF. Months earlier, with absolutely no logistics plan in place whatsoever to distribute supplies (outside of Baghdad, anyway), it was becoming clearer the 3rd Armored Cavalry Regiment and 94th MPs were on their own in organizing the budding IPF of the restless Anbar Province. Elements from the 94th headquarter section had been stopping into the 18th MP Brigade's offices in Baghdad during our mail runs over the past few months, and just grabbing police uniforms and any equipment items that they could find. It would be passed out later on, under our own supervision and directives, in and around Anbar. That informal distribution network was the best we could do at the time, but even as this was taking place, we were still responsible for reporting to the CPA the status of Al Anbar's IPF units—their training, equipment and weapons issued, vehicle procurement, additional uniforms, even the actual conditions of their police stations. Needless to say, the information we provided indicated the need for some heavy investment. However, even after more than five months of reports, nothing had been done. No one was paying attention, even though the 94th was, up until the arrival of the 82nd Airborne in October of 2003, the unit informally in charge of training the IPF in Al Anbar.

More administrators leading the way.

Captain Bentley's comments at each IPF meeting he attended with the powers that be was exactly the same—Al Anbar needs more support, and the concerns we have this month are the same damn ones we had 30 days ago.[41] The meeting would eventually end, ultimately resolving nothing. The attendees would again file out of the room, patting each other on the back and congratulating themselves on the PowerPoint presentations they'd put together.

The trend continued, and our concerns were categorically ignored. That is, until the 82nd Airborne Division came on the scene in October 2003 and created the Al Anbar Police

---

41 At that same meeting in July with the CPA, CJTF7 and 18th MP Brigade, the beginning of a much more dangerous tactical precedent was also beginning to take root; the case for using MPs assets for convoy escorts rather than patrols.

Academy. With its *own* budget, it sought approval from neither the CPA nor CJTF7.

The only CPA idea that garnished any attention from the MP corps was a potential contract to supply the Iraqi Police Force with hi-performance Motorola radios, which would increase the communication ability between the Americans and Iraqis tenfold. But for some unknown reason, that particular project was suspended.

The Glock program was a great idea and a morale builder, but no thought was going into their distribution. We were all for getting as many cops armed and ready as possible, but this clearly wasn't the answer. If anything, the 82nd, 94th and 855th were pushing for *longer* training classes, not shorter ones, and the Glock was major leverage to entice qualified cadets into the academy. The CPA, to get as many guns into the IPF's hands and onto the street in the shortest possible time, threw the program together in haste. Unfortunately, there was no way to ensure, outside of two days of instruction, that the police would even be qualified to use it. It took the U.S. military *months* to learn even our own weapon systems. Worse, we wouldn't even have a chance to vet these guys for associations with the insurgency. In less than 48 hours after arriving at *Junction City*, they'd be given a certificate, a handshake, and a sidearm that was leaps and bounds better than even those the Army was carrying.

A front-page article in the *Stars and Stripes* in June of 2004 would go on to detail the mistakes made in training the Iraqi Police.[42] We were telling them that on November 11th *the year before*. What was the CPA thinking? Soon after the introduc-

---

42 Associated Press, *US Admits Mistakes in Iraqi Police Training*, Stars and Stripes Middle East edition, June 11, 2004

tion of this little program, figures would be thrown around the Administration back home concerning the number of trained officers. As we suspected, in an attempt to show the world the security force inside Iraq was growing, the number of "trained" police was being inflated. The numbers were blatantly inaccurate; an arbitrary figure that was being used to pad the CPA's increasingly disparaging résumé. Again, we weren't doing what we needed to do to win; we were only doing enough to give the appearance of progress. And numbers, themselves, aren't progress.

Months later, those numbers would be questioned by Congress and ultimately cut in half. The police weren't being trained: they were being handed guns, uniforms and a handful of rounds.

The only redeeming factor behind the decision to start issuing Glocks after a lousy two-day crash course was that every scumbag Iraqi Police officer who wanted to forego real training for near-immediate gratification would be coming out of the woodwork and clamoring at our door. Just before the start of the first two-day program, I started checking the incoming student rosters against the names that had made our *people of interest* list. To my amazement, two names were conspicuously on *both* lists, and it brought a huge smile to my thinning, tanned face.

The bullet-stealing captain and Fallujah's chief of police would be here in a couple of days.

Forty eight hours later, the new class arrived at our gates. Before the captain even in-processed, the interrogators cornered him and starting peppering him with questions about the attack on the station. After a brief Q&A session, he was released and began his training with the others. However, the intel shop filled me in on what was discussed a few minutes later, and it contained a surprising twist: the captain never once said he'd been threatened for the bullets. He just went on to deny everything altogether. The handful of Iraqi police that told us he was fighting alongside his comrades on the day of the attack weren't exactly credible, and we had half the Fallujah department telling us otherwise. The captain's fate was slowly being sealed.

That was enough for me. By the end of the day, both the captain and chief were arrested. Before they were shipped off to the JC Bed & Breakfast and interrogated, we handcuffed each to a chair, in separate rooms, and went to work. Having grown close to a lot of these police—several who had already been killed in their service—we had questions of our own. Over the next two hours, I and Sergeants Couture, DiTrapano and Rawls bounced between both rooms constantly, poring over every second of what had happened before, during and after the February 14th attack, as well as the accusations of their links to the insurgency. Neither had satisfactory answers and it only enraged us more.

It was disturbing to think the last thing some good Iraqi cops saw as the insurgency closed in were shitty bullets jamming their already-cheaply made weapons. And the guys who caused it were sitting right here in front of me. That was the second time in this conflict the thought of killing a prisoner crossed my mind.

We later found out the intel team had been trying to get the chief for quite a while, and we were pretty sure the CIA wanted to speak with him as well. Knowing full well our cases weren't exactly airtight, but with enough anecdotal evidence from the more reliable cops we'd worked with, we fired the captain that night with a strong warning to the Fallujah department not to rehire him. If he showed up again, in Fallujah or anywhere else, those responsible would have to deal with us.

The intelligence guys got enough out of the chief and decided to put him back into the station, allegedly as an informant. The day he left, I gave him a hard stare and let him know, via the interpreters, he was being watched, and that we had spies everywhere. Again, not exactly true, but it was enough to rattle his cage a bit, as he began to understand not every Iraqi cop in his department was playing by the old rules.

His name was one of the first I passed up to the Marines after Naquib was murdered.

The academy wasn't the ultimate answer to the Coalition's prayers, but it was a start. We took a relatively simple mission and did our best to develop it as we went along. The soldiers from the 94th and 855th did an incredible job in teaching those men, putting in the hours to make sure they were prepared to take the fight to Zarqawi and his band of psychotic thugs. Sergeants Craig Ladd and Scott Couture, both well trained in unarmed self-defense, volunteered to teach the new cadets these skills, a class that wasn't originally part of the program. Craig knew some kind of Brazilian Jujitsu, having violently proved it by throwing me to the ground like a rag doll during a building-clearing exercise back at Ft. Polk (I was role playing as a bad guy who'd taken hostages). The fact Craig was scary-looking and about 225 pounds of pure muscle didn't hurt, either.

Every day, soldiers went well above what was asked of them, taking the time to make sure these guys were trained for their dangerous new task. Just before we left Ramadi in March of 2004, Marines from the 1st Marine Division came in to "train up" on the mission, observing our classes and getting to know the computer database of cadets that our own John Bachman had tirelessly put together. A few weeks prior to that, when we discovered they'd be replacing us, Travis and I drafted up a two-page assessment of the IPF of Anbar and forwarded it up to the Marine in charge, Lieutenant Colonel Cooper, who we'd have the pleasure of meeting a week later. The Marines took it seriously, committing two lieutenant colonels and a counterintelligence team to the academy's staff.

With all of the results this place was producing, the 82nd never put in the effort to expand on our intelligence and training program. The sergeant major was too busy with his little soap opera, and *his* boss, Captain Brown, had only visited the academy twice in six months. He had come for a tour of the place in November and then to speak at a graduation in March. I found it hard to believe he couldn't find the time to look into what we were doing. He lived next door at *Champion Main*, and we were sending info up to his staff almost every day. More importantly, it was the 82nd Airborne's troops on the ground in Al Anbar's cities now, serving alongside the IPF officers who were coming from our academy. Some of these cops wouldn't only save the lives of our men in women on the ground in actual combat; they also had information on men who were no doubt plotting to kill the 82nd's own troops.

Still, with all of the bullshit that went on there, the place wasn't without its charm and comforts. We'd gone from two MREs a day to more than eight different types of salad dressing at the Halliburton-sponsored dining facility. At the time, I couldn't care less about the claims of price gouging or abuse by Kellogg, Brown & Root. The food was good, and I was slowly replacing the 20 pounds I'd lost from the heat, a horrible diet, and bacteria-induced intestinal havoc over the past six months. With a makeshift gym and a lot of room to run, the platoon was keeping in great health. In a good week, I was looking at 20 miles. The shower point even had hot water (if there was electricity), and there were Porto-potties galore. The PX was nicer than the one in Baghdad, and best of all, we weren't the ones driving all over hell any more when something went down outside the gates. With the ACR, we had been the Quick Reaction Force when anything happened, and I do mean anything. Being heavily armed and highly mobile had its pros and cons. If there was an attack, an IED or an arrest, we got the call and had to be ready at a moment's notice. Those days were over. For now, anyway.

The dining hall was even open now for "midnight chow," a meal for those who were either working late or on a night shift that made it difficult to grab dinner during normal hours. On February 1st, a couple of our guys made it to the 3 a.m. showing of Super Bowl XXXVIII on the chow hall's big screen TV, where our beloved New England Patriots went on to top the Carolina Panthers 32-29, thanks to a last-second field goal by our own Adam Vinatieri. All of the soldiers who ventured out to watch in the early morning hours of the 1st were treated to Janet Jackson's wardrobe malfunction, compliments of Justin Timberlake, and were introduced to *Terry Tate, Office Linebacker*; a hilarious Reebok commercial featuring a football player violently enforcing office policies.[43]

Over our six-month tour at the academy, we made some real progress. A lot of Iraqi Police had recognized us from the different towns we'd worked in nearly a year before, excited to

---

43 *Terry Tate* was the creation of Rawson Thurber, of *Dodgeball* fame, a fellow graduate of Union College's class of 1997.

see we hadn't abandoned them in their own fight against those who wanted to see them fail. In a time when the turnover of units and a lack of "doctrinal continuity" were cutting down the efforts made by Coalition Forces, *especially* in the dangerous areas of Anbar—where the civil affairs, intelligence and military police teams had managed to gain and hold ground—our extension was well justified.

And the police were not letting us down. Just before we left in March, a group of cops in the very troubled town of Khaldiya (near Fallujah) raided a house and, using the tactics we'd taught them, nabbed a couple of known insurgents and killed a few others. And this was days after a car bomb killed a bunch of kids outside of their police station. Word got back to the schoolhouse almost every night that it was our instruction that gave them the edge. That news made my month, if not my entire tour. Weeks later in early April, the Ramadi police would eventually calm a riot without a shot fired, demonstrating an incredible amount of restraint and diplomacy on their part.

The Iraqi Police were in a very difficult position. Their success, and eventually the success of our own efforts in Iraq, depended on our unconditional support of these men. We couldn't afford not to.

In March of 2004, our year was over and we were ready to go home. Again. The platoon had spent a week or so planning *Operation Cannonball Run*, a no holds barred drive from Ramadi, down past Baghdad and eventually into Kuwait. We were packing up our gear at *Junction City*, carefully stuffing and cramming everything we owned into our trailers, and tying the rest down inside our Humvees for the daylong road trip to the

Kuwaiti border. It was amazing the amount of crap a soldier could collect over the course of a year in Iraq.

Just before we took off around 0700 that morning, we burst into our interpreters' shack and woke them up, shaking their bunks and singing stupid songs. Fond of the cheap Iraqi "sexy whiskey" they smuggled into our post on a weekly basis, they were probably sleeping one off, and I'm sure our intrusion was not a welcome one. We managed to drag them out of their bunks long enough to give them some manly hugs, back-slaps and handshakes. The mood took on a more somber tone when I looked over at Jack a few moments later. His eyes were starting to tear up. Mine were too, and a few others quickly followed suit. The smiles fading from our faces, we shook their hands and with a meaningful embrace, wished each one the best of luck.

If we made it to Kuwait in one piece—which was still a big *if*—we'd be going home in a few weeks. These guys lived here, and all the wrong people knew who they were. I prayed they'd be okay, and that I'd see them again someday.[44]

It was time to go. Our trucks, neatly parked in a straight line, pulled one by one into a column, slogged through the patches of thick mud towards *Junction City*'s main gate, and onto the highway. If all went well, 1st platoon would meet up with 2nd and 3rd near Fallujah, and make the final push to Kuwait together, just as we did nearly a year ago. Of course, we weren't about to leave Iraq that easily, compliments of yet another unit following the path of least resistance.

We pulled into the troubled Abu Ghraib district of Baghdad

---

44 I would. Two would end up working in the United States, and as of the date of this writing, they're in the process of receiving their visas via the State Department's Special Immigrant Visa program for Iraqi interpreters.

in the hazy, late morning hours of the 22nd, and ran into a convoy of about 30 fuel trucks stopped in the middle of the road. I took a few teams and went ahead to the front to find out what was up. We found that an MP squad had spotted an IED on the shoulder and blocked all traffic. Fair enough, but they needed to find us another route; this area was prime mortar territory, and 30 fuel trucks were quickly becoming 40, 50, 60 and then 70, neatly organizing themselves into one massive target.

I grew concerned as I began to recall all of the reports I'd read about this district in the past year. The area around Abu Ghraib was a haven for the insurgency, with lots of palm groves, reed thickets and fields. Intel was compiling stats about mortars landing in the same area every night for a few nights in a row, but oddly weren't part of any organized ambush. They were simply falling out of the clear blue sky. It turned out those mortars weren't misfires or accidents—insurgent teams were "zeroing" their artillery on select points on the highway to give them more precise and predictable killing power in an ambush. A few well-placed mortar tubes, pre-positioned and targeted properly, could rain explosives down on a stalled convoy within seconds. I wasn't sure if this was one of those areas, but given the IED was fairly conspicuous, I didn't want to take any chances. There was no room for error here, especially this late in the game.

I found the MP in charge, a staff sergeant, and started talking through some options. This was a four-lane highway; they could easily stop traffic in one of the opposite lanes and send these trucks around. Hell, we'd even do it for them. Even if the thing went off, the damage would be minimal at that distance. Nope. His orders were clear: halt traffic. I became insistent we move, and move now. Who was giving him such screwed up orders? Those tankers, on top of sheer numbers, were parked less than a *few yards* from each other. I couldn't think of a better mortar or car bomb target. They looked dominos; a Heaven-sent target of opportunity for any mid-level terrorist looking for a promotion. I remember thinking, "*A few well-placed shells and satellites are going to see this explosion from space.*"

While I was fighting with the staff sergeant, two of our teams set up a checkpoint a quarter of a mile behind the last fuel truck, stopping any and all traffic. It also served to spread us out a bit, reducing our exposure to the hot metal projectiles I was sure were going to be falling on us at any second.

This was ludicrous. The Marines lost men to indirect fire in their *first couple of days* in country, during their convoy movements up from Kuwait just last week. Units had come up en masse, with huge groups of trucks and vehicles that often had to stop (breakdowns, attacks, traffic, etc…) and received plenty of mortar fire. People were killed before they even had a chance to fight, for crying out loud, within hours of stepping foot into Iraq. And here *we* were, pushing our luck after a year, with about ten hours to go before we'd leave this country forever; surrounded by more than a million pounds of JP8 fuel, a handful of mindless robot soldiers, and God knows who hiding in the fields all around us.

I was done with this. If they wanted to sit here and get killed, fine, but we weren't going to die along with them just because some idiot was following orders; orders probably issued by some half-wit who'd never been on a road in Iraq. It was a stupid Standard Operating Procedure that was going to get people killed. And the fact that it was "standard" made us even more predictable; if the entire Army was doing the same thing every time in a situation like this, there was little doubt the insurgency had picked up on it. They probably knew our next move better than we did. The military was getting people killed all the time using this by-the-book approach, for the sake of simplicity.

Well in our world, "by the book" was quickly becoming "by the soldier" as we found better ways to do things. I'd long ago began working under the assumption SOPs don't win wars, people do.

Fuck this. I had two teams search ahead and find a way around them. After about 20 minutes, they returned with good news; they had found a narrow dirt path about a mile up the road that ran parallel to the highway. I figured it was a little too far out of the way to be considered a trap; if the insurgency wanted us down a road that concealed a really big bomb, the IED would've been set up much closer its entrance. However, at the time, I was willing to take the risk.

In what I thought would be my last defiant act of common sense, I courteously advised the staff sergeant and his team to step aside. Our trucks moved smartly and with a purpose around our MP brothers, took the dirt path, circumvented the highway, and again made our way south to freedom. I felt better and better as the images of those trucks got smaller and smaller in our Humvees side view mirrors.

Unfortunately, our 1st squad, only hours behind us (traveling from Al Asad) weren't as lucky. They were stopped dead in their tracks by the MP unit we blew past that morning, trying the same thing. The MPs who had stopped traffic immediately recognized the distinctive 94th unit patch and pulled in front of them. The IED was finally cleared soon after, thankfully without incident.

There were no mortar attacks, no ambushes and no IEDs for the rest of the haul out of the danger zone. Not even a flat tire. We fueled up at combat support center *Scania*, a roadside "truck stop" of sorts for convoying soldiers south of Baghdad, and the unofficial boundary between the wicked roads of the Sunni Triangle and the fairly docile highways of southern Iraq. With our combat tour coming to an end and our liberation growing closer by the hour, we felt ourselves more and more relieved with each passing mile. Pulling my weapon inside of the truck after about an hour, I hopped on the radio and told our gunners to step down from their blistering turrets and have a drink. I took off my Kevlar for a few seconds, briefly enjoying the breeze whipping through the Humvee, cooling the sweat from my shaved head.

I'd forgotten what that had felt like; the simple pleasure of driving with the windows down on a warm day, the wind in your hair and sun on your face. Staring out at the barren, lifeless desert, I closed my eyes and drifted off to sleep. Waking about 20 minutes later, it was the best nap of my life. We were done.

It was all coming to an end, with only a few hoops to jump through in Kuwait over the next two weeks or so. As we rolled further south, it felt as if the weight of the world was collectively being lifted off of our shoulders.

The entire platoon made it to the Kuwaiti border about 12 hours later, with the rest of the company crossing the finish line the next morning. By 10 a.m. that day, we'd all be at *Camp Victory*, the military's massive post in northern Kuwait serving as a holding pen for eager soldiers, sailors, airmen and Marines making their way back home. Their year-long tours over, most of the units we entered Iraq with that first fateful week of May 2003 had already boarded a plane and taken their freedom flight back to the United States. In about two weeks, we'd be taking ours.

PART 3:
When Bullets Meet Bureaucracy

IN APRIL OF 2004, the insurgency made a huge comeback in Iraq, organizing itself almost overnight and putting some serious hurt on our operations. Their timing was impeccable. We, along with several other units, were only a few days away from flying home—of leaving Iraq forever—having survived hundreds of thousands of miles of driving on and through some of the worst roads and cities on Earth. Mentally and physically exhausted, we were ready to go home. It sucks to say it, but all that was someone else's problem now.

We were enjoying some well deserved down time at Camp Victory and were looking forward to taking off. And although everyone was over the moon excited about getting home, our exhilaration was often tempered by the news of yet another soldier killed, sometimes in an area we'd been working in only days before. One of the worst was a mortar round that struck the mess hall at *Junction City* about a week after we'd left Ramadi. Nine Marines were killed as they ate their evening meals, sitting at the same tables we had been just a few nights ago.

Having been deprived of any decent fast food for almost a year, most soldiers gladly waited in 30-minute lines for burgers and ice cream. A few would spend a ridiculous amount of money on jewelry, clothes, trinkets and useless camel figurines; not so much because they actually wanted them, but only because it felt so good to spend money again. After all, you could only blow through so much of your cash at the PXs in Iraq on soda and chips. Almost everywhere I went, I ran into a soldier I'd worked with. With most, I'd stop, say hello, and recall the fonder memories of our time working together. With others, I was a bit more cautious. I'd had my fair share of run-ins with plenty of people, and the last memory some had of me in Iraq was either screaming at them over the radio or bitching them out in person. But in almost every case, the relief was palpable. All was forgiven. The war was over for us. Hugs and handshakes were dispensed freely and without reservation, and for good reason; by the grace of God we'd survived, only narrowly escaping death on a handful of occasions we'd all rather forget. In a few short days, we wouldn't have a care in the world. Every day of the rest of our lives was gravy after an experience like this.

Not feeling entirely at ease, I was enjoying myself, but very much aware nothing was concrete yet. This wasn't some extended field exercise; this was the real world, and the Army didn't owe us shit. Images of Muqtada al Sadr's black-clad Mahdi Army were starting to fill the TV at the dining facility, along with pictures of burning Army trucks, masked men with AKs and kidnapped contractors. That's when I really started to get the feeling that I was a cheap, plastic pawn on a giant, sandy, bomb-filled chessboard. The 94th was not a civilian corporation whose contract was up. We were still part of the Army—with all of our equipment on-site—and could be ordered virtually anywhere in the world. Until our plane was wheels-down in the States, I wasn't convinced it was over. Even then I'd still be a little worried. In the military, nothing is *ever* guaranteed.

While walking to the local PX with Sergeant Couture one afternoon a few days later, feeling a little better about our situation as the redeployment process rolled along, we noticed a bunch of new arrivals, prepping their equipment for that awful ride north. Like so many we had passed on our way to Kuwait last week, in a few days they'd be in Iraq, their new home for at least the next 12 months.

"Look at those poor bastards," Scott said.

"Yeah, sucks to be them," I replied.

"I would break down and start sobbing if I actually had to go back," said Scott.

"Me too."

Scott was the strong, silent type, and the fact he actually said that to me—both as a friend and an officer—was surprising. He'd rarely gotten frustrated the entire tour, and seldom wore his heart on his sleeve. He was tired, and his statement drove it home for me as well. We not only wanted to leave; we had to. We were simply drained.

Scott didn't start sobbing when he heard, but we both came pretty damn close.

CHAPTER 9:

"When we're airborne, with Germany behind us, then I'll share that sentiment."

Sean Connery as *Henry Jones*
Indiana Jones and the Last Crusade

I told you it wouldn't be the last Indy quote. Here, Indy and his father are leaving Germany after a successful rescue mission of Henry's diary. Having boarded a zeppelin that would take them to freedom, Indy's already starting to relax, enjoying the victory. Henry's much more skeptical. Still on the ground, they both notice the Nazi colonel who was tracking them approach the aircraft just before takeoff.

The ultimate case of counting your chickens before they hatch. The 94th would not be able to escape by jumping into a tiny plane, anchored to the bottom of a Nazi blimp, and flying away.

The 94th was two hours away from boarding four of those big, beautiful charter buses that would ferry us to Kuwait

International Airport. We had packed our bags and lined them up neatly outside, stuffing every last possession into our green canvas duffels. In a few hours we'd receive our customs inspection: Active duty MPs would pick through our belongings to make sure we weren't taking any restricted items (Iraqi weapons, maps, porn, etc...) back to the States. Our CONEXES—the large metal containers we used to ship our equipment around—were carefully packed and waiting in "the yard." By sunrise the next day we'd be somewhere over Egypt, 35,000 feet in the air on a plane that would bring us back to our friends and families. The redeployment would end our year of combat in Iraq, and our year and a half deployment in support of the war on terror.

Our troops were busting; smiling from ear to ear, bags full of souvenirs draped over their arms, skipping from place to place. Everywhere they went on that last day in the Middle East they looked like spastic 'tweeners coming back from a party at the mall. Camp Victory was awash in Kuwaiti salesmen with SUVs loaded with knockoff or stolen watches & jewelry, eager to get a chunk of the thousands of dollars burning a collective hole in the camouflage pants of redeploying soldiers. The call center was abuzz with conversations of exotic honeymoons. Finally, lush weddings could be planned. Reservations for expensive steakhouses could be made. High-class strip clubs could again be frequented. A few of our people might even make it back home in time to see their kids' first steps. Assuming our plane didn't crash, the rest of our lives was indeed ours for the taking.

As we joyfully began taking our duffels down to the inspection area, we'd seen a helicopter fly in low and land suspiciously close to our tent. There were rumors shooting back and forth about what was going on, but we optimistically kept to our schedule and got our bags ready. Before long, a few polished, official-looking guys in uniform started walking towards our tent. *Top men*, I remember thinking. The 82nd was already gone, as were most of the other soldiers in the neighboring tents. It was clear anyone walking our way was looking for us.

A colonel from Combined Forces Land Component Command, or *CFLCC*, walked over to our pad with his security entourage and pulled our commander aside. They started talking about something; with a lot of nervous smiles, slowly shaking heads and speechless stares into the distance, it didn't look good.

We had heard the stories about a few units who were scheduled to leave Iraq but had been put on hold. No one said their tours had been extended yet, but we'd been told by some reliable sources that all military flights out of Kuwait were suspended. I figured it was a knee-jerk reaction to the surge in violence in southern Iraq and around Fallujah. The night before, I was on the phone with my parents at the telephone center, discussing my tentative plans upon returning to New York. My dad had seen the uprisings around Iraq on the news, and nervously asked if it were possible we'd be sent back. Reluctantly, I told him the odds were slim. My own words stank of desperation; I could sense I was trying to convince myself it wasn't going to happen. I think my dad knew it, too.

As the top men drew nearer, our operations sergeant said, "Maybe he's looking to see us off." I didn't share his hopefulness. After about 30 anxiety-filled minutes of quiet pacing and gentle nail biting, the entire company was formed and brought to attention. I started half-joking with a couple of guys while the platoon was being assembled, asking them if they were ready to head back north and start fighting again. "Don't you dare say that," one of them said, I can't remember who it was.

The colonel took the formation, told us to fall out and to gather around him. It didn't take him long to break the news.

"I've got some bad news in my hip pocket."

That's all he needed to say. He went on to tell us, that after a year in combat in Iraq, with less than 11 hours to our flight back to the United States, the problem with the insurgency was getting out of hand and certain units had to be extended to deal with it. The 94th had been put on the list and would have to stay behind for another three months.

Silence. I looked down, stared at my boots for a second, and then took a look around. A few people started to weep, their quiet sobs suffocated by the deceptively gentle desert wind.

I didn't know how to feel, but for some reason I wasn't surprised. Given what was going on in Iraq, it wouldn't make sense *not* to keep us. I didn't know all of the facts, but the mental calculus was telling me a week ago this was the only answer. Don't get me wrong, it was still the biggest kick in the nuts I had ever received, but it all added up.

I asked the colonel where we'd be sent and who we'd be attached to. He replied, "most likely Baghdad, with the 1st Armored Division." We had survived the past year only to be stopped in our tracks and sent straight back into the lion's den.

As you might recall from the news, April of 2004 was a disturbing time for the U.S. military in Iraq. We were losing control of our routes and our patrols, and cities all over the country were plagued by heavy fighting. The Army had even surrounded Najaf and was preparing to assault the city. We'd all felt the visceral anger following the barbaric murder and mutilation of those Blackwater contractors. My God how that made our blood boil, seeing those poor guys strung up from a bridge in Fallujah and those animals dancing around the charred bodies in celebration. We had seen the new wave of kidnappings and attacks on convoys in and around Baghdad, and were sympathetic to the problem. However, extending a group of mentally and physically exhausted soldiers with half-broken equipment was not the answer; fresh troops with new equipment was.

Worst of all, I had just thrown away all of my "snivel gear." I had finally managed to get a hold of some niceties; a comfortable mattress, a pillow and a couple of blankets. But now they were all collecting sand, old food and tobacco spit at the bottom of our dumpster. I'd have to buy all of that stuff all over again.

That was one of the first things I thought about. It wasn't the three months of hell we'd go on to face, the combat we'd find ourselves in, or the brand new thoughts of death, similar to the ones that had filled my head every day for the past year. It was a few replaceable items. I have no idea why. I'd read Andy Rooney's book a few months prior, *My War*, about his experiences in World War II and remembered some of his comments about depression when he was thrown into Europe following D-Day.[45] He went on to say, and I'm paraphrasing here, that the human mind is only capable of handling so much anxiety and despair. After a while you were numb, you simply didn't feel anything. You'd maybe even find some twisted humor in it. I guess this was one of those times. My head was officially full, and I was feeling my "500 yard stare" coming on. I wasn't quite at 1000 yet.

Within minutes our troops—experiencing a precarious blend of rage, shock and depression—stampeded towards the phone center. I was right behind them. But before we left,

---

45 Andy Rooney, *My War* (New York, NY: Public Affairs Books, 2000)

Reggie had a good, practical idea. We were all pretty damn hot, but we had to be careful about what we said to people on the phone, to protect our operational security *and* image as professionals. Our message was clear enough—we were just as upset as anybody, but calling home and badmouthing the Army was not going to help. It would only hurt our efforts in the long run and serve to damage the morale of the soldiers fighting in Iraq. Yes, it was difficult, but we had to display a little intestinal fortitude and discipline, and handle this like professional men and women. We couldn't afford to come off as a bunch of whiners. If anyone wanted to bitch, we suggested they come to Reggie or me. Our tent flap was always open. Don't dump it on your families who were helpless over 8000 miles away *and* undoubtedly much more frustrated, angry and in the dark than we'd ever be. With another 90 sleepless nights and fearing the worst every time the phone rang, they had it bad enough. It was a mini pre-emptive strike on our part; the press was sure to pick up on the story, and would most likely try to contact our families.

Within hours, the American media had focused in on the small Army Reserve unit from New England. A few parents appeared on national television in an interview with NBC's *The Today Show* a few days later, and *Time Magazine* had picked up on our story.[46] Maine's political machine roared to life, as Senators Susan Collins and Olympia Snowe began contacting the Department of Defense regarding both our extension and our deployment, now in its 17th month.

Over the past year, they had sent us copies of correspondence they'd passed up to the Department of the Army through the Senate Armed Services Committee, regarding the plight of

---

46 Nancy Gibbs, *Digging in for a Fight*, Time Magazine, May 3, 2004

our equipment and the lack of reinforcements during our tour. Their sincere concern and valiancy in the face of a very powerful Secretary of Defense and resolute Bush Administration were appreciated. Being so accustomed to "detached" representation here in Iraq—men and women in our own *service*—it actually made me rethink the way I looked at State Government. However we all knew the Army had made up its mind on this one. We weren't going home any time soon.

Our attempt to restrain our troops' rage didn't go over very well with some people, and I could understand why. We couldn't censor everyone, and people had a right to speak to their families, but the fact was our family support group back home wasn't exactly united. Some were sure to run with this one, and run they did. We could only hope they could keep their cool long enough to get their facts straight about our extension, and not give the media more fuel against the war, the Army or the Administration. The support group, with the exception of a few rogue members who went to the press with every instance of military evil, did okay.

Our guys were handling it better than I ever could have hoped. For the most part, there were just a lot of sullen faces, forced smiles and long drags on cigarettes. However, some dealt with their frustration in other, more unique ways. Our own Staff Sergeant Todd Libby decided it would be best to strip down to a tight purple man-thong, run from our tent area to *Victory*'s main roadway, and chase after five or six buses full of troops on their way to Kuwait International. Jesus, what a gangly, pasty mess he was, darting in and out of those buses, waving and smiling like a lunatic. I should mention Libby's 6'4" and all legs. As if that wasn't bad enough, he was wearing a matching blue shower cap with flowers on it.

Reggie and I just let him be. We'd lost all control of Todd

months ago. Captain Bentley stared on, yet again completely unfazed by Todd's unusual behavior.

The reality set in that evening. The sun had barely set by this point and the entire camp turned an eerie, almost smoke-grey color. I was walking to the chow hall. Yesterday, there were a thousand footprints in the sand on this path. Today, only a few, and they were ours. Everyone in our section of the camp had gone home.

I again passed those "poor bastards" Scott and I had been taking pity on only hours before. In a few days, we'd be right behind them.

We were going back. Poop.

I felt my eyes start to tear up. We had accomplished so much in the last year, and nearly broken ourselves in the process. On top of it all, we had made it this far without losing anyone. Given the shape we were in, what was happening in Iraq and the nature of our anticipated mission, we were going to suffer losses. I choked back the tears and, in my second sincere conversation with God—frankly with any deity who happened to be working the Help Desk at the moment—I prayed for the strength to lead my men and women through this. That was all I was asking for.

One thing was for certain, and offered a tiny bit of solace in an otherwise depressing situation: No matter what happened, where we went, or to whom we were assigned, we were a team. The 94th was very good at its job, and we'd continue to do things the way we saw fit. Period.

With an acceptance of the fact we were going to be there for another three months, the 94th went on to re-group, re-arm and re-think our 90-day strategy.

CHAPTER 10

"My men are not expendable."

Arnold Schwarzenegger as *Major Alan "Dutch" Schaefer*
Predator

People die in war, and it's not always because of any one specific, identifiable factor. There are simply too many variables. I can't reiterate this enough. You could do everything "perfectly" in combat and still become a casualty. While we were prepared to *accept* losses, we were careful not to *assume* they had to happen. If we were going to lose someone, it would be due to a higher power, circumstances outside of our control. God was going to reach down and pluck one of us up. However, no one was going to die because of something we were able to prevent, and it damn sure wasn't going to happen because of a decision to blindly buy into some cold, economic theory regarding eventual human casualties in war.

In my view, the more officers were willing to accept losses in their counterinsurgency operations, the more it eventually crept into their thinking, and subsequently, their planning. I'd seen it happen more than a few times over the past year, and somewhere down the line a 19-year-old kid in a turret paid for it. Shit, indeed, rolls downhill. Without even knowing it, they'd put people in harm's way needlessly because of decisions based on this flawed assumption. Our new job was inherently dangerous, but that didn't mean we couldn't mitigate some of the risk. For Chrissake, there were risks and then there were bad decisions and terrible habits. We'd gotten very good at separating the three, and made a pact to continue to do so.

No one was sure what our new mission would be. From what we were reading in *Stars and Stripes*, the generals were reviewing their troop strength and deliberating as to what kind of forces were needed back in Iraq. I was expecting any day for them to come out and say more troops were required, and we had two hours to pack our gear and move out to Baghdad. After nearly a week of fitfully tossing and turning in our bunks, placating ourselves with *Family Guy* DVDs and glued to the radio & newspapers, it was announced CJTF-7 wouldn't need any additional troops in Iraq. The 1st Armored and 1st Cavalry Divisions would take care of it.

Holy shit, was that a relief. For the past week I was certain they were just going to throw us into some burning section of Baghdad, Fallujah or Ramadi and tell us to get it under control. I had already emailed our interpreters from Baghdad and inquired if they'd like to work with us again. Within a few hours most had replied "yes," along with some strong language indicating their support (Jack had written "we will follow you into the Hell" in his reply email to me). It nearly brought a tear to my eye. However, we weren't needed back in theater. CJTF7 had enough troops in-country to put down this uprising.

That being said, God Bless both the 1st Cavalry Division

and 1st Armored Division for bearing the brunt of the chaos that defined Iraq in the spring of 2004. The 1st Cav came in just as things were getting out of control, and the 1st Armored Division was in the same boat we were. Leaders from both had commented on the strength and tenacity of the insurgency, but went on to criticize its organizational and planning abilities: if the insurgents had only waited a few weeks, the 1st Armored Division would have completed its rotation back to Germany. Without the men, weapons and machines of the 17,000-soldier division to deal with this new insurrection, U.S. military manpower would've been stretched even thinner than it was. It wasn't like their redeployment was a secret; it was major news in almost every paper in the free world. Given the fact the military would most likely have to recall the 1st Armored Division from Germany to Iraq, the insurgency would have scored a one-two punch against the ability of the U.S. military *and* to the morale of the troops returning to Iraq who'd just gotten home. That was the first real indication for me the insurgency wasn't as cohesive and structured as we once thought, and that each rebel group had their own fractured objectives.

I'll forever have a tremendous amount of respect for those units and what they went on to accomplish over the next three months. The 1st Armored Division lost several soldiers to a car bomb a few days after the extension, troops who were originally slated to return home just days before. The emotion was overwhelming. There was a similar, heartbreaking story of an 82nd Airborne medic near Fallujah who was killed by a mortar *two days* before he was scheduled to leave for Kuwait. Forty-eight hours. Later on in our extension, a fellow MP would be killed in a rocket attack at *Anaconda* the night before he was to fly home. Those were some of the worst war stories imaginable, and given our situation, they felt incredibly relevant.

Today, I find myself thinking about what kind of men and women they would have turned out to be if they'd survived their tours—what careers they might have taken when they returned, what they might have done for mankind, if they would have become parents. Then I start thinking about the thousands of others who were lost in this war and start asking the same questions. After a couple of minutes, I have to make myself stop. Those who've never known someone killed in combat might give each a passing thought when hearing about them in the news, and then go on with their lives. Those of us who have known someone killed in combat have spent countless hours staring at the ceilings above our beds on quiet nights, thinking of nothing but.

While the brass at Combined Joint Task Force 7 decided we weren't needed, the CFLCC, based there in Kuwait, had different ideas.[47] They needed more troops and, seeing us in their pool of available resources, grabbed us. We were attached to them soon after and were given the mission of escorting supply convoys north into Iraq. The 1st Armored Division would eventually move out of Baghdad to points further south, their mission also being to protect convoys moving from Kuwait into central Iraq.

What a welcome relief that was. Our new mission, although one of the more dangerous in Iraq, would take us straight

---

47 After its replacement by CJTF-7 as the operational headquarters for all ground units in the CENTCOM theater, the Combined Forces Land Component Command became the primary logistics hub for military forces in Kuwait and Iraq. CFLCC still remained in charge of logistics for all land forces in theater, and remained the headquarters for U.S. Army Central Command, managing Army service component issues in the CENTCOM theater.

through 1st Armored Division territory. That was going to be a comforting feeling, riding on a road with Abrams tanks up and down the whole damn thing; if all went as planned, we could literally leapfrog the M1s on our way to Baghdad.

Soon after our reassignment, we did get a bit of good news. According to a one-star general, the provost marshal of CFLCC, we were only needed to escort our elements through the more peaceful roads of southern Iraq and into Convoy Support Center (CSC) *Scania;* the sleepy little military truck stop I spoke of earlier. *Scania* was considered by most of the military community who worked in Kuwait and South-Central Iraq as the last safe combat outpost before heading into the real rough areas. Everything north of this support center—which had suffered very few, if any, attacks to date—was considered very hostile territory. Most of southern Iraq, at least the route we preferred, was wide-open space with few known troublemakers.

Before we began our new missions, the Army was using *Military Professional Resources, International* (MPRI), a consulting group hired by the Department of Defense to offer some additional training. Comprised of former servicemen from Special Forces, Navy SEALs and other elite groups, they reviewed some convoy basics with the units that would be guarding the major shipments north. Most of us were pretty skeptical right off the bat—the first guy we met talked to us like we were fifth graders, and the last combat most of these guys saw was probably Desert Storm. And unless you had experience running convoys, I didn't want your advice. However the fellers at MPRI turned out to be a talented, down-to-earth group of instructors whose sensible guidance really hit home. Making it clear they were teaching *a* way, not *the* way, we appreciated their solid knowledge of unconventional tactics and sincere respect for our experiences, as well as the steps the Army was taking to help us. There was always more to learn.

In about a week, we'd be helping to protect the men and women of the U.S. Army's 375th Transportation Group; the truck drivers and logistics soldiers who were providing valuable material to those fighting the good fight in some of the most violent towns in Iraq. The Marines were starting their first offensive in Fallujah, Coalition Forces had Muqtada al-Sadr's fighters surrounded in Najaf, and the 1st Cavalry Division was poised to re-take Baghdad. They needed supplies and needed them now.

The 94th was about to work with some extremely brave people who'd witnessed more shots fired in anger than all of us combined. We were also about to become spectators to the most disturbing levels of incompetence and cowardice we'd seen since crossing the border over a year before.

Every soldier a rifleman

There are three main tenets of combat: be able to shoot, move and communicate. They were the top "Three Commandments" for any operator. The rest was just details, and those were always subject to change anyway—few battle plans survived the first contact, intact. However, you were absolutely screwed without those three. No engagement was going to be won if you weren't proficient with your weapon. If you couldn't drive, run or walk, you could wait for some air support and hope for the best, but otherwise you were sitting ducks on the defensive. And if you couldn't talk to your men and women, especially under stress, that would arguably be the worst of all. Rarely did this doctrine work well in *peacetime* training; I could only imagine the unimaginable chaos in store for those who didn't subscribe to it in Iraq.

That said, the leadership of the 375th was criminally negligent in their ignorance of this creed. Over the next three months, we saw so many flagrant and bizarre errors in judgment by these men and women it was hard to believe any one of these people had survived so far. Honestly, I couldn't figure out how they made it through grade school, let alone into the Army, with such poor instincts. And at any given time, they were a sneeze away from us murdering them.

There was no attention paid to even the most basic of plans; choosing their routes, what to do if a tire blew or engine went kaput, or *actions on contact*—the "holy shit" plan if bombs started going off and bullets started flying. Their gear was a mess and rarely ready. Radio checks weren't being done prior to moving out. Few even knew what they were hauling. Too many of their leaders had the telltale "yeah, yeah, yeah" look permanently pasted on their faces. My parents put ten times more thought and energy into our summertime drives from upstate New York to Boston when I was a kid.

The disconnect between our two units could not have been more pronounced. On top of that, most of the units we were working with hadn't been in theater more than a few weeks. Even *worse*, these units now had tactical control of the military police—battle-hardened MPs were to be under the command of a bunch of brand new truck drivers from Kuwait. To put it in civilian terms, the State Police were now at the beck and call of the local Teamsters Union.

It ended up being painfully obvious the leadership of the 375th had never expected their units to see "real" combat. I mean, who signs up to lead truck drivers and actually expects to shoot at someone? Or get shot at? On top of it all, if you didn't hold a combat or combat support position in the U.S. Army, you'd probably only been given some basic weapons training with little emphasis on tactics.[48] It wasn't anyone's fault; it was just the way it was.

I didn't expect every soldier to be a killing machine—I'm very aware each specialty in the military has its own niche in war, and some won't receive the training afforded to other units. On a more personal note, I wasn't going to start complaining about the U.S. Army Transportation Corps while enjoying the food and ammunition they risked their lives to bring us: After my very first convoy, back in May of 2003, I never wasted a bit of food at the mess hall or took any item at the PX for granted again. To this day, a cold Pepsi *still* tastes what I think a million bucks would taste like, and a bag of Doritos is like gold-plated Heaven in my mouth.

However I *did* expect every troop to keep up with what was going on, and to be prepared. Our lives were riding on it. Get on the ball, for Chrissake. Soldiers who hadn't anticipated the risks of their mission were now on the front lines of this conflict. The roads—with the ambushes, car bombs, and IEDs—were by far the most dangerous places to be in Iraq. The war was moving towards a conflict of attrition, with thousands of soldiers carefully moving along Iraq's roads in one of the most tactically challenging environments imaginable. Supply lines were being hammered by an enemy who'd discovered new ways to challenge us. Convoy ambushes were becoming the tactic du jour of the insurgency. Why? Because convoys were easy targets. We were foolishly making them easier targets. With

---

48 Fortunately, that's being changed in basic and advanced training—lesson learned after the disastrous attack on Jessica Lynch's unit, the 507th Maintenance Company, in March 2003.

a combat patrol, you could count on some close air support, maybe even some tanks backing you up of things got really bad. Your mission was *somewhat* offensive in nature. With a convoy, you were just another row of slow-moving targets shuffling north, outsiders to those who worked in the area, with clear orders to keep moving if you were fired on. You were, quite simply, a sitting duck, a "bullet magnet" if you will. The 375th, I'm sure, was well aware of this. So was our enemy. But I was concerned that most still didn't know what they were in for, and hadn't been briefed on the changing threat. Even worse, I was getting the impression from the leaders at all levels they just weren't listening.

Be careful what you wish for

During our entire year of combat in Iraq, we were always bitching about having no higher military police command that would go to bat for us. Most other MP units were part of a battalion; a unit made up of three or four companies with a lieutenant colonel who could exercise a little influence over how they were to be applied. The 94th had *two captains*, and we were Reservists. We clearly didn't have the sway a higher rank had, even when presenting rock-solid cases as to why certain things should or should not be done after more than a year of hard-earned experience.[49]

But now, we had a bona-fide lieutenant colonel and an entire battalion staff to help us. Finally, someone was there to give us a hand with these clowns. The 94th, along with four other MP companies, would now fall under the 125th Military

---

49 For a sizable portion of our tour with the ACR, Dave and I were the "senior" MPs in the Anbar Province.

Police Battalion, a National Guard unit from Puerto Rico. Complete with a lieutenant colonel and a couple of majors, we were sure to command a little more respect.

Little did we know at the time, we were quickly becoming someone's learning experience. The 125th would have full administrative control of every MP company and of every new mission. In turn, the 125th was under the command of the 375th, the overlords that kept an eye on each and every convoy from Kuwait into Iraq.

Within weeks of hearing the news, we were sent from *Camp Victory* to another Kuwaiti post, *Camp Udari*. *Udari*, which later had its name changed to *Camp Beuhring*, was a staging area for new units who were on their way into Iraq. We moved in and initially set up shop in tents, but eventually moved to nicer, air-conditioned trailers. Despite our missions, living at *Udari* made it easier—there were no mortars, the gym was well equipped, the mess hall was huge, and there was usually something to do after hours. It even had a coffee shop. But it was so damn hot. Our tents were air-conditioned, but every time I stepped outside it felt like a hair dryer was blowing in my face. Even my eyelids burned from the searing wind.

But the most vital of *Udari's* gifts was the new Level 2, or *add-on*, armor packages provided by the Army. The request for better armor for our 90-day extension was honored, and our mechanics went to work bolting and welding the half-ton of steel onto our Humvees. The gorgeous, sand-colored new metal slabs now meant we were at least protected from our enemy's 7.62mm rounds, whereas before they'd cut through the Humvee's thin frame with ease. The new ballistic-resistant windows would do the same. And although a great deal safer than our older, conventional Humvees, IEDs and car bombs could still blow Level 2 armor into a twisted, fractured mess. A massive improvement, this was a step in the right direction and helped to restore our floundering confidence in the vehicles we were trusting with our lives.

And yet there were people up the chain of command sincerely worried the added armor would lead to "greater brake wear and increased fuel consumption." Fucking unbelievable.

Now, for the missions: Imagine the worst road trip you've ever had. Now multiply that frustration, fear and anger by ten trillion. This is the best comparison I can give you to what it was like taking a convoy through Iraq. Couple that with a command worried more about brake pads than MANPADs, and it didn't take long for us to start getting uncomfortable again.

Our first mission was to be a 24-vehicle convoy escort to Logistic Staging Area *Anaconda*, a large military post an hour north of Baghdad and another three hours past *Scania*, our initial handover point. A little dismayed about our new destination—which took us directly through the heart of the Sunni Triangle—I went to the 125th and asked them what the plan was. Obviously, *Scania* was no longer our turnaround point. Fine, but that would mean they'd really have to get their act together to help us.

This was now one of the most dangerous missions in the U.S. Army. We'd be taking supplies through Baghdad, Fallujah, Ramadi, Mosul, everywhere; no place was off limits now, I'd assumed that much. But how did the 125th plan to help us? They hadn't given us any information—no points of contacts, no call signs, no frequencies, nothing so far. They didn't even tell us where their tent was.

That was going to be the norm from now on. If we wanted something, we'd have to get it ourselves. Here we were, tasked with taking 20 vehicles, less than half of them driven by U.S.

Army soldiers—a quarter of those, MPs—through and around Baghdad for the next three months. That was rough enough in itself, made worse by the presence of what was turning out to be a bunch of 9-to-5 pikers from the Transportation Group.

The only redeeming quality of the 125th was their intelligence officer, a really sharp first lieutenant, who put in a lot of effort to find out what was going on in the areas we'd be driving through. He actually came to us with the newest intelligence, almost every day. The rest formed a robotic human chain through which to pass down more morale-shredding missions to our commander. That's all they were good for.

I'd be taking most of the platoon on our first mission of the extension from *Udari* to *Anaconda*. Just before we headed out the gate and rumbled toward the border once again, we were warned insurgent attacks manage to shut down large stretches of the primary route north, known as Main Supply Route *Tampa*. Cutting straight up the middle of Iraq, it was one of the fastest, most easily defendable, wide-open routes to Baghdad and points north, to include our objective in Balad, the site of *Anaconda*. Intel had alerted us parts of the route were now designated *red*, meaning they were unsafe for travel due to frequent attacks, so we'd be taking an alternate route up into Balad.[50]

Our new route would skirt the outer edges of Baghdad, half of them through town, and half through the countryside. Regardless, almost every road on the map was either red or amber.

The alternate path had us driving on narrow roads with no

---

[50] Routes were designated daily by the Movement Control Teams (MCTs) as green (permissive), amber (recent violence) or red (closed, under attack or use at risk) each day, based on the most recent intelligence.

shoulders, lined with large piles of dirt and debris full of who knows what, in the middle of nowhere, miles from support of any kind. Our radios often couldn't reach anyone outside of our convoy. I had no way to talk to all of my *own* guys, and any wrong turn could put us into a dead-end street with no way to turn around. We were responsible for 20 vehicles, most of them huge civilian tractor-trailers. The maps we were using were twenty years old, and no one had traveled our route in days, if not weeks. Half of the civilian drivers were 19-year old "third country nationals" from Bangladesh or Pakistan who couldn't speak a lick of English, drove their 18-bald-wheeled semis four feet from each other, and sped around corners like over-caffeinated, wide-eyed kids playing a video game.

This, more or less, would be our mission template for the next three months.

It was critical our cargo move north to *Anaconda*, but now we'd be heading there on untested routes, much to our disadvantage. The drive to *Anaconda* was a dangerous enough trip, but made even worse by the absence of even *basic* intelligence on the new roads and lackluster planning on the part of our new friends, the Movement Control Teams, or "MCTs." They would prove nearly fatal in their work, or lack thereof.

We were seeing a gross amount of negligence from the transportation planners we were coming across, and the MCTs were no different. Because of the Army's failure to protect its major supply routes, we were now forced to use roads no one had ever taken before, streets potentially in much worse shape than those that had been attacked. Sure, they might have been patrolled once or twice, and weren't exactly in downtown Baghdad, but no one had looked at their patrol schedules, capability of handling tractor-trailers, or thought about their accessibility by insurgents. Our convoys were usually between

15 and 25 trucks and were a huge target of opportunity for our enemy to do some serious damage.

Before we moved out from *Scania* on our first mission, starting the first of what would be many trips into deadly territory with our cargo, our movement control commanders told us the alternate routes had been checked out, were being patrolled, were fit to handle heavy traffic, and marked with spray paint. There were so many small turns—which alone made it a ridiculous route for a large convoy—it was nearly impossible to use even GPS precision to label them. And there were no Google Maps back then to help us through this. MCT's sole purpose in life was to provide us with this critical information.

Every one of these claims proved untrue. Over the next 24 hours, like a blind rat in a lethal maze, we'd have to feel our way to *Anaconda* over a complex, unmarked country route with no visible patrols and roads barely wide enough for a Humvee. Since there were only two main highways that headed north other than the main supply route, it was simple for our enemy to know we'd soon be coming up one of the three or four other routes. Plus, we would be easy enough to see with so many trucks. We were being set up for failure in the worst possible way.

The first IED, on the southeastern edge of Baghdad, sent a huge cloud of dirt and concrete into the clear blue sky. I saw the blast from my Humvee, about 200 yards away. The first few Humvees disappeared behind a cloud of smoke and sand. After a few moments, I radioed up to the lead trucks for the report. I hadn't heard any shooting, and the vehicles were still moving. One of the truck drivers was slightly hurt, his forearm slashed by debris. Other than some ringing in their ears, everyone was otherwise ok.

Scott later said they were so close to the massive explosion, he felt the back end of his 3-½ ton vehicle slide sideways on the asphalt.

We pushed on to *Anaconda*, heading out of Baghdad on a narrow concrete road that cut right through one of Iraq's large grazing fields, just east of Baghdad. We'd noticed a few shepherds with their flocks around us, roaming through the open plains.

Less than 30 minutes later, another IED exploded, hurtling shrapnel into the lead trucks. I gave the order to start laying down some suppressive fire, just in case this was the beginning of an ambush. Seconds later, my Humvee was passing through the stretch of road the IED had been hidden in. The shoulder was flanked on both sides by huge piles of dirt and rocks that could have held just about anything. My gunner yelled "IED!" and ducked down into the truck. I told my guys to floor it. Drive! There was nothing we could do but haul ass as fast as we could and hope for the best. This new armor would be no match for God knows how many 155mm artillery shells exploding less than five yards away. At this moment, speed was our only ally.

For the first time in the war, I thought this was the end. I don't think I've ever felt as helpless, and it enraged me. I was going to die, angry, in the middle of an otherwise beautiful field right here in the Iraqi countryside—not fighting or shooting, but waiting. At the mercy of whatever force was in control of the universe at the moment, I grabbed the top of my helmet with my left hand and clutched my M16 in my lap with my right, anticipating the explosion that would tear through the truck and blow me into the afterlife.

It never came. We continued our slow, agonizing march toward Balad.

You Bet My Life

So there we were; getting hit with IEDs, trying to keep control of 20 trucks in Iraq's most rural areas, out of contact with any support elements, and on slender dirt roads where it would be virtually impossible for a semi to pass a destroyed vehicle. We managed to get out of there without another attack and made our way around Baqubah to *Anaconda*.

When we got back to *Scania* a week or so later, we let the movement control team guys know what had happened: no markings, no patrols, nothing. They had no explanation.

I did. The MCTs simply didn't bother to check out all of the routes they were sending people on, and then bullshitted us about doing so. No one had the cojones to actually get into their Humvee, make the drive and map out the routes they were charged with surveying. It was their job, *their only job*.

They hadn't even requested the lone MP units available at *Scania* to recon the route that would be used for the sole purpose of transporting large vehicles and equipment. They hadn't contacted the units in that Area of Operations for updated intelligence or patrol times (we tried to time our movement with patrol schedules when possible). Again, we were at the mercy of "soldiers," comfortably situated in their all-inclusive command resort, who had mastered the despicable art of checking the box. They didn't have to escort these convoys; all they had to do was let us know which routes were open and which were not, and then guess as to which one they felt would be better. Based on what, you ask? I haven't a clue. Maybe third- or fourth-hand intelligence, I guess.[51] They

---

51 It would ironically come to be based off of the reports of our own MPs

might as well have just thrown a dart at the map, made their choice, and then handed us a blindfold and a fucking cigarette.

From that point on, the only instructions the Movement Control Teams gave my men were the times at which we could leave. They were not in a position to give qualified orders, so in my estimation, were no longer relevant in our planning. They were a rest stop, staffed with know-nothing tour guides, and nothing more. Unless a specific road could *physically* not be driven, they wouldn't be telling us where to go. If they tried, I'd be telling them where to go—straight to Hell in a hand basket. And with the enraged convoy escort units they were pissing off, coupled with the disastrous instructions they were giving us, we'd all be meeting up there soon enough.

The MCTs would go on to rely on others to do their dangerous work. One officer even had the nerve to ask me to take a photo of a pontoon bridge connecting two roads near *Anaconda*. Instead of rising to the challenge of actually supporting our movement the way they were supposed to—with real data and usable information—the leaders earning their combat pay settled into their comfortable environment, completely at ease with the fact their own critical tasks were being performed entirely by other maneuver units. We depended on them for vital information and got nothing. In essence, the music had stopped, and they had their chairs.

What a complete waste of manpower, let alone resources. Here we were, scrounging for as many bodies as we could find to keep these convoys moving north in one of the most trying times of this war. Yet when I walked from the parking lot to *Scania*'s main gate on our first mission, I was halted by three

---

in the battalion and those of the heavily armored Stryker units, who usually ended up escorting the heavier loads of weapons and ammunition.

MPs at a small checkpoint. Their job? To watch me check my weapon at the clearing barrel. It took three men to make sure my weapon was cleared. An *entire MP team* was somehow mysteriously required to watch me pull my pistol out of its holster, work the action and check for rounds. Looking back, given how many convoying soldiers wanted to flat out kill the MCT guys, this probably was a good idea.

The unforgivable mistakes and absolute cowardice being made on a daily basis—those that could have been avoided by some grit and intestinal fortitude on behalf of the MCT officers, not to mention better management of their own personnel—would end up getting young soldiers hurt. Nearly every convoy coming out of Kuwait was rolling through *Scania*, some being led by men and women who, up until a few hours before, had never stepped foot in Iraq. The critical firsthand intel the MCT were supposed to be providing—detours, weight limits, routes and ambush points—just wasn't there. Less than a few hours north, IEDs were being detonated at a frenetic pace, killing and maiming our men and women every hour. The casualty rate had nearly *tripled* since March, and the only thing between these new convoy commanders and the insurgency—hiding in wait and becoming more battle-hardened by the day—were these toy soldiers in their cushy offices.

My, oh my, does shit roll downhill.

Our situation was summarily getting worse. On top of our ineffectual command, some of the leaders of the transportation units we were assigned to escort were making very dangerous tactical decisions on the roads. We were starting all over again with the problems we had with the *Muleskinner* guys over a year ago, and these cats were about as enthusiastic as the ACR was in changing their ways. Of course, they had a few inexperienced officers who insisted on coming on these convoys, who'd go on to mouth off about how much they'd learned about convoy security in a school somewhere back in the States. It was as if they were *trying* to get us killed: taking more dangerous routes for the sake of saving time, ignoring our advice when traveling together, and confrontations—actual screaming matches—with us on the highways. Here we were, an MP unit with over a year's worth of combat experience, dealing with stubborn renegades who were fighting us tooth and nail over no-brainer decisions. What the hell was happening? I felt so sorry for the lower enlisted, the young guys and gals who actually did the loading and driving, who were forced to listen to these pinheads day in and day out.

For instance, most transportation units were consistently taking one of the worst routes in Iraq when traveling into Baghdad, one that led them through the car bomb- and IED-ridden towns of Al Hillah and Al Iskandariyah, in order to save some time. They were taking a route easily ten times more dangerous than a relatively safer one to save, literally, a few minutes.

Convoy commanders were also ordering their drivers to travel within about 25 meters of one another when on the road—straight out of the Transportation Corps manual—even after we explained to them a tight group of large vehicles was an ideal target for an insurgent looking to maximize damage with a rocket grenade, IED or car bomb. I insisted they be more proactive; think about how these ambushes were going down. A big gun was no use to anyone if it was in the kill zone with a dead soldier behind it. These guys thought the closer they got to one another, the safer they'd be. No one was going to get kidnapped and beheaded as long as they were near their friends. It was abhorrent to see the insurgency's influence on the actions of a bunch of American soldiers, their paranoia driving them further into a trap our enemy was slowly constructing, whether they intended to or not.

The Military Police Corps, among other branches of the U.S. Army, had learned its lessons over the past year. We knew better—the new guys didn't. No one was going to get killed over some jackass's willful mistake. After hundreds of futile attempts to employ some sound decisions, it would sadly come down to this: if you want to kill yourself, fine. We're not going to hold your hand while you do it. The MPs will be within small arms distance (a quarter of a mile or so) of the convoy. If you need something, call us on the radio, if you're even on it—some transportation commanders didn't even monitor their own frequencies. Otherwise, we'll be way out front or way in the back. If we saw any sign of an ambush, we'd engage the flanks with our MK19s, and our highly trained gunners were up for the task. I had every confidence any one of them could completely destroy a car, truck, or person a half-mile away in less than ten seconds.

This particular one really pissed me off. Not to offend the religious aspect of war, but most of our convoy commanders insisted on praying prior to their departure, only to ignore a review of basic tactics in the event of an incident—for example, what to do if we were ambushed, if someone broke down, if someone got a flat, if there was an IED, if there was a casualty. And there almost always was. Although the convoy commander was officially "in charge," the MPs would take care of stuff like that. They'd be in control when it was convenient for them, only *after* the fact. And they wondered why they were having such a hard time.

The practice of giving transportation units tactical control over their military police attachments is one of the worst in conventional military thinking.

Logistical Staging Area *Anaconda* was its own nightmare. For anyone reading this who served there, I'm so sorry. *Anaconda* was located near the Iraqi town of Balad, and was formerly an Iraqi Air Force base. Housing the U.S. military's largest amount of supplies and soldiers outside of Kuwait—with more than 12,000 people—it was a hub for just about every transportation unit in-country. Stocked full of equipment, contracted workers and American troops, it was one of the most heavily mortared and rocketed bases in Iraq.

At the conclusion of that first convoy of our new extension, in the first ten minutes of pulling up to Anaconda's main entrance, we, for some unknown reason, were made to wait for "clearance" to pull onto the post. Here we were, about 15 trucks waiting outside this camp, all parked much too close together. Iraqi day laborers, permitted to work on or near the post on construction jobs, huddled around the "search area" about 50 yards away from the post's entrance. They just stared at us. I recognized that unsteady, piercing look; it was the same one I'd seen in Ramadi and Hit all last year. Some were being searched, most were smoking. A few were on cell phones. *What in the world were we waiting for*, I remembered thinking. The gate guard was shuffling through paperwork and called someone on the radio. If I survived the next 20 minutes, I was going to find out who was on the other end of that radio and choke the living shit out of them both.

A mortar round slammed into the sand and exploded less than 50 yards from us. Someone knew we'd just arrived, and probably also knew we'd be staying put for a while. Now we're understandably frustrated. We all crowded into a little concrete shack and waited. No one was hurt, but we all knew *Anaconda's* infamous reputation; people were injured or killed here by incoming rounds almost every week.

Again, WHAT *THE FUCK* ARE WE WAITING FOR!?

A few minutes later, we were allowed on post. Great, thank you. Some administrator decided they'd make a convoy sit motionless for 30 minutes so they could figure out where they should have us park. For crying out loud, the place was big enough to park anywhere—and with the frequency of incoming rounds, I would much rather have stayed away from any bottlenecks on post anyway. Sometimes you *were* safer by yourself, especially at a place like *Anaconda*, where mortars were flying in like planes into Los Angeles Airport. It didn't take a genius to figure out there were Iraqi spotters everywhere, especially at the front gate, and that Iraqi mortarmen had most likely zeroed in on some key spots, to include, just maybe, the entrance to the post.

I soon found out, first hand, what an incredible exercise in tragedy *Anaconda* was. It was the most reactive post in Iraq, an absolute shitshow of incompetence. On top of the incredibly important task of waiting at the gates while mortars were lobbed at us, we had standing orders that no one was to leave the tents (tents that were barely standing) without a weapon, Kevlar and vest. This in itself wasn't the worst idea I've heard of, but that one's coming up in a few minutes.

The fact you couldn't walk from point A to point B without 30 lbs of body armor on such a large post should have been an indicator that something was very wrong. You had one hell of a problem outside the gates, and the fact *Anaconda* was constantly being peppered with mortars told me our shadowy insurgent foes weren't too far away, probably within a few miles. After the rounds hit, air raid sirens would go off for a few minutes to let everyone know the base was now "under attack." What a morale killer that was; having an alarm go off *after* some harassment fire that got everyone riled up, freezing all movement on or off post for a good ten minutes, and pinning down soldiers wherever they might be, to include the PX and chow hall—the two largest, most concentrated targets on base. Meanwhile the insurgency was laughing their collective ass off at the thought of the commotion they've been allowed to raise, made worse with our ridiculous alarms letting them know they've hit their mark.

And now for the worst part. Balad Airbase and the surrounding areas were some of the least populated places in Iraq. With a lot of open fields, palm groves and rolling hills, it was a "movement to contact" (read "search and destroy") paradise. No cities, no open desert; just a lot of trees, fields and hiding places—an ideal perch for our enemy, but a hell of a great place to hunt them, too. It was the most conventional battleground scenario within 50 miles.

However, instead of letting them into the surrounding hills to hunt these mortar teams, the military police assigned to Balad Airbase were given the most important task of all—traffic control. They'd be handing out tickets and telling people to put their seatbelts on. The post commander, Command Sergeant Major Dan Elder, wanted to show "there are still risks associated with operating motor vehicles without the proper safety gear and seat restraints." [52] Whatever you say, you jackass administrator.

---

52 MSG Jack Gordon (Public Affairs Acquisition Team, USAR), *Better Watch Out…Anaconda MPs Conducting Traffic Safety Checks*, Army Reserve Magazine, Winter 2004-05

What an abhorrent waste of manpower, equipment and talent—hundreds of motivated young troops, pulsating with the primal urge to seek and destroy those bastards shooting rockets into our post and wreaking havoc on the biggest logistical area in Iraq, being assigned traffic duty. They were pulling the figurative plug on the slowly dying morale of *Anaconda's* military units. Even worse, good people—American troops, contractors and Iraqi interpreters—were being dismembered or killed weekly by insurgents who should have been cut in half by a barrage of hot American lead months ago.

There *was* an armor battalion and a Black Hawk unit tasked to respond to mortar attacks; *Anaconda* even had the coveted counter battery radar. However the conventional approaches of the tankers made it too easy for insurgents to pick up on their patterns. *Anaconda* had an active airfield that made it dangerous to dispatch helicopters quickly, and the understandable safety precautions that accompanied the launch of a Black Hawk took several minutes.

Months later, I read an article on the website of the late Colonel David "Hack" Hackworth—a military hero, gifted author and champion of soldier's rights—about "General Jimmie," General James E. Chambers, the commanding general of the 13th Corps Support Command at Balad. Shameful. The general was hardening his own trailer at *Anaconda* with huge concrete barriers a full two months before even 10% of the troops at Balad had any blast protection whatsoever.[53] Meanwhile, after a year in Iraq, most of the MPs and transpor-

---

53 David H. Hackworth, *Balad's General Jimmie*, from the *Defending America* archives, September 13, 2004, courtesy of *Soldiers for the Truth* and *DefenseWatch*, (www.sftt.org); the article can be found on Colonel Hackworth's website, www.hackworth.com/archive

tation units still couldn't get fully armored vehicles, and were sleeping in transient tents full of holes that offered no protection, not even from the rain.

It's what my old boss at American Express use to call "advanced rationalization:" focusing on something which was *somewhat* important and ignoring that which was *absolutely critical*. We've lost far more soldiers to mortars in Iraq than to on-post traffic accidents. But I guess the MPs were better off pulling people over who were going a little too fast or weren't, God forbid, wearing their seatbelts.

And the mortars just kept on coming.

After a few missions north, we'd developed a pretty good strategy on how to carry out these escorts. We kept up the safety briefs, got to know our drivers, refined our actions on contact, started carrying extra weapons that weren't being used by other squads, and went over which trucks we could ditch if we had to (some were carrying ammunition and water, others DVDs and magazines; guess which one we wouldn't be defending?). We'd already been hit a few times—a couple of RPGs and small arms attacks, nothing too bad—and were dealing with it well. We'd adjusted.

Around the end of June that year, CFLCC decided the ratio of MP vehicles to trucks escorted was to be 1 to 4. One MP truck to every four vehicles was a good balance. However in our experience, it would be ideal to have at least four MP vehicles for each convoy, meaning there would be at least 16 escorted trucks on each trip. A bigger target, yes, but with four MP teams, we felt much more comfortable—I'd much rather have four MP teams than three.

First, the firepower was overwhelming. Ten MPs carry

more weaponry than an infantry squad, and we'd be able to achieve fire superiority in an ambush that much more quickly. Yes, it's not always the deciding factor, but it just felt better to have more guns. And second, there was the mobility factor. If one MP vehicle broke down or was damaged, which was happening on average every other mission, it could be towed without taking too much away from the ability to at least defend ourselves. There was no tow truck service on the Iraqi highways; we recovered our own vehicles. So if one broke down, another MP vehicle would be the one to tow it. One damaged truck would, in essence, destroy the effectiveness of two. There had already been a steady stream of reports of convoys being so badly hit it took *hours* to get them moving again, some on the very roads we were traveling. When you could well find yourself with a destroyed Humvee (often full of weapons and gear), a crippled semi tractor trailer, troops understandably dazed both by explosions and the fact people were trying to kill them, *and* tending to casualties, it made for one hell of a mess. And it was happening, on average, at least once per day. With convoys trained to keep moving in the event of an ambush, the thought of three teams slugging it out in an ambush on Baghdad's mean streets as their trucks sped on was even more troubling.

With three trucks, given our breakdown ratio, we were looking at the possibility of having only one combat effective MP vehicle for those escort missions requiring three MP teams. Not a good situation. For the basic safety of these convoys, we needed at least four.

Around mid July, CFLCC decided the roads around Iraq were now "safer," and the ratio was dropped to 1 to 5. I don't know how they'd know that; most of the people making these decisions had never even been in Iraq. Worse yet, they decided

15 trucks would be the limit for each convoy. However we'd go on to work out side deals with the convoy commanders to shift some loads around and get the 16 vehicles when crossing into consistently dangerous territory. On the more hazardous missions, those being anything north of Baghdad International Airport, we'd have our four trucks.

We weren't asking for much. We had the assets. We'd gladly do more escorts than planned, and we'd go further north than anticipated, but we needed to use some common sense in planning these things. Keep the ratio, but up the convoy limit. Again, rear-echelon leaders in Kuwait were calling the shots; they never even ran it past us. No "Hey MPs; you've been on the road, every day, for over a year, doing *exactly* this kind of work. What do you think?" Nothing. And the response from our battalion? The faint sound of chirping crickets and tumbleweed blowing in the wind. Not a word.

The gravity of our potential problems really hit me while on our third escort mission, barely three weeks into our extension. Traveling roughly 150 yards behind the lead Humvee with over 20 trucks in our convoy, I watch in horror as an RPG screamed out from an alleyway on the northwest edge of Baghdad towards one of our Humvees. Seconds later, it smashed into the road and exploded just behind our lead vehicle, its ghostly-white smoke trail the only thing that remained of it.

If that RPG was fired a half a second earlier, it would have hit the driver's side door and most likely killed everyone inside the lead Humvee. With three MP trucks, I started to think how screwed we'd be if one of our Humvees was hit and needed to be towed out. With two teams struggling to secure the downed truck, there would be effectively one MP team fighting if we were hit. Three men. Not very comforting, and that's *without* any injuries.

This very scenario was beginning to kill a lot of people in Iraq.

CHAPTER 11

"Transportation is a precise business."

Jason Statham as *Frank Martin*
The Transporter

Our main route north from Kuwait, skirted the town of Safwan (just over the border of Kuwait and Iraq), and ran well west of Basrah and east of Iskandariyah and Hillah. It shot straight up and across the open desert through some of the most barren parts in Iraq. In other words, the perfect route—not a soul for miles, for literally fifty miles. The desert was a three-day walk in almost every direction.

As you approached Baghdad from the south, there were some bridges and overpasses, what military planners call "key terrain" because of their importance to Army operations. There weren't too many of them, and if one of those bridges was destroyed, you could forget about going north on that road. You'd be forced to take one of three or four other much more dangerous alternate routes, often dirt roads through troubled towns (like the ones we took on our first mission). You can see what I'm leading into.

Insurgents destroyed a key bridge on our main supply route in April of 2004, shutting down all movement north into Baghdad and Fallujah. Worse, it was blown up less than a half mile from a military outpost. Of course, with the Army's predictable, reactive nature, only *then* were key bridges and intersections protected.

Meanwhile, the Marines in our old stomping grounds in Al Anbar were doing things a bit differently, at least as far as mobility support was concerned. They'd learned from our mistakes. After we left in the spring, instead of waiting for the next IED or ambush from an intersection (or for a bridge to be taken out), they put Marines *on* the roads, *on* these bridges and *on* the key terrain. Backed up by tanks, Humvees and foot patrols, they constantly surveyed the main supply routes. They were protecting terrain instead of doing what the Army was often guilty of; concentrating their fighting forces on a big post and then taking their chances when traveling outside the gates. Of course, you can't defend every inch of road, but the Marines did all they could, and they did what they had to do. The results were very impressive and predictable; far fewer IEDs were being emplaced, and a lot of the insurgent teams were meeting their makers on the dimly lit roads around Fallujah.

One of the most dangerous was the "cloverleaf," a major intersection at the northeast edge of Fallujah, notorious for its frequent attacks. Units traveling to and from Baghdad up until then had been constantly bombarded by ambushes in and around the place. Even worse, after the 82nd Airborne left Fallujah, a disturbing discovery was made, just off of the roads in and around the cloverleaf.

Just after the Marines relieved the 82nd, they uncovered

caches of weapons *and food*, complete with trenches, mere yards off of the main highway. The U.S. Army, using another tool from their infinite arsenal of reactive ideas, allowed our enemy to live, work and plan (as well as eat) right there near the road. The Marines decided instead to park a few units right on top of it. Needless to say, few attacks occurred in that part of town from then on.

Months later, CFLCC got the brilliant idea—"in order to confuse our enemies"—to start alternating the routes they were using to travel north. If there were a hundred different roads heading to our varying destinations, this may have done some good. But we only had *three total routes*. Three. If we weren't on one, all it took was a simple process of elimination by our enemy as to where we'd eventually be. It wasn't rocket surgery. The fact that a bridge on main supply route *Tampa* was down narrowed the choices even further. Our lives, yet again, were in the hands of unqualified planners who were naively oversimplifying a very complex tactical environment.

To no one's surprise, it didn't take long for the insurgency to figure out what was going on. Convoy attacks and casualties began to climb, and the command elements in Kuwait were letting it happen. The sheer tonnage of men, material and vehicles that had to go to the military posts in and around Baghdad was staggering. Varying routes would only serve to spread our forces thinner and put greater strain on convoy security. It was simple math. But somehow this asinine rationale was supposed to "trick" the insurgency into thinking, what, we had stopped sending convoys? That we were one step ahead of them? That we'd somehow fly under their radar? Trying to sneak us down a road that was rarely patrolled and in no shape to handle heavy trucks was going to fool someone?

Just fix the fucking bridge already.

Bad guys were everywhere in Iraq, not just around major supply routes. All it took was a guy on a cell phone placing a call to a couple of his friends ready with an IED or rocket propelled grenade to confirm our route. For Chrissake, we saw them all the time outside of these bigger logistical posts, the ones with few active combat units, yakking away on their phones to someone. Again, right in our driveway. However in this case, we could only do so much. I couldn't go around killing people on cell phones. We reported it back to the post and simply hoped someone was paying attention.

In our case, it was usually a road near Baqubah, one that was rarely used by the U.S. military and miles from any type of support. With narrow roads filled with twists, turns and piles of rocks on the shoulder, they were insurgent playgrounds. So good in fact, it was probably where they took their new guys to train. I shudder to think what would have happened if the Iraqi resistance was more prepared for our arrival on our first mission. With four MP teams and some truckers, having no real contact with support, we'd have a tough time fighting off any organized ambush. We'd be gone for days before anyone besides our own command checked the paperwork and noticed we were missing.

The Army recklessly left its main routes unsecured, and the units forced to travel Iraq's roads were paying the price for it daily. For crying out loud, we were receiving reports IEDs were even being found strapped to the HESCO barriers on main supply route *Tampa*. [54] Carelessly left behind by American

---

54 The *Hercules Engineering Solutions Consortium* (HESCO) Barrier was often used for blast protection at checkpoints, at the front gates of major military posts, and in populated troop areas (i.e., surrounding mess halls and sleeping quarters). For MSR checkpoints, they would be staggered on opposite

military units manning traffic control posts, the unguarded barriers provided the perfect lair for an IED. Military vehicles maneuvering their way through the tight, S-shaped roadblock created by the reinforced concrete barriers were slowed to a crawl. An IED rigged to the inner walls of a HESCO could explode *inches* away from Coalition soldiers, moving at about five miles per hour around the very walls meant to protect them. Again, we were aiding the insurgency with our inexcusable negligence, furnishing them with ambush points literally of our own making.

If we were not able or willing to send another 25,000 troops to guard and patrol all of the roads we were using for supply travel, we needed to *choose a route and fucking own it*. My God, we were playing right into the enemy's hands. But even worse, the movement control staff just didn't have the courage to explore and know the routes they were sending thousands of soldiers on every day, relying on second-hand intelligence to guide their recommendations. I mean, convoy movement was *big* business in Iraq in April of 2004. Supplies were at critical lows due to all of the attacks: gunners couldn't find .50 caliber bullets, units were running out of fresh water, Humvees needed parts, and fuel was at a premium. Stuff just wasn't getting into Iraq from Kuwait. The tours of thousands of soldiers had been extended for this specific purpose, and it wasn't being taken seriously. As I have said many, many times before—and this was the doctrine by which we survived in Iraq—we were responsible for our own safety and security.

---

sides of the road, forcing oncoming traffic to slowly snake their way through an "S" shaped lane. Consisting of wire and burlap baskets filled with reinforced concrete or sand, standing about 3 feet high, they were designed to protect soldiers by containing the blast and absorbing the shrapnel from an exploding artillery round or car bomb (www.hesco.com)

CHAPTER 12

"I'm the guy who does his job. You must be the other guy."

Mark Wahlberg as *Sergeant Dignam*
The Departed

One of the best soldiers in my unit, SGT Eric Giles, summed our situation up best when he mentioned something he'd read scrawled on a Porto-potty wall, often a source for simplistic virtue: "*Do you remember the days in the Army when people did their jobs?*"

I hadn't been in the Army long enough to really know if this was true or not, but one thing was becoming painfully obvious; some soldiers wouldn't do their part in this war if it meant even the slightest threat to their own safety. In some jobs, simply showing up was half the battle. This wasn't one of them. Simply arriving at your workplace was all well and good if you were the night watchman at a library, but you weren't going to cut it as a soldier.

Or were you? Too many people had been let off the hook

by this point in our deployment. Maybe it was the result of the common belief that service in the Army wasn't so much for Duty, Honor, and Country as it was a way to pay for school, or to make a little extra cash on the weekends. We all like to think we're "serving" by joining the military; but after all the oaths, drill & ceremony, cool gear and target practice, this is where the rubber met the road. Do you have the guts to do your job for the mission at hand, and for the man or woman next to you?

Maybe it stemmed from the fact the military, for the past decade, often over-rewarded people who simply came to work. It was becoming clearer to me that too many leaders in Iraq were gladly placing someone's life in danger if it meant less risk to their own. And as long as those leaders were producing something—anything—no one higher up the chain would expect anything more. There was no accountability for those who didn't want to step up to the plate and get their hands dirty, maybe with the exception of this book and others like it. There were too few leaders looking to take action where it really counted. The MCTs at *Scania* were proving that in spades.

Simply being in Iraq was dangerous, but some were in much more vulnerable positions than others. As I said before, we all took our chances with the occasional mortar round or rocket while on post, but the guys on the roads and towns were bearing the brunt of the casualties. A lot of soldiers were not serving in ultra-risky positions, and that was perfectly fine—every military occupation plays a role in combat. But that's the key word: serving. Some just didn't want to put in the time, to be all they could be, at their particular task. That wasn't sitting well with me. It's still doesn't, as young kids and brave troops continue to pay the price for another's lack of work ethic, foresight and courage. The inaction of one could easily mean the death of another ten.

For those who did all they could for the war efforts in Iraq and Afghanistan; who engaged in the conflict and learned how to do things better, who made it their mission in life to give 100% in saving troops and defeating our enemy, and who might have gladly given a portion of their sanity in these efforts, thank you. If we ever meet, you'll never pay for another drink for the rest of your life. You have my eternal gratitude for your service, and you know who you are.

For those of you who didn't; who performed your work barely to standard, who checked the box for your own career, and who let others pay the price for your lack of courage, fucking kill yourself. The world will be that much better off without you, and the U.S. military that much more efficient moving forward. Best yet, young soldiers won't have to die for your complacency and cowardice.

You know who you are, too.

The return trip from *Anaconda* sent us through the northern and western edges of Baghdad, some dicey areas where several attacks were taking place several times each week. Trusting our experience, knowledge and discipline would carry the day, we drove vigilantly through Baghdad, keeping our distance from each other, trying our best to make ourselves a low-yield target in our defensive task.

However, we all knew that all of the tactical skill, experience and luck in the world wasn't going to save us from a guy in a car with a hundred pounds of explosives in his trunk and the will to die. Some things were simply left to chance. Given the fact we had made it this far without incident, and that some other units had lost men and women *within a few days* of being in Iraq, I was convinced somebody's number was up. We were heavily armed, seasoned professionals by this point and would probably win in a firefight, but that wasn't the point. It was the problem. Our enemy didn't fight that way. A passing car was going to explode, blasting me into a million pieces, and I wouldn't feel a thing. Or I'd watch helplessly as one of my own teams was blown into the next world by a violent fireball, leaving nothing but two charred, smoldering wrecks on the side of the road.

In the rush to get supplies moving north, it was apparent no leader in the 375th Transportation Group in Kuwait—the element of the military that had found itself on the front lines of this war almost overnight—was taking the time to re-prioritize shipments. If they were, they were terrible at it. Our second mission had us shipping Humanitarian Daily Rations, those small meals wrapped in yellow plastic, for the Iraqis. Sure it was a nice gesture, but not exactly critical. In my estimation, they were simply clearing out some unwanted crap from their storage areas, but when it came to the business end of logistics, once the huge gears were put into motion, they were very difficult to stop or alter. Schedules had been made, and a massive amount of goods, vehicles and manpower had been committed to the task of moving this stuff into Iraq. The tactical situation was changing by the minute, but the method by which we supplied the troops hadn't changed in years.

Again, most of the planners had no vested interest in triaging the materials we were taking into Iraq. They wouldn't be the ones shipping it. Just load it onto the flatbed and the MPs and truck drivers will risk their lives to move it. Check the box and *get 'er done*—one of the stupidest damn sayings I've ever heard, and one perfectly representing the reckless attitude of the Transportation Group. As long as convoys were moving north, everything was hunky-dory.

In October of 2004, someone finally put their foot down. Some of you might remember reading about the 343rd Quartermaster Company who, upon discovering they'd be hauling contaminated fuel, told the Transportation Group they weren't going anywhere. Their equipment was a mess, and so was the TG's ability to plan anything other than their own dinners. What you heard was only the tip of the iceberg.

A policy came down from Combined Joint Task Force 7 just after our first mission that neither the Transportation Group or MPs would transport or escort any *rolling stock*; equipment with wheels that could be driven on its own. It took a while for the order to be issued, but I understood why. The Coalition was getting used to the conditions around Iraq, and was moving as fast as they could. After a few weeks, they decided it wasn't worth the dangers for extended units to transport new, state-of-the-art equipment with broken trucks like ours. Good news for us, and a smart move to boot.

However, thanks to the ignorance of our Transportation Group leaders, we ended up shipping, among other things, the coveted "up-armored" Humvees to units in Baghdad. The up-armored hummers were considered rolling stock, and it didn't make much sense to escort them with our ailing equipment. But at least soldiers were getting the equipment they needed, serving in much more dangerous places than we were, and more often.

It wasn't the fact we were escorting better equipment to soldiers who needed it. For Chrissake, the guys patrolling Sadr City were in a much worse position than we were. They were battling it out every day in some of Baghdad's worst neighborhoods, and we had a Starbucks in Kuwait. It was the fact the transportation staff, once again, didn't give a shit about us or any other soldiers in their own command. Why weren't they following CJTF7's directive concerning the rolling stock? These units up north had plenty of rear detachment personnel—soldiers living in Kuwait who supported their units with additional duties—who were more than qualified to take this equipment directly to them. You have a gun and can drive a truck, right? Well grab your gear and move out!

The ammunition, the food, the diesel fuel: we'd gladly take that stuff to where it was needed. However there was no reason we should be taking this new equipment into Iraq. After asking why the Transportation Group wasn't making any progress in getting combat units to move their own equipment, they were telling us they'd hit some dead ends. I feared it a nominal attempt on their part, at best.

The staffers in Transportation had it made. They didn't give a damn about the guys and gals on the road. When we went to them with even the most *basic*, critical requests, the response was more of the same; that infuriating "Hey, we gave it our best shot and lost, so I guess it's okay to give up now" attitude we were growing so used to. In their eyes, we were just a bunch of whining brats.

In mine, they were traitors. Once in a while we'd make the trip down to *Camp Arifjan*, the massive Army post in Kuwait where most of the transportation leadership was housed. The place was a ghost town after 5 p.m. every day. I couldn't find anyone. We were in a 24/7 war, and yet everyone had gone home for the night, their lights off and offices locked.

I kept trying to think of what I was going to say to the parents of one of my 18-year-old soldiers if they were killed escorting these up-armored Humvees with our crappy, 1987 model trucks that had to be repaired every other day, with turrets so rusted they couldn't spin right, and often couldn't keep up with the trucks we were protecting. Just shut your mouth and drive; no one wanted to hear about your problems. The only thing that matters is keeping things moving on a tidy schedule. To Hell with safety and logic.

Don't worry about the MPs who had up-armored Humvees stationed at the safest base in Iraq, and who wouldn't be held accountable for lying about patrolling or marking convoy routes. Disregard the ruling from *the* authority in Iraq that said no rolling stock would be escorted. Don't concern yourself with the rows and rows of up-armored Humvees sitting idle in Kuwait, waiting to be moved north, some for months at a time. Go ahead and forget about the young drivers with the Transportation, Maintenance or Quartermaster Corps who were still waiting for their truck cabs to be armored. Try not to think of the kids who would be shredded by IEDs or RPGs because their vehicles were in such disrepair and lacked even basic spare parts. Ignore the fact there were hundreds of up-armored Humvees still parked unused in Kosovo, barely being used in a much less dangerous mission.

The 375th didn't bother to put up even a token fight in anyone's defense. These were the men and women we were depending on for our lives, legislating their rules and schedules from an office in one of the safest places in the world.

Sometimes a troop has to "suck it up" in less than ideal conditions. Totally fine, I get it. For example, when we first arrived at Hit in May of 2003, we didn't have the Interceptor Body Armor we were promised, but the 94th had missions and had to make due. Instead, I wore a standard issue police vest with a ceramic plate in the chest pocket, underneath my outdated flak jacket. A couple of older vests strapped to my back were better than nothing. It was early on in the war and, understandably, errors in judgment had been made. No one knew what to expect, and we were aware of the logistical restrictions of the U.S. military. You got over it, and did your best. Our troops improvised, adapted and overcame.

But now here we were, almost a full 14 months after the end of the actual ground war, still dealing with this shit. Enough was enough.

After the 343rd Quartermaster Company refused their order to move north, *Anaconda*'s own "General Jimmie" would eventually go on to lead the investigation.[55]

God help us all.

Every day of our extension was the same. No matter how we tried to remedy our situation, every day we woke up to the same thing, over, and over, and over. It was like our own personal *Groundhog Day*.

Each MP leader, after returning from an escort mission, would submit an *After Action Review*. In short, it was a brief explanation of the mission, with what went right and what went wrong, and suggestions for improvement. Each review, about three per week, was forwarded to the 375th's commander, Colonel Cory Youmans. However after a few weeks, it was obvious they weren't being addressed. A later meeting would end up proving they weren't even being read.

---

55 Regarding the condition of the quartermaster vehicles being used in their escorts, Brigadier General James E. Chambers was quoted as saying, "Not all of their trucks are completely armored. In their case, they haven't had the chance to get armored." (Source: CBS News National Security Correspondent David Martin and the Associated Press, *Refusing Reservists Face Charges*, November 16, 2004).

It came to the point where we asked for—better yet, demanded—more action on the part of our battalion commander, Lieutenant Colonel Rosado. Godammit old man, talk to Youmans and fight for us! Seriously, we were being bent over the barrel here on a daily basis, and some very significant concerns were being tossed aside. It was becoming so problematic, MP officers or senior non commissioned officers were continuously called upon to step in and lead convoys after discovering some of the more incompetent transportation commanders would be in charge.

Two in particular were a major and a captain from the 1175th Transportation Company. The major was a renegade cowboy-type who was convinced he was the best thing to happen to convoy security. After one of the worst prep speeches I had ever heard—on his first mission, mind you—he went on to give some horrendous tactical advice: everyone just stay as close together as you can.

He was saying, in essence, make yourself a larger target. That always works, right?

He didn't notice the almost exclusive use of car bombs and IEDs against American patrols and convoys. Given the fact we were working on very busy roads in and around Baghdad, where it was impossible to control the flow of traffic given our assets, vehicles following his advice would be a perfect target. Vehicles too close together were at risk for just about any type of attack, but spreading out a bit enabled all units to keep a watchful eye over a greater area, to support each other with direct fire if any of us were hit. An MP team, if out of the kill zone anyway, could reach out and touch someone with some serious firepower and protect a downed truck until we figured something out. Anyone with a crew-served weapon could. I went to speak with him afterward about it and got the usual

"I've been here two months and I know what I'm doing" reply. I went on to respectfully explain our experience and how we'd never lost a soldier in our escorts (I looked for wood to knock on, but found none). After all, he was new and I was willing to give him some room. It's not as if I wanted to make him look like an idiot in front of his own guys. We had more discretion than that, if just barely. Still, he just wouldn't budge.

After giving him a couple of likely "oh shit" scenarios, I asked him what he would expect from the MPs. Jesus, I did not like the answers he gave, something about "blasting them to Hell." Here we go again, with that simplistic Hollywood kill 'em all routine. At that point in the Iraq war, an ounce of prevention was worth about 5 tons of cure.

I was convinced he wouldn't last long, and he didn't. He was hit by a Humvee in southern Iraq, driven by one of his own men in some stupid accident that could have been prevented. He ended up being okay, but as the MEDEVAC chopper flew out with his battered body, I couldn't help but feel relieved he was out of our hair.

The captain from the 1175th was just a fucking bonehead; falling asleep for hours during the convoys, forgetting to fuel vehicles before moving out, and allowing no time for his soldiers to eat or rest. He possessed no redeeming qualities that anyone could think of. I was so pleased we shared the same rank, and that my men and women were forced to salute him each day.

We had to do something to protect our guys and gals who were continually at the mercy of these people. We were continually hearing reports about other convoys and patrols being hit all around our escorts near Baghdad. However, with the steps we were taking, we weren't experiencing nearly the same level of activity. We were either incredibly fortunate or we were doing something right. Not wanting to chalk everything up to luck, we knew we were making good decisions on the road. We'd recon by fire into known ambush areas, an art we perfected during our audacious night patrols through Ramadi and Hit. We spread our vehicles out to just within small arms range of each other, offering better protection and making us a less desirable target. We constantly scanned our frequencies for air assets who could do a quick flyover of our route. We radioed ahead to maneuver units already in the area and let them know we were coming through. And we always took charge of our situation.

It wasn't always enough. With so many escorts, it was impossible to have an MP officer or senior non commissioned officer on all of them to keep them running somewhat trouble-free. The junior officers were doing all they could with some success, but there were too many flagrant abuses of even the most commonsensical security procedures. Our commander, Dave Bentley, the well-mannered boy from Worcester who kept his cool in even the most trying situations to date, was furious. He decided to sit down with the platoon leaders and draft up an MP "Bill of Rights" to be used while on convoy escort. Quite simply, it was a list of safety and security rules, to be signed by Lieutenant Colonel Rosado, that could be used by our leadership to stop any serious safety violation (which we went on to define) being committed by a transportation NCO or officer. The Department of the Army had extended us over a year in Iraq only to hand us over to the most thoroughly inept commanders in the military, who were unable to provide these convoys with the security they were in such desperate need of. If we were extended to defend these vehicles, we would do just that. No more dicking around. From now on, we were going to take control over *every* safety aspect of *every* convoy. Period.

As we drafted our Bill, we learned later some of our worst fears were confirmed. There were actually informal contests being conducted between transportation units as to who could perform the mission the fastest. I don't have to tell you the endless possibilities to get yourself killed acting like this. I'm all for speed, but when that kind of practice starts to influence the way you do business in the most lethal towns in the Middle East—places that could end your life in the blink of an eye—someone has to put an end to it. Another transportation unit had already lost a lieutenant that way; after trying to take a shorter route south around the city of Hillah, a thoroughly rotten town south of Baghdad, the commander made a wrong turn, a mistake that put the entire convoy in the center of the city. Insurgents were waiting, the road blocked with a large tractor. They were ambushed, and one of "OIF 2.0's" most massive firefights ensued in the downtown area. When I read the report in Kuwait, I thought the number was a typo: there were an estimated 40 rocket propelled grenade rounds fired by the enemy in that engagement alone.

Shot in the leg, their convoy commander, a lieutenant, managed to drive his vehicle out of the kill zone just before bleeding to death. He left behind a pregnant wife, due in a few months.

CHAPTER 13

"You're such a coward. I can't believe they let you wear a uniform."

Wolfgang Bodison as *Lance Corporal Harold Dawson*
A Few Good Men

On yet another unworldly hot Kuwaiti afternoon in mid-July 2004, Colonel Youmans decided to call a "town meeting" of his own to talk over some issues between the MPs and transportation. We were finally going to get to the bottom of this mess. Youmans took center stage under one of *Udari*'s massive recreation tents and got the ball rolling.

"I hear we're having some problems."

I have to give him credit. It took a lot of nuts to get up in front of a hundred or so MPs from four different companies and get hammered by just about everyone. However, it was an excellent forum to air our grievances, and better yet, put this guy on the spot. Of course, a few troops who didn't know any better went on to spout off a few ridiculous, shortsighted questions, like "Why were we extended and others got to go home?," questions the colonel couldn't possibly have an answer for. The decision to extend us was made by people well above his pay grade, but questions about our vehicles, equipment and missions were brought up time and time again. I had one, too.

"Why am I hearing some of your convoy commanders are having 'contests' to see who can get home the fastest?"

I received a curt, but polite, "That's not the first time I've heard that."

I asked him what the plan was. He said he'd look into it. We also asked why we hadn't even been given a courtesy reply to the issues we'd brought up in our *After Action Reviews*. The colonel casually remarked no such reports had reached his office.

My heart pounded. I saw red, and had to walk out.

The only thing we wanted from the sea of people between the soldiers leading the convoys and the colonel was to pass up a few fucking pieces of paper; well organized, thought-out summaries of what was happening on the roads around Iraq. It was much worse than I thought. Either the colonel was derelict in his duty, or our battalion was. I was starting to think they both were.

I did feel a bit better having at least talked to Colonel Youmans *directly* about what was going on with these escorts. We must have said something right. About a week before we were to leave, the infamous problem captain was relieved of duty, and the injured major was given a harmless staff job, which I'm sure he went on to fuck up. On behalf of all the great soldiers who would end up working for the 1175th, thank you for putting up with what I would reasonably consider some of the worst leadership I've ever seen in both my business and military careers. Ever. Just spineless, robotic zombies. It's almost as if they wanted to fail, or were actively trying to lose. I was in Iraq's version of *The Twilight Zone*.

Dave and I went to Rosado with our little Bill of Rights a few days later, and gave him a rundown of what we thought the best courses of action would be if the transportation convoy commanders couldn't keep their shit together on the road. We took it a step further and pretty much told our new MP Battalion to put up or shut up. In a meeting with the battalion executive officer, I insisted a member of the staff accompany us on our next escort, to witness *personally* the ridiculous decisions being made by the "leadership" of the Transportation Group. It was tough, time and time again, as junior officers like me and Dave tried talking directly with Colonel Youmans about what was going on out on the roads, only to be summarily ignored. Sometimes on the road, it simply came down to rank. We were being ignored by this command, and now we had proof our trip reviews weren't even being read. Here was the perfect opportunity for our battalion to get involved, to do more than hang out in their tents all day and pass along missions to the MPs. Their presence on the road could potentially make a large difference in the way we could do business and would no doubt save lives. On top of it all, it would give us a much-needed morale booster.

I asked the 125th's executive officer point-blank if he'd come out with us on our next mission, so he could get a first-hand feel as to the problems we faced. After some tough guy talk from the staff about what they'd do if they were in our shoes, no one stepped up to the plate and volunteered to come along with us. No one was willing to go. No one.

Not *one* member of that battalion went with us the entire time we were there, not even the lower-ranking officers who actually planned our missions and heard our concerns. The higher-ranking officers, charged to protect our basic interests, folded. Absolutely disgraceful. It was a stomach-turning brand of counterfeit leadership I never thought I'd see in the U.S. military. Now we knew just what kind of armchair warriors we were working with.

Way to stand up for the cause, ladies and gentlemen. It wasn't a *specific* requirement of your job, so I guess you're off the hook. However it *was* an implied task of your career, the one you began by raising your right hand and taking an oath, as you took responsibility for the safety and men and women in your care.

I hope you can look yourself in the mirror every day, because I sure as hell wouldn't be able to.

Good luck guarding Puerto Rico.

A few weeks later after our little shake-up, we were getting somewhere by working with other MP units experiencing the same concerns. Better yet, the transportation guys and MPs were beginning to understand one another.

With that said, I definitely don't want to make all of these truckers sound like little punks. Most of the drivers had shown real courage and were a pleasure to work with. We'd spend a lot of our down time together and had gotten to know quite a few of these brave young men and women who were, like us, doing the best they could with what they had. A few we spoke with were involved in that ambush in Hillah with some of the 1st Armored Division's elements a few months back, and had fought so heroically they were awarded the combat patch by the division commander, even though they weren't officially attached to his command. That didn't happen every day. I just wished they hadn't wound up there in the first place.

However some didn't fit that description, and it was worse than just not "getting along." It was bad enough that we started barking a little louder at our battalion leadership, demanding more action on their part. There was a light at the end of the tunnel, as our redeployment looked more and more definite with each passing day. And even if these changes weren't going to take effect during our tour, we'd lay down the tracks for other MP units after the 94th left theater.

The battalion was taking supplies from Kuwait to most of the larger cities in Iraq—Fallujah, Najaf, Tikrit, Taji, Baghdad and Ramadi—driving thousands of miles on each mission in an effort to reclaim the roads and get supplies moving to our men and women fighting horrid urban battles. Our average mission mileage was more than 1000 miles; that was like driving from New York City to Toledo, Ohio and back. Our teams were coming in for a day's rest, and then heading out for another week or so on the roads.

Worse yet, at about the two-month mark of our extension, CJTF 7 decided to cut two MP companies from their command and send them home. Why did they release these companies—over 300 MP soldiers—from the roster at such a critical time in this conflict? Convoys needed protection, and these two companies were extremely valuable assets. Worse, we'd been in-country much longer. We were driving into battle space on a daily basis and were dependent on the patrols. Dave contacted some higher-ups and poked around for answers. No one knew why the units had been released. On top of being a serious tactical mistake, it was the first real indicator CJTF 7 and the Coalition Forces Land Component Command weren't talking with each other.

There had to be a good reason behind the decision, but at this stage of the game, I wasn't so sure there was.[56]

---

[56] Allegedly, the two MP units were released early due to the demands of a state Senator back in the United States.

CHAPTER 14

"Next time you get a bright idea just put it in a memo."

Alec Baldwin as *Jack Ryan*
The Hunt for Red October

Our time in Kuwait wasn't without its sick comedy. There we were, in the spring and summer of 2004, in one of the biggest crises of the war. Insurgent bravado was at an all time high. Convoy attacks were becoming more frequent and more intense. Soldier morale was dropping exponentially by the day, and we had no real control of our tactical environment. The answer from our brave commanders leading the way? More memos. Throw more paper at our troops!

In the middle of all of this, instead of dealing with the growing problems with these Iraqi-bound convoys, we received memo after memo from everyone but Santa Claus about what we should or shouldn't be doing on post or on the roads. My personal favorite: *If any soldier is preparing to drive a military vehicle in just a T-shirt under their bulletproof vest* (meaning their camouflage uniform top was removed), *that convoy is not to leave the post.*

Oh yeah? Make me.

I didn't want my guys in their boxers and a pair of sneakers, but when it's over 130 degrees Fahrenheit in a Humvee, leadership should cut some slack for the sake of soldiers' comfort. For crying out loud, these trips often ran in excess of ten hours. Some jackass who'd never ventured out of his or her air-conditioned office during the day, who was outside the wire *maybe* once a month, would make that decision for us. Fine! Then I guess this convoy isn't going anywhere, is it? Another: *Off duty soldiers can't wear sleeveless shirts while on post.* And don't even *think* about taking a dump in the chemical toilet before reading this field sanitation memo.

The best one was compliments of our own 125th MP Battalion, from a command that had been in Kuwait less than three months and hadn't spent one day in Iraq: it was a memo requiring those MPs who were about to take their two-week vacations to write an explanation as to why they should be allowed to leave. At this point, a little more than half of our company had the chance to take some R&R. But a majority of the 94th, as well as the other MP companies in the battalion, had been in Iraq for over a year with no *mention* of a break. Between planning, preparing for, and actually going on missions, most hadn't had more than a few days off. The 125th were already sending their people on leave, and then had the nerve to ask our guys for a memo explaining why they thought they deserved to take a breather. Needless to say, some of the responses were hilarious and blatantly disrespectful. At that point, what in the world did we have to lose?

Less than three months into his tour, during one of the most challenging times the military police faced in the war so far, the command sergeant major of the 125th decided he needed a little time off and went home for two weeks. And you wonder why we didn't rely on anyone. We couldn't. This was the best the U.S. Army National Guard had to offer. Utterly pathetic.

And then things got worse.

About a month into our new mission, I got an email from Tom, one of our interpreters at the academy. It was only one line. That's all it needed to be.

They killed Captain Laith last night. I'm sorry.

Captain Laith Faaris, a man I had grown to admire and respect, a man who was the closest thing to an Iraqi brother I'd met, had been gunned down outside of Hit while traveling in his car with his cousins, who were also badly wounded. He'd been shot 18 times.

All of us knew an American who had been killed in action. It was always in the back of your mind someone you were close to, someone you might have just had lunch with, might be dead by the end of the day. It was something you simply got used to. But this was, for me, the most personal and upsetting look at what the Iraqi police and Army were going through every day; the danger they and their families faced, the personal sacrifices they made, the fragile trust they were helping to build. I began to really appreciate their situation when I was at the academy months before, where men lost their brothers, fathers and friends, went to their funerals, and came back the next day with tears still fresh in their eyes, ready to train and fight.

Laith was a friend, and in a lot of ways more of a soldier than anyone gave him credit for. He put in the courage and strength to lead his town, his province and his country in the right direction, standing up to these spineless men who threatened his new Iraq. I'll never forget him. Nor will I ever forget our sunset chats back at the train platform in Mohamadi and at the Hit police station, smoking cigarettes and talking about what we were going to do when the war was over.

He left behind a grieving wife and five-year old son, just like so many here in America. That night, for the first time since I was ten, I cried myself to sleep.

I would've liked nothing more than to see him again. Perhaps I will someday.

The unit was keeping up a high level of motivation and spirit since being delivered to Iraq in May of 2003, even after our first and second extensions. Everyone was performing so admirably, taking a bad situation and working through it with pure grit and fortitude. However, after more than a month working with the 375th and 125th, with all of the flagrant errors being committed on an hourly basis, our patience and good nature were long gone. The only thing that mattered now was getting everyone home alive. No one was going to die because of something we were able to prevent, no matter how difficult the task. We were fighting a purely defensive war at this point, and we were losing control of the way we could fight it. Back in Hit, at least we knew the police, we knew the roads, we had informants, and we recognized neighborhoods. We were zipping into town and grabbing targets, or cruising through Ramadi at night ready to blast some IED team to smithereens. Now, we rarely knew anything about the routes we were traveling on, with the exception of intelligence passed down from our own unit or the other MP companies in our command. Moreover, the men and women charged with our supervision weren't lifting a finger to help us. Something had to be done. It was the pivotal point in the deployment for me, for all of us. We were too close to the end.

If this is the way it was going to be, I didn't belong in today's military, certainly not with leaders like this. I had little to look forward to if I progressed through the ranks. At this point, if I lost my career defending my platoon against these half-wits, so be it. Let's get this shit over with now, and I'll take the court martial when this is all over. *If* I made it back, that is. I think all of us felt that way. Even our First Sergeant, Dennis Mawn, a man I didn't much care for at first but developed a grudging respect for, was losing his cool. Dennis had a level head, and his military bearing with our higher commands was remarkable. He usually knew how to talk to people to make them see things our way.

However these people were beyond talking to. If we found ourselves on the road again, with convoy commanders making stupid decisions, what was our recourse? We all came to the conclusion the potential disciplinary shitstorm was well worth it; we'd have to ignore these ludicrous tactical orders if we wanted to bring our men and women home in one piece. It wasn't as though we "somewhat disagreed" with a few of their judgment calls—their choices were just plain dangerous.

That decision separated the men from the boys. We all crammed together in our little four-man room one night; the platoon leaders, Dave, the first sergeant, and Master Sergeant Greg Carder. Most of us were in agreement something needed to be done. The one dissenter who stands out in my memory was Greg, and his argument was sickening: orders were to be followed, regardless of how thoughtless they were. Glaring at him, I asked how the fuck he could say something like that. His argument boiled down to this: if we lost troops, at least we wouldn't get into any more trouble with the military. My heart sank. It was the ultimate and most painful act of covering your own ass I'd ever seen. This wasn't a split-second, last-minute plan to grab Saddam. We were on a regular schedule of safeguarding cargo, some of it completely unnecessary, lead by officers who didn't even know who we were.

Greg hadn't once been on an escort during our extension. And although it wasn't his "job" to physically help us move these convoys north, he was a master sergeant and should have been looking out for his troops. He didn't do what he needed to do when it really mattered. As is the case with thousands of other complacent, single-minded soldiers just like him, he was clearly part of the problem, not the solution.

We weren't defenseless by any means, but our whole situation was spinning beyond our control. More than a little uncomfortable with the complacency of both our new battalion and our transportation bosses, it was time to do something. We gave the word to the entire 94th they, alone, were in charge of all security matters on the road, with or without full approval from our own battalion or transportation leadership. The blame would come to rest with the 94th command, including myself, a decision I couldn't have been happier with. Besides, at that point, what's the worst that could happen? They'd send us to Iraq? Extend us twice? Give us this mission with the worst equipment and worst possible leadership?

There I was, putting my rank, my career and potentially my own freedom on the line. However, after this experience, what kind of career could I expect? And why would I want to protect it, only to take my chances of working under people like this again? What I had originally thought were a few isolated incidents of cowardice and idiocy was quickly becoming the norm. My superficial rank of *captain* was just that—my *rank*. It was a label. But my *role* was of an Army officer, and that had implications far beyond any rank or title I'd ever wear on my collar. My job—my life—for my time there was to defend my soldiers while completing a mission, not to be promoted to major. Fortunately, the leadership of the 94th saw it the same way.

Career progression in the military isn't always about your performance on the job. This comes as a big surprise for most readers, I'm sure. Far too many soldiers try to engineer a respectable profession by taking the path of least resistance, only to embellish their accomplishments with carefully crafted phrases and buzzwords on their reports. If everything went as planned, they'd get promoted. I understand the same tends to be true in a lot of careers in the civilian world, but in the military the bottom line is: performance talks and bullshit walks. But if the bullshit was talking in wartime, someone was going to wind up dead. No one cared if you "ensured a 100% participation rate" in some battalion training exercise, or "exceeded expectations during an annual inspection" if you didn't have any common sense when the shit hit the fan.

This abject self-interest serves no purpose in combat. War is a blinding spotlight that shines on your character, your courage and your capabilities. Flaws will eventually be exposed quickly, irreversibly, and sometimes violently. That is assuming, of course, you're actually engaged and fighting one.

I wasn't about to become one of those officers. Neither was Dave, nor Chris, nor Jim, nor Dean, nor the First Sergeant. They could have easily sat back in Kuwait and let their sergeants take those missions north, shrugging their shoulders and leaving them to duke it out with whatever asshole was leading the convoy that day. But they didn't. We went on to take those convoys ourselves and, on several occasions, defied the orders of several officers and senior enlisted who were making potentially fatal decisions. You want to take that more dangerous route to save a few hours? Good luck, you're going alone. You'd like to take a break right here, in the middle of nowhere, surrounded by rolling hills with no protection? Knock yourself out; we'll be up the road a few miles and taking ours near more defendable terrain. You're going to start screaming at my MPs during a convoy in front of everyone? I have a duffel bag *full* of plastic zip-tie handcuffs and we'd be more than happy to use them. And then we'll stuff you into said duffel bag for good measure. Just try us—we're right, you're wrong. We have nothing to lose but each other.

Fortunately, we never had to use the zip-ties.

One MP was lost during the extension; Specialist Craig Frank from the 1775th MP CO, Michigan National Guard. He was killed by an RPG near Baghdad. I'm unaware of any specific details of how it happened, but his girlfriend received word of his death on the same day his last letter to her arrived.

Clearly, I had never in a million years expected any of this to happen. I *never* expected to be fighting the leadership in my own Army like this. Never. Even the worst people I'd met in the Army, up to this point, were somewhat reliable. They'd usually do the right thing. However, I was beginning to understand there were plenty of people in the U.S. military who shouldn't be there. We were being forced to put our lives in the hands of individuals who were either totally asleep at the wheel, or just weren't putting in the effort. I sincerely believe we are the best military on Earth, and not simply because of the technology, weapons and spirit de corps. It's because of the thousands of lesser-known incidents of tremendous courage displayed by the young men and women in today's military. The stories in this book—while arguably more commonplace than not—far from sum up our entire experience, one filled with story after story of soldiers making sacrifices so willingly and critical decisions so adeptly, in every military specialty. It's because of guys and girls like that, the ones who continually adjust to changing conditions and find better ways to do things, why we win wars.

Simply put, it's because of the operators who exercise initiative, not the administrators who hide in their tents.

However, the polarization of duty, courage and common sense in this conflict was quickly coming to a head. It was a division that was representing the weakest link in our ability to conquer a very determined enemy, and the troops on the roads of Iraq were the ones paying the price. I felt like a gladiator fighting to earn my freedom, with those officers who owned me looking down from their privileged seats cheering for my success, if only for their own gains.

It was then that I started hearing a common theme in the advice most junior officers were giving me in our bitch sessions. Several, without fail, said I should "stay in, make some rank, and then you can change things." I used to be a big subscriber to that theory. After all, I was a captain, and had used my rank effectively to bring about some substantial changes. Hell, what did I have to lose? A lot of the men and women I was trained to respect and admire were turning out to be complete disappointments. And no amount of self-flattery laced with the latest military lingo could change the fact some leaders didn't have the balls to take charge where the Kevlar and rubber Humvee tires met the IED-filled road. Since most of the MP officers had been "in the shit," we could cash in some of this capital to force some action when we got back to the States. However, within minutes after leaving a meeting with Lieutenant General James

Helmly—the Chief of the Army Reserve—in July of 2004, my subscription to this theory was abruptly cancelled.

Now, here is *the* guy in charge of us, of the *entire* United States Army Reserve, standing here in Kuwait. He came specifically to speak with the Reserve Component, regarding both the conditions surrounding our deployment and his future plans for the Reserve system. A two-tour Vietnam veteran with the 101st Airborne Division, he'd done his time and qualified himself as a leader. Better yet, he spoke directly to us, and us only. His willingness to have a dialogue with the 94th showed us he understood exactly what Reserve units in combat were up against, and his speech confirmed it.

I'll never forget something he said to us in that meeting: his colleagues at the Pentagon and Washington D.C. were "often insensitive to the responsibilities of leadership." How fitting and true that statement was. Not only was it a strong argument against excessive political and civilian involvement in this conflict, it represented an institutional condition that, on a similar scale, was plaguing the planning and execution of convoy movements around Iraq. The "top men" in transportation and our own battalion were calling the shots with little knowledge of the situation on the ground, and worse yet, without the guts to find out. The constraints on the Reserve system, no matter how real or delusional they were, were working their way from the top down. And in our case, without a doubt, the chickens were coming home to roost.

General Helmly had some very smart plans on how to deal with the issues at hand, and with those that were sure to come up in the near future. He asked for our input, which we gladly and respectfully offered. We were way beyond whining about our extension; that was old news. Someone had to stay behind, and it just happened to be us. Tough luck, I guess. Anyway, with a somewhat concrete date when we'd be leaving theater, we were now looking at future deployments, equipment problems, training considerations, and promotions, to name a few. He had a solid reply to all of our questions—I mean he hit it right on the head with every issue. He was candid, sincere, and we respected the fact he came to Kuwait to talk with us. Our own commanding General of the 94th, Major General Dennis Laich, never bothered to pay us even a token visit. I'd later discover General Laich had never deployed overseas in support of a combat mission.[57] How could an Army officer earn a star for his uniform without ever having been to war, I thought.

The general wasn't blowing any smoke either, a refreshing change from what we were used to. But he went on to say, in essence, he was frustrated by those in Washington and at the Pentagon who were too hesitant to enact any of his recommendations. General Helmly's inability to make any significant, common sense adjustments to the Reserve system certainly wasn't due to a lack of effort or competence; but rather to budgets, politics, personalities, or the fear of the efforts involved in bringing sizable changes to this massive, ancient organization.

In what would make up the bulk of a December 2004 memo to the Pentagon from the general himself, we had a candid discussion that afternoon concerning the lack of any long term planning or manpower management within the U.S. Army Reserve, the fact we were on a fast-track to becoming a "broken force," and the insistence on a business as usual attitude. The

---

57 United States Army Reserve Command (USARC), 94th Regional Readiness Command (94th RRC) Leadership webpage, *http://www.usar.army. mil/USARC/RRC/0094RRC/0094_RRC_Bio_Laich.htm*

United States Army Reserve was clearly in trouble, but nothing was being done.[58]

I wasn't going to wait around to find out what happened next. With the accidental advice given to me by the most senior officer in my chain of command, I decided then and there I had served my country and soldiers under these conditions long enough, and with any luck—if I got home alive—I'd resign my commission next June, the end of my eight year obligation to the United States Army.[59]

The 94th's last mission was the quintessential nail-biter. Third platoon had five teams escorting some trucks to *Camp Speicher* near Tikrit, on roads that had seen some incredible violence over the past few months. There had been so many attacks on the highway between Taji and Baghdad that everyone was on edge, especially our turret gunners. Exposed from the chest up, constantly on the lookout for hidden dangers, they had to be on their toes every second of every mission. They were our first line of defense against IEDs and ambushes, and when on these highways, the "Vehicle-Borne Improvised Explosive Device;" the new buzzword for car bomb.

We often were traveling on these roads during the equivalent of rush hour traffic, bumper to bumper sometimes. The more popular parts of Baghdad (the roads anyway) looked like any large American city at 5 o'clock in the afternoon. Most Iraqi drivers would give the American patrols and convoys some

---

[58] Bradley Graham, *General Says Army Reserve Is Becoming a 'Broken' Force*, The Washington Post, January 6, 2005

[59] My resignation was submitted June 5, 2005, and was accepted soon after with an effective date of October 7, 2005.

room, keeping back 50 yards or so, but once in a while they'd get a little too close or drive a little too suspiciously. A quick burst from a machine gun over the hood of the Iraqi version of a New York City taxi usually stopped them in their tracks. Anyone who kept coming had nothing to lose. If that were the case, at least we'd have a chance to get a few shots off before any would-be bomber in his '88 Toyota could martyr himself.

The rest of the 94th had wrapped up their missions over the past few days, and was now silently on pins and needles watching the elements of our own 3rd platoon work their way into and through central Iraq. Back at *Udari*, we were following their movement on our secure computer network known as the *Blue Force Tracker*. Using GPS chips to track vehicle movement, *Blue Force Tracker* could pinpoint the location of these trucks to within a few meters, and then superimpose their position on a computer-generated map of Iraq. Our convoys were marked by little blue rectangles.

Each night the teams from 3rd platoon would radio in with their status. In one considerably unsettling update, they'd been stopped at an Iraqi police checkpoint near Balad. While sitting there a few hundred meters back, they saw a man dart from his car seconds before it exploded in a massive orange and black mushroom cloud. Third platoon's convoy passed by the charred wreck a few minutes later, and pushed on to deliver their Tikrit-bound cargo, shaken but unharmed.

A few days later, they made the return trip back to Kuwait, cautiously passing through the treacherous corridors that had killed and maimed so many soldiers and Marines. I followed the journey of our comrades on the *Blue Force Tracker's* cold, topographical map. Every two minutes or so, the rectangles would tick a few millimeters south on the screen. Inching their way through western Baghdad on *Route Sword*, they were moving through the heart of this war's casualty machine. Over the course of an hour that morning, I intently watched the little blue boxes tick their way through Baghdad, and eventually out of the Sunni Triangle. They hadn't radioed in, but they'd never stopped moving. That was a good sign. By the end of the day, they were well south of Baghdad, about five hours from the border. Barring any unseen complications on the desolate road leading to Kuwait, they should be out of harm's way later that afternoon.

Not too long after, the five teams from 3rd platoon pulled into *Udari* and our 15-month deployment in Iraq unofficially came to an end. After an unremarkable 30-second celebration of handshakes and one-armed embraces with a few of us who went to greet them, they dumped what was left of the ice from their coolers, cleaned their trucks of empty Gatorade bottles and MRE wrappers, and brought their weapons inside.

Just like that, it was over.

Each of the 94th's soldiers, called to duty on the snow-covered fields of upstate New York in December of 2002, returned home to the very same tarmac at Ft. Drum almost two years later. Although there were several Purple Hearts earned during the 94th's tour in Iraq, everyone survived. After more than twenty months of service, the tour of these 166 soldiers—men and women who had killed people, been shot at, hit with exploding shrapnel, driven thousands of miles on dangerous roads, and seen some of the worst behavior mankind was capable of, all the while managing to somehow evade death in the darkest cities in the world—would all come to an end in less than a few weeks. The longest serving Army Reserve unit since World War II was going home. To say that life would never be the same again is an understatement.

After running all around *Camp Arifjan* over the next few

weeks to get the signatures needed to ship out—literally checking each box on our stupid little military forms—we flew out of Kuwait International Airport on July 31, 2004, at a little before 2 in the morning.

A few soldiers in the 94th will have permanent physical reminders of our time there. Everyone has memories they'd rather forget, but never will. In the end, we made it home to tell our stories, hug our families and get on with life. A special thanks to the courageous troops who served in Iraq in 2003 and 2004 for the privilege.

I'll end with a quote, but not from some silly movie this time. An author by the name of Robert Byrne said it years ago, and I've heard it's one of General Stanley McChrystal's favorites:

"The purpose of life is a life with purpose."

For me, it sums up perfectly the precious responsibility I have of living a better, more meaningful life in honor of those men and women killed in their service to this great nation. That's *my* purpose, and I'll live the rest of my life doing just that.

The rest of my life.

Afterthoughts

"I'm pretty sure I have PTS."

It's something a lot of veterans have said, and even more have thought about. Several have been professionally diagnosed. The truth is all veterans have it, to some degree. The only variable is in which form it reveals itself.

I was spared the worst of it—I have friends that still have panic attacks or nightmares, even after a decade of being home. Mine took a different form, one that affected my life greatly, but in a direction I didn't expect. A precarious blend of survivor guilt, "horizon chasing," and hypersensitivity to even the smallest things, it was a driving factor behind the creation of this book.

Survivor guilt is the easiest one to describe. I survived this conflict, other men and women—ten times the person I am, or ever will be—did not. It's not overwhelming by any means, but it's always on the back burner. I hear their collective voice, constantly reminding me I owe it to them to live a better life, to make the absolute best of my own while I'm here. Trying to reconcile two different, often opposing forces—doing all you can for those who never could again, and throwing caution to the wind because you survived a war—is a mental line that is tough to define.

We're all chasing a horizon in some way. Mine happens to be doing all I can for wounded vets and their families. I can't sit still because I feel like I'm wasting time when I do, time that is more of a gift than I'll ever know. As you can imagine, it can make you a bit restless.

The hyperawareness is one nearly every vet has: You just had to pay attention more overseas. It's not always easy to turn off. The military mantra "stay alert, stay alive" is a simple one that doesn't always work, but who would want to take the chance, even in a country with so many safeguards? Years of watching pedestrians crossing New York City streets barely a step behind a speeding cab—risking their lives to save 4 seconds out of their day—drove me nuts, as did fellow passengers ignoring the flight safety brief before takeoff. It takes two minutes! Pay attention and read the damn pamphlet, it could save your life! It can be an exhaustive habit, even when most of it might not be necessary—but old habits die hard.

If you want to see where some (certainly not all) PTS can develop, you will here in this book, and it's not always from places you might expect. It's difficult to forget memories, both good and bad, stained by the constant threat of death. You see someone die, sometimes gruesomely, and it flips a switch in your head that you sometimes can't turn off. You lose a friend, and you forever wonder what kind of parent he or she would've made, or miss their companionship dearly. You see bad habits from troops, and it requires that much more mental bandwidth to constantly correct it. You bear witness to mismanagement or cowardice from your leadership, and years of expectations of your military come crumbling down. You watch ISIS storm across Iraq and capture towns in you fought, bled and killed for, and realize your sacrifices were in vain; the result from a decision made by politicians who were never there, to appease a population who just doesn't know any better. Or worse, a choice made by men you risked your life to train so they could allegedly defend their own country.

Any one of these, or a combination of all of them, can and will influence what impact PTS will have.

And you might've noticed I dropped the "D" from PTSD, because in my mind, it's not a disorder. Attention Deficit Disorder is a disorder. Obsessive-Compulsive Disorder is a disorder. Post Traumatic Stress is not. It's stress. And to call it a disorder is like jumping into a building that's on fire to rescue a kid, and then calling the resulting burns a "skin disorder." It's not something you're born with, nor is it something you catch. It's not a disorder. It's a reaction your mind has when it's been through something trying. And to call it a "disorder" often insults the men and women who deal with it because they chose to do something brave, something few others could or would handle.

I began writing *Taking Anbar* in October of 2004, about two months after the 94th Military Police Company returned from the ruthless Iraqi desert to the lush forests of New England. It's a book that, among others, looks to chronicle our relatively unique wartime experiences. However, for that first year, writing served as my therapy, helping me to cope with the jarring memories of our tour in Al Anbar Province that surrounded my thoughts just about every day.

I remember very well that afternoon I first began to write. My girlfriend, Kate, and I were enjoying the view of downtown Chicago from the small balcony of her condo on a beautiful, sun-drenched afternoon. She had moved from Boston earlier that year, bought the place about halfway through our tour and, assuming everything went as planned, asked me to move in with her when I got back. Just a few weeks earlier, after a wild and slightly self-destructive decompression period drinking with some friends in several of Boston's seediest clubs and bars, I took her up on the offer. I quickly collected my belongings—scattered over three states—packed everything I owned into my '99 Volkswagen Jetta, and made the mind-numbing 12-hour drive from my parents' house in Upstate New York to my new home in Illinois.

I also remember, quite well, the incident during that trip that made me want to write, which occurred just a few weeks before.

I was driving back to Chicago on I-90, and had pulled off at a rest stop somewhere in Ohio. Having shuffled around Boston from apartment to apartment in the late 90's, I knew all too well the frustration and aggravation that came with a major move. This one was no different, and after just three days I was ready to blow my top. The details were overwhelming, and all I wanted to do was get settled. I got out of the car and started rummaging around for a couple of items that I was afraid I might've forgotten. After a few seconds of searching, I immediately noticed I'd left a few things behind. A split second later, I remembered exactly where I'd left them in my parents' house, now over 500 miles away.

This was just perfect. Swearing to myself and shaking my head, I slammed the door, leaned against the car and stared at the highway traffic. How could have I forgotten that stuff? And I had the money, why didn't I just pay for a move? After about a minute of fuming over my petty ordeal, I took a step back from the car, looked at my reflection in the driver's side window and began to feel ashamed of myself. There I was, in front of a McDonald's, complaining about a stupid pair of running shoes and a few missing dress shirts back in New York. It was pathetic.

I'd been in the States a little less than a month and life was slowly returning to normal. However it wasn't until that little incident in a McDonald's parking lot that the enormity of what I'd experienced struck me. After more than a year at war in Iraq, having participated in one of the most brutal and complex acts of the human condition, I survived. I lived to see the faces and feel the touch of my family and friends again. About a thousand of my comrades had not. Another ten times that would return horrifically maimed, barely recognizable to anyone they knew. And here I was, perfectly fine, on a gorgeous day in the United States of America, in front of a fast food restaurant—complaining about something absolutely fucking ridiculous and, even worse, letting it get the best of me.

I was free to live the rest of my life in relative peace because some of America's finest young men and women had given theirs on a desert road or in an ancient city a half a world away, killed in a violent storm of shrapnel or deafening volley of gunfire. Some hadn't yet seen their twentieth birthday.

I thought about where I was when I turned 20—nearly ten years ago at this point, at a party back in college, swimming in alcohol and friends without a care in the world.

If this was life returning to normal, I didn't like where normal was headed. My eyes started to well up. This foolish little problem I was having, along with the thousands of others like it that had been such a source of irritation for me in my life before the war, seemed decidedly less burdensome now.

I not only wanted to write this book, I needed to. The experience in Iraq, itself, wasn't enough. I needed to give the public an accurate account of just what happened there. I needed to revisit our tour and get some perspective on life, before I wasted it complaining about shirts and sneakers. I needed to tell a story that both praised the men and women who fought with unreal courage, and shamed the ones who turned their backs on their Oath to the troops in their charge. I needed to get some things off my chest.

As a result, a lot of its content comes from a place of sadness, disbelief, humor and rage. I've done my best to accurately describe what we went through as soldiers while at war in Anbar Province in 2003 and 2004, immediately following the formal end of the conflict. However, I'm sure a few dates or names are off, only because a lot of this was from notes I took when I had a chance, letters written to friends and family, or the collective memories of my platoon. It's taken nearly a decade to finish, but the lessons learned in combat are timeless enough.

So in conclusion, thank you for purchasing this book. In case you didn't see it, proceeds from its sales are funding **OnBehalf.org**, a national, all-volunteer nonprofit that aims to provide wounded veterans with financial and professional assistance, to include those dealing with PTS. Regardless of your opinions of the wars in Iraq or Afghanistan, you're helping some brave young men and women get back on their feet. And for that, you have my eternal gratitude.

Michael J. Gifford

Captain, U.S. Army Reserve

1997-2005

August 2015

Epilogue

A Pawn's View of the Chessboard

People understandably ask me why I decided to leave the Army. My answer is reasonably simple—I was a square peg in a round hole. Sooner or later, I would've met my match and been booted out. Today's military doesn't always look favorably on those who are a little too outspoken. If you don't believe me, you will soon enough.

However despite some of the stories I've written over the course of the book, I couldn't be more proud of the United States military, my unit, and my service to this nation. My writings aren't intended to dissuade young men and women from serving their country; rather I want them to be able to recognize the problems within the military so they don't repeat the same mistakes we made. I also want to make it perfectly clear that my story isn't meant to be an all out rant against the leadership in America's Armed Forces, and the specific people I discuss over the course of the writing represent only a small minority. The institutional issues I bring to light—while much more prevalent, and certainly nothing new—I'm confident will be remedied with time.

I also wanted to give a responsible perspective of the war from some of the people who fought it, a moderate view that falls between the two extremes that I'm sure you've heard.

On one hand, there are those who believe the war was a mistake from the beginning and are quick to claim that it became the hopeless quagmire that they predicted it would all along; "We're in over our heads, need to leave now, and any peace is better than any war. Another terrorist thug will just step up and replace Saddam anyway."

On the other, there's the overconfident rhetoric from those who think the U.S. military is indestructible and can do no wrong, that if we just stay in it for a little while longer, things will work out just fine; "These trivial security problems in Iraq are the unavoidable results of war, and our minor oversights are inconsequential in the glorious march towards absolute victory." Continually trying to spin each extreme and ignoring the realities of both is only bound to lead to trouble.

I don't like either one, and have an opinion of each.

First, the "Defeatists."

There was a good cartoon in the *Stars and Stripes* back in 2004, one that I think sums up their view of the war. It showed a man screaming out to the soldiers from the back of a landing craft as they stormed the beaches at Normandy, during the first few minutes of D-Day. He was crying out, "Stop! Don't go! It's too hard!" His t-shirt read, "Liberal Left."

To this day, there are no shortage of critics of this war, on both sides of the isle, and I'm sure not every liberal holds this opinion—I don't mean to split this straight down political party lines. As a soldier and citizen of the United States, I'm a *big* believer in free speech, that it must be encouraged and protected. And while some have offered a more sensible, level-headed and apolitical view of our work in Iraq, I feel the most ardent opponents were using this war for their own gains, and simply masking their contempt for President Bush.

We had access to cable television news in Iraq once we'd made the move to Ramadi in October of 2003, and I made a point of watching for a few minutes when I could each night at dinner. The mess halls were often flowing with commentary from Fox News and CNN, among others, with opinions from both the left and right. A believer in healthy debate, I wasn't asking the American people to blindly follow the Bush Administration without question. However the irresponsible attacks on our President—specifically the one that claimed he'd gotten us into an unwinnable war, or that it was too difficult an undertaking—genuinely made my stomach turn and insulted me as a soldier.

Constantly trying to place the blame for the troubles in Iraq square the President's shoulders was a blatant smear campaign orchestrated by the liberals of this country, looking to score political points at the expense of our military men and women. Their ideology of "support the troops but not the war" rang hollow and insincere to me, regardless if it was because they resented Bush or actually thought the war unwinnable. In any event, it looked as if these fair-weather politicians were capitalizing on the military's perceived failures, in a cheap attempt to enlist the newest wave of potential constituents whose growing resentment of the war represented an easy target.

I found CNN's several-daily updates of just how many troops had been killed in Iraq since "major combat operations had ended" appalling. There it was, every few minutes or so, in the crawler on the bottom of the television screen. It was like the media was trying to make some kind of sick, empty point. Thanks for the breaking news.

I'm from New York, one of the bluest states in the Union, but I consider myself a conservative and, dare I say it, a Republican. And while I'm a firm supporter of free speech, I'm also equally as supportive of—and insistent on—personal responsibility. To put it more bluntly, feel free to speak about whatever you please, but do your homework before you open your mouth and be prepared to defend your words. Most importantly, if you're going to complain about a problem, at least be ready with an answer. Have a plan, not just another smartass bumper sticker or t-shirt.

And that's just the problem. With each irresponsible insult and shortsighted comment from America's complainers, there's rarely a solution offered. It's been the way of too many in this country for years. They've made quite a living for themselves scaring people and pointing out the mistakes of others from their offices in Washington, or from their perfect little insulated communities in New York, Connecticut or Massachusetts. Being a "professional complainer" does nothing for the American way or for the advancement of our society, and the excuses to why they continually have no answers are starting to anger me.

I'll say the same thing to them as I said to my troops overseas—"if you're gonna bitch about something, let's hear *your* answer."

I'm still listening.

Second, the "Supermen."

While a supporter of the Administration and the war in general, I questioned some of our motives, the way the war's being fought, and the belief that things were "just fine." They weren't fine. And while post-war Iraq was not entirely impossible to manage, the fact that some didn't (or wouldn't) learn from history's lessons makes things so much more tragic than they had to be. Dismissing the problems we were having as simple, negligent side effects of war while attempting to make way for more positive news is a dangerous display of ignorance. You can't keep covering your ears and eyes to the reality on the ground. Marginalizing major issues and celebrate nominal successes with ingratiating pats on the back is not a healthy approach to warfare *or* public affairs. "Staying the course" and insisting on this course of action will never work. I'm forever the optimist, but I learned two hard facts overseas—not every soldier is a hero, and not every mission ends in success.

When I read that article in the *Stars and Stripes* in June of 2004 about the mistakes being made in training the Iraqi Police, I wanted to explode. We'd been screaming the same thing for the better part of a year and no one was listening. We all knew that there weren't that many cops truly ready to take on their new security tasks, but in order to show "progress" in Iraq, the DoD and Administration misrepresented the number of available Iraqi security forces.[60] You might be able to get away with fluffing the numbers of new bridges built or oil wells secured, but not with IPF and Iraqi soldiers fit for duty. Our bosses wanted to paint a pretty picture for *their* bosses and that's about it. It's also funny how when we were running one of the largest police academies in Iraq, the 82nd Airborne's gen-

---

60 United States Government Accountability Office, *Rebuilding Iraq, Preliminary Observations on Challenges in Transferring Security Responsibilities to Iraqi Military and Police*, Statement of Joseph A. Christoff, Director, International Affairs and Trade, before the Committee on Government Reform; Subcommittee on National Security, Emerging Threats and International Relations; House of Representatives, March 14, 2005

eral only showed up once, one less time than the 82nd captain who allegedly ran the place. We could see just how seriously it was being taken.

We couldn't go on building new schools for Iraq's kids indefinitely if there were still major problems with security. Hospitals in Iraq lacked even the most basic supplies as innocent people flooded their emergency rooms on a daily basis. Military intelligence officers who look like they just learned how to shave can't be responsible for the questioning of detainees if we want real information.

I'm not one to harp on mistakes in judgment where no one new any better—that's not what this is about. We underestimated the strength of the insurgency. Fine, no one really knew what would happen. We shouldn't have disbanded Iraq's military after the war. OK, I can understand why that decision was made. We didn't capitalize quickly enough on the jubilation immediately surrounding the fall of Baghdad, ironically discussed in a paper written by the Army War College and published in February 2003, just before the invasion.[61] Lesson learned. Pretty soon, we could argue it all the way back to not invading Iraq in the first place. Those issues are long gone and inconsequential to what's happening today, but some will no doubt resurface in other conflicts and look us straight in the eye everyday, no matter what's being said in the newspapers, on the radio, or from the White House press room.

---

61 Conrad C. Crane and W. Andrew Terrill, *Reconstructing Iraq; Insights, Challenges, and Missions for Military Forces in a Post-Conflict Scenario*, Army War College, February 2003.

The "Other" Case for Invasion

No one followed the reasons for going to war with Iraq as closely as the members of the United States military, and everyone had an opinion. For some, it was transparent; it was a war for oil, revenge or to satisfy the bloodlust of the Administration following 9/11. For others, it was even simpler; Saddam was a bad guy and the people of Iraq desperately needed our help. In either case, once it was clear that our military was heading into battle, everyone prepared themselves emotionally. Justifying the invasion in our own minds was a necessary part of that process.

I certainly can't speak for everyone, but here's what was going through my head in the spring of 2003, a view I shared with many officers in my position.

In my humble opinion—given the information at the time—this war was legal, just and necessary. I could never go as far as to say if it was clearly "right" or "wrong;" that's entirely subjective anyway. However, it was (and still is) my thorough belief that any proactive steps taken by this, or any future President, to defend the United States need *never* be validated through a unanimous vote by the world's countries, *especially* U.N. Member States. The President and Congress, working with the best intelligence and information available, make the decision. Period.

In the months leading up to the invasion, the U.N. had become, through their own inaction, an "irrelevant debating society" who I likened to a pathetic group of defenseless schoolchildren dealing with a bully who paid no attention to their pleads. Saddam didn't care about how many resolutions were passed condemning his tyrannical exploits. He didn't care about the world's opinion regarding his alleged weapons of mass destruction developments. He didn't care how much his people suffered as money was made hand over fist with the U.N.'s failed Oil for Food program, which in my opinion was just another token act that only served to punish the people of Iraq. He wasn't going anywhere—so he thought, anyway—and the more he rattled our cages, the more he enjoyed it. The governments of the world were quick to point out his murderous activities, but no one was prepared to do anything about it. What he was allowed to get away with at the expense of his own citizens, how his sons were quickly earning their reputations as animals, and his overt funding of terrorism around the globe over the past 20 years were enough for most American soldiers to steel themselves for war. And if we had to go it alone, so be it.

However, despite the incredible failures of the UN, I came to resent most those Americans that believed we could act on Iraq if, and only if, the entire world was in agreement—that absolute compliance with international opinion was somehow the key to legitimacy in our quest for military action. The President of the United States was much more capable of leading our military than Kofi Annan and his do-nothing minions, who in my estimation disastrously mishandled the mass murder in Bosnia at the height of the Balkan war, were avoiding any real action against North Korea or Iran's nuclear program, all but ignoring the Israeli peace process, and trivializing the explosive growth of genocidal campaigns in Africa. And at the time, Slobodan Milosevic was looking happy and healthy, ridiculing justice at The Hague. I expected nothing less in any U.N.-sponsored trial of Saddam. Anan continued to "strongly condemn" terrorist action with empty rhetoric and ineptitude—since we won't move for meaningful military action, I guess we'd have to shame tyrants and terrorists into giving up.

At the end of the day however, Saddam Hussein needed

to be removed, and not because of the relatively simplistic case put forth by the U.S. Government. No amount of talk or diplomacy was going to change this man and his plans, and any future efforts to convince him to comply with international law would've certainly proved useless. Based on all I've heard, I'm convinced that a containment policy wouldn't address the fundamental problems within the Middle East, and our little threats only served to embolden Hussein and reinforce his image as a rebel against Western oppression.[62] And I can't imagine what kind of hell Iraq would fall into if one of his son's took over.

So after all is said and done, what drove me to support the invasion? Contrary to what you may be thinking, it wasn't to spite the U.N. or their supporters. It was based much more on fact.

Saddam had the art of screwing with other countries down to a science. His sons were a menace. He was openly funding the campaign of terror in Israel.[63] He brazenly defied the enforcement of international law, shot at Coalition aircraft almost daily when on patrol in the north and south "no-fly zones,"[64] killed hundreds of thousands of his own people,[65] was

---

[62] Senator John McCain, *Containing Saddam has Failed; Regime Change Only Path to Disarmament*, February 13, 2003 (courtesy of Center for Strategic and International Studies; www.csis.org)

[63] Kern Lane, *Saddam Pays 25K for Palestinian Bombers*, Fox News, March 26, 2002 (www.foxnews.com)

[64] Prepared Testimony of U.S. Secretary of Defense Donald H. Rumsfeld before the House and Senate Armed Services Committees regarding Iraq, Washington, D.C., September 18-19, 2002 (www.defenselink.mil)

[65] US Department of State Fact Sheet, April 4, 2003 (www.state.gov)

harboring known terrorists,[66] and ignored the betterment of his country in the relentless search for better weaponry—all the while sitting on top of the world's second largest oil reserves.[67] Saddam Hussein was the bully in the global neighborhood that needed his lights punched out—for the long-term good of the world and humanity. The only effective containment policy was the one we were enforcing with Hussein on trial and under U.S. control, confined to a small prison cell.

So here I am now, years after the invasion, watching Fox News and leafing through the New York Times in my office. Like an interested fan watching the game from the sidelines, I anxiously absorb the commentary from red state Republicans and blue state Democrats, right wing conservatives and left-leaning liberals, wealthy corporate types and elite academic pundits. Having been there and done that, I now I feel the need to run out onto the field with some responsible commentary of my own.

On one hand, the thought that President Bush "lied" to the American people about Iraq's WMD or potential link to 9/11 in order to start a war is *ridiculous*. It's one of the weakest

---

[66] Abu Abbas, the Palestinian terrorist who organized the *Achille Lauro* cruise ship hijacking in 1985 and murdered US citizen Leon Klinghoffer, was captured by US forces outside of Baghdad in April of 2003. Abbas was the general director of the Palestinian Liberation Front, designated a terrorist organization by the US State Department (David Ensor, *US captures mastermind of Achille Lauro hijacking*, CNN, April 16, 2003; www.cnn.com). It was known that Abu Musab al-Zarqawi's terror network, linked to Al Qaeda in a February 2003 speech by Colin Powell to the United Nations Security Council, was working within Iraq prior to the March 2003 invasion.

[67] Gal Luft, Co-Director, Institute for the Analysis of Global Security, The Brookings Institute, *Iraq memo #16*, May 12, 2003 (www.brookings.edu)

anti-war arguments I've ever heard (and I've heard them all), and consider it an irresponsible accusation from the President's liberal critics. But on the other hand, I'm very concerned with some of the beliefs behind the Administration's case for war. In my opinion, the broken record of claims coming from both the White House and its conservative base that lead America to believe we were on the verge of a Saddam-sponsored terrorist attack are arguably exaggerated. They only serve to hurt the President's push for regime change in the Middle East. Appealing to the American public and their sense of justice and freedom makes more sense than constantly telling the world that Saddam gassed his own people or reminding people of September 11th. No soldier's grieving mother or father gives a damn about some Kurds who were killed 20 years ago, or the remote chance of a State-sponsored nuclear, biological or chemical attack on the United States.

And while I believe Iraq would eventually pursue some kind of intercontinental munitions delivery system, I'm not convinced they would ever be a direct threat against the U.S. The components needed to build these weapons aren't exactly abundant—nor are the machinery, know-how or technology—and the international community has developed sophisticated programs to counter the proliferation of just about all of them. Even if Iraq were to *somehow* construct or purchase a nuclear weapon or similar WMD, it would be inviting its own destruction with any real or perceived threat by the United States or Israel. I'd be surprised if Tel Aviv didn't have its own unapologetic Baghdad-bound missiles in the air *long* before our government's response. As for a biological or chemical attack, the "weaponization" and subsequent dispersal of such materials is an extremely difficult process and, given the development of our own protective mechanisms, the intended results of such an attack are questionable. While the psychological effects of an

Captain Michael J. Gifford

attack using any of the three would no doubt be significant—potentially greater than any actual physical casualties they may yield—the production, smuggling or outright purchase of such material would represent a lopsided risk to any group who was looking to do us harm. In my opinion, you'd strike much more death, fear and panic with cheap explosives in a backpack at a bus stop than with some kind of doomsday nerve agent or "bug bomb."

And it just didn't fit Saddam's profile. His possession of WMD was more or less being used to frighten the Iranians, objectify his own virility and rile up the West. In addition, I find the argument that Iraq's WMD would somehow find itself in Al Qaeda's hands threadbare. Given the fact that Saddam was a megalomaniacal secular leader and Al Qaeda a zealous fundamental faction—two groups with very different aims—it struck me as highly unlikely that Hussein would risk his power for such a haphazard collaborative effort.[68] Our intelligence capabilities would eventually find the link, paving the way for an all-out, clear-cut conventional attack against the Iraqi regime. It just didn't make sense he'd trade his throne for the detonation of a potentially unreliable weapon and hand the U.S. an easy victory, and the presence of such a belief throughout the country underscores our misunderstanding of threats abroad.

I'm an ardent supporter of our former president and of our military, and consider myself a steadfast conservative. But

---

68 Mohamed Atta, a 9/11 hijacker and ringleader, believed Saddam Hussein to be "an American stooge set up to give Washington an excuse to intervene in the Middle East." (*The 9/11 Commission Report, Final Report of the National Commission on Terrorist Attacks Upon the United States,* New York, NY: W.W. Norton & Co., 2004), p. 161

as you've seen, the book is critical of both the Armed Forces and the Bush Administration. In my opinion, it's best to learn from what's been done rather than sweep the past under the rug, regardless of political affiliation. And for the sake of the military—an increasingly apolitical organization that often finds itself caught between partisan bickering—it's critical that America learn from its faults, for the well being of our fighting men and women tasked to put in motion the violent machines of failed diplomacy. This certainly won't be our last war, and the odds of entering another where everyone's in total agreement are slim, at best.

Tom Brokaw's "Greatest Generation" answered the call to arms and sent its men and women overseas into a colossal fight to purge the Earth of fascism and Nazism. That generation recognized both the direct military threat the growing war in Europe posed to the American people, *and* to the principles of freedom around the world. They played the hand that was dealt to them, as must we. Continually scrutinizing the decisions behind our war with Iraq, rather than learning from our errors and looking forward to better ways of dealing with future threats, is counterproductive at the least.

Taking Anbar deals with the common thread to each—learning from our mistakes in Iraq, and finding solutions to the problems that will no doubt resurface in current conflicts.

The Soapbox

Where the Army, the U.S. Government and Americans can do better

HERE'S THE SECTION where I *do* rant a bit.

The U.S. Army is an all-volunteer service, so it's hard to fault anyone who's willing to sacrifice so much to fight for this country and its ideals. But sometimes even good leadership supports bad policy, and those issues need to be addressed.

The fact is that we were supporting the trend, *especially* in the Reserves, that "showing up" was good enough. I can't tell you how many award ceremonies I attended over my eight year career, both Active and Reserve, which overly-celebrated basic participation. While it's important we recognize those who've elected to serve, those who serve must recognize that they've joined an organization that holds itself to a higher standard. Signing up and filling the ranks isn't good enough, and that goes ten-fold for leadership. But it's happening all too often, and within a few short weeks, some of these people may be handed a rifle and head off to war. The actions, or inactions, of these people represent the weakest link in a chain of events that eventually lead to failed missions—missions that mean the difference between winning and losing our campaigns, and life and death to those around them.

I'd noticed that the initial invasion of Afghanistan in October of 2001 had already begun to clear out some of the military's "dead weight." I was hearing that a lot of students were dropping out of ROTC programs across the country, Reservists were reneging on their commitments and so on, and I was relieved that the military was allowing itself to be purged. I for one didn't want to be forced into a war zone with a bunch of people that were there simply because of some contractual obligation. Analysts were saying that this new World War would require a lot of focus and energy, not just troops taking up space on some real estate in Southwest Asia, an opinion that I wholeheartedly agreed with. If anyone wanted to run, now was the time. I say let them all go—sometimes a forest fire is just what the forest needs.

I was so fortunate to be with the 94th MP Company. Just after I officially transferred to the 94th, I knew I was with a special bunch. Most of the troops were excited at the prospect of going to war, but not *too* excited. They were ready to jump off of the plane in Kuwait ready to fight, but not *too* gung-ho about the whole thing. They had a levelheaded approach to what they were getting into, a real down to Earth view that I found refreshing. They didn't have anything to prove, the leadership wasn't trying to impress anyone, and no one struck me as a bloodthirsty Hollywood killing machine. Then it hit me—the commander of the 94th MP CO, Captain Dave Bentley, a tremendous officer and leader, was an engineer with no military police training. My own primary and official MOS was not of an MP, either. There were other military police officers in the Reserve Command. The 94th MPs had been short two platoon leaders for some time now, and were prepared to deploy without them. What was wrong with this picture?

Our Reserve Command was no different than the national trend. Soldiers in our own little corner of the world were already bailing out, with some leaders turning their backs on the more sacred obligation of leading young troops. I'll be perfectly honest—I had no idea exactly what I'd be getting into when I volunteered for this whole thing. Yes, I wanted more experience. Yes, I wanted the combat patch. Yes, I was thinking about my career. However, most importantly, I wanted to "cut my teeth" as a junior officer and lead soldiers in a tactical mission, and if they had the guts to go, so would I. The fact that the 94th was ready to deploy without two platoon leaders disturbed me. There were MP officers in the command sitting idly by while young kids were set to deploy into war with no leadership. While there was no doubt some troops would have been just fine without another officer tagging along (and most likely would've done well with only the guidance of senior enlisted), it wasn't the point. Where were these officers, and why hadn't they volunteered for this?

There's no getting around it today. Officers shouldn't elect a combat or combat support MOS without expecting to apply it at sometime in your career—every officer should be jumping at the chance for some tactical experience, rather than shuttling around from desk job to desk job.

Joining the military as an officer just for the benefits is like deciding to be a doctor for the salary. It's going to take more than a desire for a decent paycheck to get you through years of service and potential conflict—it's a passion and commitment for what you want to do in life. An officer in the Army should be in for a higher purpose than money for school or for a little extra cash on the weekends (for Reservists, anyway). And here I was seeing captains and lieutenants sloughing off their commitments—not so much to the 8-year contract they signed when they became officers, but to their Oath of Office.

This had a huge impact on the wars in Iraq & Afghanistan, and in the military in general.

I'm not the best officer in the world, and I don't pretend to be. Far from it. I'm not very good with paperwork, I don't know the regulations like I should, I'm horrible at taking criticism, and I'm usually guilty of thinking the worst of people. However I know the fundamentals in and out. And to tell you the truth, it doesn't take an officer to recognize the institutional problems within the Army.

Officers have a choice to make upon their commissioning which will determine the fate of their careers. Over the eight years I was in, well before we even went into Iraq or Afghanistan, I saw too many men and women do everything in their power to evade their duties, to just barely meet the already low standards to prevent being kicked out. I've seen too many officers take no action, and avoid making the difficult decisions in their military lives. Instead of learning the art and science of good leadership, they simply do what they're told and go with the flow in hopes of being handed greater rank and responsibility. Is this the environment we should be fostering? Would *you* want a leader who's afraid to make a decision because of the potential impact on their career? What kind of career would that be? One that would not lead to any circumstance that's good for professional growth, or to the strong leadership of soldiers.

Would you want your son or daughter being led by someone like this?

I wouldn't, and I can safely assume that anyone who has a

child in the Armed Forces today to answer the same. I would be skeptical of anyone who had to be forced to fulfill their military commitment, just as I would be of anyone who was pushed into war for the solitary reason of furthering their own career. Either way, they're probably not doing it for the right reasons, a gamble that shouldn't involve the lives of those you're expected to lead competently.

*

"My only real motivation is not to get hassled, and the fear of losing my job. But you know what, Bob? That will only make someone work just hard enough to not get fired."

Ron Livingston as *Peter Gibbons*
Office Space

With combat time almost a certainty now to any officer entering the Army, the military needs to more closely look at an officer's qualification for leadership. Back in the late 90's, the military had something for everyone. There was always a small, armed conflict in some "Fifth-World" nation somewhere that was making the news, and could give an infantry officer some trigger time. There were programs in Europe that could introduce young officers to strategic and operational intelligence across the globe. There was a unit somewhere in California or Texas that was badly in need of someone who could straighten out their pay and administrative problems. You could pick and choose your assignment, with a reasonable expectation that you'd find a job you really enjoyed and could almost tailor to your liking. Now, and moving forward, the needs of the military far outweigh those who want a little Army experience to complement their resumes. Things are much different now, and it's a real test for officers. They can either define their career as a bold decision to train and lead those troops into this war on terror, or they can let it be guided by a fear of making the wrong decision and perfecting the art of keeping a low profile. With so many overbearing guidelines and regulations, I can see how so many people choose the latter, but it's not a decision that's going to lead to successful leadership.

Right from the get-go I was never concerned with what higher leadership thought of me. It was one of the benefits of not being a career military officer. Besides, I'd already dealt with most of the "superior officers" in my Reserve command and was not impressed in the least (and I'm easily impressed). Of course there were a couple of exceptions; there were a select few I had gotten to know well and develop a great deal of respect for. In those isolated cases, I was very concerned about what they thought of me, and did my best to learn from and with them. But for the most part, I wasn't worried. As I said, I'm not super-good at taking criticism, and the more it dawned on me that I was accepting it from increasingly unqualified people, the worse I became at it. And in my eyes, it was a good thing. I wasn't about to listen to anyone who had continually wasted opportunities to do their duty and qualify themselves as leaders, no matter what the assignment or excuse. A lot of officers in the military may be "school qualified" to do their job, but still are in no way fit to lead or give direction to junior officers or soldiers.

Not every leader's going to have the chance to go to war, but there are some who continually evade the more difficult aspects of their careers. This tested my patience over and over again in Iraq. It's a fundamental problem dangerously amplified by war, where you have junior officers and NCOs putting in an extraordinary effort, only to have it undermined by the spineless inaction of a few officers or senior enlisted. For instance, there was a major at *Junction City* back in Ramadi, who told us all one night that he was forced to deploy because, self-admittedly, he couldn't get out of it. Worse, he's hastily giving me tactical orders about a situation he had no knowledge of concerning the area around our post, and never once came along with us on a patrol, an IED sweep, *any* mission outside of the compound. He never put in the effort. If I'm the one with the responsibility to follow the orders of my superior officers, shouldn't *he* have the responsibility to qualify *himself* as a leader? Here's a man (or woman) who has an assignment that doesn't require him to leave the relative safety of an Army post, who has the ability—but not the desire—to join us on a patrol of a dangerous section of a troubled town. The first-hand experience of that patrol would enhance the effectiveness and competence of their decisions, and would no doubt aid in the safety of troops under their command. However, because of the fear for their own safety, they won't go. They've refused to make the more difficult—but necessary—choice to qualify themselves. And by substituting the right schools for tough real world assignments, putting forth just enough of a nominal effort to advance their careers, they've made the rank and are now calling the shots. What a damn nightmare, to be lead by armchair warriors who never took a real risk in their life.

Will this problem ever be completely addressed? Probably not. Cowardice and rationalization are human traits the world over, and no organization is exempt. If his boss had a clue, he or she would've insisted the major travel with our units to get a better picture of things, or stuck him in a staff position that wouldn't impact our operations. Clearly, he or she didn't.

This unequal balance of bravery and sense of duty is most certain to rear its ugly head again sooner or later. We're facing a determined foe, an enemy so driven that he'll slip on his own blood to run out and shoot at an American tank. We can't fight these fundamental extremists with lackluster doctrine. What do we need? Stricter standards, better training, more purpose. How do we do it? Lose some of the older, antiquated notions that are lessening the effectiveness of the United States Army, and for God's sake, start losing some people that are holding it back.

"And what are you prepared to do now?"

Sean Connery as *beat-cop Jim Malone*
The Untouchables

Since we can't always depend on the best equipment, let's get down to the nitty gritty, to where the rubber meets the road—training, specifically on weapons and tactics.

In the U.S. military, in order to be "qualified" on your assigned weapon, you have to hit a number of targets at various distances within a specific amount of time. Easy enough, but it doesn't really qualify you for combat shooting. I can only speak from the experience of being a Reservist, but from what I've heard the Active component could use some work in this area, too—in Iraq and Afghanistan, the Active and Reserves shared many of the same challenges anyway.

Everyone, not just the Rangers or Special Forces guys, need more specific training. I'm not talking about sending an 18-year-old supply clerk into a room full of hostages with live rounds, but a certain degree of "danger" would increase the confidence with our weapons that this Army is often slow to dole out. Yes it's more difficult, dangerous and time-consuming; but war is difficult, dangerous and time-consuming.

I'm a huge believer in *every soldier a rifleman*, the principle behind the Warrior Ethos that's been so passionately endorsed by Army leadership for more than a decade. Currently Army doctrine calls for Reservists to visit the rifle range twice a year with their weapons systems in order to become qualified to operate them in a safe and effective manner. Unfortunately the Army's definition of "qualified" often differs with mine, and most soldiers whose lives depend on knowing how to use the extraordinary killing devices the Army provides us to defend ourselves are in agreement. The mechanics of a weapon are easy enough to learn. You put the bullets in here, the safety switch is this right here and the trigger is this thing here. Aim through this and shoot. However the circumstances and situations that troops will face overseas are much more demanding than what's being taught on the ranges at our Reserve and Active posts nationwide. Learning what is going to be realistically required of our young troops in combat takes more than two opportunities a year, and goes well beyond firing at a few stationary targets.

Basic training has incorporated a lot of practical scenarios into its programs that mimic those encountered in the Middle East over the past few years, which I applaud. However, too often that's the end of a young soldier's training before the newly-minted killer plods off to their respective Reserve units to combat an ancient ritual of paperwork and antique approaches to combat training.

Let me give you a little information on how the military conducts its weapons ranges. The small arms ranges, like the M16 and 9mm courses, involve little green targets in the shape of enemy silhouettes that pop up at specific times and at specific distances. In the Army (it's a little different in the Marine Corps), everyone gets in a line, marches off to their foxhole, hops in, and follows specific directions from the "range master" in the tower. The range master gives specific instructions via a loudspeaker on exactly when to load your magazine, exactly when to chamber a round, exactly when to move your selector switch from "safe" to "fire" and when to fire the weapon. When the command is given, you shoot 20 rounds while standing in a foxhole. After that's done, you'll hop out of the foxhole and fire 20 rounds from the prone. Your targets are between 25 and 300 yards away and stay up only for a few seconds. After it's over, you pick up your expended brass shells and march off the range. With sometimes as many as 20 soldiers at a time, it's understandably a very controlled environment, and any "unauthorized movement," like touching your weapon after it's been set down, can lead to one hell of an ass-chewing. And while it can be quite challenging and does give you some good mechanical experience with your weapon, something's still missing.

A perfect example was our weapons qualification day at Ft. Drum back in December of 2002. For three days straight, Watertown, the city closest to Ft. Drum, was the coldest place in the contiguous 48 states. We wrapped ourselves up in Gore-Tex, our chemical suits, anything to stay warm. Trudging through the snow in the 7-degree weather, we'd face blinding snow and ice on the ranges to fire our weapons. I couldn't even see the M16 course, but it didn't matter, because I knew the procedure down cold, pardon the pun. Because it was that predictable and I'm a pretty good shot, I could almost do it with my eyes closed (with the blowing snow I had to).

The next day it had cleared up a bit, and we hit the 9mm range. However it was more of the same. Being military police, readying ourselves for possible close-quarter combat, I wondered why we were learning to shoot the way we were. In the

9mm handgun qualification course, the same small green targets pop up between 5 and 25 yards away, at predictable times and intervals just like the M16 course. A single round is fired into the target and drops when it's hit. Most of us had 9mm training before, and knew the weapon well—too well to simply fire one round at shapeless green targets. But that's what we were doing. We were being sent off to war with the bare standards. This was not the real training I was looking for, and it was just another way for the Army to check the box in preparing its soldiers for war.

After I "qualified" the Army way, I grabbed a few spare rounds (which are often hard to find) and a couple of guys straight out of basic for some more realistic shooting. I owned my own 9mm and was familiar with it, so I wanted a few of the younger kids to get some trigger time with the weapon they'd be carrying 24 hours a day for the next year. Before we started, I went over how a pistol would most likely be used in a combat situation. The 9mm is a close range firearm, and if you pulled it out with intent to use it, it usually meant someone was only a few yards away. You wouldn't be shooting one shot at a time until someone stopped coming at you—you'd probably empty at least three or four rounds, and in one hell of a hurry, until "the threat was eliminated." Clearing a building would be a perfect example; a situation we could easily find ourselves in overseas.

We reset the targets after the qualification, but this time we fired three rounds as fast as we could, from different positions and different stances, at the targets when they popped up. Is it a bit more dangerous? Yes, it is, but far more practical and confidence-building than the Army's way. The younger troops later thanked me later on for the additional training, now with more "muscle memory" on the 9mm that may help save a life.

Combat isn't always about simply being able to aim a weapon and pull the trigger. The war in Iraq tested our tactics each day, as our engagements got closer and closer and more and more dangerous. Handing some kid an M16, having them fire it at stationary targets for a few hours and then sending them overseas into a very complicated engagement is not the way to go. It's like handing a 17-year-old kid fresh out of driver's education a set of keys to the fastest car you can find, and telling him to start racing on the NASCAR circuit.

One exception I was glad to see was MPRI's training in Kuwait after our extension. Just before resuming our mission of convoy escort, this company comprised of retired contracted Special Operations soldiers devised a handful of tactical scenarios for us to practice on. One that sticks out in my mind was a close-quarter ambush, one where we were "attacked" by an RPG round. A puff of smoke would indicate the ambush, we'd radio each other of the contact, set up our vehicles in the best possible position, bound from our trucks and start sending some rounds downrange towards our "enemy."

What a refreshing change from the M16 range. Instead of being processed on a qualification assembly line, constantly being instructed on what to do next, we were tossed into a situation that required some actual thought on our part. Yes, it was quite dangerous—we had live rounds, no idea when or where our attack would come from and we're exiting our vehicles in a hurry in order to start laying down some lead.

And guess what—that pretty much describes one of the most frequent combat situations in Iraq, and a template I'm sure other foreign insurgents would pick up on.

While our exercise with MPRI wasn't *entirely* lifelike, it was good training and made me feel more like a soldier with a brain, and less like some robotic moving target.

If we want troops heading into the next hot zone with the knowledge and confidence they'll need to survive and beat our enemy, we need more realistic training. People may get hurt in this one, but rather here on a controlled range than in the middle of yet another hostile, Third World city.

Another factor that contributes to the lack of strong combat training is the endless stream of paperwork that drives the Reserve and Active components. The incredible focus on ridiculous peacetime activities is chipping away at our Warrior Ethos, as our preparedness for actual combat atrophies under tons of useless training and administrative duties.

During my eight years as a Reserve officer, I attended countless classes on "FormFiller" and "PowerPoint," the military's main weapons for producing documents and communicating with other soldiers. Through such dynamic, inspirational training I discovered that that there were so many wonderful ways to obtain blank Army forms to fill in and push up the chain of command, adding to the infinite problems the military was already having with keeping order. In contrast, I also learned that it literally takes an Act of Congress to procure "blank" ammunition for our M16 rifles (the ones that made noise but didn't house an actual bullet) and land for a training area on which to practice our life-saving combat skills.

The Army Reserves (and some Active commands) are a bubbling stew of paperwork and bureaucracy that offers lots of fat and yields very little lean, practical combat training. The Active component is much better off, but the institutional problems persist. A perfect example was the TSIRT for the 94th in March of 2003 just before we shipped out to Iraq. It was just another check the box exercise that showed just how much our readiness had dulled as a result of the paper-pushing bureaucrats—those who'd never been to combat were telling us what we needed to do. Apparently the Army deemed that was all the training we needed to become "qualified" for combat duty. The only useful information I gleaned off of our TSIRT was that it was very important not to eat any depleted uranium rounds I found lying around.

In an effort to be fair, I'll say this "training" occurred before the rise of the insurgency in Iraq, so we had no idea what specific problems we'd face. However the fact that the Army said we were qualified to go to war after a few minutes of firing our weapons and watching a stupid movie like that was unnerving to say the least.

The fix is simple enough in theory but lamentably hard in actual practice—hammering home basic soldier skills over and over again. The fundamentals of soldiering must be made "muscle memory," the factor that will make the difference between life and death. One thing is for sure—our enemy doesn't discriminate between the Active and Reserve components, and either branch of our military will find itself in combat if deployed to the war zones regardless of MOS. In Iraq, the 94th escorted convoys and patrolled around the Al Anbar Province and Baghdad for over a year. We worked with several transportation, quartermaster, and maintenance units who had previously never considered that one day they might discover themselves actually pulling a trigger in combat, but that's what happened. Almost overnight, they found themselves on the front lines in Iraq. Bottom line—we can learn the paperwork and other nonsense on the job, but everyone needs to know the basics of unconventional combat and the potential scenarios they may find themselves in.

The U.S. military as a whole needs to trash the path of least resistance—the forms, the paperwork, the other meaningless indices that measure a soldier's training—and start getting down to the business of tactical basics. "Train like you fight" is a simple enough doctrine to print off on yet another useless Army manual or pamphlet, but is rarely being put into actual practice.

We were incredibly fortunate to have the collective attitude we did before heading to Iraq. If we didn't like something, we spoke up and said something about it. As Reservists, we had that unique view of the Army; able to see it from both the inside and outside. Even though we weren't full-timers like our counterparts, a lot of our guys were older with experience. With the Active side, it was often fresh young kids just learning about life, with few speaking up for fear of getting into trouble, despite their bright and active minds.

It was that perspective that allowed us to speak our minds, and in my opinion was a huge factor in bringing us all back home. Our mantra was simple—we were responsible for our own safety and security. We'd go on to put together our own tactical training, and didn't rely on "Army standards" to get us through this combat tour in Iraq.

Cheap, Fast, Good—pick two, Mr. Rumsfeld.

"You go to war with the Army you have, not the Army you might want or wish to have at a later time." [69]

What the holy fuck Rumsfeld meant by this answer to a soldier's question, one asked during a "town hall meeting" with troops preparing to head into Iraq in December of 2004, I

---

69 *Secretary Rumsfeld Town Hall Meeting in Kuwait*, US Department of Defense, Office of the Assistant Secretary of Defense (Public Affairs) News Transcript, December 8, 2004

haven't the foggiest. However the question posed by Specialist Thomas Wilson, a soldier with the Tennessee National Guard, drove home a point that was on the minds of Active and Reserve personnel alike; after almost two years since the invasion, why was the U.S. military still driving around Iraq with substandard equipment? Why were we still being forced to salvage scrap armor to weld onto our Humvees for better protection? [70]

Way to go, Tommy. I have no doubt your question saved lives.

Rumsfeld was pretty good at throwing his nonsensical, bullshit riddle-speak at the press during his briefings, but it's a little tougher when you're in the Middle East staring down 2000 soldiers who want answers—especially one who wasn't frozen in fear by Rumsfeld's presence or concerned with what an off-color question would do to his career. Rumsfeld's answer, that the lack of new up-armored Humvees was the result of limits on production—not money, or the Army's desire to procure new ones—turned out to be untrue. The *sole* company that produces these Humvees, O' Gara-Hess & Eisenhardt (purchased by Armor Holdings Aerospace & Defense Group in August 2001), stated in December of 2004 that they were fully capable of cranking out additional hummers, *by more than 22%*, but was waiting for the Pentagon's order.[71] Only *after* the meeting did the order come for more Humvees, and only *afterwards* did the Pentagon increase the production of armored plating

---

70 Thomas E. Ricks, *Rumsfeld Gets Earful From Troops*, The Washington Post, December 9, 2004

71 *Armor Holdings Could Boost Humvee Armor Output 22%*, Bloomberg News, December 9, 2004 (www.bloomberg.com)

at its Rock Island arsenal in Illinois by ordering a 24-hour shift.[72]

So what was the problem? As you might have guessed, it's far from a simple one.

My first concern was the accuracy of the reporting of ground conditions to the Pentagon and DoD—were combat leaders in Iraq candid with the Department of Defense about the problems we were having?

As an eyewitness to severe communication breakdowns within Iraq—sometimes regarding events that took place *only a few miles away*—I could see how signals could've been crossed when trying to get information all the way from Iraq back to the States; by the time reports were reaching the Pentagon, who knows what they might have looked like. And knowing that some of our leadership in Iraq might have been looking to protect their reputation as those who could "make do with the materials they'd been given," it seems plausible that commanders might not have as up front as they could have been concerning the growing problems on the roads.

However a DoD briefing by Major General Stephen Speakes in December of 2004, specifically outlining the in-progress plan to armor combat vehicles, doesn't support this theory. His testimony to the Department of Defense was very thorough and highlighted the shortcomings of vehicle armor in the Iraqi theater of operations.[73] Prior to his testimony, the

---

72 Bryan Bender and Boston Globe Staff, *Army orders increase in armor production*, The Boston Globe, December 11, 2004 (www.boston.com)

73 *Special Defense Department Briefing on Uparmoring HMMWV*, U.S. Department of Defense, Office of the Assistant Secretary of Defense (Public Affairs) News Transcript, Presenters: Major General Stephen Speakes,

leadership of the 94th MPs had an opportunity to discuss this and several other issues personally with General Speakes while in Kuwait during a meeting in the summer of 2004—impressed with his sincerity, willingness to help and attention to detail, I am quite certain his reporting was accurate.

So who *was* behind this shortage of up-armored Humvees; trucks that thousands of soldiers had been screaming for over the last 12 months?

Before we begin, let's take a brief look at the process behind the acquisition of the M1114 "up-armored Humvee," from the ground up. Operational items, such as the M1114, that are needed to support rapidly changing conditions in combat, are developed outside of what are considered "normal" supply forecasting procedures. Because of their sudden increase in demand, combat units in Iraq or Afghanistan submitted "Operational Needs Statements" for the up-armored, which were then converted in to *theater requirements* by Combined Forces Land Component Command (CFLCC) and CENTCOM. From there, they're passed up to the Department of the Army, where they are validated and eventually passed to the program managers that oversee the procurement process. Since the M1114 variant is a brand new item still in its initial issuance, funding must be obtained for their production; program managers secure the funding through Congress (which can take months) and orders are then placed with the industrial base.

U.S. Army G-8, Force Development; Brigadier General (*Promotable*) Jeffrey Sorenson, Deputy for Acquisition Systems Management to the Assistant Secretary of the Army for Acquisition, Logistics, and Technology; Colonel John Rooney, Chief of Staff, Army Test and Development Command, December 15, 2004 (www.defenselink.mil)

So, who was responsible for the scarcity? While hardly a simple issue, the United States Government Accountability Office (GAO) puts it rather bluntly. According to the GAO's report, the shortage resulted because "*a decision was made* [by the Department of Defense] *to pace production rather than use the maximum available capacity*," and that "*funding allocations did not keep up with rapidly increasing requirements.*" The report goes on to say that the DoD did not "*give Congress visibility over the basis for its acquisition solution,*" and that the "*acquisition challenges impeded DoD's ability to respond to rapidly increasing demands.*"[74]

Translation—the DoD ordered just enough Humvees to meet demand, but it planned on meeting its target number of M1114s over a certain period of time. Furthermore, the money needed to pay for them was based off of this projected number. Instead of taking advantage of the maximum monthly capacity of the industrial base (in this case, O'Gara-Hess Eisenhardt), it paced the production of the up-armored over a span of months, looking to reach a specific number by a specific date. However the demand for M1114s spiked mid-production, and the Department of Defense, specifically the Department of the Army, had to adjust their numbers. As demand for the M1114 rose, so did the pace of production—but still not to O'Gara-Hess's maximum capacity. Efforts were then made to appropriate funding for the additional orders, an often complicated and time consuming Congressional affair. By the time funding was secured and orders were placed, the demand would spike yet again. This represented the frustrating gap to units

---

[74] United States Government Accountability Office Report to Congressional Committees, *Defense Logistics, Actions Needed to Improve the Availability of Critical Items during Current and Future Operations* (GAO-05-275, April 2005).

like mine who, after 12 months at war in Al Anbar as military police with outdated equipment, were still pleading for armored Humvees.

An interesting point, however; according to the GAO, the Department of Defense did not inform Congress of the total available production capacity. If Congress had known about the capabilities of the industrial base, it's possible they could've delivered funds faster to secure their production. Given that it currently takes *four months* just for the industrial base to procure the materials needed for the production of a M1114 (that's a separate issue in itself), we're talking about quite a few months in going from demand to actual supply.

In a nutshell, that was the deal.

Here's how it broke down in Iraq: In August of 2003, right around the time the IED was becoming a formidable weapon, CENTCOM was asking for just over fourteen hundred M1114s. At the time, the guys and gals at the O'Gara-Hess assembly line were cranking out 51 of the M1114s per month to meet the need. Congress had already appropriated $1.2 billion for soldier and vehicular armor that August, but the Pentagon held the money until it was decided just how many vehicles it should order. In February of 2004, the Army made a deal with O'Gara to produce 460 per month—an almost ten-fold increase in pace to meet the new demand. However, in September of 2004, just over a year later, the requirement was 8105.

I've heard the government's side of the story. But in order to get a better view of the situation, I contacted Mr. Robert Mecredy, President of the Armor Holdings' Aerospace and Defense Group, the man who originally gave the statement to the press concerning the available capacity to manufacture the M1114. Our conversation was lengthy, with some surprising details.

A theme repeated in our conversation was all too telling—no one saw this coming. No one saw a protracted war in Iraq. No one could predict that 54% of the ground personnel in Iraq would consist of Reserve and National Guard personnel, the units that were often working with outdated equipment. Mr. Mecredy, himself a former soldier, was approached by the Chief of the National Guard to discuss the future need of up-armored Humvee variants. Instead of accepting a figure put forth by Mr. Mecredy based on the number of Humvees currently fielded by the Guard and Reserve components, the Chief looked into the possibility of having a "pool" of Humvees to draw from for units. Why? It's expensive to build these things, and the Guard didn't want to pay for them. Mr. Mecredy went on to explain that the Guard itself was not "embracing the need" for this vehicle.

My position stated in previous articles written for SFTT.org are clear—the new wars of the 21st century will not be won with the ultra-expensive gadgets purchased by the United States military. They will be won one step at a time, against a foe that already knows how to beat a conventional enemy. Long gone are the days of the lone bombing campaigns and missile strikes. If real change is to be affected in the world, troops will have to be on the ground, rooting out the bad guys, door-to-door if need be. While neither perfect nor infallible, equipment such as the M1114 are vital to that mission, and will provide the edge in a fast-paced unconventional war.

So what caused the fire behind the increased production of the M1114? Simply put, members of Congress attending the funerals of a growing number of servicemen and women.

According to Mr. Mecredy, Congress was insistent on

getting answers to the mounting number of casualties in Iraq, and in finding out why wasn't more being done. The Department of Defense's less-than-transparent acquisition process wasn't offering Congress the details it wanted. Only after the GAO report was state legislature made aware of the DoD's process by which it purchased and fielded the M1114.

The reality that the number of deaths provided to those on the home front, coupled with growing pressures from field commanders in Iraq, led to the boom in funding and production of the up-armored Humvee—Specialist Williams' remarks sealed the deal.

Thanks to the public holding their leaders to account, much has been learned—and exposed—about the process behind buying new military equipment. Since the GAO investigation, communication between the government and the industrial base has increased markedly. Military leaders are now in better touch with industry, each gauging the other's requirements. However, according to the GAO report, the DoD has not taken the actions necessary to fulfill their recommendations, nor did they address how they intend to improve their current practices.

Somewhere between the ground truth in Iraq and the Secretary of Defense, there was a huge breakdown. In any event, it's extremely troubling to think that someone in the military chain of command either didn't think it necessary to address this pressing problem, didn't think it a major "war stopper," or worse, didn't even know about it. After all, it was a *specialist*, not a general or colonel, who caused the fallout and led to an increase in the production of more armored Humvees.

One thing is for certain; the American press—and a soldier with a point—can do wonders for the efforts of those on the ground. And it's to this great truth we owe the introduction of more up-armored Humvees to Iraq; in my opinion, a vehicle that has saved, and will continue to save, the lives of American servicemen and women all over the world.

"[Rumsfeld's] beloved shock-and-awe whiz-bang wonder weapons worked well enough initially in Afghanistan and Iraq, but as we saw on the tube last week, we're once again back to the age-old struggle of man against man—with grunts [personnel], not machines, taking and holding ground." [75]

Logic told me when I entered the Army Reserves in 1997 that the Department of Defense was not going to spend billions of their budget dollars on equipment that was only used a few days a month by bunch of Reservists. And because I understood the situation, I was willing to wear the "hand-me-downs" afforded to us by our Active duty counterparts.

I was even somewhat accepting of that fact—sort of—when we first entered Iraq, Reservists were driving around in the older, 1987-model Humvees with little or no protective armor that required almost constant maintenance. I even understood that the Army just couldn't move that fast and that flak jackets taped to the doors would have to suffice for the moment. But after about six months, an engineer unit at Al Asad tested the metal sheets from salvaged Iraqi vehicles for ballistic defense, with impressive results. They would stop a bullet from both an M16 and an AK. Unfortunately it was never applied, due in

---

75 David H. Hackworth, *With Deepest Sympathy*, from the *Defending America* archives, November 22, 2004. Courtesy of *Soldiers for the Truth* and *DefenseWatch* (www.sftt.org), the article can be found on Colonel Hackworth's website, www.hackworth.com/archive

part because the engineer officers, feeling the pressure exerted by their commanders, didn't want to get into trouble for modifying government vehicles. I guess they preferred another government vehicle, an American soldier, getting "modified" instead—by an IED or other bomb.

However over a year later, when we were tasked with the perilous mission of escorting convoys through Baghdad, we still didn't have what we needed, and we were on the roads constantly. Only after a *year* of bitching about our equipment, something was done about it. Our older trucks finally had the "add on armor kits" installed—large bulletproof sheets of metal bolted to our cab, along with ballistic side windows—just before our mission. But we still didn't have ballistic windshields.[76] What was taking so damn long? For a lot of soldiers on the ground in Iraq, surviving the daily onslaught of ambushes and IEDs *was* the war. What the hell is wrong with this picture?

The fundamental issue here isn't so much re-allocating the available equipment to allow for better protection for soldiers in the Reserves (although it's a good temporary fix). It is really a question of how the money is spent in the first place. Former Secretary of Defense (SECDEF) Donald Rumsfeld insisted on spending billions of dollars on conventional warfare technology—missiles, aerospace technology and larger weapon systems were getting the cash as SECDEF Rumsfeld looked to

---

76 We eventually procured ballistic windshields for our humvees, save a few. During our many escorts to *Anaconda*, we sought out a maintenance company that might've been able to help us obtain the ballistic glass. We found one, and they were courageous enough to provide us with their excess windshields, circumventing the bungling paperwork shuffle that was holding up their acquisition in Kuwait—a great example of resourcefulness and cooperation trumping a mechanical bureaucracy.

transform our military into a smaller, more elite, more technologically advanced fighting force, literally at the expense of soldiers on the ground in Iraq and Afghanistan.[77]

SECDEF Rumsfeld's approach was flawed from the start. Perhaps it was borne from a naïve and overly conventional view of combat, one I'd expect from a man who's never been to war (or from a former pilot, as Rumsfeld is). While the integration of air-ground combat operations have had some stunning successes, this campaign against terror, this new World War, isn't going to be won by spending more money on bombers or missiles, the use of which is playing an increasingly limited role in low intensity conflicts.[78] A smart bomb isn't smart enough to patrol a neighborhood, escort a convoy, and kick down a door in a raid that's meant to find a specific person, a person that looks like everyone else in his neighborhood. A smart bomb can't find a terrorist in a town of millions. And any man or woman who doesn't have a good understanding of the priorities needed to win this brand of conflict—priorities that could help influence much needed public support and troop morale—shouldn't be calling the shots.

---

77 Navy and Air Force budgets (fiscal year 2006) appropriate a total of almost $10 billion for fighter aircraft alone, a figure more than *three times* what was allocated for the weapons, tracked combat vehicles (*M1 Abrams tanks, Bradley Fighting Vehicles and Stryker infantry carrier vehicles*), and other combat vehicles for the Army and Marine Corps combined (Source: *Department of Defense Budget, Fiscal Year 2006 Procurement Programs (P-1)*, pages 14, 22, 37, 67 and 74, presented February 2005).

78 *The "Post Conflict" Lessons of Iraq and Afghanistan*, Testimony to the Senate Foreign Relations Committee by Anthony H. Cordesman, Arleigh A. Burke Chair in Strategy, Center for Strategic and International Studies, May 19, 2004, pgs. 5-7

The war on terror isn't going to be won at 25,000 feet—it's going to be won at 200 meters, fighting insurgents shooting at us with good old, Russian-made AK47s in the cities around Iraq, Afghanistan or wherever we find ourselves next. The over-conventional approach by the DoD is costing the lives of hundreds of young American men and women who need basic equipment to take this fight to our enemy—killed by the very insurgents that have eluded our current inventory of ultra-expensive bombs, missiles and planes. While I'd love to sit here and tell you the Army is involved with nothing but offensive operations that require this equipment, more often it is not. The operations revolving around simply sustaining an Army are massive, and involve an incredible amount of movement and travel. There's always a soldier in need of food, water and ammunition. A million-dollar bomber can't get it to him.

The best technology and equipment isn't always the answer; tactics, techniques, and procedures count for a lot. I don't think I'm alone in thinking that troops on the ground ultimately win wars, and deserve the best, most practical equipment we have. I can understand the need for a sophisticated arsenal to serve as a deterrent for other countries that pose a greater conventional threat, but running a new "arms race" while ignoring the basics of what's needed to fight a very-current global war on terror isn't a sound long-term strategy.

Instead of rubber-stamping a signature on the sympathy notes to the families of those who gave their lives in this war, the former SECDEF should've given the guys and gals on the ground in Iraq and Afghanistan, Reserve or Active, the basics they needed to defeat the insurgency.

The third issue before us is the readiness of the Reserve

system. In one of my first assignments in the Reserves as a platoon leader I was asked by my commander to draft an Officer Evaluation Report (OER) Support Form that listed some of the tasks I looked to accomplish for the platoon over the next rating period.

My plan offered some challenging options—a series of tactical training exercises, an obstacle course, a competitive weapons range, and a list of tactical-related events. My commander responded with, "Why don't you just shoot for an 80% attendance rate at all drills for the platoon."

Not exactly the standard I was looking for, and, as that became the status quo by our command, it came to represent the sad state of affairs of the Reserve system as a whole when it came to readiness.

Now I realize that something like readiness cannot be quantified easily. Even so it didn't take a rocket scientist to discover that the system prior to our deployment was abysmal at best. The only thing the Army was looking for when we deployed was an acceptable number of troops to go overseas. While we did have acceptable "T" and "E" ratings, (training and equipment), they weren't as important to the Army as the coveted "P" (personnel) rating which simply says if you had enough people, you're ready for war. That was by far the most influential factor in evaluating a unit for readiness. While the unit may have been ready in a numerical sense, the soldiers were not. In a rush to make numbers look good, soldiers are thrown into slots without the proper training and pushed off into combat.

This may come to a shock to some readers, but believe it or not the Army will send you to war even if your paperwork is imperfect or incomplete. USAR leadership at all levels should not fret over checking every box when it comes to deployment.

When it comes to readiness the USAR must move its focus from filling every rank with warm bodies to actual, realistic, combat training. For any military leaders reading this that are preparing to deploy, keep in mind it is a cold hard fact that the DoD is not nearly as concerned with soldier readiness as it is with numbers. It's up to Reserve leadership to drop the numbers game and build soldier skill, morale and confidence by developing more practical standards of readiness.

Like the old adage says, "no combat-ready unit ever passes inspection."

Leadership is the fourth and largest issue that faces the Reserves, if not the entire military. While it's an age-old problem that isn't going to be resolved here, I do what I can to bring the problems to light. Succinctly stated, the more leadership flaws that are exposed, the more difficult it becomes to correct the problems that are revealed.

It should be clear to anyone who has jumped through the Army's hoops that the USAR doesn't challenge its leadership hard enough, and that subsequent lack of training leads to horrible consequences. The first part of this equation goes back to the training issue—too many leaders become paper-pushers who lose their tactical edge.

I joined the Army to defend my country and its ideals, knowing full well that I might be asked to pick up a weapon and take a shot at somebody someday. Like it or not, that's what the Army is all about. It can't be hidden behind paperwork, manuals, publications or regulations. War is dangerous business and good leadership is the only assurance of victory. How the troops will ultimately perform comes down to how well the leaders handled themselves, their subordinates and their weapons. Leaders who reject this basic fact will find themselves in a world of hurt overseas against an unconventional and adaptive enemy, regardless of what job they were specifically trained by the Army to do.

I can't say for sure with the Active component, but the USAR's promotion record reveals that far too many leaders are promoted, especially in the officer corps, by substituting real world experience with the right schools. I can tell you that it is a universal law in the military that what goes around comes around. Those who take shortcuts on their way to greater rank and responsibility will ultimately pay for it with their own life or, even worse, with the blood of the soldiers they've taken an oath to defend in this unrelenting, no-quarter war on terror. Now that any Reservist can expect to head overseas, make sure they're ready to go. Allowing Reservists to be promoted to fill a leadership position without proper training, at any level, is a deadly mistake.

For example: about half way through our tour, I began to notice articles in various military publications discussing the removal of the "conditional promotion" policy with U.S. Army sergeants. Normally, a specialist could be conditionally promoted to sergeant as long as he or she completed Primary Leader Development Course, PLDC, within a certain time. Being that an E5 is considered the first real leadership position within the NCO Corps, it made sense that they'd have to attend a course to learn how to do it. PLDC is no joke, and can be quite challenging. The same went for E5 to E6 and E6 to E7 with the attendance of the Basic and Advanced Non-Commissioned Officer Courses (BNOC and ANOC, respectfully).[79]

However, the article was stating that E5s could now be

---

79 Association of the United States Army, Institute of Land Warfare, *Saying*

conditionally promoted to E6—E4s would no longer need to attend PLDC to "earn their stripes." Sergeants are now in leadership positions with no real leadership training. This is not the best course of action for the USAR to take. I can only speak from experience, but as a Reservist, our weekend drills or even two-week annual training events (ATs) weren't really enough to get us in fighting shape. Usually it was more of a paperwork exercise than anything else; trying to stuff in as much as you can into two days was tough, even with a small, full-time staff. There is a certain amount of "on the job" training you can expect when deployed, but too many times I saw soldiers in the Reserves promoted that weren't ready, or even qualified, to lead troops. And before you know it, literally overnight, they're doing so *in combat*. While the war may have started on a time and date of our choosing, our *enemies* have initiated the battles that followed, battles that a lot of unprepared soldiers found themselves in. Like I said before, and many others have said it too, the enemy ALWAYS gets a vote.

Stricter standards must be met in the Reserves before troops are promoted. PLDC is a school that all E4s should attend, with similar schools, regardless of MOS, for each rank. The same goes for officers. Simple fundamentals need to be reinforced year after year. You can learn the paperwork and regulations as you go—you can't be taught the "Warrior Ethos," the basics that make you an effective soldier, twice a year when you pick up your weapon. Every soldier *has* to be a rifleman first, even those—especially those—who think they'll never pick up a weapon in combat. Ask any transportation soldier who has ever been in Iraq.

Good-Bye to Conditional Promotions, First Quarter, 2004, February 2, 2004 (www.ausa.org)

The Reserve system and its soldiers must take these facts to heart—the days of the "one weekend a month" approach to duty are over. The days of ticket punching need to end. The USAR has to get back to critical soldier fundamentals and relieve those leaders who have allowed complacency to become standard practice. It is past time to "train like you fight and fight like you trained," otherwise disaster instead of victory looms over the horizon.

Can it all be done with one weekend a month and two weeks a year? We did it, and I'm confident most other units can do it, too. Most Reservists have extensive prior Active duty experience, which will no doubt be an important factor in training the next generation of citizen-soldiers.

Technology isn't a substitute for awareness

There's been a lot of talk regarding the Transportation Security Administration's infamous "no-fly" list, a register of people who are considered a threat to airline security and should not be allowed on commercial aircraft. The ACLU even argued a case in 2003 challenging its very existence after a few people were wrongly "flagged" for allegedly being involved in terrorist activities.[80] Typical—everyone's supportive of the war on terror until they're personally involved. The ultimate "not in my backyard" rationale. Wasn't it just a few years ago when we all rallied around the flag and pledged our support and sacrifice? Now we can't even wait in the security line at the airport without getting pissed off, and a little embarrassment is enough to send someone running to the ACLU.

---

80 *The ACLU in the courts since 9/11, Rebecca Gordon, et al v. FBI, et al*, April 22, 2003 (www.aclu.org)

I agree in having a list that defines those who might pose a danger to commercial aircraft, even if the system isn't exactly perfect. It makes a lot of sense to me, and while it hasn't lead to the capture of any known terrorists, the no-fly list may provide a deterrent to those who have been selected to carry out missions. Then there's the computer assisted passenger pre-screening system, or CAPPS. This system uses technology to identify a passenger's travel habits and ticket purchases (among other things—the specific criteria used are classified), and alerts security personnel to any suspicious fliers. Again, while not perfect systems, they represent a line of defense for the traveling public, and I support them fully—there are bound to be problems, but I believe they will be fixed over time. But all of this technology is worthless if people aren't paying attention.

In 2005 alone there were two incidents of planes being forced to land *after* it was discovered that one or more of the members of these lists were already on board.[81] For some reason the no-fly list is only being reviewed *after* the plane has taken off. Regardless if the people were a threat or not, if it isn't being reviewed before the plane flies, then tell me, what is the point of even having it? "We regret to inform you, Mr. & Mrs. Joe Public, that your daughter was aboard an airliner that crashed earlier today, most likely due to terrorist activity. The good news is we're pretty sure it was this guy, who was on board and on our list."

An article printed in the late winter of 2004 demonstrates a point where an over-reliance on technology isn't always the problem; sometimes it's simply a glaring oversight. After

---

81 Alan Levin and the Associate Press, *Diverted Flight False Alarm*, USA Today, May 12, 2005; Alan Levin, *Boston-bound passenger on 'no-fly' list*, USA Today, May 17, 2005

running the name Osama Bin Laden—the world's most wanted fugitive—through some gazillion-dollar-state-of-the-art-wiz-bang-super-tech airport security device, his name wasn't flagged. Osama Bin Laden is allowed to board.[82] While I believe that he'd be spotted *long* before he was able to make his way to the United Airlines counter at LaGuardia, it's a little frightening that such an error had been made.

There's obviously a need for a little overlap in our security measures, a "security blanket" if you will.

However, let's not put all of our security eggs in the airport checkpoint and no-fly list basket. Let us rather put some trust in the strength of the average American, rather than in technology, and make damn sure this doesn't happen again. Vigilance is the key to success in any war, and sometimes it comes in a controversial package. New breakthroughs in computer software, surveillance cameras or retinal scans don't mean a thing if no one's watching. And let's face facts: our techno-fueled complacency will yield yet another opportunity for another attack; especially for anyone named bin Laden, who already has an advantage.

Let's also remember that beyond all of the diabolical plots, sinister scheming and shortcomings of the CIA, FBI and the Pentagon, it wasn't just a "failure of imagination" that precipitated September 11th; it was a couple of 4-inch blades—carried by men who had, ironically, been flagged by the CAPPS system.[83]

---

82 Timothy W. Maier, *Homeland Insecurity, Mr. bin Laden, you're clear to fly*, Insight/News World Communications Inc., WorldNetDaily, February 18, 2004 (www.worldnetdaily.com)

83 *Congressional Quarterly*, Congressional Hearings, June 29, 2005, *House Homeland Security Subcommittee on Economic Security, Infrastructure Protection*

The Patriot Act

Ben Franklin said, "People willing to trade their freedom for security deserve neither and will lose both." I respectfully disagree.

I tend to follow the advice of another Founding Father, Thomas Jefferson, that being "The price of liberty is eternal vigilance."

First of all, I don't regard The Patriot Act as a sacrifice of our freedoms, and tend to resent those in our society that rush to judgment over the measures our government has taken. The "big brother" bullshit is an overblown concern. But of course, every wannabe militiaman or civil liberties zealot somewhere is screaming bloody murder, convinced their rights are being infringed and they'll finally prove their little point by challenging the government that somehow unjustly oppresses them. While civil liberties make this country what it is, and their defense is paramount, the irresponsible attacks against these reasonable measures that intend to make us safer are beyond the pale—the "professional complainers" again offering no solutions, only background noise.

Are we really that paranoid of our own government that we wouldn't want our Department of Justice to go the extra mile in nabbing some guys here in the United States, some of them *our own citizens*, who are looking to do some bad stuff? And are those who over-complain ready to lose a family member in a terrorist attack that could have been prevented? "It's too bad Uncle Joe was killed in that car bomb the other day in New York, but I'm glad the American who did it didn't have to

---

and Cybersecurity Holds Hearing on Improving Pre-Screening of Aviation Passengers (www.cq.com)

endure the great injustice of having his phone tapped out of an abundance of caution."

There are people here in the U.S., *citizens*, which have trained in camps overseas. There are people here that have made known their hatred of our government and our way of life. If one of these people are involved with some activities that otherwise would be difficult to track or investigate, and they were stopped before they could act, isn't that the proactive defense work we're looking for? What if something happened that we could have prevented? We can't leave anything to chance now, or a lot more innocent people will die. It's just a matter of time. You might ruffle a few feathers—it's bound to happen, and we can't just cave into the pressures of those professional complainers who see the world in black and white. I said to my guys in Iraq, I'm not an "I told you so" kind of guy—I'd rather act and be wrong than not act at all. At least you could learn from a mistake that way.

Put a little faith in your government in not letting things get out of hand, and in the judicial system charged with its oversight.

That being said, the ACLU can shut the hell up and go back to their righteous defense of the North American Man/Boy Love Association (NAMBLA) and their cause.[84]

"The guerrilla wins by not losing. The Army loses by not winning." [85]

---

84 Correspondent Kathy Slobogin, *Parents of murdered child sue child-sex advocates*, January 8, 2001 (www.cnn.com)

85 A quote from former US Secretary of State Henry Kissinger regarding the Vietnam War, 1969

I love it when al-Zarqawi and his buddy Osama were considered "masterminds" of their craft—like it takes a fucking mastermind when you look like everyone else, drive the same cars, hide behind women & kids, and send troubled young men to do your dirty work to serve your own ends. It takes a mastermind to load a bunch of explosives into a car and drive it into a mosque, checkpoint or military base. It takes a mastermind to train someone to bury explosives and blow them up when Iraqi police, soldiers or Marines drive by, only to disappear into a crowd. Wow, how do they figure this shit out?

There is no such thing as a terrorist mastermind. They're competent logisticians, at best. Why are we making these people out to more than they are, a bunch of pathetic men looking to use kids and religion for their own gains? A letter in April of 2004 the military seized a letter from Iraqi insurgents believed to be intended for Zarqawi noting low morale among followers and weakening support for the insurgency.[86] The letter barely made the news. Why is that? Other reports stated the morale of insurgents in Afghanistan was low following the initial invasion as well, complaining they were left to rot out in the mountains while their leaders drive around in air-conditioned SUVs.[87] Stuff like this has to be capitalized on, hard and quickly.

We have to pound away on ANY insurgency that it's just not worth it to fight us. Articles like these need to be front-page news, over and over again. This enemy we face is an army, too,

---

86 Kevin Flower, Geoff Hiscock, Kathleen Koch, Octavia Nasr and Mohammed Tawfeeq, *U.S.: Possible letter to al-Zarqawi cites low morale*, May 3, 2005 (www.cnn.com)

87 Tim McGirk, *War in the Shadows*, Time Magazine, October 10, 2005

Islam, Terrorism and the West

"Just as we did in the Cold War, we need to defend our ideals abroad vigorously. America does stand up for its values. The United States defended, and still defends, Muslims against tyrants and criminals in Somalia, Bosnia, Kosovo, Afghanistan, and Iraq. If the United States does not act aggressively to define itself in the Islamic world, the extremists will gladly do the job for us." [88]

There have been thousands of books analyzing the division between the West and Islam and it will no doubt be the subject of debate for centuries. But despite the past conflicts, a great majority of the world's one billion Muslims have condemned the terrorist acts that have come about since 9/11. Some brave followers of Islam have organized themselves into groups and provided specific examples in the Koran that condemn the acts of these terrorists. Although the past two thousand years have been witness to many atrocities committed by zealous followers of *all* religions, it's widely accepted that the justifications behind more recent acts of terror represent a distorted view of Islam, not a literal interpretation of any text.[89]

While I realize that the majority has nothing in common with the murderous people responsible for terrorism, the fact

---

88 *The 9/11 Commission Report*, page 377

89 Harun Yahya, *Murdering innocent people in the name of religion is unacceptable*, from *Islam For Today*, date unknown (www.islamfortoday.com)

that the governments of "moderate" Muslim countries ignore the violence committed in the name of Islam troubles me. It almost appears to be a passive support of the violence in Iraq and Afghanistan as well as in the rest of the world.

Where is the Muslim outrage at the destructive use of their religion?

The countries of the Coalition continually find themselves under the microscope and must constantly defend their roles in this war on terror. Every decision is picked apart by other governments, the press, critics, everyone. But what about when some atrocious act is committed in the name of Islam? Sure, we see the cookie-cutter answer from the U.S., the U.K. and the U.N. of how "barbaric" they are, but how about the Muslim populations in Jordan? Pakistan? Egypt? Morocco? Frankly, I'm starting to believe the U.S. Government cares more about its reputation as Americans than followers of Islam care about their religion. I can't help but feel like they readily accept violence as an understandable and justifiable component of their culture. For crying out loud, there are Sunni clerics in Iraq that issue fatwas condemning the modern clothes worn by Muslim women, but ignore the mass killings and beheadings committed in their country each day. And while it's important to note that the popular support of terrorism in some Muslim countries is diminishing, too many sanction violence in the defense of Islam. Some even saw Osama bin Laden as a hero.[90] So the question is—what is the intention of those who support or commit violence? What is the ultimate goal of these people, really, in the end?

---

90 *Islamic Extremism: Common Concern for Muslim and Western Publics*, Pew Global Attitudes Project, the Pew Research Center, July 14, 2005 (www.pewglobal.org).

Some say it's the somewhat legitimate aim of establishing an Islamic state. Others say it's for expelling the infidels from the holy lands in the Middle East. Yet others claim it's an attempt to protect the Islamic culture and way of life against the decadent West. But when someone's murdered in the name of Islam, is that considered "defending" the faith? Is a car bomb that kills fellow Muslims or the beheading of a British contractor going to lead to a successful Islamic nation?

First, let's start taking a close look at the ultimate reward for these suicide operatives of the Muslim faith. They never speak of serving a loftier purpose of advancing their society or protecting their religion, but rather gaining a spot in paradise—their own selfish goal of a personal heaven at the expense of both their religion and anyone who gets in their way. Doesn't sound like a struggle for a "homeland" to me.

Second, some just are sick people that enjoy killing. Period. It doesn't matter why people think they do it, that their actions are justified "because we're the invaders," or "we're destroying their religion." The odds of these people winning a Nobel Prize or advancing world society if we hadn't invaded Iraq are slim. Take away the thin veil of their faith and all you have are psychopathic murderers. If you need some convincing, force yourself to watch the videotaped executions of Eugene Armstrong, Nick Berg or Kim Sun-il. You'll get an idea of the inhuman acts these people are capable of. There were even reports that some of these videos were doctored to better amplify the sounds of pain and suffering in their victim's final moments. A strike at the decadent West? Yeah, I don't think so.

Third, to think that some Muslims around the world—especially the governments of more moderate Arab countries—even *tacitly* support these vile acts of savagery scares the shit out of me. A huge bomb shreds 50 kids on a street in Baghdad and no one bats an eye. Someone gets their head chopped off *while they're still alive*, and no one says a word. Yet they jump over some poor Indonesian model in a mini-skirt. What bodes worse for the world opinion of Islam—the extremists who cut someone's head off, or the moderates who stay quiet about it?[91]

But let's just go ahead and remove the religious component and see these people for who they are—narrow-minded, short-sighted, ruthless, self-serving people with no better purpose in life than to achieve their own selfish aims. Somehow, the United States is responsible for all of the ills of the world and an attack against us is their ticket to paradise. I can't listen to any more babble by these "radicals" that say the U.S. mistreats Muslims after we risked life and limb to help them in Bosnia, or when they implicate Christians in crimes against Islam dating back over a thousand years to justify terrorism. Or those mysterious U.S. policies that somehow oppress Muslims? Funny, I know of none that sanction the wanton murder of innocent civilians in the name of religion, some being Muslims themselves.

It isn't a war for Islam; it's a war for power and control. Don't think the free world doesn't see the manipulation of impressionable young men, rich or poor, to achieve the means of those who seek to rule. The Nazis, Imperial Japan, Fascist Italy; they all tried it and wound up a pile of ashes in "history's unmarked grave of discarded lies." Sound familiar?

The only redeeming factor I can think of with fundamentalist Islam is the fact that they'll *never* go on to set up a functional government. It's like *The Lord of the Flies* with these people—a bunch of bickering kids that can't even work out

---

[91] Anthony King, *One in four Muslims sympathizes with motives of terrorists*, Daily Telegraph, July 23, 2005 (www.telegraph.co.uk)

the most basic problems between themselves, and yet expect to realize this fantasy of an all-powerful Islamic nation. If it's not Sunni versus Shi'ite, it's tribe against tribe. If it's not tribe against tribe, it's town against town. If it's not town against town, it's neighbor against neighbor. The endless civil war between each sect is one reason why they'll never evolve. The fact they have the nerve to call themselves men after the cowardly, self-serving acts they commit is another.

Obviously we have some hearts and minds to win. While I support the war against radical fundamentalism, we have to be careful not to alienate the populations of those countries who might not be supportive of "everything American," but may be drawn to our economy, government and social freedoms—the foundations of liberty. Sending missiles into foreign countries in an attempt to knock off every oppressive leader (who doesn't represent an immediate threat) will only serve to galvanize resentment against the United States, and alienate those who might have been willing to give us a chance. The world's oppressive Islamic theological autocracies are like three-legged stools—fracture their legs with sweeping social change, lean on it with a developing free economy and it will eventually fall over. But we need the balls to do it first, and see it through to the end.

If we foster the more moderate beliefs of their people, we'll eventually lead them away from the extremist views that are turning the Islamic religion, in some nations, into the world's largest street gang.

"If you beat this prick long enough, he'll tell you he started the goddamn Chicago fire, but it don't necessarily make it fucking so!"

Chris Penn as *Nice Guy Eddie*
Reservoir Dogs

In memory of one of the most underrated actors of all time, Chris Penn, I'd like to begin with a memorable quote from one of his most famous movies, *Reservoir Dogs*, which best sums up my opinion of the use of torture in war to get information.

It's a quote somewhat relevant to debates among bloggers, lawmakers, military personnel and government representatives alike over reports of detainee abuse. As a former soldier, who's seen up close the fruits of our often-controversial labors, I'd like to put this and other similar issues in perspective, and demonstrate how they're affecting the broader global conflict, our reputation abroad, and the way we should be dealing with our critics.

This war on terror is unlike any other we've ever experienced. A precarious blend of intelligence challenges, invisible warriors, actual combat, criminal acts and religion, we can't always expect our ancient laws of land warfare to dovetail with our current POW situation. But with that being said, torture isn't going to get us anywhere. Torture isn't about getting information. It's about domination and a desire to hurt. Don't get me wrong; there were times in Iraq where I wanted to beat a prisoner to within an inch of his life. But beating a captive senseless—especially out of frustration or retribution—isn't going to help, and only serves to harm our cause in the worst possible way.[92] In addition, the flawed assumption behind the

---

92 Ibn al-Shaykh al-Libi, a Libyan and al Qaeda operative captured in

use of torture—that the more you hurt a prisoner, the more and better the information you'll get—is much too simplistic, anyhow. That's just not how it works. Maybe in the movies, but not in a detention cell in Iraq, Afghanistan or, I would assume, Cuba. Most of our higher-quality extremist enemies are prepared to die as martyrs anyway, and probably won't see threats of harm or death as anything to be avoided. And in regards to any traditional questioning, the Koran permits a Muslim to lie when he feels his life is in danger. Either way, you're not going to get any good intelligence.

In my estimation, there are better ways to get people to talk—don't work 'em over *harder*; work 'em over *smarter*.

The Cold War spy games are over (mostly), and times have indeed changed. Information that's taken from someone today may mean life or death on the ground for our guys tomorrow. As far as effective techniques are concerned, take a look at the conditions surrounding the questioning of Gitmo's detainee 063, the infamous 20th *hijacker*, a Saudi by the name of al-Qahtani. Turned away by alert immigration officials at Tampa International Airport in the summer of 2001, it's now widely believed he was destined to be the 5th hijacker aboard United Airlines flight 93 on September 11th. Captured in Afghanistan in late 2001—and after it was determined that he, indeed, was the man detained, questioned and set back to Saudi Arabia

---

Pakistan, was handed over to the Egyptians by the CIA in January 2002 for interrogation. While in Egyptian custody, al-Libi gave information that indicated Iraq had a hand in the 9/11 attacks; intelligence that helped justify the war with Iraq. In January 2004, he began to recant his statements, claiming that he fabricated evidence of the link to avoid further abuse by his Egyptian interrogators (Source: Douglas Jehl, *Qaeda-Iraq link U.S. cited is tied to coercion claim*, The New York Times, December 9, 2005)

from Tampa International in August 2001—al-Qahtani was sent to Guantanamo Bay for interrogation. Instead of using physical violence, the might of the American military applied a certain degree of psychological aggravation to find out what they wanted to know about al Qaeda's worldwide operations.

Now this is the way it should be done—detainee 063 was never beaten, strangled, cut or threatened with major bodily harm. Instead, he was broken down by precision professionals—the interrogator teams at Gitmo used a more "human" approach, managing to convince him of how alone he was, how no one loved him, but how he was somehow "spared" by Allah to reveal the true meaning of the Koran and destroy bin Laden.[93] To a certain extent, it worked—we gained a much better understanding of al Qaeda in Afghanistan through their method of questioning. By no means the magic bullet technique, it's apparent that getting into these guys' heads *is* a solution. And what's the best way to rile them up? Religion. It's a hot button that we should be pushing much, much more often. And while it's hardly a black and white issue, we have to let our enemies know we mean business. It's an effective alternative to some of our more antiquated methods—reports from the field have even suggested that Al Qaeda has trained its operatives to withstand traditional American interrogation techniques.[94]

And although this method of questioning may technically constitute "degrading treatment," it's by far the best way to elicit usable information. If we're to follow the torture laws to

---

[93] Adam Zagorin and Michael Duffy, *Inside the Interrogation of Detainee 063*, Time Magazine, June 20, 2005

[94] John Keegan, *Intelligence in War; The value—and limitations—of what the military can learn about the enemy* (New York, NY: Vintage Books, a division of Random House, 2003), p. 316

the absolute letter, every interrogator serving in the war on terror should pack their bags and go home—according to the United Nations, any method of questioning that can even liberally be interpreted as "cruel" is a violation of human rights.[95]

To think we'd rather focus our efforts and manpower on handling the Koran with kid gloves, rather than in finding more sophisticated ways to get info from a detainee that may hold the answer to bringing down the next terror leader and his thugs, is beyond sickening. This isn't some kind of game where we score more points by treating our detainees better. We need this information to save lives, and if that comes as an inconvenience to the sleeping habits of a Taliban militant or an Iraqi insurgent's call to prayer time, too fucking bad. In my opinion, intentionally causing distress in our enemies by chipping away at *select* religious beliefs is warranted in the quest for actionable intelligence.

Unfortunately, it often appears that members of Congress and the Department of Defense bend over *backwards* to follow the rules that have been set forth by the Geneva Convention regarding the treatment of our Enemy Prisoners of War, often to the point where we've taken to extremes to pacify universal, and often unfounded, criticisms. The living conditions for the detainees at Gitmo are often much better than those of our troops fighting in Iraq, even years after the invasion. They get volleyball courts and top of the line medical care; I couldn't even get bulletproof armor for my Humvee for 12 months as a soldier working for the wealthiest country on the planet. And from what I've read, in both classified and open source reports,

---

[95] *Office of the United Nations High Commissioner for Human Rights, Convention against Torture and Other Cruel, Inhuman or Degrading Treatment or Punishment*, ratified June 26, 1987 (www.ohchr.org)

pledging my fraternity back in college was *10 times worse* than what these guys are experiencing in Cuba.

There's a fact that everyone needs to wake up to—the men we've detained at Gitmo are not common soldiers. They aren't conscripts fighting as part of an Army, captured in some obscure battle like so many of the Iraqi soldiers you saw surrender en masse during war. These people are out to bring down the United States at all costs, and often have information that can help destroy the network that's out to destroy us. They will never fight by the same rules we do, and they know how to use our rules of warfare against America, Britain or anyone they consider an enemy.[96] We're not the bad guys here—they are—but in our panic to be completely fair, I'm afraid we're going to make deadly and potentially irreversible concessions.

And while the United States and its practices may not always be perfect, let's turn our attention to the real crimes being committed—the acts of violent jihad committed each day around the globe, and the people and governments who support it. While there have been plenty of instances of inexcusable abuse at the hands of the U.S. military—and there will continue to be—it isn't routine practice as is the case with our Islamic counterparts. Tell me, how do a few humiliating pictures of some Iraqi inmates fit into the big picture of this war? Believe me, I was just as upset as anyone with the treatment of the prisoners at Abu Ghraib, not so much because I was an American soldier, but rather because I was a military police officer. I'd spent countless hours of manpower, sweat equity and risk to life and limb to nab the guys we were sending to Abu Ghraib, only to have them "softened up" by people with

---

96 Staff Writers Dan Eggen and Josh White, *Inmates Alleged Koran Abuse*, The Washington Post, May 26, 2005

no discipline, real experience or involvement with the actual process that led to the capture of these men in the first place. Yes, I was upset—but eventually my anger yielded to the fact that we often don't hold others accountable for their actions, or beliefs.

> *"The best intentions? Some of the worst things imaginable have been done with the best intentions."*
>
> Sam Neill as *Dr. Alan Grant*
> *Jurassic Park 3*

That being said, imagine this: You're gagged and bound in a room in front of a camera and a couple of armed, masked men start to read a message in Arabic. Throwing you to the ground, one pulls a knife, plunges it into your neck and begins to saw your head off while you're still breathing. Your screams stop as the blade cuts through your larynx. You're alive long enough to see your own blood spill on to the floor and feel the blade slice all the way to your spinal cord. Your highly publicized killing is taken from an Islamic website, with select bits immediately reported on Al Jazeera. A few governments around the world, including the United States', make a few remarks on how horrible these murderous acts are. The rest, including those who practice the very religion that somehow condones the killing, say a few token words or nothing at all.

Now imagine this: You're a prisoner at Abu Ghraib, and someone ties a leash around your neck and takes some pictures. Your captors are now part of an international investigation. The entire world jumps on the bandwagon, including those Muslim governments that are somehow offended by the "atrocious" pictures of Abu Ghraib—the same people who think nothing, and say nothing, of civilians being brutally murdered in the name of their religion.

So why are the cries of injustice from these Muslim countries so much louder when the United States screws up? Why are we held to account when others are not? Most importantly, why are we so influenced by international opinion?

At one time not too long ago, Congress was looking to shut Gitmo down; not so much for the belief that it's not yielding results, but because it's supposedly ruining our reputation internationally. Tell me, who in the hell are we trying to impress? Is there any country in the world, outside of our allies, in a position to draw a credible conclusion about what American interrogators are doing in Cuba, whether from a human rights standpoint or their involvement in the role on terror? Those *in* a position to judge are up against the same threats that we are, and I'm sure are more or less supportive. But of course, every spineless government in the world finds it fashionable to bash the U.S. and its policies at every opportunity, so why not get their punches in, too? And while I appreciate what some other countries have to say about the treatment of our prisoners, no one—no one—has earned the right to criticize us at that level yet.

We're not going to get the world to agree with us on anything, so we shouldn't apologize for treating terrorists like terrorists. While issues surrounding due process and human rights will always be a factor, we need to remain aware that the prisoners at Gitmo are often the "cream of the crop," intelligence-wise, of our prisoners. Of course, that doesn't mean that they should be beaten without mercy because they represent the worst of the worst; but it does mean more aggressive techniques should be used in eliciting information.

We hold ourselves to a higher standard than just about

every country on the face of the Earth when dealing with human rights, and in my opinion we're doing just fine, despite the actions of a few power-hungry, over-zealous prison guards or CIA numbskulls. I've been face to face with men in Iraq who were responsible for the deaths of tens of soldiers and Marines, and served with soldiers who worked with trash like this every day and still kept their cool. If that's not discipline, I don't know what is.

And what are we getting in return? Flak from some no-name country with a horrible human rights record and the bodies of headless men in orange jumpsuits. And the response to the atrocities from the countries and critics that boo-hoo over Gitmo and Abu Ghraib? Silence.

The bottom line is this: we need to be brutally proactive and unapologetic in dealing with our extremist enemies—from issues surrounding interrogation, to potential future acts of preemptive aggression—no matter how severe the backlash from our critics may be. Enough with trying to do things with the "best intentions," no matter how flowery and ideal they might appear to be.

A few key events in the war on terror thus far have taught us that taking an over-simplified, unrealistic, politically popular approach to world affairs will inevitably lead to greater danger, losses and criticism—whether to actual combat planning or actions taken in the interest of public perception. For instance, the 9/11 Commission Report has more than a few stories on how we specifically could have stopped bin Laden in the late 90's, but didn't because such a strike would have apparently offended the Muslim community.[97] We had Zarqawi in our sites just before the war in Iraq started, but we didn't want to

---

[97] *The 9/11 Commission Report, Final Report of the National Commission on Terrorist*

scare off our potential European allies.[98] And I'm afraid that a Pollyannaish view of the war in Iraq just prior to the invasion led Americans—and the world—to believe that the global war on terror would be much more "tidy" than it's proving to be.[99]

I realize this view takes into account a heavy degree of 20/20 hindsight. However, if we follow this trend with future decisions and let our fears and the opinions of others guide us, we're in for a lot more trouble than we bargained for. It only underscores the need for the U.S. government to approach the war on terror from a sensible, pragmatic point of view, rather than develop strategies based on the potential reactions of others, especially those in the Arab world. We can either pay the butcher's bill now, or later with compounded interest. Despite what you've heard, their guys started this war, not us.

We've been playing by so many intricate, self-imposed rules for many, many years; rules meant to deflect criticism and soothe the rougher edges of our military operations. And while we certainly "mean well," sometimes it's best just to do what we need to do without concern with what others think of us. Our global efforts to rid the world of terrorism have somehow been misinterpreted as a war against Islam. Yet despite our efforts to prove otherwise, despite our efforts to protect

---

Attacks Upon the United States, (New York, NY: W.W. Norton & Company, Inc., 2004), pgs.108-143

98 Correspondent Jim Miklaszewski, *Avoiding attacking suspected terrorist mastermind*, NBC News, March 2, 2004 (www.msnbc.com)

99 Michael E. O' Hanlon, Senior Fellow, Foreign Policy Studies, The Brookings Institute, *Iraq Without a Plan*, from *Policy Review*, a publication of the Hoover Institution, Stanford University, December 2004 and January 2005, No. 128 (www.policyreview.org and www.hoover.org)

our image abroad, our reputation in most Islamic countries was at alarming lows.[100]

This idealistic, overly-accommodating diplomatic climate not only left a bad taste in the mouths of Muslim governments overseas, it effectively destroyed our ability to capitalize on the momentum of military operations in key Iraq and Afghan battles. Several times we permitted al Qaeda members slip through our fingers into Pakistan because we bowed to pressure not to cross the border, or by allowing the Afghan or Pakistani military forces to pursue our enemy in our stead. The Iraqi Governing Council convinced us to abide to a mid-assault cease-fire in Fallujah in April of 2004, strangling an opportunity for the Marines to strike while the iron was hot, literally "snatching defeat from the jaws of victory." [101] The Iraqi Prime Minister, Ibrahim al-Jafaari, called for a tactical "pause" on military activity in Tall 'Afar in the fall of 2004, again taking away our advantage.[102] Both no doubt lead to the escape of hundreds of insurgents, damaged the imposing image of the U.S. military in the minds of Iraqis and gave the insurgents a pivotal, symbolic victory. And for what? A better relationship with these people or their governments, the ones that have no respect for what we're doing or maybe even supporting our enemies? We just didn't have the balls to lead where we needed

---

100 *U.S. Image Up Slightly, But Still Negative, American Character Gets Mixed Reviews*, Pew Global Attitudes Project, The Pew Research Center, June 23, 2005 (www.pewglobal.org)

101 Robert D. Kaplan, *The Media and Medievalism*, from *Policy Review*, a publication of the Hoover Institution, Stanford University, December 1, 2004, No. 128 (www.policyreview.org and www.hoover.org)

102 Michael Ware, *Chasing the Ghosts*, Time Magazine, September 26, 2005

to most; to say the most "ideal" solution was not the one that was going to work.

These were all poor decisions, to say the least. But the common lesson learned from each is quite recognizable. When opportunity knocks—whether in regards to preemptive military action, interrogation opportunities or in key battles—we shouldn't let anyone convince us that answering the door isn't a good idea. If we have our enemy cornered, the military should be left to do what it does best as a blunt, hard-hitting instrument of foreign policy. And we shouldn't apologize for it.

We shouldn't pussyfoot around these subjects, nor should we kowtow to the "squeaky wheels" both inside and outside of our borders. We need to do what we have to do to win. Should we let the opinions of other nations—or the loudest within our own country—sway our resolve or actions in this global war on terror? Absolutely not. Easier said than done, but can you imagine missing an opportunity to kill a terrorist leader because we caved to pressures from Pakistan to restrict Predator Drone flights after last month's missile strike? What would Iraq look like right now if we'd never interrogated that prisoner who ultimately led us to Saddam Hussein? How would you feel if a prisoner released from Gitmo under international pressure returns to the battlefield and kills a soldier, airman, Marine or sailor?

According to the Office of the Director of National Intelligence, as of July 2014, of the 620 detainees transferred out of Guantanamo, 107 have been "confirmed of re-engaging," and 77 are "suspected of re-engaging" in terrorist or insurgent activities.[103]

---

103 https://en.wikipedia.org/wiki/Lists_of_former_Guantanamo_Bay_detainees_alleged_to_have_returned_to_terrorism

The Iraqi Point of View

In the fall of 2004, I was at home in Chicago when my cell phone rang. It was a lieutenant from the 1st Cavalry Division, on a foot patrol with his platoon in a neighborhood in Baghdad. He was using the phone given to him by Sam, one of the interpreters from the police academy, who'd come out of his house to chat with the soldiers. Sam explained to the lieutenant how he'd worked with the Army, and how he was still in touch with a few of us back in the States. After informing the LT that Sam was "on our side" and was a man he could go to for information, I wished him the best of luck and he resumed his patrol. That was the second strangest phone call I'd ever been a part of, the first being the conversation with my girlfriend and sister that night along the Euphrates the previous summer on Laith's satellite phone.

I keep in touch with most of the interpreters back in Iraq, and often pick their brains to get their views of what's happening there and what we should, or shouldn't, be doing. I wrote to a few of them in the summer of 2005, looking for their opinions and comments regarding postwar Iraq—how they felt about our presence, the Sunnis, the new government, and so on. The following are actual emails from three of them, with a few corrections and explanations noted in [brackets]. I wanted to keep most of it intact, so the grammar's a little choppy. The parts concerning their whereabouts and careers have been omitted.

In a book chock full o' my own opinion, I'll give them the last word.

Dear Mike

Regarding answering the questions mentioned in your previous email I would like to tell you:

1- According to the situation in Iraq I believe that the US Military should stay not less than 25 years from now, the Iraqi people are tough to be controlled by democratic government I am not saying that to tell you that Saddam was the right solution for Iraqis I am saying that because Iraq will never be a stable, secure country until a tough diplomatic smart talented guy have full authority to control this country. The Iraqis since 1958 (revolution year against King Faisal II) since that time they lives in fear and that fear proved it's the best way to control such people like Iraqis. If the US Military leaves Iraq now or in the soon later the Iraqi people will have nothing to fear from, this will lead to a disaster in the whole area. Our government now is not tough enough to play that role. That is why it is not right from my point of view to see the US Military leaving Iraq soon. From another point of view it was a smart move for the American government to move the battle field to Iraq it is better than making direct contact with the US enemy on an American land, but still that point makes Iraq as a place for all American enemies to make there war against America here in Iraq, and the Iraqi people paid the price.

You asked me what are we doing right or wrong answering that makes me confused because too many things are right and too many things are wrong as an example the right things are the US military being so rude and tough with the bad guys and showing mercy to the good people " sometimes LOL ". One of the great things that you saved us from the old regime opening new hope for the next generation.

The wrong things is that you kept some of the bad guys doing what ever they want claiming that there is no solid evidence to capture them. Do I need an evidence to stop killing people? Giving you an example RAGHAD is the daughter of Saddam Hussein as an Iraqi (me) and all the Iraqi people knows that she is financing the majority of terrorism in Iraq against Iraqis and America from Jordan, do I need an evidence to stop her? What about the other high ranks in the old Al Ba'ath socialist party in Iraq, Syria, Jordan and Iran. Do I need an other evidence for these people (there should be no roles for engagement) it is a war against terrorism I should do what ever it takes to save a solder or innocent child.

Moreover, not only the terrorist are fighting US military and Iraqi people in Iraq there is something more important and dangerous which is the intelligence agencies for Iran, Syria, Al Qaeda, North Korea and more others, which makes the situation in Iraq is the worst, Iraq will never be secured until the united state Army occupy Syria for the time being.

2- Regarding to the new Iraqi government I believe that the government should focus more on the infrastructure of the country: can you imagine a country with no power supplies (Electricity), clean water to drink the weather is so hot it reaches sometimes 55 C [over 130 Fahrenheit], no fuel in the land if oil Iraq, what about industry, roads and cold winters.

All the above without getting deep into details makes a simple Iraqi hate any government even if he feels more free now but he still have the right of any human being and that makes him forget all the bad memories in Saddam's days because at least at that time he use to get these basic needs.

What about the high-class people in Iraq who have the

opportunity & privilege to leave such hell like that. I love my country but I cant live in it any more if everybody goes like me what will it end up like?

3- Kurdish, Shi'ites & Sunnis are the major categories in Iraq, the Kurdish and Shi'ites used to suffer since 1969 and the history of Iraq tells it all, on the other hand the Sunnis got it all. Nowadays the best solution in my opinion is a new federal country that divides Iraq into three major states North (Kurdish), Middle (Sunnis) and South Shi'ites.

The enemy of both Iraqis and US Military is the Sunnis why? Because they used to get it all now they have nothing. They want to control the country like they used to do. If we make the federal country look at the Iraqi map you will see 95 or more of the natural resources (oil, red mercury, uranium, agriculture water, sulfur, phosphate ... etc) could be found in North and south of Iraq, why do we have to suffer our life and we have everything (me as a Shi'ite) while the Sunnis killing us with no mercy and they know they will have nothing if that happens they will lose the fortune of Iraq because they have nothing and that will lead them to lose there war against other Iraqis and the US Army , because of that they will fight badly.

Can I trust the Sunnis? I will never trust a Sunni why? Because after 35 years (almost a full generation) of having power and control of Iraq they believe that the Sunnis own the country and there is no place for other Iraqis in Iraq, that way of thinking was built in there minds and makes them look at me as an enemy even if I never hurt them.

If I want to talk about Iraqis and Iraq that will take ages to explain why this area in the Middle East will never be like other places.

If you need any type of information you think it will help you writing your book please let me know but what I want from you is to be specific in your questions and never hesitate asking. I wish you good luck with your book and I want you to wish me luck with my new starting life. Dude if you go to church next Sunday please pray for me because I need it badly.

Thanks and Best regards,

Sam

And the second:

Hello Sir;

I really want to come to America and work I feel that whatever I did here in Iraq I have no future and I looking for your help in that. And I'm very happy that you writing a book about Iraq and I will help you as much as I can.

In the beginning I don't think there is a typical Iraqi but if there is a classification I believe there is the educated Iraqi and the ignorant Iraqi and I will start with the educated Iraqi and by educate I don't mean he finished his high school or college but I mean mentally educated, [the open minded people] and the people who had seen other countries and the people who know how is [to really live]. [You're going to have to make them feel] that some thing happened in Iraq not only Saddam's regime collapsed because he wasn't a good follower to Americans but because that the Americans wanted to help the Iraqi's and you can show them that by the good treatment and the [good behavior] of the troops in the street and by respecting the humanity of the people and by showing to the that the Iraqi's and the Americas in the same side against the terrorists. A knowledge of the way of thinking of the Iraqi's is very important it's very nice to start your conversations with a Iraq by using the phrase " ALSALAM ALAYKUM." It means in English that "peace on you " and it's the formal greeting for Muslims its shows that you people don't have any problems with the Muslims. All your problem are with the terrorist and with the bad people and if you trying to say some Arabic words that will helps a lots.

That's all for the educated people and now the uneducated people. Those people the majority of them believe that most of the boomer cars [car bombs] are made by the Americans (notice how dump are they); do you remember [another interpreter at the academy]? He was pretty sure that some special forces (from the CIA) attack the Americans to give them a reason to attack the civilian and the cities and they ambush the Iraqi Police and kill them and made the other people afraid of joining the police forces and Iraq. All the time will need the Americans to stay around.

By the way [a former interpreter] didn't give back his gun " the Glock " when he quit the work. He said when he first took it from you he would never give it back. So I consider him as ignorant guy although he is an engineer. Those kind of people there is no specific way to treat them because [they believe what they are going to believe]. With other ignorant people, I think that the best way the deal with them is by saying to them "that we came here to help you, but if you mess with us we can be really tough."

And about what happened in Fallujah [during the first aborted assault on the city in the spring of 2004] because I know a lot of people from that area; they were showing off that they kicked the Americans ass and the Americans are afraid of them and they all say that if any one of the MUGAHEDEN come and try to hide in my house I will let him because those guys are very good and have their principles. But after that when the US Army attack Fallujah (and I mean the second time not the first time because the first time sucked because the first time you guys did nothing just gave the MUGAHEDEN a great credit) and the people got hurt because they did help the MUGAHEDEN; after that when they came back to their home after the evacuation and they saw all the destructions in their houses and their property, if you only mention the word MUGAHEDEN they will rip your mouth because they got enough of them and that's what [another interpreter]told me and other couple guys I know them from Fallujah so that's what these kind of people they need, some one to show them the power when it's necessary.

Most of them as you saw them have no dreams they just want to live (eat , fuck , drink , sleep) and they happy after that but they need some kind of system to follow and their system is the power and there is some thing very popular among the countryside. People that the American Army are coward (you know because they wear armor vest and Kevlar helmets) some they need some one to prove them wrong and if you offered them jobs you will see how helpful to you they can be.

What you did wrong when you first come to Iraq I can make

you imagine it by tell you this (you have a child and you never let him drive and suddenly you just gave him the key and told him you can do whatever you want what you think he will do??) that's what happened in Iraq we were had several security systems and no one can do anything. Before he think of it thousands of times and in one minute all the Iraqi people can do whatever and whenever they want it's not about freedom it's about the people and who they think and with who you dealing and his mentality, you remember the guys you were training them in Ramadi [the Iraqi police] they don't even know how to read and write how can you give them a freedom or how you can give them freedom like the people in any where else?

This is the answer for your first question, and I will sent to you soon the answers for the rest of the questions. Hope what I sent is helpful for you.

Your brother

Jack

The third:

Hi Cpt; you asked to give you my opinion about what happened in Iraq ok, It was a big mistake to occupy a country without knowing anything about this country customs and traditions this made and still makes a lots of misunderstandings which are unfortunately led to massacres and violence events.

It was a big mistake to discharge the Iraqi Army and the security, intelligence agency these people have a grate experience in dealing with terrorism field and any kind of defense.

The people lost the trust in you and a lot of them lost the confidence in themselves.

So based on above what do you need to do:

1- the USA institutions should train the soldiers on the Iraqi customs and traditions and how to respect them and respect the people (the Iraqi peoples are very ancient and proud) and this training must be bereaved on the Hands of the Iraqi people qualified living in the states (I will be on of them).

2- bringing back the good and fine reputation individuals of Iraqi Army ……Etc.

3- Rebuild the trust and confidence again by protect and serve and good dealings.

That is my opinion Sir, It a very disastrous and dangerous situation there I'm not writing to you because you asked only but I believe that you are man could somebody trust on. Ok mun, take care and God bless you.

Dave

CPSIA information can be obtained
at www.ICGtesting.com
Printed in the USA
LVOW01s1411150317
527318LV00013B/214/P